JESUS' PARABLE OF THE RICH FOOL

Society of Biblical Literature

Early Christianity and Its Literature

Number 6

JESUS' PARABLE OF THE RICH FOOL

Luke 12:13–34 among Ancient Conversations on Death and Possessions

JESUS' PARABLE OF THE RICH FOOL

LUKE 12:13–34 AMONG ANCIENT CONVERSATIONS ON DEATH AND POSSESSIONS

By

Matthew S. Rindge

Society of Biblical Literature
Atlanta

JESUS' PARABLE OF THE RICH FOOL
Luke 12:13–34 among Ancient Conversations on Death and Possessions

Library of Congress Cataloging-in-Publication Data

Rindge, Matthew S.
Jesus' parable of the rich fool : Luke 12:13–34 among ancient conversations on death and possessions / by Matthew S. Rindge.
p. cm. — (Society of Biblical Literature early Christianity and its literature ; 6)
Includes bibliographical references and index.
ISBN 978-1-58983-614-3 (paper binding : alk. paper) — ISBN 978-1-58983-615-0 (electronic format)
1. Rich fool (Parable) 2. Bible. N.T. Luke XII, 13–34—Criticism, interpretation, etc. 3. Death. 4. Wealth. 5. Literature, Ancient. I. Title.
BT378.R5R56 2011
226.8'06—dc22 2011038860

Printed on acid-free, recycled paper conforming to
ANSI/NISO Z39.48-1992 (R1997) and ISO 9706:1994
standards for paper permanence.

For
Shannon,
Ava, and Sophia

"*Aimer ou avoir aimé, cela suffit. Ne demandez rien en-suite. On n'a pas d'autre perle à trouver dans les plis ténébreux de la vie. Aimer est un accomplissement.*"
— Victor Hugo, *Les Misérables*

Contents

Acknowledgments

Many people have contributed and collaborated in helping to bring this project to fruition, and this book owes much to their considerable time and energy. I here offer them a modicum of gratitude and recognition.

This book is a revision of a doctoral dissertation completed in 2008 at Emory University ("Illustrating Wisdom: Luke 12:16–21 and the Interplay of Death and Possessions in Sapiential Literature"). For its completion and strengths I am primarily indebted to Gail O'Day, who served as an invaluable thesis director. She supported this project from its inception, and her insights, questions, and challenges consistently helped me to deepen, sharpen, and clarify my arguments. Her editing skills helped transform passable prose into coherence and cogency. I could not have asked for a more helpful advisor.

The other members of my dissertation committee, Luke Timothy Johnson, Carol Newsom, and Walter Wilson, provided thoughtful (and timely) feedback on my chapters. Their astute queries and suggestions shaped the dissertation in significant ways. Carol's guidance with Second Temple Jewish literature was especially instructive, as were the recommendations by Luke and Walter regarding Greco-Roman texts and Luke's Gospel.

Fellow doctoral students at Emory proved to be colleagues in the best sense of the word. Robert von Thaden and Bart Bruehler provided helpful comments on the dissertation proposal and overall goals of the project. Elizabeth Shively's response to a draft of chapter 5 (now chapters 5–7) at a New Testament colloquium was constructive and informative. Conversations with Robert Williamson Jr. helped me think more clearly about various aspects of the project, especially the material on Qoheleth. I thank Eric Barreto for serving as a scribe at my proposal and dissertation defenses.

I commend the staff at Pitts Theological Library at Emory, and especially John Weaver, for helping me locate and obtain numerous items of significance. Emory's Graduate School of Arts and Sciences provided five years of funding, enabling me to finish sooner than later.

My parents, Samuel and Kathy, supported me throughout my time at Emory. I thank them for their kindness and generosity.

Many people have been involved during the transformation of the project from dissertation to book. The Society of Biblical Literature was my first choice of publication for this book, and I am honored to publish with them. I thank the editorial committee of SBL's Early Christianity and Its Literature Series, both for accepting the book and for providing helpful comments. I thank Leigh Andersen, Bob Buller, Kathie Klein, and others at SBL for taking care of the myriad details necessary to ensure the book's publication. I continue to appreciate Gail O'Day's advice and assistance.

My colleagues in Gonzaga University's department of Religious Studies have expressed support both generally and in regard to this specific project. I presented a portion of chapter 2 in a departmental colloquy and received profitable feedback. Rob Hauck and Richard Goodrich helped me find certain patristic and Reformation texts, and Kevin McCruden provided useful advice regarding the indices. I am genuinely grateful to teach in a department comprised of so many decent, friendly, and interesting human beings.

Material in chapter 2 on death and possessions in Qoheleth appeared recently—in a slightly revised form—in *Catholic Biblical Quarterly*. I thank Linda Day and Joseph Jensen for granting permission to republish this material.

I dedicate this book to Shannon, Ava, and Sophia. They unwittingly but graciously endured far too many absences from home and the undue stress that I sometimes brought there. Their presence throughout this project sustained and enlivened me, and served not only as a primary incentive to finish but also as a continual reminder of where—and how—meaning can be realized. I thank Shannon for her tenacious love and support; I could not ask for a better partner with whom to share this meaning-filled journey of life. I thank Ava and Sophia, in whom I already see so much life and wisdom, for the privilege of being their father.

Abbreviations

Primary Works

1QpHab	Pesher Habakkuk
1QS	Rule of the Community
4QD[e]	Damascus Document
4Q109	4QQohelet[a]
4Q110	4QQohelet[b]
4Q185	Sapiential Work
4Q424	Instruction-Like Composition B
4Q468l	fragment mentioning Qoh 1:8–9
4Q525	Beatitudes
4QShirShabb[f]	Songs of the Sabbath Sacrifice
'Abot R. Nat.	'Abot de Rabbi Nathan
Ambrose	
Ep.	*Epistulae* (*Letters*)
Apollodorus Comicus	
Frag.	*Fragment*
Aristotle	
Eth. nic.	*Ethica Nichomachea* (*Nichomachean Ethics*)
Athanasius	
Fug.	*Apologia de fuga sua* (*Defense of His Flight*)
Augustine	
Doct. chr.	*De doctrina christiana* (*Christian Instruction*)
Enarrat. Ps.	*Enarrationes in Psalmos* (*Enarrations on the Psalms*)
Serm.	*Sermones*
Serm. Dom.	*De sermone Domini in monte* (*Sermon on the Mount*)
Trin.	*De Trinitate* (*The Trinity*)
b.	Babylonian Talmud
Ceb. Tab.	*The Tabula of Cebes*

Clement of Alexandria
Paed. — *Paedagogus* (*Christ the Educator*)
Quis div. — *Quis dives salvetur* (*Who Is the Rich Man Who Shall Be Saved?*)
Strom. — *Stromata* (*Miscellanies*)
Cyprian
Dom. or. — *De dominica oratione* (*The Lord's Prayer*)
Eleem. — *De opere et eleemosynis* (*Works and Almsgiving*)
Test. — *Ad Quirinum testimonia adversus Judaeos* (*To Quirinius: Testimonies against the Jews*)
Dialogues — Lucian, *Dialogues of the Dead*
Dio Chrysostom
Avar. — *De avaritia (Or. 17)* (*Covetousness*)
Diogenes
Ep. — *Epistulae* (*Letters*)
'Erub. — 'Erubin
Euripides
Alc. — *Alcestis*
Eusebius
Hist. eccl. — *Historia ecclesiastica* (*Ecclesiastical History*)
Heraclitus
Ep. — *Epistulae* (*Letters*)
Herodotus
Hist. — *Historiae* (*Histories*)
Hippocrates
Ep. — *Epistulae* (*Letters*)
Homer
Il. — *Ilias* (*Iliad*)
Horace
Sat. — *Satirae* (*Satires*)
Irenaeus
Haer. — *Adversus haereses* (*Against Heresies*)
Jerome
Epist. — *Epistulae* (*Letters*)
John Chrysostom
Eutrop. — *In Eutropium*
Hom. Matt. — *Homiliae in Matthaeum*
Josephus
Ant. — *Antiquitates judaicae* (*Jewish Antiquities*)

Lucian	
Bis acc.	*Bis accusatus* (*The Double Indictment*)
Cat.	*Cataplus* (*The Downward Journey, or The Tyrant*)
Char.	*Charon*
Demon.	*Demonax*
Dial. mort.	*Diologi mortuorum* (*Dialogues of the Dead*)
Dom.	*De domo* (*The Hall*)
Gall.	*Gallus* (*The Dream, or The Cock*)
Icar.	*Icaromenippus*
Ind.	*Adversus indoctum* (*The Ignorant Book-Collector*)
Jupp. conf.	*Juppiter confutatus* (*Zeus Catechized*)
Jupp. trag.	*Juppiter tragoedus* (*Zeus Rants*)
Luct.	*De luctu* (*Funerals*)
Men.	*Menippus, or Descent into Hades*
Nigr.	*Nigrinus*
Par.	*De parasito* (*The Parasite*)
Pereg.	*De morte Peregrini* (*The Passing of Peregrinus*)
Philops.	*Philopseudes* (*The Lover of Lies*)
Pisc.	*Piscator* (*The Dead Come to Life, or The Fisherman*)
Sacr.	*De sacrificiis* (*Sacrifices*)
Sat.	*Saturnalia* (*Conversation with Cronos*)
Symp.	*Symposium* (*The Carousal, or The Lapiths*)
Tim.	*Timon*
Tox.	*Toxaris*
Vit. auct.	*Vitarum auctio* (*Philosophies for Sale*)
LXX	Septuagint
Meg.	Megillah
Menander	
Frag.	*Fragment*
MT	Masoretic Text
Origen	
Princ.	*De principiis* (*First Principles*)
Ovid	
Metam.	*Metamorphoses*
P. Ins.	Papyrus Insinger
Philo	
Leg.	*Legum allegoriae* (*Allegorical Interpretation*)
Plato	
Leg.	*Leges* (*Laws*)

Pliny the Younger
Ep. — *Epistulae*
Plutarch
Cupid. divit. — *De cupiditate divitiarum*
Polycarp
Phil. — *To the Philippians*
Qidd. — Qiddušin
Šabb. — Šabbat
Seneca
Ep. — *Epistulae Morales* (Moral Letters)
Stobaeus
Ecl. — *Eclogae (Anthology)*
Strabo
Geog. — *Geographica* (*Geography*)
T. Ab. — Testament of Abraham
Tertullian
Marc. — *Adversus Marcionem* (*Against Marcion*)
Or. — *De oratione* (*Prayer*)
Paen. — *De paenitentia* (*Repentance*)
Pud. — *De pudicitia* (*Modesty*)
Virgil
Aen. — *Aeneid*
y. — Jerusalem Talmud

Secondary Works

AB — Anchor Bible
AEL — *Ancient Egyptian Literature.* Miriam Lichtheim. 3 vols. Berkeley: University of California Press, 1971–1980.
AnBib — Analecta biblica
ANRW — *Aufstieg und Niedergang der römischen Welt: Geschichte und Kultur Roms im Spiegel der neueren Forschung.* Part 2, *Principat*. Edited by Hildegard Temporini and Wolfgang Haase. Berlin: de Gruyter, 1972–.
ANTC — Abingdon New Testament Commentaries
ATLA — American Theological Library Association
BASOR — *Bulletin of the American Schools of Oriental Research*
Bib — *Biblica*

BBB	*Bulletin de bibliographie biblique*
BDAG	Bauer, Walter, Frederick Danker, W. F. Arndt, and F. W. Gingrich. *Greek-English Lexicon of the New Testament and Other Early Christian Literature.* 3rd ed. Chicago: University of Chicago Press, 1999.
BDB	Brown, Francis, Samuel Rolles Driver, and Charles A. Briggs. *A Hebrew and English Lexicon of the Old Testament.* Oxford: Oxford University Press, 1907.
BHS	*Biblia Hebraica Stuttgartensia.* Edited by Karl Elliger and Wilhelm Rudolph. Stuttgart: Deutsche Bibelgesellschaft, 1983.
BJS	Brown Judaic Studies
BN	*Biblische Notizen*
BZAW	Beihefte zur Zeitschrift für die alttestamentliche Wissenschaft
BZNW	Beihefte zur Zeitschrift für die neutestamentliche Wissenschaft
CBET	Contributions to Biblical Exegesis and Theology
CEJL	Commentaries on Early Jewish Literature
CBQ	*Catholic Biblical Quarterly*
CNT	Commentaire du Nouveau Testament
CCSL	Corpus Christianorum: Series latina
DCH	*Dictionary of Classical Hebrew.* Edited by David J. A. Clines. Sheffield: Sheffield Academic Press, 1993–.
EvQ	*Evangelical Quarterly*
FzB	Forschung zur Bibel
Gesenius, *Thesaurus*	Gesenius, Wilhelm. *Thesaurus philologicus criticus linguae hebraeae et Thesaurus chaldaeae Veteris Testamenti.* 3 vols. Leipzig: Vogel, 1829–1842.
HALOT	Koehler, Ludwig, Walter Baumgartner, and J. J. Stamm, *The Hebrew and Aramaic Lexicon of the Old Testament.* Translated and edited under the supervision of M. E. J. Richardson. 4 vols. Leiden: Brill, 1994–1999.
HeyJ	*Heythrop Journal*
HNT	Handbuch zum Neuen Testament
HTR	*Harvard Theological Review*
HUCA	*Hebrew Union College Annual*
IBC	Interpretation: A Bible Commentary for Teaching and Preaching

ICC	International Critical Commentary
JAAR	*Journal of the American Academy of Religion*
JBL	*Journal of Biblical Literature*
JJS	*Journal of Jewish Studies*
JPS	Jewish Publication Society
JQR	*Jewish Quarterly Review*
JRS	*Journal of Roman Studies*
JSJ	*Journal for the Study of Judaism in the Persian, Hellenistic, and Roman Periods*
JSJSup	Journal for the Study of Judaism in the Persian, Hellenistic, and Roman Periods Supplement Series
JSNTSup	Journal for the Study of the New Testament Supplement Series
JSOT	*Journal for the Study of the Old Testament*
JSOTSup	Journal for the Study of the Old Testament Supplement Series
JSP	*Journal for the Study of the Pseudepigrapha*
JSPSup	Journal for the Study of the Pseudepigrapha Supplement Series
KTU	*Die keilalphabetischen Texte aus Ugarit.* Edited by Manfried Dietrich, Oswald Loretz, and Joaquín Sanmartín. AOAT 24.1. Neukirchen-Vluyn: Neukirchener, 1976.
LCL	Loeb Classical Library
LSJ	Liddell, Henry George, Robert Scott, and Henry Stuart Jones, *A Greek-English Lexicon.* 9th ed. with revised supplement. Oxford: Oxford University Press, 1996.
NAB	New American Bible
NCBC	New Century Bible Commentary
NIBC	New International Biblical Commentary
NICNT	New International Commentary on the New Testament
NJPS	*Tanakh: The Holy Scriptures: The New JPS Translation according to the Traditional Hebrew Text*
NRSV	New Revised Standard Version
NovT	*Novum Testamentum*
NovTSup	Supplements to Novum Testamentum
NTG	New Testament Guides
NTM	New Testament Monographs
NTS	*New Testament Studies*
OBO	Orbis biblicus et orientalis

OTL	Old Testament Library
PG	Patrologia graeca. Edited by Jacques-Paul Migne. 162 vols. Paris: Migne: 1857–1886.
RevExp	*Review and Expositor*
SBLDS	Society of Biblical Literature Dissertation Series
SBLEJL	Society of Biblical Literature Early Judaism and Its Literature
SBLit	Studies in Biblical Literature
SBLMS	Society of Biblical Literature Monograph Series
SBLSBS	Society of Biblical Literature Sources for Biblical Study
SBLSCS	Society of Biblical Literature Septuagint and Cognate Studies
SBLSymS	Society of Biblical Literature Symposium Series
SBLTT	Society of Biblical Literature Texts and Translations
SBT	Studies in Biblical Theology
SC	Sources chrétiennes
SHR	Studies in the History of Religions (supplement to *Numen*)
SP	Sacra pagina
SSS	Semitic Study Series
SVTP	Studia in Veteris Testamenti pseudepigraphica
TDNT	*Theological Dictionary of the New Testament.* Edited by Gerhard Kittel and Gerhard Friedrich. Translated by G. W. Bromiley. 10 vols. Grand Rapids: Eerdmans, 1964–1976.
TLZ	*Theologische Literaturzeitung*
TPINTC	TPI New Testament Commentaries
TS	Texts and Studies
TSAJ	Texte und Studien zum antiken Judentum
TU	Texte und Untersuchungen
TUGAL	Texte und Untersuchungen zur Geschichte der altchristlichen Literatur
VT	*Vetus Testamentum*
VTSup	Supplements to Vetus Testamentum
WUNT	Wissenschaftliche Untersuchungen zum Neuen Testament
ZTK	*Zeitschrift für Theologie und Kirche*

Introduction

Luke 12:16–21 is one of the most neglected parables in the Synoptic Gospels. Several modern studies of the parables omit Luke's parable of the Rich Fool,[1] and it is even absent in a study of Lukan parables.[2] When the parable is treated, it often receives scant attention, meriting only a sentence or two of comment.[3] Bernard Brendan Scott aptly summarizes the parable's negligible treatment: "[This parable] has not been of major interest in the history of parable interpretation, nor has it been at the center of controversy. Its interpretation has been stable, predictable, and unafflicted by the obscurities that so torment other parables."[4]

The lack of scholarly interest in Luke 12:16–21 is due in part to a perception that the parable offers little else beyond a simple and straightforward critique of avarice. The parable itself tells a somewhat different story. Extant only in Luke and Thomas (Gos. Thom. 63), the parable is situated in Luke's travel narrative (9:51–19:44), during which Jesus journeys to

---

1. See, e.g., Alexander Balmain Bruce, *The Parabolic Teaching of Christ. A Systematic and Critical Study of the Parables of our Lord* (3rd ed.; New York: Armstrong & Son, 1898); C. H. Dodd, *The Parables of the Kingdom* (rev. ed.; New York: Charles Scribner's Sons, 1961); Dan Otto Via Jr., *The Parables: Their Literary and Existential Dimension* (Philadelphia: Fortress, 1967); Eta Linnemann, *Parables of Jesus: Introduction and Exposition* (London: SPCK, 1975); Pheme Perkins, *Hearing the Parables of Jesus* (New York: Paulist, 1981); Robert W. Funk, *Parables and Presence* (Philadelphia: Fortress, 1982); William R. Herzog, *Parables as Subversive Speech: Jesus as Pedagogue of the Oppressed* (Louisville: Westminster John Knox, 1994); Luise Schottroff, *Die Gleichnisse Jesu* (Gütersloh: Gütersloher Verlaghaus, 2005).

2. Kenneth Bailey, *Poet and Peasant* (Grand Rapids: Eerdmans, 1976).

3. John Dominic Crossan, *In Parables: The Challenge of the Historical Jesus* (Sonoma, Calif.: Polebridge, 1992), 83; Linnemann, *Parables of Jesus*, does not treat Luke 12:16–21 as one of the eleven parables in her study, but she does comment briefly on it.

4. Bernard Brandon Scott, *Hear Then the Parable: A Commentary on the Parables of Jesus* (Minneapolis: Fortress, 1989), 127.

Jerusalem.[5] The parable follows a short dialogue regarding an inheritance (12:13–15) and precedes a discourse about anxiety, God, and possessions (12:22–34). After rejecting a request to intervene in a fraternal dispute over an inheritance (12:13–14), Jesus offers a warning against greed, claiming that one's life does not consist in the abundance of possessions (12:15). He then tells the following story that the narrator identifies as a parable (παραβολή) (12:16a):

> The land of a certain rich person produced fruitfully. And he began to converse with himself, saying: "What shall I do, for I do not have [a place] where I will gather together my crops?" And he said, "This I will do: I will pull down my barns, and I will build larger ones, and I will gather together there all my grain and goods. And I will say to myself, 'Self, you have many goods laid up for many years; rest, eat, drink, enjoy.' But God said to him, "Fool! On this night they are demanding your life from you; and the things you prepared, whose will they be?" So is the one who stores up for oneself and is not rich toward God. (12:16b–21)[6]

Several basic features of the parable are noteworthy. This is the first of three ἄνθρωπός τις πλούσιος ("a certain rich person") parables in Luke (see 16:1–8, 19–31) and one of seven or eight ἄνθρωπός τις ("a certain person") parables.[7] Yet this is the only parable unique to Luke whose subject in the opening line is not a person. The man's initial response to his perceived dilemma is to ask a question (τί ποιήσω, "What shall I do?") that many of Luke's characters ask.[8] The man's monologue, which provides access to his

---

5. Luke periodically reminds readers/hearers that Jesus is on his way to Jerusalem (9:51, 53; 13:22; 17:11; 18:31; 19:28). On Luke's travel narrative, see Filip Noël, *The Travel Narrative in the Gospel of Luke: Interpretation of Lk 9,51–19,28* (Collectanea Biblica et Religiosa Antiqua 5; Brussels: Koninklijke Vlaamse Academie van België voor Wetenschappen en Kunsten, 2004). There is fairly uniform agreement about where the travel narrative begins (9:51). Although most defend either 19:27 or 19:44 as the conclusion to the journey narrative, several other endings have also been proposed (18:14, 30, 34; 19:10, 28, 46, 48; 21:38).

6. My translation is based on the Greek text in Barbara Aland, Kurt Aland, Eberhard Nestle, and Erwin Nestle, eds., *Nestle-Aland Novum Testamentum Graece* (27th ed.; Stuttgart: Deutsche Bibelgesellschaft, 1993). See chapter 5 for some of the text-critical issues involved in Luke 12:16–21.

7. Luke 10:30; 14:16; 15:11; 16:1, 19; 19:12; cf. 20:9. Many manuscripts omit τις in 20:9.

8. Luke 3:10, 12, 14; 10:25; 16:3; 18:18, 41; 20:13, 15; Acts 2:37; 4:16; 22:10.

mindset, contains an allusion to a Hebrew Bible text, Qoh 8:15. The parable also shares many similarities with Sir 11:14–19 and 1 En. 97:8–10. Luke 12:16–21 is unique in being the only parable in the Synoptic tradition in which God appears as a character and speaks (12:20).[9] This is, moreover, the only time the author of Luke-Acts attributes direct speech to God (θεός). The three elements in God's announcement (epithet, statement, question) are striking. God does not provide an explicit reason for calling the man a "fool." God tells the man, cryptically, that an unspecified "they" are demanding his ψυχή (life/soul/self). The encounter between God and the man ends with an enigmatic question regarding the future ownership of the man's goods. The parable's conclusion (spoken by Jesus or a comment by the narrator?) appears to interpret the rich man's plans in theological terms.

These fundamental features of the parable raise questions and warrant closer scrutiny. Is there a reason that the rich man is not the subject in the parable's introductory line? In what ways does making the "land" the subject change one's reading of the parable? Why is God a character in the parable, and what is the function of God's appearance? Are there particular elements of this parable that help explain God's inclusion? How is one to read God's announcement in 12:20? Is God informing the man of his imminent death, or is God punishing the man? What specifically does the man do (or not do) that results in being labeled a fool (12:20)? In the Greek Bible, the term "fool" (ἄφρων) occurs almost exclusively in sapiential texts. Is this suggestive for how one should understand the use of ἄφρων in the parable? Should this term, moreover, be interpreted in light of its only other occurrence in Luke (11:40)?

The parable leaves other questions unanswered as well. Who or what is the unspecified subject of ἀπαιτοῦσιν ("they are taking [back]") (12:20a)? Are they demanding the man's ψυχή or demanding it *back*? How should one translate the three occurrences of ψυχή ("self," "life," or "soul")? How is one to understand God's final question to the man (12:20b)? Is the question rhetorical? Is there an expected answer? In what precise way was the man not rich toward God (12:21)? What, in other words, does being rich toward God entail? Does Luke provide a positive corollary to the explicit

9. God is mentioned in Luke's parable of the Widow and the Judge (18:2, 4) but does not appear there as a character. Nor is God a character in the subsequent parable (18:9–14), although the Pharisee and tax collector both pray to God (18:11, 13).

critique in 12:20 and 12:21? Is there a constructive alternative to the rich man's folly and his failure to be rich toward God? A related question concerns the relationship between the parable proper (12:16–20) and its literary frame (12:13–15, 21; more broadly, 12:13–34). Should the parable be interpreted apart from its current literary context? If not, does the literary context interpret the parable or vice versa?

Additional elements of the parable are unclear and raise further questions. Does Jesus address the parable to the crowd *and* the disciples, or is the parable told only to the crowd? What is one to make of the similarities and differences between Luke's version and that found in Thomas? Does reading Luke's parable in light of Thomas significantly illuminate either version?

Interpreters of the parable frequently ignore or cursorily treat such questions. In what follows, chapter 1 shows that the neglect and marginalization of Luke's parable of the Rich Fool is due primarily to a mischaracterization of the parable as a simple and straightforward tale. Construing the parable in this manner is frequently the result of reading the parable through a "prophetic" lens. Interpreters who read the parable as a "prophetic" text typically conclude that it offers little more than a critique of avarice. This reading practice is the standard mode of understanding the parable among premodern and modern interpreters.

Yet reading the parable in this manner fails to acknowledge, among other things, the significance of the parable's own allusions and echoes to sapiential texts (Qoh 8:15; Sir 11:14–19; 1 En. 97:8–10). What is the significance of these resonances, and what function do they serve in the parable? Does Luke's parable engage these intertexts (or traditions represented by these intertexts), and, if so, how? Finally, what is one to make of the fact that each of these three intertexts is both sapiential and concerned with the interplay of death and possessions? Interpreters who recognize the parable's allusions to texts such as Qoh 8:15 or Sir 11:14–19 often fail either to acknowledge the diverse range of perspectives within wisdom texts or to explain how the parable's connections to such texts might influence an understanding of the parable.

This book demonstrates the multiple ways in which Luke's parable engages a Second Temple conversation regarding the interplay of death and possessions. This conversation frequently appears in sapiential texts. Reading the parable in concert with Second Temple texts whose focus is the intersection of death and possessions makes sense, given the allusions and echoes to wisdom texts within the parable (and its broader literary context), and provides insight to the kinds of questions engendered by a close reading of the parable. Such insight advances the conversation more than that offered by readers who do not read the parable in light of texts whose focus is the interplay of death and possessions.

The operating assumption of this book is that Luke's parable of the Rich Fool is situated within a (largely sapiential) Second Temple conversation on death and possessions and cannot be read properly apart from its dialogue with such texts. Although the conversation on death and possessions is featured most prominently in sapiential texts, it also finds expression in texts not technically designated as "wisdom literature."[10] I will therefore treat some nonsapiential texts that devote significant attention to the interplay of death and possessions. A close reading of four Hellenistic Jewish texts (Qoheleth, Ben Sira, 1 Enoch, and Testament of Abraham) will explicate this conversation and its contested nature (chs. 2 and 3). Analyzing two Greco-Roman authors (Lucian and Seneca) who treat these twinned motifs will broaden and nuance our understanding of this conversation (ch. 4).

I will situate Luke's parable of the Rich Fool within this spectrum of texts, showing how the parable participates in, illustrates, appropriates, and reconfigures this contested conversation on the interplay of death and possessions (chs. 5–7).[11] I will contend that central to this conversation are concerns for the meaningful use of possessions given various uncontrollable facets of death (e.g., its inevitability and uncertain timing). I will conclude by considering two specific implications of this project for reading and understanding other Lukan parables.

10. The phrase "sapiential conversation" is used throughout the book and reflects the fact that the concern in Second Temple texts with the interplay of death and possessions appears far more frequently in wisdom literature than in other literary genres. This concern, however, is not limited to texts officially designated "wisdom." As such, I do not intend the phrase "sapiential conversation" to be understood in an exclusive manner, but rather as an indication of the prevalence with which such texts appear in sapiential literature. Similarly, I use "Second Temple" regularly to refer to the time span in which most of the books that I explicate emerged. Although I do examine certain texts outside of this time span, (e.g., Lucian and certain ancient Egyptian literature), I cannot think of a more helpful term than "Second Temple."

11. This book treats the parable as it appears in its final form in Luke's Gospel. I do not inquire into the parable's *Sitz im Leben* in the life of Jesus or what the parable may have looked like in its pre-Lukan stage.

A chapter in my dissertation that treated the interplay of death and possessions in ancient Egyptian literature does not reappear in this book. I will, however, occasionally refer to perspectives on death and possessions in ancient Egyptian texts when they are germane either to Luke 12 or other texts I analyze. Ancient Egyptian literature gives sustained attention to the interplay of death and possessions and shares numerous perspectives related to death and possessions with Hellenistic Jewish texts, Greco-Roman texts, and Luke 12:13–34.[12] Egyptian culture, moreover, influenced Hellenistic Judaism and the general Hellenistic milieu out of which Luke's literary work developed.[13] Furthermore, specific Egyptian

---

12. On the role of death, see, e.g., Alan H. Gardiner, *The Attitude of the Ancient Egyptians to Death and the Dead* (Cambridge: Cambridge University Press, 1935); Jan Zandee, *Death as an Enemy: According to Ancient Egyptian Conceptions* (SHR 5; Leiden: Brill, 1960); Alan Jeffrey Spencer, *Death in Ancient Egypt* (2nd ed.; Harmondsworth: Penguin, 1984); Philippe Derchain, "Death in Egyptian Religion," in *Mythologies* (ed. Yves Bonnefoy; 2 vols.; Chicago: University of Chicago Press, 1991), 1:111–15; Henk Milde, "'Going out into the Day': Ancient Egyptian Beliefs and Practices concerning Death," in *Hidden Futures: Death and Immortality in Ancient Egypt, Anatolia, the Classical, Biblical and Arabic-Islamic World* (ed. J. M. Bremmer, Th. P. J. van den Hout, and R. Peters; Amsterdam: Amsterdam University Press, 1994), 15–34; Jan Assman, *Death and Salvation in Ancient Egypt* (trans. David Lorton; Ithaca, N.Y.: Cornell University Press, 2005).

13. See, e.g., John J. Collins, *Jewish Wisdom in the Hellenistic Age* (OTL; Louisville: Westminster John Knox, 1997), 136–40; Christina Riggs, *The Beautiful Burial in Roman Egypt: Art, Identity, and Funerary Religion* (Oxford: Oxford University Press, 2005); Garth Fowden, *Egyptian Hermes: A Historical Approach to the Late Pagan Mind* (Cambridge: Cambridge University Press, 1986); Jacco Dieleman, *Priests, Tongues, and Rites: The London-Leiden Magical Manuscripts and Translation in Egyptian Ritual (100–300 CE)* (Leiden: Brill, 2005); Jan Quaegebeur, "Cultes égyptiens et grecs en Egypte hellénistique: L'exploitation des sources," in *Egypt and the Hellenistic World: Proceedings of the International Colloquium, Leuven, 24–26 May 1982* (ed. E. van't Dack, P. van Dessel, and W. van Guch; Leuven: Orientaliste, 1983), 303–24; Marjorie S. Venit, *Monumental Tombs of Ancient Alexandria: The Theater of the Dead* (New York: Cambridge University Press, 2002). Artapanus's claims (that Abraham taught astronomy to Pharaoh and that Moses introduced the cult of Isis and invented the hydraulic lift and alphabet) show that some Jews argued for compatibility between aspects of Egyptian culture and Judaism (so Collins, *Jewish Wisdom*, 157). For a historical treatment of the Jews in Egypt, see Aryeh Kasher, *The Jews in Hellenistic and Roman Egypt* (TSAJ 7; Tübingen: Mohr Siebeck, 1985); J. M. G. Barclay, *Jews in the Mediterranean Diaspora, from Alexander to Trajan (323 BCE—117 CE)* (Edinburgh: T&T Clark, 1996).

parallels have been noted in Luke's parables of the Rich Fool and Lazarus and the Rich Man.[14]

14. On parallels with the Rich Fool, see Erich Klostermann and Hugo Gressmann, *Das Lukasevangelium* (HNT 2.1; Tübingen: Mohr Siebeck, 1919), 497; Christopher F. Evans, *Saint Luke* (TPINTC; Philadelphia: Trinity Press International, 1990), 522. On parallels with Lazarus and the Rich Man, see Hugo Gressmann, *Vom reichen Mann und armen Lazarus: Eine literargeschichtliche Studie* (Abhandlungen der Königlich Preussischen Akademie der Wissenschaften, Philosophisch-Historische Klasse, 1918, 7; Berlin: Königlichte Akademie der Wissenschaften, 1918); Kendrick Grobel, "'...Whose Name Was Neves,'" *NTS* 10 (1963–64): 373–82; Joseph. A. Fitzmyer, *The Gospel according to Luke: Introduction, Translation, and Notes* (2 vols.; AB 28–28A; Garden City, N.Y.: Doubleday, 1981–1985), 2:1126–27. Although most references to Egyptian texts will be from the Late Period, I will occasionally refer to earlier materials, since many texts contemporary to Luke-Acts, such as Papyrus Insinger, emerge from and are in conversation with a lengthy and influential trajectory.

1
Luke's Parable of the Rich Fool (12:16–21): Interpreting Its History of Interpretation

The Early–Medieval Periods

Luke's parable of the Rich Fool receives minimal attention in the early and medieval periods.[1] Most interpreters during this time who do cite the parable refer to only a portion of it and do so to bolster their denunciation of luxury and avarice. Clement of Alexandria cites 12:19–20 as one of several texts in his diatribe against those who "garishly squander wealth—for shame—and ignoring beauty they falsify God's gifts, rivaling the cunning of the evil one" (*Paed.* 2.12.125).[2] He identifies such people with the rich man in the parable. By pairing Luke 12:20 with Matt 16:26 ("For what will it profit a person if one gains the whole world..."), Clement seems to understand the rich man's fault to be related to an enormous accumulation

1. François Bovon does not find knowledge of Luke's Gospel among "most authors and apologists, especially those who were educated and orthodox ... until the middle of the second century" ("The Reception and Use of the Gospel of Luke in the Second Century," in *Reading Luke: Interpretation, Reflection, Formation* [ed. Craig G. Bartholomew, Joel B. Green, and Anthony C. Thiselton; Grand Rapids: Zondervan, 2005], 395). He considers Justin to be the first apologist who shows knowledge of Luke (395–96). For a critical response to Bovon, see Andrew Gregory, "Looking for Luke in the Second Century: A Dialogue with François Bovon," in Bartholomew, Green, and Thiselton, *Reading Luke*, 401–15; cf. idem, *The Reception of Luke and Acts in the Period before Irenaeus* (WUNT 2/169; Tübingen: Mohr Siebeck, 2003). Especially noteworthy is the parable's absence in Clement, *Who Is the Rich Man That Shall Be Saved?* Irenaeus does not discuss the parable despite his awareness of its existence; he cites 12:20 as a verse unique to Luke (*Haer.* 3.14.3).

2. Unless otherwise indicated, translations of ancient texts are my own. For the Greek text, see Clément d'Alexandrie, *Le Pédagogue* (SC; Paris: Cerf, 1965). For this and the other references to Clement of Alexandria, I use the citation system in SC.

of goods (*Strom.* 4.6.34).[3] In a chapter devoted to the spirit of the love of money (*filargyria*), Cassian cites Luke 12:20 as his final illustration in support of his admonition against the "disease of avarice [*filargyriae morbo*]" and the "madness of covetousness [*rabies cupiditatis*]" (*Institutes* 7.23–24, 30).[4] When used in this manner, the parable is reduced to a hortatory warning against the twin dangers of greed and luxury.

Understanding the parable in this manner may explain (and be influenced by?) its placement in Tatian's *Diatessaron*, one of the parable's earliest appearances outside Luke and Thomas.[5] Luke 12:13–21 follows John 7:2–31 and precedes the episode of the "rich young ruler" (a conflation of the three Synoptics). The parable of Lazarus and the Rich Man occurs shortly thereafter. In light of the "rich young man" episode, the rich man in Luke 12:16–21 seems to be positioned as someone who intentionally chooses his wealth over God. Subsequent interpreters ("premodern" and "modern") understand the parable's rich man in precisely this way and fault him for preferring wealth to God. Placing the parables of the Rich Fool and Lazarus and the Rich Man in close proximity also invites readers to consider whether the man in 12:16–21 neglects to care for the poor. Such a question becomes common throughout the parable's history of interpretation.[6] On the other hand, the absence in the *Diatessaron* of the discourse immediately following Luke's parable (Luke 12:22–34) may explain the scarce attention interpreters give to the link between the rich man and anxiety.[7]

On several occasions Cyprian utilizes the parable, like Clement and

3. Ephrem the Syrian pairs Luke 12:19–20 with Matt 16:26 in order to illustrate and warn readers of the future judgment (*Letter to Publius* 16; FC 91).

4. For the Latin text, see Jean Cassien, *Institutions Cénobitiques* (SC 109; Paris: Cerf, 2001), 324–26, 330. Cf. Richard Newhauser, *The Early History of Greed: The Sin of Avarice in Early Medieval Thought and Literature* (Cambridge: Cambridge University Press, 2000).

5. Cf. Gos. Thom. 63. See chapter 7 for a comparison of the versions in Luke and Thomas.

6. Cyprian, Cyril, and Erasmus refer to the rich man's failure to care for the poor. See below for details. The juxtaposition of the parables of the Rich Fool and Lazarus and the Rich Man (Luke 16:19–31) begins a trend that is repeated frequently by later interpreters. I am not arguing for literary dependence by these readers on the *Diatessaron*.

7. Tertullian (*Or.* 6) is an exception. Martin Luther also links the parable to the motif of anxiety (*Commentary on Isaiah 1: Lectures on Isaiah Chapters 1–39* [vol. 16 of *Luther's Works*; ed. Jaroslav Pelikan; Saint Louis: Concordia, 1969]).

Cassian, as a warning against luxury and greed. After citing 1 Tim 6:10—"for lust of money is the root of all evil"[8]—he refers to Luke 12:20 to aver that riches (*divitiae*) are the "root of seductive evils [*radicem malorum blandientium*]" (*Dom. or.* 19–20, CCSL 3A). In *Works and Almsgiving*, he cites 12:20 when warning his reader against being a slave and prisoner to money, one who has been "fettered by the chains and bonds of avarice [*catenis cupiditatis et vinculis alligatus*]" (*Eleem.* 13).[9] He similarly adduces Luke 12:20 in a catena of other biblical texts to assert that one should seek neither the desire to possess nor wealth ([*p*]*ossidendi concupiscentiam et pecuniam*; *Test.* 3.61, CCSL 3). For Cyprian, the parable highlights the potential peril of wealth.[10] Gregory Nazianzen sees in the parable a warning to those who hoard their treasures and fail to share their goods with the poor (*Or.* 14.18).

Cyprian's attention to the parable's broader literary context leads him to find not only a critique of the misuse of goods but also a recommendation regarding how to use possessions. Jesus teaches in the parable, on the one hand, that riches are dangerous (the "root of seductive evils") and that "with hidden deceit they deceive the blindness of the human mind" (*Dom. or.* 20). For this reason God "rebukes the foolish rich man who ponders on his worldly wealth and boasts of the abundance of his overflowing harvests" (*Dom. or.* 20). On the other hand, Cyprian observes that Jesus "teaches that he becomes perfect and complete who by selling all his possessions and distributing them for the use of the poor lays up for himself a treasure in heaven" (*Dom. or.* 20; cf. *Eleem.* 7). Cyprian thus sees in Luke 12:33 a constructive alternative to the negative example of the rich man in the parable. On another occasion, Cyprian reads the parable in light of 12:21, identifying the man's storage of earthly goods as poverty toward God.[11] Cyprian is also one of the first to highlight the man's loneliness as a possible fault.[12]

---

8. "Radix enim omnium malorum est cupiditas."

9. CCSL 3A; cf. Cyprien de Carthage, *La Bienfaisance et Les Aumônes* (ed. Michel Poirer; SC 440; Paris: Cerf, 1999), 110–11.

10. By claiming that the rich man was "rejoicing" in his stores (*Dom. or.* 4.20), Cyprian also begins a pattern—followed by other interpreters—of attributing vices to the rich man not made explicit in Luke's text (cf. *Eleem.* 13).

11. "Why do you heap up for your punishment the burden of an inheritance, that the richer you have been with the world, the poorer you become with God? Divide your revenue with your God; share your profits with Christ; make Christ a partner in your earthly possessions" (*Eleem.* 13).

12. "Why do you brood alone [*solus incubas*] over your riches?" (*Eleem.* 13).

Cyril of Alexandria's interest in the parable's literary context leads him to focus on a number of issues in addition to greed and luxury. The parable illustrates the principle in Luke 12:15 that one's life does not consist in one's possessions.[13] Cyril's other critique, that the man fails to raise his eyes to God and does not cherish love for the poor, is possibly due to reading the parable in conjunction with Luke 12:21 and 12:33. Like Cyprian, he notes the solitary nature of the rich man, identifying the man's plans to enjoy the fruits of his field by himself as one of his errors.

Prophetic texts are the most frequent choice for interpreters who read the parable in light of other biblical texts. Tertullian compares the rich man in the parable to Hezekiah (see Isa 39) and likens God's speech in 12:20 to Isaiah's harsh proclamation to Hezekiah (*Marc.* 4.28; cf. Isa 39:5–7).[14] Jerome links the rich man in Luke 12 to Nabal of 1 Sam 25:38 (*Epist.* 125.10). In berating those who oppress the poor, Gregory Nazianzen cites both Isa 58 and Luke 12. For Gregory, Isa 58 refers to people who show no pity to the widow or orphan, and the rich man in the parable is "the most unjust of all" (*On His Father's Silence* 18).

Concomitant with reading Luke's parable in light of prophetic texts is an emphasis on luxury or greed. Tertullian, in the example cited above, cites the parable—and 12:20 specifically—to underscore his point that God condemns boasting over riches (*divitiarum gloriam*; *Marc.* 4.28.11, CCSL 1). Cyril places the brother's request for Jesus to intervene in the inheritance dispute (12:13–15) into conversation with Amos 5:11 and Isa 5:8. Reading Luke 12:15 through these prophetic lenses, he concludes that the primary point of this dialogue and Jesus' response is the danger of covetousness.[15]

Clement of Alexandria's remarks on the connection between prophetic and parabolic discourse may suggest one possible reason for the prevailing tendency in this period to read Luke's parable in concert with prophetic texts. Clement asserts that the "character [χαρακτὴρ] of the Scriptures is parabolic [παραβολικὸς]" and subsequently claims that this parabolic "nature" (εἶδος) of the Scripture is "most ancient" and "naturally

13. Cyril of Alexandria, *The Gospel of Saint Luke* (trans. R. Payne Smith; n.p.: Studion, 1983), 360–61.

14. Tertullian comments extensively on the three parables in Luke 15 (*Paen.* 8; *Pud.* 7–9; cf. *Marc.* 4.32) but does not engage substantively the Rich Fool parable.

15. Cyril of Alexandria, *The Gospel of Saint Luke*, 360.

abounded most of all in the prophets" (*Strom.* 6.15.126–127).[16] Furthermore, neither prophecy (προφητεία) nor Jesus "declared the divine mysteries simply so as to be understood easily by any who encounter [them], but [rather each] conversed in parables [ἐν παραβολαῖς διελέξατο]" (*Strom.* 6.15.124). Prophecy was spoken by Jesus "in parables," and "the holy mysteries of the prophecies are veiled [ἐγχαλύπτεται] in the parables" (*Strom.* 6.15.125–126).[17] Clement's view of the similarity between the style of Jesus' parables and the prophets, if shared by others, may have influenced the practice of reading Luke's parable with prophetic texts in mind (cf. *Strom.* 6.15.129–130).

What is clear is that reading Luke's parable in light of sapiential texts yields noticeably disparate results from reading it in light of prophetic texts. Reading the parable in concert with wisdom texts leads interpreters to focus not only upon luxury and avarice but also upon other issues germane to the parable such as death and inheritance.[18] Only two interpreters from this period cite the parable in conjunction with a wisdom text. Athanasius adduces Qoh 9:12 and Luke 12:20 to support his claim that, although everyone's time is "measured" (μετρέω), no one knows the *end* of one's time (τὸ τέλος τοῦ χρόνου) (*Fug.* 15). The rich man thus errs by "thinking he still has a little time to live." On two separate occasions Augustine juxtaposes Luke's parable with a psalm. He suggests that Luke 12:20 fulfills Ps 49:16–17, the latter of which describes how a rich person will neither receive anything nor maintain glory in death (*Enarrat. Ps.* 2.6).[19] Augustine seems to link these two texts because of the common

16. I was alerted to these references in Warren S. Kissinger, *The Parables of Jesus: A History of Interpretation and Bibliography* (ATLA Bibliography Series 4; Metuchen, N.J.: American Theological Library Association, 1979).

17. The prophecies are veiled in this manner because it is not suitable for "all to understand." Clement may likely have been influenced by Mark 4 and Isa 6 here.

18. Chrysostom is an exception and one of the only interpreters who comments on death without reading the parable in light of sapiential texts. In an admonition to give away one's riches, he cites the parable's conclusion to stress that death's timing is uncertain and that the "tenure" of possessions is insecure (*Eutrop.* 2.5). He elsewhere refers to the parable to make the point that a soul, once torn from the body, can no longer wander the earth (*Hom. Matt.* 28.3). Although not explicitly raised in the *Recognitions of Clement* (10.45), the motif of death is intimated in the reference to the parable to support the argument that rich people should not delay their conversion.

19. Psalm 49 is widely regarded as a wisdom psalm. See, e.g., Gerhard von Rad, *Wisdom in Israel* (Nashville: Abingdon, 1972), 49.

motif of the death of a rich person. He also finds similarities between Luke 12:20 and the description in Ps 39:6 of one who heaps up treasures but is uncertain who will gather them (*Trin.* 14.14.19). Here Augustine highlights the uncertainty of the recipient of one's inheritance. It is unclear if Augustine attends to death and the uncertainty of inheritance because of reading the parable in light of these psalms or if this pairing is a consequence of motifs he perceives they share in common. Important for our purposes is the identification of themes (death, the uncertainty of inheritance) by Athanasius and Augustine that tend to be neglected when the parable is read with prophetic texts.[20]

Scant attention is given to the parable of the Rich Fool in the medieval era. It is one of the only parables unique to Luke that was not included in the first printed missal for the Roman rite (published in Milan in 1474). Its absence in the list is noteworthy, given the presence in the missal of most of Luke's other parables (the Lost Sheep, Samaritan, Friend at Midnight, Lost Coin, Father and Two Sons, Unjust Steward, Rich Man and Lazarus, and Pharisee and the Publican).[21] In his extensive study of allegorical treatments of parables in the medieval period, Stephen Wailes concludes that medieval sources "contain no thorough allegory" for the parable of the Rich Fool. He finds that medieval interpreters treat the parable as an "illustration of the dangers of avarice … and an exhortation to almsgiving."[22]

These twin concerns mirror two of the predominant emphases given

---

20. Augustine cites most of the parable in a sermon on Matt 19:21. Curiously, instead of "eat, drink, be merry" (12:19), he has: "Soul, you have many goods; be satisfied; be delighted [*Anima habes multa bona, satiare, iocundare*]" (*Serm.* 36.9, CCSL 41). This difference in phrasing makes identification of the allusion with Qoh 8:15 more difficult. (In a separate sermon on Luke 12:15, he does cite Luke 12:19 as "eat, drink, be merry" [*Serm.* 57].) Augustine links the rich man in the parable to the other "luxurious" rich man in Luke's parable of Lazarus and the Rich Man (*Serm.* 36.16). In a sermon on Luke 12:15, Augustine writes that the rich man had no concern for the needs of the poor (*Serm.* 57.6). Although these last two remarks occur in different sermons, it is possible that his pairing of the parable with that in Luke 16:19–31 helps explain his comment regarding the man's lack of regard for the poor. Augustine understands God's speech to the rich man as God's attempt to put an end to the folly of the man's avarice (*Serm. Dom.* 2.33).

21. Stephen L. Wailes, *Medieval Allegories of Jesus' Parables* (Publications of the UCLA Center for Medieval and Renaissance Studies 23; Berkeley: University of California Press, 1987), 6–7.

22. Ibid., 220.

to the parable in the early church, indicating a certain consistency regarding the treatment of the parable in both periods. The focus on avarice and almsgiving, moreover, underscores the likelihood that the lack of interest in the parable was due in no small part to the perception—shared by many early and medieval readers—that it offered little more than a simple critique of greed. The absence of any allegorical treatment of the parable in the medieval era reflects an assumption that everything to be learned from the parable could be discerned from a surface reading.

The predominant attention in the early and medieval periods on reading the parable in light of prophetic, rather than wisdom, texts helps explain the dominant moral focus on the proper use of possessions and the corresponding neglect of the theme of death. It is uncertain whether reading Luke's parable as a critique of avarice is a necessary consequence of placing it into conversation with prophetic texts—in which avarice is frequently castigated—or whether the parable is placed into dialogue with prophetic texts because it is understood to be chiefly concerned with avarice. In either case, readers highlight greed and luxury and ignore or downplay death and several other significant motifs. Although some wisdom texts are adduced as parallels to the parable, no extant text mentions the parable's internal allusions to Qoh 8:15 or Sir 11:14–19, an oversight contributing to the predominant focus on greed and possessions. Pertinent as well for our purposes is the absence of interest in the parable as an illustration of an attempt to wrestle with whether—and how—possessions might be used meaningfully in light of death.

Reformation

Erasmus, Luther, and Calvin continue the practice of reading the parable primarily as a warning against the twin dangers of greed and luxury. Yet these three readers also display an interest in other elements in the parable, such as death and anxiety.

Erasmus focuses on the role of possessions in the parable. He follows some earlier interpreters by faulting the rich man for responding to the growth of his fields with a selfishness that did not consider the needs of his poor neighbors.[23] In what is likely influence from the discourse following

23. Erasmus, *Paraphrase on Luke 11–24* (vol. 48 of *Collected Works of Erasmus*; trans. Jane E. Phillips; Toronto: University of Toronto Press, 2003), 33.

the parable (Luke 12:22–34), Erasmus observes that, rather than thinking about how he might meet such needs, the rich man instead worries about storing his goods. Erasmus suggests that, if the rich man had been guided by love, he would have become aware of the needs of those around him. As a blessing from God, the man's lands are to be used for generosity. The rich man thus fails because he prefers to be guided by folly rather than love.

Erasmus also sees in the parable a focus on death. He modifies God's speech to the rich man so that God chastises him for assuming that he has many years left to live.[24] Erasmus may be influenced here by the rich man's soliloquy (in which he anticipates enjoying his goods for many years to come) and the insistence in 12:22–34 that one cannot prolong one's life. The speech Erasmus inserts into God's mouth highlights the uncertain timing of death, moving it to the forefront of the parable.

In Erasmus's version of the speech, God informs the rich man that his possessions will no longer belong to him but rather to his "heir, or to anyone else who seizes them."[25] Erasmus here answers a question the parable asks (Luke 12:20b) but leaves unanswered ("And the things you prepared, whose will they be?"). The man could have acquired "spiritual riches," which would have accompanied him into death, if only he had disbursed his wealth to others. Erasmus concludes his commentary by reiterating that God desires the rich to give relief to the needy. Those who become monetarily poor in giving away their goods are "more blessedly rich."[26] It is possible that Erasmus is influenced by Luke 12:33, in which the giving of alms is prescribed as an ideal use of goods.

The general neglect of Luke's parable in the early and medieval periods is replicated in its relative marginal treatment by Luther; it is one of the only parables unique to Luke on which he apparently did not preach.[27] He only refers to the parable when commenting on other biblical texts, in order to buttress or illustrate points he finds in these texts. He twice cites

24. Ibid., 34: "You fool, since life itself is not guaranteed you, why are you storing up for years to come? For only in this life can you enjoy the things you are putting away, and no one is guaranteed life for even a single day. Why are you promising yourself many years?"

25. Ibid.

26. Ibid.

27. Luther preached on the parables of the Samaritan, the Lost Coin, the Steward, Lazarus and the Rich Man, and the Pharisee and the Tax Collector. See Eugene F. A. Klug, ed., *Sermons of Martin Luther: The House Postils* (trans. Eugene F. A. Klug et al.; 3 vols.; Grand Rapids: Baker, 1996).

the parable when discussing a prophetic text to illustrate the danger of avarice.[28] The parable thus seems to merit attention not in its own right but rather as an adjunct to other texts.

Luther does, however, highlight elements in the parable often neglected by other interpreters (e.g., death and uncertainty regarding both inheritance and the future). His attention to these motifs correlates with, and may partially result from, pairing the parable with sapiential texts. He twice cites Luke's parable to defend his related claims that one cannot know the future and that God condemns human presumption about the future.[29] He follows the latter comment in *Trade and Usury* with a note that nearly the entire book of Ecclesiastes is devoted to this principle of not knowing the future.[30] He also cites another wisdom text here, Prov 27:1, to bolster his claim of presumption about the future.

On two occasions Luther refers to the parable to illustrate the general impossibility of determining the recipient of one's inheritance.[31] Luther here echoes—whether intentionally or not—Qoheleth's stress on the twin inability to take goods beyond death and the uncertainty regarding who would inherit one's goods. Qoheleth complains about the uncertainties involved in leaving one's inheritance to another (2:18–19, 21) and the possibility of leaving it to a stranger (6:1–2).

Luther's attention to the role of death in the parable also appears to be influenced by readings of sapiential texts. He refers to Luke 12:20 while commenting on Qoh 7:16–17 to stress the potential imminence of death and divine judgment.[32] In a comment on Matt 6:19–21, he claims that "what Christ describes in Luke 12:16–21" depicts the lesson he finds in Ps

28. Luther, *Commentary on Isaiah 1*, 341; idem, *Commentary on Habakkuk* (vol. 19 of *Luther's Works*; ed. Hilton C. Oswald; trans. Martin H. Bertram; Saint Louis: Concordia, 1955), 214.

29. Martin Luther, *Fourteen Consolations* (vol. 42 of *Luther's Works*; ed. Martin O. Dietrich; trans. Martin H. Bertram; Philadelphia: Fortress, 1969), 148; idem, *Trade and Usury* (vol. 45 of *Luther's Works*; ed. Walther I. Brandt; trans. Charles M. Jacobs; Philadelphia: Muhlenberg, 1962), 254–55.

30. Luther, *Trade and Usury*, 255.

31. Martin Luther, *The Sermon on the Mount* (vol. 21 of *Luther's Works*; ed. and trans. Jaroslav Pelikan; Saint Louis: Concordia, 1956), 174–75; idem, *1 Timothy* (vol. 28 of *Luther's* Works; ed. Hilton C. Oswald; trans. Richard J. Dinda; Saint Louis: Concordia, 1973), 370.

32. Martin Luther, *Notes on Ecclesiastes* (vol. 15 of *Luther's Works*; ed. and trans. Jaroslav Pelikan; Saint Louis: Concordia, 1972), 123.

76:5, namely, that riches cannot be carried into death by those who serve them in life.[33]

Diverging sharply from previous readings of the parable, Luther identifies the parable as an illustration of *poor* people's greed. Luther's focus on the man's avarice, coupled with his belief that poor people are the greediest of all, leads him to apply the parable to the poor and to describe the rich man's monologue as "the peasant's song that all the greedy bellies sing."[34] Wealth, Luther insists, is not the rich man's problem.

Jean Calvin considers Luke's parable and its meaning to be fairly simple and straightforward. There is, he writes, "nothing here but what is perfectly common, and what every man has constantly in his mouth," namely, that accumulating great wealth cannot prevent one's life from suddenly being taken away.[35] Calvin's claim regarding the parable's simplicity both echoes previous interpretations and anticipates assumptions (explicit and tacit) that become common in subsequent centuries.

Calvin's perception of the parable as "perfectly common" may be due to his failure to cite any wisdom texts as pertinent to the parable and to read it in concert with such texts. Although he notes that the phrase "eat, drink, enjoy" (Luke 12:19b) is a "Hebrew idiom"—even adding that "there is greater force and propriety than the words appear at first"—he neither specifies the source of this Hebrew idiom (Qoh 8:15) nor clarifies what this "greater force" is. His identification of 12:19b as a "Hebrew idiom" neither illuminates the parable nor influences his reading of it.

Calvin finds three primary messages in the parable: the warning of the danger of covetousness; the demonstration that the "present life is short and transitory"; and the message that "riches are of no avail for prolonging life."[36] His emphasis on covetousness reiterates the prevailing interpretive

---

33. Luther, *Sermon on the Mount*, 174; cf. 14.

34. Ibid., 174. Cf. 12–13: "There is many a beggar getting bread at our door more arrogant and wicked than any rich man, and many a miserable, stingy peasant who is harder to get along with than any lord or prince." Again: "the poorest and most miserable beggars are the worst and most desperate rascals and dare to commit every kind of mischief and evil tricks, which fine, upstanding people, rich citizens or lords and princes, do not do." These remarks may reflect influence of the peasant revolt in 1525, to which he responded harshly. The published commentary on the Sermon on the Mount (1532) was based on his preaching in 1530.

35. Jean Calvin, *Commentary on a Harmony of the Evangelists, Matthew, Mark, and Luke* (trans. William Pringle; 3 vols.; Grand Rapids: Eerdmans, 1949), 2:148.

36. Ibid. Calvin claims the parable was "intended" to show that "vain are the

trends in the patristic period.[37] Like Erasmus and Luther, Calvin highlights the role of death, but he also discerns a certain link between death and possessions.[38]

Nineteenth Century

David Friedrich Strauss exemplifies Calvin's claim regarding the simple and straightforward nature of the parable. The parable's perceived simplicity may explain the thirteen words Strauss spends describing it, compared with the two pages he devotes to the parable of the Unjust Steward.[39] The former, he claims, is one of five parables unique to Luke that has a "definite, clear signification."[40] His minimal attention to the parable echoes Calvin's perception of it as revealing nothing but what is "perfectly common." Like Calvin, Strauss reflects and anticipates the primary way in which the parable will be understood, as an uncomplicated story requiring little if any interpretation.

Just such an interpretation appears in Alexander Balmain Bruce's tome on the parables. Bruce chooses not to examine the parable of the Rich Fool in his self-titled "systematic" study, since he considers it to be of

deliberations and foolish attempts of those who, trusting to the abundance of their wealth, do not rely on God alone, and are not satisfied with their own share, or prepared for whatever may befall them; and finally, that such persons will suffer the penalty of their own folly" (2:150–51).

37. The rich man, "agitated by insatiable desire," enlarges his barns "as if his belly, which had been filled with his former barns, had not got enough" (2:149). Calvin considers the man's storage of his produce to be a positive character trait. The man is instead condemned for his "ravenous desire [which] like a deep whirlpool, swallows up and devours many barns." The man's greed shows that he "does not comprehend the proper use of an abundant produce" (2:149). Calvin does not, however, clarify what this alternative use might entail.

38. The rich man, avers Calvin, "lengthens out his expectation of life in proportion to his large income, and drives far away from him the remembrance of death" (2:149).

39. David Friedrich Strauss, *The Life of Jesus Critically Examined* (trans. from the 4th German edition by George Eliot; Philadelphia: Fortress, 1972), 348–50. In a parenthetical comment (349), he suggests that one compare Luke's parable with Sir 11:17ff. (Strauss writes "Wis 11:17ff," but I understand him to refer to Ben Sira). He does not, however, comment upon how this parallel text might help elucidate Luke's parable.

40. Ibid., 348–49. The other four parables he cites are the Two Debtors, Samaritan, Friend at Midnight, and Widow and Judge.

no "independent didactic importance."[41] The parable's absence in Bruce's study is significant given the (perceived) stature of his work at the time.[42] For Bruce, the parable "simply teaches in concrete lively form a moral commonplace" and contains "no new or abstruse lesson." Such parables, he avers, were not distinctive to Jesus and can be found among the rabbis; indeed, Jesus speaks the parable of the rich fool as a "Jewish moralist."[43] Bruce prefers instead to focus on parables that "embody truths deep, unfamiliar or unwelcome," those that reflect "mysteries of the Kingdom."[44] Bruce thus continues a trajectory that sees little in the parable other than a "simplistic" tale.

Adolf Jülicher: A Turning Point in Scholarship?

In some ways, Adolf Jülicher anticipates future scholarship on the parable of the Rich Fool. Such is the case with his classification of the parable (and three others) as an "example narrative" (*Beispielerzählung*).[45] Jülicher is also one of the first to identify Qoh 8:15 as a parallel text to Luke 12:19, noting that both share the same three verbs in common (ἐσθίω, πίνω, εὐφραίνω).[46] Yet like Calvin, Jülicher fails to mention why or how the parallel he identifies is significant for understanding Luke's parable.[47] He establishes a pattern in which the identification of a parallel text is presented as meaningful in its own right.[48] Yet citing information is not

41. Bruce, *The Parabolic Teaching of Christ*, 9.

42. Adolf Jülicher lauds Bruce for certain aspects of his work (*Die Gleichnisreden Jesu* [2 vols.; Tübingen: Mohr Siebeck, vol. 1, 1888; vols. 1–2, 1899; repr., 1910], 1:300). Gerant Vaughan Jones wrote in 1964 that Bruce's work "has not been surpassed in English" (*The Art and Truth of the Parables: A Study in Their Literary Form and Modern Interpretation* [London: SPCK, 1964], 9).

43. Bruce, *The Parabolic Teaching of Christ*, 9.

44. Ibid.

45. Jülicher, *Die Gleichnisreden Jesu*, 2:viii. The other three are the Samaritan, Lazarus and the Rich Man, and the Pharisee and the Tax Collector.

46. Ibid., 2:611–12. He also notes the similarity with Tob 7:10 (φάγε, πίε καὶ ἡδέως γίνου).

47. He does cite the Qoh 8:15 parallel to suggest that Rönsch may be incorrect in thinking Luke based the rich man's speech on Roman funeral rites formula (*Parentationsformel*) (2:611).

48. Abraham J. Malherbe ("Hellenistic Moralists and the New Testament," *ANRW* 2.26.1:275–76) speaks of citing parallels "without allowing the exposition of those books to be substantially influenced by the parallels." His critique of the "uncritical

tantamount to illumination, nor does it constitute legitimate interpretation.[49]

Jülicher's interpretation comports in other ways with previous patterns of reading the parable.[50] Of the four "example stories," he gives the least attention to the "Foolish Rich Man," thereby continuing the parable's negligible treatment.[51] Moreover, although his classification of the parable as a *Beispielerzählung* is often heralded as a monumental shift in the history of parable interpretation, such classification does not significantly alter how subsequent scholars read the parable of the Rich Fool. Jülicher's (allegedly) stark departure from reading parables allegorically has had far less impact upon the interpretation of Luke 12:16–21, perhaps because this parable (up until Jülicher's time) was not commonly read allegorically. Understanding Luke 12:16–21 as a "negative example" mimics reading practices of the parable in the early church. Jülicher's description of the story as "highly simple" resembles the remarks of Calvin and Bruce regarding the parable's complete lack of complexity.[52] If anything, Jülicher's classification of the parable as a *Beispielerzählung* merely provided a *terminus technicus* to what was already an established pattern for treating this parable.

"Modern" Readers

The general neglect of the Rich Fool parable in the early and middle twentieth century is consonant with its reception in the early, medieval, and Reformation periods. Many modern parable scholars fail to treat the par-

---

use of parallels" (regarding Hellenistic moral philosophers and the New Testament) is apropos to readings of Luke's parable.

49. Jülicher echoes Calvin in two additional ways. The latter states that his goal is to find the "one" primary meaning of each parable, and he displays a disdain for speculative readings: "To inquire with great exactness into every minute part of a parable is an absurd mode of philosophizing" (Calvin, *Commentary on a Harmony*, 176).

50. For an anticipation of Jülicher's rejection of allegory and his focus upon one primary meaning of the parable, see C. E. van Koetsveld, *De Gelijkenissen van den Zaligmaker* (2 vols.; Utrecht: Schoonhoven, 1869); E. P. Gould, *St Mark* (ICC; New York: Charles Scribner's Sons, 1896), 74.

51. Jülicher, *Die Gleichnisreden Jesu*, 2:611. His remarks on the parable focus on grammar and textual parallels. He cites, for example, certain psalms that contain speeches to one's own person.

52. Ibid., 2:608.

able. It is absent, for example, in C. H. Dodd's work on the parables.[53] Nor is it one of the eleven parables that Linnemann analyzes.[54] The parable is absent in most theologies of the New Testament[55] and even in a book on Lukan theology.[56]

The perception of the parable as simple and straightforward is one of the primary reasons for its lack of attention by past and present scholars.[57] In her brief remarks on the parable, Linnemann reinforces the notion that discovering the parable's message requires little thinking or imagination on the part of the reader.[58] As noted previously, Jülicher's designation of the parable as a *Beispielerzählung* merely provided a *de jure* classification for what was already a *de facto* practice. But the importance of his classification is significant, since it has seemed to provide further warrant for scholars to dismiss the parable as a "simple" tale. Many scholars (German, French, and American) have followed Jülicher's classification of the par-

53. Dodd, *The Parables of the Kingdom.*

54. Linnemann, *Parables of Jesus.*

55. Rudolf Bultmann refers to several Lukan parables (Luke 10:30–37; 15:11–32; 18:2–5, 10–13) but omits the Rich Fool (*Theology of the New Testament* [trans. Kendrick Grobel; 2 vols.; New York: Charles Scriber's Sons, 1951–1955], 1:14, 17, 24). George Bradford Caird does not cite the parable, but he neglects most of Luke's parables (despite his reliance on Luke as the primary text upon which he constructs his theology) (*New Testament Theology* [ed. L. D. Hurst; Oxford: Clarendon, 1994]). Adolf Schlatter twice refers to the parable in a section entitled "Jesus' Dispute with the Rich" (*The History of the Christ: The Foundation for New Testament Theology* [trans. Andreas J. Köstenberger; Grand Rapids: Baker, 1997], 166–70). He joins other interpreters in understanding the potential danger of wealth as the parable's chief concern (167). Schlatter anticipates a future scholarly emphasis with his identification of the rich man's fault as his willful hedonism. Werner Georg Kümmel refers to the parable only once, and he does so to support his claim that Jesus believed God would play the role of judge in the future (*The Theology of the New Testament: According to Its Major Witnesses: Jesus, Paul, John* [trans. John E. Steely; Nashville: Abingdon, 1973], 40).

56. Hans Conzelmann, *Die Mitte Der Zeit* (Tubingen: Mohr Siebeck, 1953).

57. Other books on the parables that omit the Rich Fool include Via, *The Parables*; Perkins, *Hearing the Parables of Jesus*; Funk, *Parables and Presence*; Herzog, *Parables as Subversive Speech*; Schottroff, *Die Gleichnisse Jesu*; Bailey, *Poet and Peasant.*

58. Linnemann (*Parables of Jesus*, 4) calls Luke's parable an "illustration," which she distinguishes from "similitudes and parables." Whereas a parable adduces a "correspondence (*analogia*)," the illustration produces an "example (*exemplum*)" (5). A parable requires one to transfer the narrative's content to "another level (from 'picture' to 'reality')." The illustration, on the other hand, "refers directly to the reality and only needs to be generalized" (5).

able as an "example story."[59] An exception is Jeffrey Tucker, who highlights some of the problems and misguided assumptions in creating a distinction between the categories "parable" and "example story."[60] Despite his refutation of Jülicher's classification, few have followed Tucker in discarding "example story" as an appropriate category for parables.[61]

Most modern interpreters who treat the parable emphasize wealth and avarice, showing considerable less interest in death, the relationship between death and possessions, and the parable's own allusions to wisdom texts. Rudolf Bultmann is somewhat representative; he does not cite any parallel Jewish wisdom texts to the parable,[62] and his title for Luke 12:13–34, "attitude to possessions in this world," suggests that wealth is the parable's chief concern. It is perhaps no coincidence that Bultmann, like Jülicher, sees the parable as an "exemplary story," one that has "no figu-

59. So, e.g., Klostermann and Gressmann, *Das Lukasevangelium*, 497; Rudolf Bultmann, *The History of the Synoptic Tradition* (trans. John Marsh; Oxford: Blackwell, 1963), 177–78; Egbert Seng, "Der Reiche Tor: Eine Untersuchung von Lk. xii 16–21 unter besonderer Berücksichtigung form- und motivgeschichtlicher Aspekte," *NovT* 20 (1978), 141, 151–52; Wolfgang Wiefel, *Das Evangelium nach Lukas* (Berlin: Evangelische Verlagasanstalt, 1988), 236; Fitzmyer, *The Gospel according to Luke*, 2:971; François Bovon, *L'Évangile Selon Saint Luc 9,51–14,35* (CNT Deuxième Série IIIb; Geneva: Labor et fides, 1996), 273.

60. Jeffrey T. Tucker, *Example Stories: Perspectives on Four Parables in the Gospel of Luke* (JSNTSup 162; Sheffield: Sheffield Academic Press, 1998). He finds that "the categorical distinction between *Parabel* and *Beispielerzählung* does not withstand scrutiny" and that the use of the category "example story" is unhelpful (42). John Dominic Crossan argues that when originally told these four narratives were parables, but secondary additions have resulted in their present form as example narratives ("Parable and Example in the Teaching of Jesus," *NTS* 18 [1971–1972]: 285–307).

61. Cf. Ernst Baasland, "Zum Beispiel der Beispielerzahlungen: Zur Formenlehre der Gleichnisse und zur Methodik der Gleichnisauslegung," *NovT* 28 (1986), 219; Klyne Snodgrass prefers using the term "single indirect parable" (*Stories with Intent: A Comprehensive Guide to the Parables of Jesus* [Grand Rapids: Eerdmans, 2008], 13–15, 350–52, 397).

62. Bultmann (*History of the Synoptic Tradition*, 204) does refer to a parallel in *Thousand and One Nights*: "A certain king, who had collected rich treasures, was summoned by the angel of death at the very moment when he was sitting at a luxurious table, and saying to himself: 'Soul, you have amassed for yourself all the good things of the world, and now you can enjoy them in a long life and good fortune.'" Bultmann fails to clarify how this parallel influences one's reading of Luke's parable.

rative element at all."[63] Arthur Cadoux identifies avarice as the parable's chief emphasis,[64] and the only parallel text he cites is a Muslim tradition attributed to Jesus that also highlights the folly of avarice.[65]

Central to this book's argument is that many concerns germane to Luke's parable are illuminated when it is read in concert with Second Temple (primarily sapiential) texts whose focus is the interplay of death and possessions. Cursory readings of the parable, such as those by Bultmann and Cadoux, usually accompany a failure to situate it within this set of texts. Evident in many other scholars is a corollary between an almost exclusive focus on wealth or avarice and a failure to consider wisdom texts as pertinent conversation partners.[66] Scholars who do cite wisdom texts usually fail to show how such texts elucidate Luke's parable.[67]

The failure to cite certain wisdom texts can result in questionable readings of the parable. Robert Tannehill, who sees possessions as the primary concern in 12:13–34, faults the rich man's plans in 12:19 as a "hedonistic" formula.[68] Tannehill adduces several parallels to Luke 12:19 (Isa 22:13; 1 Cor 15:32; Sir 11:19) but omits Qoh 8:15 from this list. Had he placed the parable into dialogue with Qoh 8:15, and considered the man's plans as an attempt to actualize this maxim, he may not have evaluated the man's behavior as wholly negative. Tannehill cites the adage "Let us eat and drink, *for tomorrow we die*" and insinuates that the man is a fool because

63. Ibid., 177–78. Bultmann's primary concern is the parable's tradition history (cf. 23, 178, 192–93, 324, 335).

64. Arthur T. Cadoux, *The Parables of Jesus: Their Art and Use* (London: Clark, 1931), 205. He sees in 12:20 ("God's epithet, demand and question") the parable's chief meaning, namely, the "*reductio ad* absurdum of selfishness."

65. Ibid., 206: "Whoso craves wealth is like a man who drinks sea-water: the more he drinks, the more he increases his thirst, and he ceases not to drink until he perishes."

66. See, e.g., Charles H. Talbert, *Reading Luke: A Literary and Theological Commentary on the Third Gospel* (New York: Crossroad, 1982), 140; Crossan, *In Parables*, 83; Fred B. Craddock, *Luke* (IBC; Louisville: John Knox, 1990), 162. Craddock reads the parable through Exod 20:17 and prophetic texts (e.g., Mic 2:2).

67. Wiefel, who also classifies the parable as a *Beispielerzählung*, notes that the parable "takes up Jewish ideas" in its description of the rich man but does not specify what such ideas might be (*Das Evangelium nach Lukas*, 236). He lists 1 En. 97:8 and Sir 11:18 as texts that bear upon Luke's parable, but his only insight about these is that "Jesus thinks of a landowner, one who expects a rich harvest" (237).

68. Robert C. Tannehill, *The Gospel according to Luke* (vol. 1 of *The Narrative Unity of Luke-Acts: A Literary Interpretation*; Philadelphia: Fortress, 1986), 246; cf. idem, *Luke*, 205–6.

he does not realize that death follows those who enjoy themselves.[69] The parable provides no indication, however, that the rich man's plans cause his death. Moreover, and as we shall see in chapter 2, Qoheleth repeatedly extols enjoyment as an ideal use of possessions.

The interpretation of Luke's parable—and of any text—is significantly influenced by the parallel texts, or conversation partners, one selects and omits. Joachim Jeremias cites one parallel to Luke's parable, Ps 14:1 ("A fool says in his heart, 'There is no God' "), claiming that the term "fool" (ἄφρων) in Luke 12:20 is used in the same sense as it is in the psalm.[70] The number of interpreters who follow Jeremias in reading the rich man's folly through the lens of Ps 14:1 is legion. Joseph Fitzmyer cites Ps 14:1 to support his claim that the "God-fool contrast" runs throughout the parable.[71] Wolfgang Wiefel maintains, in light of Ps 14:1, that the rich man has forgotten God.[72] Frederick Danker sees in Luke's description of the farmer a fitting application to "persons who forget God."[73] Tannehill, referring to Ps 14:1, declares that the rich man "is a fool because he is thinking of his own pleasures and behaving as if there is no God."[74] That God calls the rich man a fool indicates to Stephen Wright that the man is "one who 'has said in his heart: "there is no God." ' "[75] Bernard Brendan Scott reads the parable through the lens of Ps 14:1, concluding that the rich man "dies a fool, one whose very activity has denied the existence of God."[76] In what likely reflects influence from Ps 14:1, I. Howard Marshall writes, "The fool is the man who feels no need of God."[77] Klyne Snodgrass similarly avers: "Like the fool in Ps 14:1 the man left God out of the picture."[78]

69. Ibid., 206.

70. Joachim Jeremias, *The Parables of Jesus* (2nd ed.; trans. S. H. Hooke; Upper Saddle River, N.J.: Prentice Hall, 1972), 165.

71. Fitzmyer, *The Gospel according to Luke*, 2:971.

72. Wiefel, *Das Evangelium nach Lukas*, 236.

73. Frederick W. Danker, *Jesus and the New Age: A Commentary on St. Luke's Gospel* (rev and exp. ed.; Philadelphia: Fortress, 1988), 247–48.

74. Robert C. Tannehill, *Luke* (ANTC; Nashville: Abingdon, 1996), 206.

75. Stephen I. Wright, "Parables on Poverty and Riches," in *The Challenge of Jesus' Parables* (ed. Richard N. Longenecker; Grand Rapids: Eerdmans, 2000), 222.

76. Bernard Brandon Scott, *Re-imagine the World: An Introduction to the Parables of Jesus* (Santa Rosa, Calif.: Polebridge, 2001), 95.

77. I. Howard Marshall, *Luke: Historian and Theologian* (Carlisle, U.K.: Paternoster, 1970).

78. Snodgrass, *Stories with Intent*, 399.

As the preceding statements suggest, reading the parable in light of Ps 14:1 leads to understanding the rich man's fault in (primarily) theological terms. Such theological readings (at least of the parable's final form) are not without merit, especially given the explicit comment in 12:21b. It is questionable, however, if the single use of ἄφρων ("fool"; 12:20) legitimates these particular theological readings. Numerous sapiential texts associate folly with motifs that are germane to Luke's parable, namely, the misuse of possessions and/or faulty perceptions of death. In chapters 5–7, I will show that these (and other) texts offer a more fruitful and illuminating context for understanding the use and function of "fool" in 12:20a. I will demonstrate, moreover, the importance and advantage of reading Luke 12:20a in light of Luke's only other use of ἄφρων (11:40).

Although not entirely neglected in the early part of the twentieth century, attention to the role of death and possessions in the parable increases notably in the latter third of the century. Jeremias argues that the initial focus on death and possessions in the parable's original version was subsequently "transformed into a warning against the wrong use of possessions."[79] He identifies the parable's focus as the approaching "eschatological catastrophe" that will be as urgent and imminent as the man's demise. For Joseph Fitzmyer, the parable illustrates the death of an individual person and, *contra* Jeremias, not an eschatological catastrophe or the coming judgment.[80] The man fails to realize that death may arrive at any time, and the "point" of the parable involves the "consideration of death" that Jesus brings "into human existence."[81]

Scholarly interest in the motif of death accompanies, and may partially result from, readings that consider the parable's immediate literary context. Although Caird understands the potential dangers of wealth as

---

79. Jeremias, *The Parables of Jesus*, 106. He sees the parable's original eschatological warning directed to a "fool obsessed by his possessions and unconscious of the sword of Damocles hanging over his head" (cf. 164). The new version of the parable, altered to have a "direct hortatory application," is more similar to the man in Matt 6:19–21 who stores up treasure for himself on earth (83, 87, 112–13). In this change he sees Jesus being turned into a "Teacher of Wisdom," a shift whose triumph he finds celebrated in Jülicher's work. Jeremias classifies Luke's parable under the category "Imminence of Catastrophe." For Jeremias, God shatters the security of the "rich fool" in a night (164).

80. Fitzmyer, *The Gospel according to Luke*, 2:971.

81. The man, Fitzmyer claims, experiences judgment at his death in the form of God's speech, and one must answer in this judgment for how one has lived one's life.

the parable's central theme, he also—as a result of reading the parable in light of Luke 12:22–34—observes the role of anxiety and, to a lesser extent, death.[82] Luke Timothy Johnson observes connections regarding death, possessions, and anxiety in the parable and its immediate literary context (Luke 12:13–34), identifying fear/anxiety and possessions as the unit's focus.[83] He sees alms in 12:33 as the alternative proposal to the critique in 12:21 of the rich man's use of goods.[84] The acknowledgment of the reality of death in the discourse on anxiety (12:22–31) influences his faulting the rich man for failing to consider the possibility of his imminent death.[85]

As is intimated above, attention to the parable's broader literary context has the potential to engender richer readings of the parable. A second way to enlarge the parable's context (and range of fruitful meanings) is to situate it within its broader cultural matrix. My approach to the parable (detailed in chs. 5–7) adopts both of these reading strategies and shows

---

82. G. B. Caird, *The Gospel of St. Luke* (New York: Seabury, 1963), 163. The rich man, Caird writes, learns the lesson Jesus conveys in the discourse, namely, that "anxiety cannot postpone for one hour the approach of death." Death discloses the rich man's "essential poverty," since the "only possessions worthy of man's striving are those death cannot take away."

83. Luke Timothy Johnson understands Luke 12:13–34 as a *qal wehomer* argument in reverse (*The Gospel of Luke* [SP 3; Collegeville, Minn.: Liturgical Press, 1991], 201). He also sees a link in 12:22–33 between death, possessions, and fear/anxiety (201–2).

84. Luke Timothy Johnson, *The Literary Function of Possessions in Luke-Acts* (SBLDS 39; Missoula, Mont.: Scholars Press, 1977), 154. He sees alms as the way of "being rich towards God, of establishing a sure treasure in heaven" (155). Cf. idem, *The Gospel of Luke*, 202.

85. Johnson, *Literary Function*, 153. Johnson also hints at the interface of fear and possessions, arguing that the rich man "thinks that once he has all his goods tidily stored away … his ψυχή will be secured and he can live the good life" (153). For Johnson, Luke shows here—and elsewhere—that acquisitiveness is rooted in fear and that this removal of fear is necessary for one to share one's goods generously (*The Gospel of Luke*, 201). In *Literary Function* (153–54), he finds similarities between the parable and the story of the strong man (11:21–22), noting that they share in common the "view of possessions as fragile, as arousing false security and requiring constant preoccupation." In both stories, "the disposition of the possessions signif[ies] the condition of the possessor." The parable illustrates a more general Lukan motif, that "[p]ossessions are what men use to preserve their life, to gain security against threat" (153). The rich man is accordingly a fool because "he thought [his possessions] secured his life 'for many years to come'" (*The Gospel of Luke*, 201). If read in light of Qoh 2:1–11, the man may be deemed a fool because he sought meaning in acquiring his possessions.

that this dual contextualization allows for a more fully textured reading of the parable. We turn now to readers who have employed the second of these approaches and whose interpretation of the parable is fundamentally shaped by reading it in light of either Greco-Roman or Jewish wisdom texts.

Reading The Parable with Greco-Roman Texts

Danker's primary strategy is to read the parable in light of Greco-Roman statements on wealth because, as with previous interpreters, he considers wealth—and specifically the critique of "private wealth"—to be the parable's central concern.[86] Luke's Greco-Roman readers, he asserts, would have recognized various elements in the parable such as the "antithesis of a public-spirited citizen" and "the awful syndrome known as satiety-insolence-infatuation."[87] Citing parallels that stress that one should not be judged until one's death,[88] Danker maintains that the rich man's plans to eat, drink, and be merry are incongruent with such maxims and a sign that the rich man failed to take such maxims to heart.[89]

Danker's identification of similarities between Luke's parable and Greco-Roman texts demonstrates a likely cultural exchange between Luke-Acts and its Greco-Roman milieu. Unfortunately, he selects parallel texts on the basis of his a priori understanding of the parable's chief concern. His citation of parallel texts suggests, moreover, that Luke's engage-

---

86. Danker, *Jesus and the New Age*, 247–48. He titles 12:13–34 "Worldly Cares."

87. Ibid., 248–49. He cites Herodes Atticus for whom the purpose of having wealth was to distribute it beneficently. He notes that for Aristotle illiberality takes the forms of stinginess and "inordinate acquisitiveness" (*Eth. nic.* 4.1.38). The man's monologue, he claims, would be familiar to many in the Greco-Roman public due to its similarity with expressions on gravestones. He cites an inscription in modern Timgade, Algeria, from the ruins of Colonia Marciana: "Make love, bathe, play, and laugh. That's living!"

88. "Prior to death and exequies/ no human being shall be called a blessed one" (Ovid, *Metam.* 3.135–137); "Judge no one happy until death" (Solon, in Herodotus, *Hist.* 1.32.5); "Look at life's last lap" (Juvenal, *Sat.* 10.274–275).

89. Danker, *Jesus and the New Age*, 248. The experience of the rich man in the parable "revealed that man receives his life temporarily on loan from God and that he cannot live only out of the resources that surround his bodily existence" (249). Danker does not cite any Greco-Roman texts that speak to this specific issue of one's life being on loan from God.

ment with Greco-Roman culture was limited merely to echoing certain motifs. I will show below that Luke 12:13–34 reflects a more dynamic process of textual appropriation and reconfiguration of a contested conversation. Finally, although Danker cites Qoh 8:15 as a parallel text, he gives no indication of its potential usefulness in explicating Luke's parable.

Abraham Malherbe argues that Luke 12:13–34 intentionally mirrors ancient Greek and Latin reflections on the topos of greed (πλεονεξία).[90] He sees the man's actions in Luke 12:17–18 as a sign that his "greed is insatiable."[91] Malherbe twice insists that Luke represents the "insatiably covetous rich man as a hedonist."[92] Reading the parable in conversation with Greco-Roman texts leads him to interpret greed as the primary concern of the parable. Malherbe does not attend to the motif of death. Building on Malherbe's article, Ronald Hock situates the parable within the "broader cultural horizon" of Greco-Roman literature, in particular the Greek novel.[93] He classifies the rich man as an "aristocrat" and, following Malherbe, characterizes him as a hedonist because he reads his plans (12:19) in light of Greco-Roman texts that critique greed.[94]

Danker, Malherbe, and Hock exemplify the extent to which interpretations of Luke's parable are shaped and determined by the texts one selects as dialogue partners. Reading the parable in light of Greco-Roman texts whose primary concern is the critique of greed results in evaluating (and condemning) the man as a hedonist. Such readings also tend to neglect the motif of death. Yet some Greco-Roman authors (e.g., Seneca, Lucian) evince a singular interest in the interplay of death and possessions, a concern also present in Luke's parable. A more richly textured and nuanced reading of Luke's parable results when it is placed into critical conversation with texts, Greco-Roman and Jewish, whose primary focus is the interplay of death and possessions. Reading Luke's parable in light of such texts highlights issues in addition to wealth, avarice, and hedonism,

90. Abraham J. Malherbe, "The Christianization of a *Topos* (Luke 12:13–34)," *NovT* 38 (1996): 123–35.

91. Ibid., 132: "This is the attitude of the typical self-centered (μου), acquisitive covetous man given to gathering (συνάγειν) superfluities."

92. Ibid., 133.

93. Ronald F. Hock, "The Parable of the Foolish Rich Man (Luke 12:16–20) and Graeco-Roman Conventions of Thought and Behavior" in *Early Christianity and Classical Culture: Comparative Studies in Honor of Abraham J. Malherbe* (ed. John T. Fitzgerald, Thomas H. Olbricht, and L. Michael White; Leiden: Brill, 2003), 181–96.

94. Ibid., 190.

thereby expanding the horizon of the parable's potential meanings.[95] Such a reading strategy is further justified by the parable's own allusions and echoes to Jewish wisdom texts (e.g., Qoh 8:15; Sir 11:14–19). I will now examine several interpreters who read Luke's parable in light of Jewish sapiential texts.

Reading the Parable with (Jewish) Wisdom Texts

Some interpreters mention wisdom or cite wisdom texts as parallels to Luke's parable but do not make it central to their interpretation. Bornkamm understands Luke's parable to be a type of wisdom expression, and he finds the absence of apocalyptic images significant.[96] Given this view, it is curious that he does not cite any parallels to wisdom texts.[97] Fitzmyer notes similarities between the parable and both 1 En. 97:8–10 and Ben Sira 11, but he discusses neither how Luke engages such texts nor how they bear on one's reading of the parable.[98] Moreover, he fails to address a significant discrepancy between the parable and 1 Enoch: whereas the latter focuses exclusively on wealth that is unjustly acquired (1 En. 97:8a, 10a), Luke's parable gives no explicit hint that the man procured his goods in such a manner.

Following Jülicher's precedent, scholars who cite parallels to Luke's parable often do not explain how such parallels illuminate the parable. At times this failure accompanies an inability to observe the diverse spectrum of voices within wisdom texts regarding the interplay of death and possessions. Despite finding prophetic and wisdom elements in the parable, Stephen Wright sees no new "message" in it. He understands it as a "transmutation into story form of the poetry of Psalm 49 … or the teaching of Sirach 11:18–21, with their emphases on the inevitability of death

95. On a text's "meaning potential," see Brian Blount, *Cultural Interpretation: Reorienting New Testament Criticism* (Minneapolis: Fortress, 1995), viii.

96. Günther Bornkamm, *Jesus of Nazareth* (trans. Irene and Fraser McLuskey with James M. Robinson; New York: Harper & Row, 1960), 88. The parable, he writes, is "in the style of the wisdom literature, which appeals to the natural understanding."

97. For Bornkamm, the parable illustrates the failure to grasp the lesson in the parable of the steward (cf. Luke 16:1–8), that one must prepare for the future (ibid.). He faults the rich man for neglecting his inevitable death, and he seems to identify the man's folly as his anxiety: the man's cares "devour body and soul instead of serving life" (ibid.).

98. Fitzmyer, *The Gospel according to Luke,* 2:971–72.

and the folly of trusting in wealth or envying the wealthy." He also cites 1 En. 97:8–10 as a relevant parallel and notes that the primary difference between these two texts is that in the parable God spoke to the rich man.[99] Wright describes the man's monologue as "the typical outlook of a hedonist" and, due to influence from Ps 14:1, understands the man as a type of atheist.[100] The man is a fool because his goods will shortly pass to others, and the "illusion of ownership he has maintained will be shattered."[101]

Wright observes some ways in which Luke's parable illustrates motifs from certain Jewish wisdom texts, but his assertion that the parable merely echoes the wisdom tradition does not take into account the many ways in which Luke 12:16–20 reconfigures sapiential motifs.[102] Wright conveys, moreover, little sense of the diversity within wisdom texts. He characterizes the "wisdom tradition" as that which extolled "common-sense instruction as something God-given and portrayed obedience as not only right but also the best and safest course of action."[103] This description applies to some wisdom texts, but certainly not all. It is more helpful—and more of an accurate reflection of the dynamic dialogue between such texts—to speak of wisdom tradition*s* rather than a single, static tradition.[104] Underlying my book's thesis is a claim that wisdom texts whose focus is the interplay of death and possessions, far from representing a monolithic voice, comprise a diverse and contested conversation.

Although François Bovon follows Jülicher and others in describing the parable as "*une histoire exemplaire*," he acknowledges the importance of wisdom parallels and identifies specific aspects of the parable as having their "equivalent" in Hebrew and Jewish wisdom.[105] He cites several such parallels (in a footnote) to show that Luke 12:15 and 16–21 fit into Israel's

99. Wright, "Parables on Poverty and Riches," 224.

100. Ibid., 222.

101. Ibid.

102. These I will detail in chapters 5–7.

103. Wright, "Parables on Poverty and Riches," 223.

104. So Walter T. Wilson, *Love without Pretense: Romans 12:9–21 and Hellenistic-Jewish Wisdom Literature* (WUNT 2/46; Tübingen: Mohr Siebeck, 1991).

105. Bovon, *L'Évangile Selon Saint Luc*, 245. These include the man's own ψυχή (soul/life) as his interlocutor; the "foolish character" resulting from a life without God; the risky and passing nature of riches; the relation between sin and death; the inconsiderate enjoyment of goods of this world; and the "formation of capital from God's perspective (as opposed to here below)." This list would have been more useful had Bovon provided specific examples from wisdom texts.

"wisdom tradition."[106] This fit appears to aid in Bovon's claim that the parable encourages one to live with an "account of one's death."[107] Bovon sees connections between Luke 12:19 and numerous texts, including Qoh 8:15, 1 Cor 15:32, and Isa 22:13.[108] The pertinence of these latter two ("Let us eat and drink for tomorrow we die") are questionable, however, given that Luke 12:20 seems to suggest that the rich man is *unaware* of his imminent death. The rich man plans to eat, drink, and be merry not because of an awareness of a sudden demise but, as we shall see, *despite* such cognizance.[109]

To understand the parable, Bovon asserts, it is necessary to "plunge into Hebrew wisdom," but he does not significantly pursue this line of inquiry.[110] His claim (that the rich man's folly lies in forgetting ethics, the fear of God, and ignoring the misery of others) is asserted rather than based upon a comparison with actual texts.[111] Although he states that numerous parallels to the parable can be found in Seneca and *A Thousand and One Nights*, he provides no specifics regarding these texts.[112] He cites Deuteronomy Rabbah 9:1 and Sir 11:18–19 but does not explain how either text relates to, or might influence one's reading of, Luke's parable.[113]

George Nickelsburg moves beyond merely identifying parallels to discussing how Luke's parable relates to such texts. Observing paral-

106. Ibid., 252 n. 65. These include Ps 49 (48):7, 11, 17–20; Sir 11:18–19; T. Jud. 18–19; 1 En. 94:6–11; 97:8–10; Jas 5:1–6. He also refers to the beatitude and woe in Luke 6:20, 24 and "all the Lucan texts on riches." Like Jerome, he cites Nabal (1 Sam 25:2–39) as a parallel to the man's large reserves of goods (254, n. 82.).

107. Ibid., 257. He equates this account of death with defining one's identity in relation with God and neighbor (citing Luke 10:25–37).

108. Ibid., 255 n. 85.

109. Ibid., 255 n. 87. Bovon notes the prevalence of this motif ("eat, drink, be merry") in Greco-Roman, Egyptian, and Assyrian culture. He mentions funerary inscriptions, Euripides, *Anthologie palatine*, Herodotus, Plutarch, Lucian, and so on. He claims that the Evangelist places "this pagan wisdom … in the heart of a man whom he calls 'Fool.'"

110. Ibid., 255.

111. Cf. his claim that the man's punishment by God resulted from his failure to respond to the success of his crops with an "evangelical attitude."

112. Bovon, *L'Évangile Selon Saint Luc*, 256.

113. Ibid., 256–57. The former is a story of a man who plans to preserve wine both for the circumcision of his newborn son and the son's future marriage. At that very moment, however, the angel of death announces to the father the imminent death of his infant son.

lels between the parable and both Sir 11:18–19 and 1 En. 92–105,[114] he argues that, in contrast to Ben Sira, Luke's parable "agrees with 1 Enoch in describing the rich in a bad light, hoarding, relying on riches, and falling under God's judgment."[115] This link, paired with verbal similarities between the two texts, suggests that Luke's parable is "closer to 1 Enoch than to Ben Sira."[116] Situating the parable in this manner reflects a more nuanced understanding of the possible relationships and levels of engagement between Luke's parable and sapiential texts.[117] Yet, like Fitzmyer, Nickelsburg does not note the important difference between Luke 12 and 1 Enoch regarding the issue of unjust goods. He also assumes that the rich man's intention of eating, drinking, and being merry is the proximate cause both of his imminent death and God's judgment.[118] But no such causal relationship is patent in the parable. The conversation between 1 Enoch and Luke's parable is richer and more contested than Nickelsburg's analysis suggests.

Kenneth Bailey moves beyond merely identifying a parallel text and provides a more nuanced treatment of how Luke's parable relates to Sir 11:19–20.[119] He sees the parable as an expansion of Ben Sira's "very short

---

114. George W. E. Nickelsburg, "Riches, the Rich and God's Judgment in *1 Enoch* 92–105 and the Gospel according to Luke," *NTS* 25 (1978–1979): 324–44. For an earlier (and less detailed) analysis of the parable in light of 1 Enoch, see Sverre Aalen, "St. Luke's Gospel and the Last Chapters of 1 Enoch," *NTS* 13 (1966–1967): 1–13.

115. Nickelsburg, "Riches, the Rich and God's Judgment," 335.

116. Ibid.

117. Following Nickelsburg and Aalen, Philip Frances Esler considers Luke in light of 1 Enoch. He differs by seeking to understand what the differences between Luke and 1 Enoch reveal about their respective audiences (*Community and Gospel in Luke-Acts: The Social and Political Motivations of Lucan Theology* [Cambridge: Cambridge University Press, 1987]).

118. Nickelsburg, "Riches, the Rich and God's Judgment," 334.

119. Kenneth Bailey, *Through Peasant Eyes: More Lucan Parables, Their Culture and Style* (Grand Rapids: Eerdmans, 1980). He also cites Ps 49 as a parallel to Luke's parable. These parallels lead Bailey to conclude that Jesus "is dealing with a theme already well-known in the literature of the audience" (63). By "audience" he seems to refer not to readers of Luke but to hearers of the historical Jesus. For Bailey's detailed work on the parable's literary structure, see *Through Peasant Eyes*, 58. Bailey's *Poet and Peasant* (Grand Rapids: Eerdmans, 1976) treats five Lukan parables (Unjust Steward, Friend at Midnight, Lost Sheep, Lost Coin, Father and Two Lost Sons) but not the Rich Fool.

story into a drama."[120] Whereas Sir 11:19–20 is "directed to the wealthy who *acquire* their possessions by sharpness and grabbing," Jesus' parable discusses wealth that is a divine gift.[121] The parable carries "subtle overtones" lacking in Ben Sira, such as the man's discovery that his soul, and possibly his wealth, was "on loan."[122] Whereas Ben Sira exposes the rich person's lifestyle (as "sharp and grabbing"), the parable reveals the man's lifestyle and the isolation that his riches create.[123] The parable differs further from Ben Sira in that the rich man's problem in the former is "what to do with unearned surpluses."[124]

Jacques Dupont's description of the parable ("a dramatic illustration of the sages' teaching on the uselessness of riches in the face of death") demonstrates the potential advantages and drawbacks of considering the parable in light of wisdom texts.[125] Dupont rightly identifies death and possessions as two significant elements in the parable, yet he construes wisdom teaching on death and possessions as a monolithic voice. Some sapiential texts certainly exhibit a concern with the *inutilité* of riches in the face of death (e.g., Ps 49), but this is one of many perspectives on death and possessions in what constitutes a richly textured—and contested—sapiential conversation. Dupont draws attention to a legitimate (and helpful) aspect of wisdom teaching on death and possessions, but he misconstrues this single aspect as representative of the whole.

Our investigation concludes with three scholars—Georg Eichholz, Egbert Seng, and Bernard Brandon Scott—who seek to contextualize Luke's parable with Jewish wisdom texts (or, in Scott's case, the "wisdom tradition").

---

120. Bailey, *Through Peasant Eyes,* 63. Bailey thus sets himself apart from Jülicher, for whom it was sufficient to cite the existence of literary parallels.

121. Emphasis original. For Bailey, Ben Sira's man reflects on "What do I do with my earnings?" Jesus' man must, however, ask, "What do I do with what I have not earned?" Much of the parable is about the man's failure to "perceive the question in this fashion" (63).

122. Ibid.

123. Ibid., 63–64.

124. Ibid., 64.

125. Jacques Dupont, *Les beatitudes 3: Les évangélistes* (Paris: Gabalda, 1973), 113, 183. He contends that the comparison with wisdom texts is "essential," and he cites Sir 11:18–19 and Ps 49:7–11, 17–20 as the most important texts; for Luke 12:20b, he cites Ps 39:7; Sir 14:15; Qoh 2:21.

Georg Eichholz

Eichholz understands the proper attitude towards possessions as a central element in Luke's parable. He affirms Jeremias's claim that the parable is eschatological, warning in view of the approaching judgment to be cautious with accumulating worldly goods.[126] The query about the inheritance (12:13) reflects the "problematic tendency of always wanting to have more [*Mehr-haben-wollens*] than one has," and the parable illustrates the reason why this tendency "is threatened in the end."[127] Central to the parable and the teaching on anxiety is the motif of "wealth [*Reichtums*], in the sense of the problem of wealth."[128] The description of the man as "rich" (12:16) is significant, since Luke's use of this term "hints always at an endangering of the person."[129] Wealth is dangerous because it "teaches a person that one's life is secure."[130] Buying into this belief is the rich man's primary fault. Despite functioning in his monologue "like a reliable guarantee of his life 'for many years,'" his wealth "cannot even guarantee his life for an hour."[131]

---

126. Georg Eichholz, "Vom reichen Kornbauern (Luk. 12, 13–21)," in idem, *Gleichnisse der Evangelien: Form, Überlieferung, Auslegung* (Neukirchen-Vluyn: Neukirchener, 1971): 179–91.

127. Ibid., 180. He defines πλεονεξία as "*Mehr-haben-wollen* (*als man hat*)." For Eichholz, the pairing of the parable and the inheritance question is one of several instances in which Luke focuses upon "the problem of wealth" (180–81), a problem Eichholz elucidates as "*der Macht des Reichtums in der Hand des Menschen zu*." In light of the discourse on anxiety (12:22–31)—and other Lukan comments on wealth—Eichholz claims that Luke's parable answers the question, "From what does a person live?" (189). He writes that both brothers (in 12:13–15) are "determined by the worry about their existence [*von der Sorge um ihre Existenz bestimmt*]" (180). The younger brother insists on his right "because the worry about his existence also drives him" (*die Sorge um seine Existenz umtreibt*). He understands Luke 12:13–21 as an "*Art Kopfstück*" to 12:22–31.

128. Ibid., 189. This emphasis anticipates Johnson's understanding of the danger posed by riches.

129. He cites Luke 1:51; 6:24; 16:19–31; 19:1–10. For Eichholz, Luke's Gospel "knows about the risk of being rich in the sense of a *real* risk" (ibid., emphasis original).

130. Ibid.

131. Ibid. Moreover, the man's wealth "conceals the gift-character of his life, so that his wealth allows him to live beyond reality." The phrase "beyond reality" is a quote from Karl Heinrich Rengstorf, *Das Evangelium nach Lukas* (Göttingen: Vandenhoeck & Ruprecht, 1952), 143. The man's delusional attitude toward his wealth prevents him from recognizing what is most real in life. "In his monologue the rich

Eichholz and I diverge in our use of certain wisdom texts as fruitful conversation partners for Luke's parable. Despite their common emphasis on eating, drinking, and enjoyment, Eichholz rejects Qoheleth's remarks on *Lebensfreude* (2:24; 3:13; 5:17; 8:15; 9:7–9) as irrelevant to the man's monologue in Luke's parable.[132] Such remarks in Qoheleth, he claims, are not pertinent to Luke's parable, since the latter fails to share Qoheleth's commitment to a joy that calls for "self-denial" (*Selbtsbescheidung*).[133] Eichholz finds, moreover, that Qoheleth's insistence on death as an inescapable reality is incompatible with the rich man's speech, in which death is overlooked (*übersehen*).[134] The man, Eichholz avers, should have been aware of the "transitoriness" (*Vergänglichkeit*) of life,[135] since this theme appears in texts such as Wis 2:4b–5a.[136] The sharp contrast regarding death in Qoheleth and the rich man's monologue need not require, however, that the former be disregarded as a helpful conversation partner with Luke's parable.

Eichholz and I both situate the parable in two contexts: its broader literary frame and certain sapiential texts.[137] Reading Luke 12:16–21 in light of these dual contexts leads us to identify similar motifs as impor-

---

farmer ... continues for himself a fragile guarantee" (Eichholz, "Vom reichen Kornbauern," 189–90).

132. Eichholz, "Vom reichen Kornbauern," 185–86. He acknowledges that Qoheleth can help us recognize the characteristics of the parable's monologue.

133. Ibid., 186. Eichholz here refers approvingly to the claim in Kurt Galling, "Das Rätsel der Zeit," *ZTK* (1961): 13.

134. Eichholz, "Vom reichen Kornbauern," 187: "Der Monolog in unserem Gleichnis verrät kein Wissen um den Tod." He cites von Rad approvingly: "Wealth is uncertain, being just is uncertain, above all the future that comes is uncertain; only death is certain" (186). See Gerhard von Rad, *Old Testament Theology* (trans. D. M. G. Stalker; 2 vols.; Louisville: Westminster John Knox, 1962), 1:458.

135. Eichholz, "Vom reichen Kornbauern," 187.

136. "Our life blows over like the trace of a cloud, and like a mist it itself is evaporated" (ibid., 188). The man's refusal to consider death means that he has "not considered God" (188). "God speaks here the speech of death because death comes in the *Auftrag* of God, because in death God meets the person" (189).

137. He notes two specific parallels between Luke's parable and James 4:13–5:6 (ibid., 190). He sees in Jas 4:13 "the monologue of the rich farmer ... translated, so to speak, in the speech of the wholesaler." As God rejects the rich man's plans, so, too, is there objection to the plans of the wholesalers (Jas 4:14). The rich man and the "wholesalers" ignore the "elementary wisdom" found in both texts, that "[n]o one has one's life at one's disposal because it is only at God's disposal."

tant features in the parable (e.g., death's inevitability, the neglect of death, greed, anxiety, the role of God). We differ methodologically, however, in four ways with regard to which sapiential texts we bring into conversation with Luke's parable. First, I include Qoh 8:15 (and other texts in Qoheleth) as a relevant parallel and important dialogue partner. In doing so, I seek to show that Luke's parable and Qoheleth participate in and contribute to a contested Second Temple conversation on death and possessions. Second, in addition to several Jewish texts that Eichholz does not consider, I also incorporate Greco-Roman texts as part of the Second Temple conversation with which Luke's parable is engaged. Third, I seek to describe the multiple ways Luke engages this contested conversation. Finally, I expand the parable's literary context beyond 12:22–31 to also include 12:32–33. Doing so draws attention to uses of possessions that function as constructive alternatives to those modeled by the rich fool.

Egbert Seng

Seng's approach consists primarily of citing parallels between Luke's parable and Hebrew Bible wisdom motifs.[138] He sees in the parable (and especially in 12:19–20) "a distinctive wisdom coloring,"[139] and he contends that "the essential features of our parable are *only* to be looked at in the context of *typical* wisdom motifs."[140] What Seng identifies as "typical" represents, however, only one side of a contested conversation within wisdom literature. He claims, for example, that wisdom texts agree that wealth is futile, ephemeral, and ineffective, and he cites a catalogue of texts that highlight wealth's fallibility, its ultimate decay, and its function as a source of arrogance and sin.[141] Such texts, he notes, depict rich people completely negatively.[142] Seng neglects sapiential texts that speak positively about wealth,

138. Seng, "Der Reiche Tor."

139. Ibid., 141–42. As evidence he points to the use of the terms ψυχή, εὐφραίνω, and ἄφρων.

140. Ibid., 142, emphasis added. He identifies six such motifs in the parable: the "dubiousness and transitory nature [*Vergänglichkeit*] of wealth"; the "laughable inheritance"; the nature of a person in the context of life and death; calling someone a fool; "unconcerned enjoyment of life"; and "having treasure in God."

141. Ibid.

142. Such texts, he avers, characterize the rich as deceitful sinners who trust in unjustly acquired fortune, greedy, tormenting themselves to gather fortune, unable to sleep due to worry, and whose health is destroyed. The wealthy incorrectly believe they

such as Qoheleth's frequent recommendations to enjoy possessions.[143] He thereby predetermines his view of Luke's parable by bringing it into dialogue with only one side of a contested conversation in Jewish wisdom.

Seng's selective reading of wisdom texts circumscribes his understanding of the parable in other ways. In light of texts that establish a "close-fitting connection between the sin of a person and death," and in which retribution is the fitting result of sinful behavior, Seng concludes that the rich man's death is justified.[144] Seng fails, however, to consider wisdom texts that reject the "act-consequence" theory in which people are punished for their sins.[145] Buttressing his belief in the justified nature of the man's death is the description of the man as a "fool" (Luke 12:20), coupled with the consistently negative portrayal of fools in wisdom texts.[146] In light of such texts, Luke's rich man is someone who "wants to provide rest for his soul and to ask for careless joys of life." His attitude is "the typical sign of the sinner, that he sees, despite the quick end, the highest aim of life in the joy of his goods."[147] Yet such a perspective is enjoined in the very wisdom tradition that Seng claims to represent. He cites texts that can be read as an encouragement to enjoy one's life (e.g., Isa 22:13; Qoh 2:24; 5:17) and even includes Qoh 8:15 in this list. He does not, however, address the apparent conflict between the admonition to enjoy oneself (in Qoh 8:15) and his insistence that the wisdom tradition eschews such enjoyment. The coher-

---

can secure life through wealth and are unable to foresee that their fortune is temporary. The rich can suddenly come into poverty; they cannot exhaust death, and their treasure is not useful on the day of wrath.

143. See, e.g., Qoh 2:24a; 3:12, 22a; 5:17; 8:15; 9:7–10; 11:8–9.

144. Seng summarizes the message in these texts: "In this sudden end wisdom sees the just retaliation for the sinful arrogance" ("Der Reiche Tor," 144–45). Since everyone is repaid according to one's work, sinners will not receive impunity. It is the conviction of wisdom that a lengthy enjoyment of happiness and joy of life goes only to the God-fearing (146). This person, in Seng's understanding of wisdom texts, will have no fault and will miss no good.

145. See, e.g., Qoh 8:14; 9:1–3.

146. Seng cites texts that describe the fool as one who denies a concrete work of God, wrongly and arrogantly believes he holds his happiness in his own hand, and follows his own way. The fool surrenders to an illusion, places excitement in dreams, and is led to deceptive speculation and self-deceptions. The fool's hope and faith are depicted, therefore, as ephemeral and like scattering smoke. The fool's efforts are unsuccessful, for he is killed by his own anger and enthusiasm. The way of folly leads irrevocably to death ("Der Reiche Tor," 145).

147. Ibid., 146.

ent harmony Seng finds in wisdom texts comes at the cost of excluding or subsuming certain sapiential perspectives.

Seng's selective omission of wisdom texts flattens not only the diversity among sapiential perspectives but also his reading of Luke's parable as a simple and straightforward tale. Adopting Jülicher's terminology, he classifies the parable as a *Beispielerzählung*, describing the rich man's actions as a "negative exemplary case [*Musterfall*], one that is *fully clear in itself* and *allows no transfer or interpretation* [*Ausdeutung*]."[148] Influencing Seng's view of the parable as a *Beispielerzählung*—and his claim that the man's death is divine punishment for sins—is his understanding of God's speech in 12:20 as an "Old Testament prophetic word of judgment to a single person."[149] He reads God's speech in 12:20 as a death sentence (*Todesurteil*), and in this sentence he sees "the point of the entire story."[150] Here is another example of how reading the parable in concert with prophetic texts contributes to seeing in the parable little more than a critique of a faulty use of possessions. As Seng concludes, the parable is a "*paränetiches Exempel* that illustrates in a model the problem of the finiteness of a person and the proper posture to earthly riches."[151]

---

148. Ibid., 141, emphasis added; cf. 151. Seng rejects Jeremias's description of Luke 12:16–20 as an "eschatological parable of judgment" (139). For Seng, Jülicher views the parable as a "religious-moral" tale, and Jeremias understands it as an example of "*reaslisierenden Eschatologie*" (138). He argues that the story must be a *Beispielerzählung* since the question about inheritance in 12:20 is incompatible with an eschatological event (151–52). He also understands the rich man as an "everyman," making him a "universal exemplary type" (152). He follows Linnemann in his use of "*Musterfall*."

149. Ibid., 139. Quoting Claus Westermann (*Grundformen prophetischer Rede* [Munich: Kaiser, 1964], 94), he notes that such judgment announcements always occur to an individual and refer to a "concrete and previously committed offense." Such prophetic speeches contain a charge that names specific offenses. "Verse 20 consists of this charge in the simple assessment: 'ἄφρων.' This invective reveals the attitude of the rich man and justifies the now-effected verdict" (139). The central emphasis in the prophetic word of judgment is the rationale for the punishment. The penalty (*Strafurteil*) in God's speech is the man's "sudden death in this night" (140). He cites the use of ψυχή in 12:20 and 12:19 as evidence for an "immediate connection between the sin [*Schuld*] and the punishment" of the rich man.

150. Seng, "Der Reiche Tor," 138.

151. Ibid., 152.

Bernard Brendan Scott

Scott sees the parable of the Rich Fool as an "illustration" of Sir 31:5–11 and notes the twin emphasis in the latter on the problems posed by riches and the use of wealth for the purpose of charity and almsgiving.[152] Scott chooses, however, to place the parable into conversation with the Joseph narrative and the Sabbath instructions in Exodus. Whereas Joseph stored surpluses in *store*houses so that others would have food, the rich man stores up goods only for himself.[153] Scott labels him an epicurean because of this selfish orientation.[154] The Joseph narrative and the Sabbath instructions enable Luke's audience to recognize that the rich man's harvest is a divine miracle that demands drastic action.[155] The rich man fails because he "mismanages the miracle" by hoarding his wealth.[156]

It is unclear why Scott neglects Qoh 8:15 or Sir 11:14–19, both of which share several similarities with Luke's parable, in favor of Hebrew Bible texts where the connections are less explicit. Given the tenuousness of these connections, one wonders if the parable would evoke the Joseph narrative and Sabbath instructions in the minds of Luke's (or Jesus') audience. More curious is Scott's imaginative reworking of the parable's ending in light of the Joseph narrative: the rich man's death will allow his harvest, like that of Joseph's, to "be available for the village."[157] The villagers, Scott envisions, will mourn for the rich man, build a statue to honor him for his foresight and planning, but will not know that God demanded the man's life. Scott supposes that God must intervene in the man's death lest the villagers starve.[158] Scott's reconstructed ending answers the question God poses to the rich man (12:20b), a question the parable is content to leave unanswered.

152. Scott, *Hear Then the Parable*, 133: "The hoarding of wealth is condemned; wealth must serve a public need."

153. Scott, *Re-imagine the World*, 94, emphasis original.

154. Ibid., 94–95.

155. Scott, *Hear Then the Parable*, 133–34.

156. Scott, *Hear Then the Parable*, 136–37. The rich man "sins against" two principles of the Mediterranean world: using wealth for community, and the perception of limited goods.

157. Scott, *Re-imagine the World*, 131. "God's purpose is fulfilled," since the "harvest will be available for the good of all" (95).

158. Ibid., 95, 131.

When Scott asserts that God's intervention in the parable "confirms the moral direction of the wisdom tradition" or that "on the theme of wealth Jesus is in agreement with the wisdom tradition," he flattens the tension regarding the use of possessions in wisdom texts.[159] Similarly, his claim that the rich man's actions run "directly contrary to the injunctions of the wisdom tradition"[160] assumes a degree of unanimity in the wisdom tradition that does not exist. The most nuance Scott provides is identifying two subsets of the "wisdom trajectory dealing with riches."[161] He assigns Luke's parable to the "minor key" of the wisdom tradition and the parallel version in Gos. Thom. 63 to the "major key."[162] Whereas the version in Thomas is "common wisdom," since it focuses on the "common" theme of accumulating money and critiquing greed, Luke's version—while drawing on a common mytheme (greed)—focuses instead on the need to dispose of wealth, an issue given little attention in the wisdom tradition.[163] Scott's oversimplification of the treatment of possessions in wisdom traditions, and his neglect of the intersection of death and possessions, weakens his analysis.

Advancing a Conversation and Filling a Gap in Scholarship

Many of the questions that shape my own book have been adumbrated in previous scholarship. The full pursuit of these questions has been hindered by preconceptions about the parable's potential meaning and purpose, frequently resulting in a myopic emphasis on possessions and wealth and a corresponding neglect of death and its existential (and ethical) significance. These latter motifs are brought to the fore, however, when the parable is read in concert with Second Temple texts whose focus is the interplay of death and possessions.

---

159. Scott, *Hear Then the Parable*, 139, 140.

160. Ibid., 139.

161. Ibid., 130.

162. Ibid., 130–31: Whereas the latter entails a "more common motif of an admonition against greed," the former is a "less common subset on the use of wealth" (cf. 140). The rich man's "problem is the disposal of his wealth" (132; cf. 133). Scott makes the same point in *Re-imagine the World*, 16. In chapter 8 I compare Luke's version with the parallel in Thomas.

163. *Hear Then the Parable*, 66.

The tendency to underestimate the diverse and conflicting voices within Jewish wisdom literature is unfortunately common to New Testament interpreters for whom the wisdom tradition too often functions as "background" material in their primary goal of explicating New Testament texts. Readers of the parable who employ a limited repertoire of wisdom texts regularly misconstrue contested sapiential conversations as a univocal tradition. Richly textured and generative readings of the parable are stymied by neglecting the diversity within and among wisdom texts. I seek to avoid this reductionistic analysis by attending to the diversity and conflicting statements regarding death and possessions within texts and by reading such texts on their own terms.

In chapters 2–4 I will delineate a spectrum of Jewish and Greco-Roman texts whose focus is the intersection of death and possessions.[164] This range of texts will reveal the existence of a contested Second Temple conversation—comprised of disparate and conflicting voices—regarding the interplay of death and possessions. Such texts evince diverse understandings of death and offer, in light of these perceptions, competing answers regarding how possessions can be used meaningfully. I will argue that Luke 12:13–34 participates in this conversation by appropriating, reconfiguring, and illustrating elements of it for Luke's own theological, ethical, and existential purposes.

164. Even within the book of Proverbs there is ambiguity regarding wealth and possessions. Timothy J. Sandoval recognizes such ambiguity but seeks to argue for a more coherent treatment of wealth in Proverbs (*The Discourse of Wealth and Poverty in the Book of Proverbs* [Biblical Interpretation Series 77; Leiden: Brill, 2006]). James L. Crenshaw finds Ben Sira to be more attentive to the ambiguity associated with wealth than previous sages (e.g., Proverbs) (*Old Testament Wisdom: An Introduction* [rev. ed; Louisville: Westminster John Knox, 1998], 147).

2
The Interplay of Death and Possessions in Qoheleth and Ben Sira

In chapters 2 and 3 I explicate four Hellenistic Jewish texts in which the intersection of death and possessions figures prominently: Qoheleth, Ben Sira, the Epistle of 1 Enoch, and Testament of Abraham.[1] I will show that

1. Most scholars see some degree of Greek influence upon Qoheleth. So Elias Bickermann, *Four Strange Books of the Bible* (New York: Schocken, 1967), 141–67; Martin Hengel, *Judaism and Hellenism* (trans. John Bowden; 2 vols.; Philadelphia: Fortress, 1974) 1:115–26; Rainer Braun, *Kohelet und die frühhellenistische Populärphilosophie* (BZAW 130; Berlin: de Gruyter, 1973); Charles Whitley, *Koheleth, His Language and Thought* (BZAW 148; Berlin: de Gruyter, 1979), 165–75; Ludger Schwienhorst-Schönberger, *Nicht im Menschen Gründet das Glück (Koh 2:24): Kohelet im Spannungsfeld jüdischer Weisheit und hellenistischer Philosophie* (Freiburg: Herder, 1994); Norbert Lohfink, *Qoheleth: A Continental Commentary* (trans. Sean McEvenue; Minneapolis: Fortress, 2003), 6–7, 13–14; Ronald E. Clements, *Wisdom in Theology* (Grand Rapids: Eerdmans, 1992) 34–35; cf. 42; Roland E. Murphy, *The Tree of Life: An Exploration of Biblical Wisdom Literature* (3rd ed.; Grand Rapids: Eerdmans, 2002), 173. For Stoic influence, see Dominic Rudman, *Determinism in the Book of* Ecclesiastes (Sheffield: Sheffield Academic Press, 2001), 173–99. Michael V. Fox cautions that general similarities between Qoheleth and Greek philosophy do not imply "direct knowledge" on Qoheleth's part (*Ecclesiastes: קהלת. The Traditional Hebrew Text with the New JPS Translation* [JPS Bible Commentary; Philadelphia: Jewish Publication Society, 2004], xii). For Mesopotamian influence, see Oswald Loretz, *Qohelet und der Alte Orient: Untersuchungen zu Stil und theologischer Thematik des Buches Qohelet* (Freiburg: Herder, 1964), 90–134.

Most scholars understand Ben Sira as a text in dialogue with Hellenism. See, e.g., Miriam Lichtheim, *Late Egyptian Wisdom Literature in the International Context* (OBO 28; Fribourg: Universitätsverlag, 1979), 185; Johann Marböck, *Weisheit im Wandel: Untersuchungen zur Weisheitstheologie bei Ben Sira* (BBB 37; Bonn: Hanstein, 1971); Hengel, *Judaism and Hellenism*, 1:131–53; Theophil Middendorp, *Die Stellung Jesu Ben Siras zwischen Judentum und Hellenismus* (Leiden: Brill, 1973), 8–24; Jack

the interplay of death and possessions is a prominent motif in each of these texts and that the perspectives on these twin motifs comprise a spectrum of diverse views. This spectrum reflects, I suggest, the existence of a lively and contested Second Temple conversation regarding the appropriate and meaningful use of possessions, given the many uncontrollable vicissitudes of death.

The four texts in these two chapters evince disparate perceptions of death and divergent recommendations regarding the use of possessions. In each text there is an integral link between its specific view(s) of death and its corresponding advice concerning possessions. I will argue, moreover, that the motif of "control" plays a central role in perceptions of death and in corresponding attitudes toward possessions and their use. Various facets of death represent a loss of control, and the diverse recommendations regarding possessions and their use represent attempts to seize control.

These four texts have been selected for analysis because they provide some of the most extensive treatments of the intersection of death and possessions in Hellenistic Jewish literature. The Hellenistic Jewish character of these texts also makes them fitting comparative texts with Luke-Acts. The sapiential features of these four texts provide additional points of commonality with Luke 12:13–34.[2] Qoheleth and Ben Sira are widely regarded as belonging to the wisdom corpus.[3] The Epistle of 1 Enoch and

---

T. Sanders, *Ben Sira and Demotic Wisdom* (SBLMS 28; Chico, Calif.: Scholars Press, 1983); Murphy, *Tree of Life*, 173–74, 214–15; John G. Gammie, "The Sage in Sirach," in *The Sage in Israel and the Ancient Near East* (ed. John G. Gammie and Leo G. Perdue; Winona Lake, Ind.: Eisenbrauns, 1990): 355–72; Clements, *Wisdom in Theology*, 35.

John J. Collins classifies Testament of Abraham as Hellenistic Jewish literature (*Jewish Wisdom in the Hellenistic Age* [OTL; Louisville: Westminster John Knox, 1997], 248–49).

2. By "sapiential features" I mean to highlight a text's inner texture rather than its technical genre classification (in this case as "wisdom literature"). On "inner texture," see Vernon K. Robbins, *Exploring the Texture of Texts: A Guide to Socio-rhetorical Interpretation* (Harrisburg, Pa.: Trinity Press International, 1996), 7–39.

3. For Qoheleth as wisdom, see Loretz, *Qohelet und der alte Orient*, 196–208; von Rad, *Wisdom in Israel*, 227; Murphy, *Tree of Life*, 1; Collins, *Jewish Wisdom*, 1; C. L. Seow, *Ecclesiastes: A New Translation with Introduction and Commentary* (AB 18c; New York: Doubleday, 1997), 67–69; Fox, *Ecclesiastes* (JPS), x. For Ben Sira as wisdom, see, e.g., Murphy, *Tree of Life*, 1; Fox, *Ecclesiastes* (JPS), xi; Shannon Burkes, *God, Self, and Death: The Shape of Religious Transformation in the Second Temple Period* (JSJSup 79; Leiden: Brill, 2003), 87; Sanders, *Ben Sira*, 11; Daniel J. Harrington, *Jesus Ben Sira of Jerusalem: A Biblical Guide to Living Wisely* (Collegeville, Minn.: Liturgical Press, 2005), 1.

Testament of Abraham also contain certain sapiential characteristics (see ch. 3). As I will argue in chapter 5, Luke 12:13–34 has several sapiential features, not least of which is the citation of Qoh 8:15 and the allusion to Sir 11:14–19 in the parable of the Rich Fool.[4]

I seek to explicate these four texts (and the ones I analyze in chapter 4) through inductive close reading, an approach intended to allow the motifs and concerns of the texts to emerge from the texts themselves.[5] I therefore seek to avoid reading them through the lens of Luke's parable, asking how they might relate to questions or concerns that are his.[6] I do, however, bring to these texts an a priori interest in determining their understanding(s) of the relationship between death and possessions.

The Interplay of Death and Possessions in Qoheleth[7]

Qoheleth displays an intense interest in the interplay of death and possessions.[8] No other book in the Hebrew Bible gives as much attention to the

4. On the complex discussion of the definition and characteristics of wisdom literature, see Crenshaw, *Old Testament Wisdom*, 3–15; von Rad, *Old Testament Theology*, 1:418–59; Walter A. Brueggemann, "The Epistemological Crisis of Israel's Two Histories (Jer 9:22–23)," in *Israelite Wisdom: Theological and Literary Essays in Honor of Samuel Terrien* (ed. John G. Gammie et al.; Missoula, Mont.: Scholars Press, 1978), 100; James C. VanderKam, *An Introduction to Early Judaism* (Grand Rapids: Eerdmans, 2001), 115.

5. Although this type of reading attends both to synchronic and diachronic features of the text, it privileges the former as a window into the text's potential meaning(s). As Vernon K. Robbins notes, the primary object of inquiry in this approach is the literary text, not "supposed realities" outside the text (*The Tapestry of Early Christian Discourse: Rhetoric, Society and Ideology* [New York: Routledge, 1996], 15). This literary focus is due to the comparative intertextual aim of this project, namely, to situate Luke's parable within the context of a specific Second Temple conversation that is comprised of, and finds expression in, a broad spectrum of texts.

6. Explicating the texts in this manner will allow a construction of a fruitful dialogue between them and Luke's parable precisely because it treats each text as a legitimate conversation partner.

7. The following material on Qoheleth appeared in a slightly revised form: Matthew S. Rindge, "Mortality and Enjoyment: The Interplay of Death and Possessions in Qoheleth," *CBQ* 73:2 (2011): 265–80. I thank Linda Day (*CBQ*'s editor) and Joseph Jensen for granting permission to republish this material.

8. The most extensive treatments are Qoh 2:1–26; 3:11–22; 5:9–6:2; 8:8–15; 9:1–10; 11:7–12:8.

intersection of these two motifs. Although scholars have not overlooked Qoheleth's interest in death,[9] few make it central to their understanding of this work.[10] An exception is Shannon Burkes, who argues that death is "the driving theme and main concern of Qoheleth."[11] She finds Qoheleth distinctive in this regard, claiming that the author has "cornered the market" on the issue of death in the Hebrew Bible.[12] In contrast, the theme of possessions in Qoheleth has received relatively little interest.[13] While Qoheleth's motif of enjoyment—closely related to that of wealth—has received ample treatment, virtually no sustained attention has been paid to the intersection of death and possessions.[14]

---

9. Von Rad, *Wisdom in Israel*, 228; M. A. Anat, "The Lament on the Death of Humanity in the Scroll of Qohelet," *Beth Mikra* 15 (1970): 375–80; James L. Crenshaw, "The Shadow of Death in Qoheleth," in Gammie et al., *Israelite Wisdom*, 205–16; Michael V. Fox, "Aging and Death in Qohelet 12," *JSOT* 42 (1988): 55–77; Joseph Blenkinsopp, *Wisdom and Law in the Old Testament: The Ordering of Life in Israel and Early Judaism* (Oxford: Oxford University Press, 1995), 72–73; Mathias Delcor, "Jewish Literature in Hebrew and Aramaic in the Greek Era," in *Introduction; The Persian Period* (vol. 2 of *The Cambridge History of Judaism*; ed. W. D. Davies and Louis Finkelstein; Cambridge: Cambridge University Press, 1984), 361; Jean-Jacques Lavoie, *La penseé du Qohélet: Étude exégétique et intertextuelle* (Quebec: Fides, 1992); Clements, *Wisdom in Theology*, 90.

10. Murphy does not list death as one of the book's "essential points" (vanity, joy, wisdom, fear of God, retribution, and God) that are "central to the author's thought," but he does claim that death "casts its shadow over all [Qoheleth's] thoughts" (*Tree of Life*, 53).

11. Shannon Burkes, *Death in Qoheleth and Egyptian Biographies of the Late Period* (SBLDS 170; Atlanta: Society of Biblical Literature, 1999), 1. Death, she maintains, "dominates the stage and forms the core of the author's melancholy" (1). Death, moreover, "represents the chief flaw that embraces and subsumes all other problems in the world" (2). Her view remains unchanged in her subsequent work, where she speaks of death in Qoheleth as "the defining and insurmountable ground of existence" (*God, Self, and Death*, 6).

12. Burkes, *Death in Qoheleth*, 1. She reiterates the assessment of Michael V. Fox, *Qohelet and His Contradictions* (JSOTSup 71; Sheffield: Almond, 1989), 294. Robert Williamson Jr. ("Death and Symbolic Immortality in Second Temple Wisdom Instructions" [Ph.D. diss., Emory University, 2011]) helpfully utilizes Terror Management Theory as a way of analyzing Qoheleth's attitude toward death.

13. Though see C. W. Reines, "Koheleth on Wisdom and Wealth," *JJS* 5 (1954): 80–84; James L. Kugel, "Qohelet and Money," *CBQ* 51 (1989): 32–49.

14. On enjoyment in Qoheleth, see Eunny P. Lee, *The Vitality of Enjoyment in Qohelet's Theological Rhetoric* (BZAW 353; Berlin: de Gruyter, 2005); R. N. Whybray, "Qoheleth, Preacher of Joy," *JSOT* 23 (1982): 87–98; Norbert Lohfink, "Qoheleth 5:17–

The respective monographs of Shannon Burkes and Eunny P. Lee demonstrate the tendency to concentrate on either death or enjoyment of possessions without recognizing the integral relationship between these two motifs. A comparison of the specific texts that each scholar highlights is revealing. In the chart below, the left column lists the texts that Burkes cites as Qoheleth's explicit references to death. The right column shows the texts Lee classifies as the seven "enjoyment" passages in Qoheleth.[15]

2:14–16	2:24–26
3:2, 19–21	3:12–13, 22
4:2–3	
5:15–16	5:17–19
6:3–6	
7:1–2, 4, 17, 26	7:14
8:8	8:15
9:2–12	9:7–10
11:8	11:7–12:7

The overlap between these two lists is striking. Ten of the thirteen texts that Burkes considers to be explicit references to death occur in close proximity to texts that Lee classifies as "enjoyment" passages. More sig-

19—Revelation by Joy," *CBQ* 52 (1990): 625–35; Ricky William Byargeon, "The Significance of the Enjoy Life Concept in Qoheleth's Challenge of the Wisdom Tradition" (Ph.D. diss., Southwestern Baptist Theological Seminary, 1991); Agustinos Gianto, "The Theme of Enjoyment in Qohelet," *Bib* 73 (1992): 528–32. For a brief comment on death and possessions, see Blenkinsopp, *Wisdom and Law*, 72–73.

15. Burkes, *Death in Qoheleth*, 59 n. 100. Lee, *Vitality of Enjoyment*, 3, 9. (On the latter page Lee cites 11:7–12:7, but on the former she cites 11:7–12:1). For similar lists of "enjoyment" passages, see William P. Brown, *Character in Crisis: A Fresh Approach to the Wisdom Literature of the Old Testament* (Grand Rapids: Eerdmans, 1996), 137; François Rousseau, "Structure de Qohélet I 4–11 et plan du livre," *VT* 31 (1981): 200–217; Thomas Krüger, *Qoheleth: A Commentary* (trans. O. C. Dean Jr.; Hermeneia; Minneapolis: Fortress, 2004), 1 n. 2.

nificant, each of the seven "enjoyment" passages cited by Lee occurs in the immediate context of an explicit reference to death.[16]

Burkes gives little attention to the link between death and possessions, only twice acknowledging the connection between the two motifs.[17] She recognizes that "Qoheleth's repeated advice amongst all these comments on death is to enjoy life to the fullest while one can."[18] Yet she does not analyze the relationship between the specific understanding of death and admonitions regarding enjoyment in Qoheleth.

Lee is more attentive to the formative role of death in Qoheleth than Burkes is to the comments on enjoyment.[19] Whereas Burkes relegates the "enjoyment" passages to the periphery of Qoheleth's thought, Lee seeks to attend to both the death and the enjoyment passages, insisting they need not be mutually exclusive and that both are authentic expressions of Qoheleth's *Weltanschauung*.[20] Lee also observes Qoheleth's pattern of placing admonitions to enjoy life in the context of reflections on death.[21]

Despite her observations concerning the close proximity of these motifs, Lee offers minimal comment on the precise relationship between death and enjoyment. The closest she comes to doing so is her observation that, when Qoheleth "reflects on the inevitability of death, he does so in order to motivate people to embrace life all the more."[22] She thus understands Qoheleth's statements on death as evidence for his argument that one should enjoy life.[23]

---

16. Though not listed as an "explicit" reference to death, Burkes considers Qoh 12:1–8 to be a "reflection" on death (*Death in Qoheleth*, 53).

17. Burkes identifies one of the three types of reflections on death to be "places where Qoheleth counsels enjoyment, but almost always in view of death" (ibid., 59).

18. Ibid., 72. She stresses that "in the vast majority of cases, these counsels lead Qoheleth back to the brevity of life, death itself, or *hebel*."

19. See, e.g., Lee, *Vitality of Enjoyment*, 56, 66.

20. Ibid., 9–10, 74.

21. Ibid., 99: "Throughout his reflections, Qohelet describes life under the sun against the backdrop of inevitable death—the days under the sun are *hebel*. But it also comes with its invigorating possibilities." She notes that the "[e]njoyment Qohelet espouses … takes place with the specter of death ever looming in the near horizon" (81). She observes that the material on enjoyment in 9:7–10 occurs after "a passage in which he broods over the inevitability of death" (62).

22. Ibid., 56. She cites Qoh 3:19–22; 5:14–19; 9:5–10; 11:7–12:8; she neglects to cite 2:1–26 and 8:8–15.

23. See also ibid., 56, 62.

Furthermore, although both Burkes and Lee discuss Qoheleth's "enjoyment" passages, they give little thought to the role of wealth and possessions as the principal means by which people are to enjoy themselves. Disregarding the role of wealth is an oversight, since possessions consistently function in Qoheleth as instruments of enjoyment. Enjoyment is not an abstract principle in Qoheleth but the result of a specific practice whereby goods are used to a certain end. In their general neglect of the relationship between death and wealth, Burkes and Lee are representative of Qoheleth scholarship.[24]

I will show that Qoheleth consistently responds to a reflection on death with specific admonitions regarding possessions. When Qoheleth reflects on death, the first practical things that come to mind are issues related to possessions (e.g., toil, inheritance, and the enjoyment of goods). An explication of six selections in which death and possessions intersect (Qoh 2:1–26; 3:11–22; 5:9–6:2; 8:8–15; 9:1–10; 11:7–12:8) will show that (1) Qoheleth's recommendations to enjoy possessions are a direct result of his perception of death as an inevitable and unjust event that destroys one's entire being; (2) the advice to enjoy possessions reflects an effort to find some way of exerting control in the face of the loss of control represented by death; (3) the perception of goods as divine gifts underscores both the appropriateness of enjoying them and the fragility of such enjoyment. What follows is a synchronic analysis of the interplay of death and possessions in Qoheleth.[25]

Qoheleth 2:1–26

The intersection of death and possessions is a thread throughout Qoh 2:1–26. The section begins with a lengthy rehearsal of Qoheleth's pursuit of enjoyment (שמחה / εὐφροσύνη; 2:1–11).[26] Although proposing to test himself with enjoyment and to experience good (טוב / ἀγαθός; 2:1),[27]

24. Crenshaw offers one comment on the relationship between "death" and enjoyment ("Shadow of Death," 205–16). Von Rad does not address the relationship between the two motifs (*Wisdom in Israel*).

25. On the socioeconomic context of Qoheleth, see Seow, *Ecclesiastes*, 21–33.

26. For various translations of שמחה, see Fox, *Ecclesiastes* (*JPS*), xx.

27. Lee (*Vitality of Enjoyment*, 38) notes that ראה connotes "to taste" or "experience." Cf. Qoh 9:7, where the same verb, δεῦρο, is used in Qoheleth's invitation to eat bread in gladness and drink wine with a good heart.

Qoheleth forewarns the reader that he will ultimately regard this enterprise as bankrupt (הבל / ματαιότης; 2:1).[28] Enjoyment (in this context) is judged to be insufficient as a source of meaning. Qoheleth calls laughter madness and, concerning enjoyment, asks, "What does this thing do?" (2:2).[29] What follows in 2:3–11 can be understood, in part, as an attempt to investigate and answer this query: Is meaningful enjoyment possible?

At the heart of his pursuit of שמחה / εὐφροσύνη is an attempt to seize control over potential vehicles of enjoyment. In addition to drinking wine in long draughts, Qoheleth sought to "become master over folly" (לאחז בסכלות / κρατῆσαι ἐπ' ἀφροσύνῃ; 2:3).[30] The itemized list describing Qoheleth's endeavor to "seize" pleasure is characterized by repeated attempts at acquisition (2:4–9). Acquired (קנה / κτάομαι) objects include slaves, maidens/courtesans, flocks, herds, silver, gold, male and female singers, and a male and female cupbearer (2:7–8). These are in addition to Qoheleth's work building and planting houses, vineyards, gardens, groves, fruit trees, and pools of water (2:4–6). The excessive nature of his acquisitiveness is reflected in the claims that his quantity of possessions surpassed that of anyone else in Jerusalem (2:7–9).

Qoheleth's acquisitiveness is a tangible manifestation of a quest for pleasure, an expression embodying (and revealing) the controlling nature of this enterprise. This search for pleasure is a quest for control, actualized in multiple attempts to acquire and possess items and people. Qoheleth's

---

28. For possible meanings of הבל, see Gregory of Nyssa, *Homélies sur l'Ecclésiaste* 1.3 (ed. P. Alexander; SC 46; Paris: Cerf, 1996), 114. Legitimate meanings include "an incomprehensible [ἀδιανόητον] word or an unprofitable activity [πρᾶγμα ἀνόνητον] or a foundationless plan [βουλὴ ἀνυπόστατος] or lacking a diligent goal/accomplishment [σπουδὴ πέρας οὐκ ἔχουσα]." Cf. Jacques Chopineau, "Hèvèl en hébreu biblique: Contribution à l'étude des rapports entre sémantique et exégèse de l'Ancien Testament" (Ph.D. diss., University of Strasbourg, 1971); Michael V. Fox, "The Meaning of HEBEL for Qohelet," *JBL* 105 (1986): 409–27; Fox, *Ecclesiastes* (*JPS*), xix; Lee, *Vitality of Enjoyment*, 1–2, 30–31; Burkes, *Death in Qoheleth*, 45–48.

29. For מהולל designating laughter mixed with despair, see Fox, *Ecclesiastes* (*JPS*), 12.

30. κρατέω can mean "conquer, lay hold of, become master of, get possession of, seize, secure" (LSJ, 991). Similarly, אחז can mean "grasp, take hold, take possession" (BDB, 28). For other uses of סכלות, see Qoh 2:12, 13; 7:25; 10:1, 13; cf. 1:17 (שכלות). The existence of εὐφροσύνῃ as a variant in some manuscripts for ἀφροσύνῃ may indicate that a scribe understood pleasure, rather than folly, to be the object of Qoheleth's control; the lack of a corresponding variant for סכלות, and the principle of *lex dificilior*, suggest that ἀφροσύνῃ is more original.

unwavering commitment to pursuing pleasure is exemplified in not denying himself anything that his eyes desired. Nor does he withhold (מנע / ἀποκωλύω) any enjoyment (שמחה / εὐφροσύνη) from his heart (2:10a).

It is possible that in the explanation for this total abandon (2:10b),[31] Qoheleth identifies enjoyment as the sole benefit of his pursuit of pleasure and laments that such enjoyment did not produce any additional meaningful benefit.[32] "All" the deeds his hands made and his toil are deemed meaningless (הבל / ματαιότης) and a "striving after wind." The net result is that there is no benefit (יתרון / περισσεία) under the sun (2:11).[33] Qoheleth thereby provides an (initial) answer to the first question posed in the book (see 1:3) regarding what benefit there is for a person who toils under the sun: none.

The discussion of pleasure leads to a reflection on death's universality and its elimination of memory.[34] Qoheleth challenges a traditional proverb (2:14a) by pointing out that the wise and foolish both succumb to death (מקרה אחד יקרה את־כלם / συνάντημα ἓν συναντήσεται τοῖς πᾶσιν αὐτοῖς; 2:14).[35] Realizing that he also will share the fate of the fool (2:15) causes him to question the point of being wise (2:15; cf. 7:16).[36] Such a

31. "For my heart made merry (שמח / εὐφράνθη) in all my toil (עמל / μόχθῳ), and this was my share (חלק / μερίς) from all my toil (עמל / μόχθου)."

32. So understands the NJPS: "rather, I got enjoyment out of all my wealth. And that was all I got out of my wealth."

33. The repetition of כל / πας in 2:11 highlights the comprehensive nature of what Qoheleth considers הבל / ματαιότης.

34. If Seow's proposed emendation is correct, then initial interest in the subject of death is conveyed with the use of "after me" in 2:12 (*Ecclesiastes*, 153).

35. R. N. Whybray finds eight "clear examples" of quotations from Proverbs in Qoheleth (Qoh 2:14a; 4:5, 6; 7:5, 6a [omitting "this is *hebel*"]; 9:17; 10:2, 12 ("The Identification and Use of Quotations in Ecclesiastes," in *Congress Volume: Vienna, 1980* [ed. J. A. Emerton; VTSup 32; Leiden: Brill, 1981], 435–51, here 435–37). Cf. Robert Gordis, "Quotations in Wisdom Literature," *JQR* 30 (1939–1940): 123–47; idem, "Quotations in Biblical, Oriental and Rabbinic Literature," *HUCA* 22 (1949): 157–219; idem, *Koheleth—The Man and His World: A Study of Ecclesiastes* (New York: Schocken, 1955), 100. For συνάντημα as death, see Qoh 3:19a. Murphy equates מקרה with death (*Tree of Life*, 54).

36. It is uncertain, as Elizabeth Huwiler notes, if Qoheleth's evaluation of this as ματαιότης refers to his being wise or to the same fate befalling the wise and the foolish (2:15) (Roland E. Murphy and Elizabeth Huwiler, *Proverbs, Ecclesiastes, Song of Songs* [NIBC; Peabody, Mass.: Hendrickson, 1999], 164).

question bespeaks a utilitarian expectation regarding the extrinsic benefits of wisdom.

Qoheleth perceives death as a destroyer of memory, since the memory of a dead person vanishes among the living. The fool retains no memory (זכרון / *μνήμη*) of a wise person, and in "the coming days all will be forgotten [נשכח / *ἐπελήσθη*]" (2:16a).[37] The importance of the erasure of memory is indicated by its appearance in the conclusion to the book's preface (1:11).[38] Memory's fragility threatens the ability to live on after death. Not only is it impossible to control *how* one will be remembered after death; one cannot determine *if* one will be remembered at all.

The inability to determine the recipient of one's inheritance is another uncontrollable consequence of no longer being alive. This lack of control and the possibility that a fool might inherit his goods lie at the root of Qoheleth's hatred of toil (עמל / *μόχθος*; 2:18–19). He is grieved because he cannot guarantee the moral stature of the recipient of his inheritance. If the results of one's hard labor are given to a fool, what purpose (and meaning) is there in toil (2:20–23)? Qoheleth here echoes the question that is posed in 1:3 and answered in 2:11.

Frustration with these uncontrollable aspects of death and inheritance leads Qoheleth to conclude that there is nothing better than eating, drinking, and experiencing (הראה / *δείκνυμι*) good in toil (2:24a).[39] In light of an uncontrollable activity (Who will receive my inheritance?), Qoheleth recommends using possessions in a way that can be controlled. By enjoying my own goods, I can become the recipient of my inheritance. Yet Qoheleth will shortly qualify the inherent limits (and benefits) of this attempt to exert control through the use of possessions.

Death relativizes the use of goods in two apparently disparate ways. On the one hand, death renders the relentless pursuit of (and attempt to control) pleasure meaningless. On the other hand, another uncontrollable

37. This niphal form of שכח can mean "fall into oblivion" (Gesenius, *Thesaurus*, 1060).

38. "There is no זכרון / *μνήμη* of the ones who were first, and indeed for the ones who came last there will not be a זכרון / *μνήμη* of them with the ones who will come after them."

39. On the "nothing is better" formula, see Graham Ogden, "Qoheleth's Use of the 'Nothing is Better'-Form," *JBL* 98 (1979): 339–50.The hiphil of ראה can mean "cause to experience" (BDB, 909).

aspect of death (inheritance) provides an impetus to derive enjoyment from the use of one's goods (food, drink, toil).[40]

Qoheleth concludes this reflection with an understanding of enjoyment that appears antithetical to his previous effort to control pleasure. The function and role of control partially explain Qoheleth's ambiguous evaluations of the merit of enjoyment. His initial pursuit of שמחה / εὐφροσύνη is described in terms of an effort to seize control (אחז / κρατέω) of it. Moreover, Qoheleth seems to have predetermined the outcome of this quest as one that will be meaningful. Enjoyment, wisdom, and toil are the three realms in which he sought to procure meaning, and he evaluates each attempt as bankrupt. What is meaninglessness may not be these items in themselves (enjoyment, wisdom, toil) but the effort to control these as projects with a predetermined result.[41] Qoheleth perceives these three things, moreover, not as intrinsically valuable but as the means to a certain extrinsic benefit.

Central to Qoheleth's recommendation of enjoyment is the identification of eating, drinking, and enjoying toil as divine gifts (2:24–26). This perception of wealth and goods as gifts of God comports with Qoheleth's view of God as a giver. God primarily (and only?) relates to people by giving gifts and—at times—the opportunity to enjoy such gifts. "Gift" terminology pervades the book.[42] Of the twenty-five uses of נתן / δίδωμι ("to give"), eleven or twelve refer to divine activity.[43] God is a giver and is not, in Qoheleth's view, a *deus absconditus*.[44]

Qoheleth underscores the divinely gifted nature of goods with an assertion (eating, drinking, and enjoying toil is "from God's hand") and a question ("for who can eat or who can enjoy [יחוש] apart from [God]"?)

---

40. Blenkinsopp sees death as the cause of Qoheleth's vain pursuit of pleasure (*Wisdom and Law*, 72).

41. Huwiler notes that הבל in 2:1 may refer either to "pleasure itself or to the experiment with pleasure" (in Murphy and Huwiler, *Proverbs, Ecclesiastes, Song of Songs*, 164).

42. See 1:13, 17; 2:21, 26; 3:10, 11; 5:5; 7:2; 8:9, 15, 16; 9:1, 9; 10:6; 11:2; 12:7, 11.

43. The third use of נתן in 2:26 may refer either to God or to a person. It is elsewhere used as a divine passive (9:9), and Qoheleth twice refers to a "gift" (מתת) of God (3:13; 5:18). With two exceptions (4:17; 7:21), the LXX of Qoheleth renders נתן as δίδωμι.

44. So Krüger, *Qoheleth*, 2; *contra* Leo G. Perdue, "Cosmology and the Social Order in the Wisdom Tradition," in Gammie and Perdue, *The Sage in Israel and the Ancient Near East*, 469.

(2:24b–25; cf. v. 26)?[45] Identifying the enjoyment of life and toil as God's gifts reflects a significant departure from Qoheleth's previous efforts at manipulating life for his own benefit. Recognizing the ability to enjoy life as a divine gift renders meaningless any efforts to control and manipulate such gifts.

Qoheleth 3:11–22

Death's universal inclusivity functions for Qoheleth as a warrant to enjoy possessions. Death is the one unavoidable event that everyone must face.[46] There is a time "to give birth and a time to die [מות / *ἀποθανεῖν*]" (3:1–2a). Not only do the wise and foolish share the same fate (מקרה / *συνάντημα*; cf. 2:14–17), but so do people and animals (3:19a): "For the fate [מקרה / *συνάντημα*] of people and the מקרה / *συνάντημα* of beasts, there is one מקרה / *συνάντημα* for them; as the death [מות / *θάνατος*] of one is, so is the death [מות / *θάνατος*] of the other" (3:19a). People consequently have no advantage over animals (3:19b). What distresses Qoheleth is that "all things go to one place" (3:20a). Dust is both the origin and destination of all things (3:20b).[47]

It is this perception of death as the common fate of all that leads Qoheleth to recommend enjoyment: "There is nothing better except that a person enjoy [ישמח / *εὐφρανθήσεται*] one's deeds, for it is one's share [חלקו / *μερίς*]" (3:22a). Qoheleth proposes finding enjoyment in one's deeds precisely because of the impossibility of knowing (or controlling) what will occur in the future (3:22b).

Qoheleth responds to the uncontrollability of death by recommending enjoyment of what one can control. In so doing he suggests that intrinsic value can be found in the activities characterized by enjoyment. The inscrutability of God's actions (3:11), for example, leads to the realization that there is nothing better than "to enjoy and do well in one's life" (לשמוח ולעשות טוב בחייו / *τοῦ εὐφρανθῆναι καὶ τοῦ ποιεῖν ἀγαθὸν ἐν ζωῇ αὐτοῦ*; 3:12).

The ability to experience enjoyment is (again) possible only because such activity is a divine gift (מתת אלהים / *δόμα θεοῦ*; 3:13). Identifying

45. The term in the LXX that renders חוש, *φείδομαι*, generally means "to spare" (LSJ, 1920).

46. So von Rad, *Old Testament Theology*, 2:458; Huwiler in Murphy and Huwiler, *Proverbs, Ecclesiastes, Song of Songs*, 159.

47. It is unclear if Qoheleth's question in 3:21 is genuine or rhetorical.

these activities as gifts of God qualifies the extent to which they may be manipulated or controlled. Because of their status as gifts, their perennial availability is unreliable. Hence the injunction to enjoy when the opportunity presents itself; such an opportunity may exist only in the present moment. Qoheleth's perception of these activities as divine gifts shows that his apophatic tendencies are not absolute. God is, if nothing else, a giver.[48]

Qoheleth 5:9–6:2

The intersection of death and possessions is a prominent motif in Qoh 5:9–6:2.[49] The section begins with reflections on the inability to control wealth and the desire for it. Whoever loves silver will not be satisfied (שבע / πίμπλημι) with it, and such insatiability is in direct proportion to one's level of material excess (5:9).[50] In addition, insomnia plagues the person satisfied with wealth (שבע לעשיר / ἐμπίπλημι πλουτέω; 5:11). Efforts to guard wealth cannot ensure its protection; a person may consequently be empty-handed when bearing a son (5:13).[51] The inability to guarantee the safety of possessions (and their transfer to progeny) underscores their inherent fragility. Any sense of control over them is illusory and temporary at best.

Qoheleth also insists on the impossibility of taking possessions beyond the grave. A person enters the world naked and will depart in the same fashion, not taking "anything in toil [עמל / μόχθῳ] that one might carry in one's hand" (5:14). This inability to carry toil's benefit beyond the grave

48. In addition to constructive gifts (such as goods and the ability to enjoy them), God also gives unhelpful and—apparently–even harmful things (Qoh 1:13; cf. 2:26; 3:10–11; 6:2). I thank Robert Williamson Jr. for drawing my attention to this aspect of Qoheleth's thought.

49. References to Qoh 5 are to the MT and LXX, whose verse numbers precede those in the NRSV by one.

50. One does not, for instance, love one's product (תבואה / γένημα) in its abundance (המון / πλῆθος) (5:9). The cryptic phrasing (καὶ τίς ἠγάπησεν ἐν πλήθει αὐτῶν γένημα;) reflects the Hebrew: ומי אהב בהמון לא תבואה. It is unclear if αὐτῶν modifies γένημα or ἐν πλήθει. The only "usefulness [כשרון / ἀνδρεία]" of abundance is that one can see it with one's eyes (5:10b). Lee finds the primary concern of 5:7–6:9 to be the "problem of human greed and insatiability" (*Vitality of Enjoyment*, 49).

51. Perhaps this undependable aspect of wealth is what the author has in mind in the preceding verse: "wealth is guarded [עשר שמור / πλοῦτον φυλασσόμενον] to the evil of its owner" (5:12).

is a "wicked sickness," since death erases (and thereby renders meaningless) the fruits of labor. Reiterating the point emphasizes its importance: "As one entered [life], so one will depart, and what is one's benefit [יתרון / περισσεία], by toiling [יעמל / μοχθεῖ] for wind?" (5:15). This permanent separation from possessions highlights wealth's ephemeral nature. Its use and any potential benefit (יתרון / περισσεία) are confined to the present life. Because the fruit of labor cannot be guaranteed to last as an inheritance for children (cf. 5:13), and since bringing the produce of toil beyond death is untenable, Qoheleth questions the purpose of engaging in distressing toil (5:15–16).[52]

Given death's finality and the uncertain advantage of toil (עמל / μόχθος), Qoheleth concludes that what he has seen to be good (טוב / ἀγαθός) and beautiful (יפה / καλός) is "to eat and drink and experience goodness [טובה / ἀγαθωσύνην] in all toil [עמל / μόχθῳ], by which one toils [יעמל / μοχθῇ] under the sun, a number of days of life that God gives, for this is one's share" (5:17). The uncontrollable vagaries associated with possessions and toil lead Qoheleth to recommend enjoying those elements (eating, drinking, finding goodness in toil) over which some modicum of control can be exercised. Since possessions cannot be enjoyed *post mortem*, one is to benefit from them while one has the opportunity, before (and because) death eliminates such a possibility.

Notwithstanding the declaration that toil is chasing after wind, Qoheleth entertains the possibility of finding goodness (טובה / ἀγαθωσύνη) in toil (cf. 5:10).[53] Eating, drinking, and finding goodness in toil is, as previously noted, predicated on his understanding of possessions as divine gifts. God gifts some people with wealth and possessions (עשר ונכסים / πλοῦτον καὶ ὑπάρχοντα), the authority to eat from them and take one's share, and the ability to rejoice in toil (שמח בעמל / εὐφρανθῆναι ἐν μόχθῳ; 5:18). The prominence of "gift" (נתן / δίδωμι) terminology (see 5:17, 18a, 18b; 6:2) functions as a warrant for the enjoyment of wealth insofar as it portrays food and drink (and the ability to enjoy them) as God's gifts.[54]

52. A similar concern might underlie his earlier question, "For whom am I toiling and depriving my life of goodness?" (Qoh 4:8).

53. That טובה / ἀγαθωσύνη can be rendered as "kindness" raises the possibility that Qoheleth here envisions generosity, and that meaning can be found in sharing with others. On generosity in Qoheleth, see Lee, *Vitality of Enjoyment*, 71, 133–35.

54. For "gift" language in Qoheleth, see 1:13, 17; 2:21, 26; 3:10, 11; 5:5; 7:2; 8:9, 15, 16; 9:1, 9; 10:6; 11:2; 12:7, 11.

This, Qoheleth reiterates, "is the gift (מתת / δόμα) of God" (5:18b). Given Qoheleth's perception of such goods as divine gifts, it is not surprising that his consequent worldview precludes asceticism as a legitimate option. The one (and only) proper response to a gift is to use and enjoy it.

The "gifted" nature of possessions comports with Qoheleth's understanding of their uncontrollable quality. If God can grant the ability to enjoy goods, this same ability can (presumably) be removed. Qoheleth envisions, and has observed, this very scenario; enjoyment, he acknowledges, is not always feasible. The antitype to the person described in 5:18 is one to whom God gives "riches, possessions, and glory [עשר ונכסים וכבוד / πλοῦτον καὶ ὑπάρχοντα καὶ δόξαν]" and who is not lacking anything that one desires (6:1–2). Yet God does not authorize (שלט / ἐξουσιάζω) this person "to eat from it [לאכל ממנו / φαγεῖν ἀπ' αὐτοῦ]," and a stranger will do so instead (6:2).[55] The opportunity to enjoy goods is, at any rate, tenuous and not guaranteed to last. This inability to secure a perennial pleasure from goods provides a further reason for enjoying them in the present moment.[56]

Qoheleth 8:8–15

Qoheleth's admonition to enjoy oneself (8:15) is rooted in his view of death as the archetypal loss of control. "Mastery [שלטון / ἐξουσία] over the day of death" is not possible (8:8). Nor is the ability to control how the dead are remembered, as evidenced by the honorable burial given to some wicked people (רשע / ἀσεβής) and the discarding of the bodies of the just (8:10).[57] Although the wicked may be lauded undeservedly in burial, they, too, hold no power over death. Nor can they control its timing; they cannot lengthen their days for a shadow (8:13; cf. 6:12).

55. He describes this circumstance as another "futile and wicked sickness [הבל וחלי רע / ματαιότης καὶ ἀρρωστία πονηρά]" (6:2; cf. 5:15).

56. References to death in subsequent comments (6:3, 6, 12) suggest that death is the tacit catalyst of the transference of possessions to a stranger (6:2). Lee sees allusions to death in this pericope and notes a connection between נפש (6:2, 3, 7, 9) and death (*Vitality of Enjoyment*, 50). Drawing on Canaanite mythology in which death "is portrayed as a monster with a wide-opened maw (*nps*)," she connects the insatiability of "Greedy Death" (citing *KTU* 1.23.61–64; cf. 1.5.2.2–4) with the reference to the insatiable נפש of "Sheol's deadliness" (citing Isa 5:14; Prov 27:20; 30:16).

57. On the difficulties involved in translating 8:10, see Seow, *Ecclesiastes*, 284–86.

The perception of death as a common fate shared by the just and the wicked leads Qoheleth to recommend enjoyment as the most meaningful use of possessions. Lamenting that death strikes everyone without regard for how a person has lived, Qoheleth anticipates a concern (cf. 9:2–3) regarding the universally inclusive, and therefore futile (הבל / ματαιότης), nature of death. Death comes equally to the just (צדיק / δίκαιος) and the wicked (רשע / ἀσεβής) despite their respective disparities in behavior (8:14). Although not precisely clarifying what happens (נגע / φθάνω) to the just and the wicked, one may infer from the preceding context that Qoheleth is alluding to death.[58]

Qoheleth responds to this uncontrollable facet of death by recommending and praising enjoyment (שמחה / εὐφροσύνη): "because there is nothing better for a person under the sun except to eat and drink and enjoy [לאכול ולשתות ולשמוח / τοῦ φαγεῖν καὶ τοῦ πιεῖν καὶ τοῦ εὐφρανθῆναι], and this will accompany a person in toil [עמל / μόχθῳ] throughout the days of life, which God gives one under the sun" (8:15). This invitation to enjoyment can be understood, in part, as a rejection of the need to pursue a just life, since the just and the wicked share the same fate. Such a view may partially inform Qoheleth's previous admonition about not being too righteous (צדיק / δίκαιος) nor acting too wise (חכם / σοφίζω; Qoh 7:16). Because almost everything lies outside the realm of one's control, Qoheleth enjoins doing those things (eating, drinking, enjoyment) that one can control.

Qoheleth 9:1–10

As in 5:9–6:2 and 8:8–15, Qoheleth's counsel to enjoy possessions in 9:7–10 results from his perception that death is everyone's inevitable destiny (9:1–6). Death's nondiscriminating power ensnares all with complete disregard for a person's lifestyle. It matters not whether one is righteous (צדיק / δίκαιος) or wicked (רשע / ἀσεβής), good (טוב / ἀγαθός) or evil (רע / κακός), clean (טהור / καθαρός) or unclean (טמא / ἀκάθαρτος), offers sacrifices (זבח / θυσιάζω) or does not offer sacrifices (9:2a).[59] Repeating this

58. So Michael V. Fox, who sees death as the primary focus in Qoh 8:11–14 (*A Time to Tear Down and a Time to Build Up: A Rereading of Ecclesiastes* [Grand Rapids: Eerdmans, 1999], 292).

59. For the text-critical issues regarding "evil" (רע), see Seow, *Ecclesiastes*, 299; Fox, *Qohelet and His Contradictions*, 257.

assertion emphasizes its importance: the same fate will befall the one who is good (טוב / ἀγαθός) and the one who sins (חטא / ἁμαρτάνω), the one who takes an oath and the one who fears it (9:2b). Enclosing this discussion between two references to מקרה / συνάντημα ("event/fate") underscores death's universality (9:2a, 3).[60] It is the "one event [מקרה אחד / συνάντημα ἓν]" for the four pairs listed in 9:2, and its universal grasp is evil (רע / πονηρός) precisely because it conquers *all* (כי מקהר אחד לכל / συνάντημα ἓν τοῖς πᾶσιν; 9:3).

Since the experience of death is not determined by a person's religious, ethical, moral, or cultic status, it is impossible to exert any influence over it. The disconnect between death and one's conduct constitutes a rejection of the "act-consequence" (*Tat-Ergehen Zusammenhang*) relationship that is defended in Proverbs and Deuteronomy.[61] Regardless of the accuracy (and heuristic value) of "act-consequence" as a *terminus technicus*, it is clear that Qoheleth is at odds with texts that champion this perspective (e.g., Prov 12:21; Ps 1:6; cf. Deut 4:1, 25–27, 40).[62]

Qoheleth's belief that death annihilates a person's being results in counsel to enjoy possessions. Death destroys all knowledge, and the memory of

60. Seow understands מקרה here to refer to death (*Ecclesiastes*, 304). Fox, *A Time to Tear Down*, 292: "Qohelet alone in the Bible complains about the universality of death."

61. On the "act-consequence" relationship, see Klaus Koch, "Gibt es ein Vergeltungsdogma im Alten Testament?" in *Um das Prinzip der Vergeltung in Religion und Recht des Alten Testaments* (ed. Klaus Koch; Wege der Forschung 125; Darmstadt: Wissenschaftliche Buchgesellschaft, 1972), 130–80. For a critique of Koch, see Roland E. Murphy, "Wisdom—Theses and Hypotheses," in Gammie et al., *Israelite Wisdom*, 35–42, esp. 36. Cf. Blenkinsopp (*Wisdom and Law*, 46–51, 75–76) for a brief overview. Qoheleth seems to reject the Deuteronomistic theory of divine retribution due to its incompatibility with (his own?) experience. See Murphy, *Tree of Life*, 57.

62. On Qoheleth's resistance to certain elements within Israel's wisdom traditions, see Murphy, *Tree of Life*, 55; Brown, *Character in Crisis*, 123. Debate exists regarding the nature and extent of this resistance. Fox situates Qoheleth squarely within wisdom literature but avers that Qoheleth "shows no awareness that his observations clash with the beliefs of *other* sages" (*Ecclesiastes* [JPS], xxii; cf. x, xiii). Explanations proposed for his rejection of certain tenets of traditional wisdom include the emergence of a "crisis" within wisdom (so Kurt Galling, *Die Krise der Aufklärung in Israel* [Mainzer Universitätsreden 19; Mainz: Gutenberg-Buchhandlung, 1952].) Seow cautions against the speculative nature of averring that Qoheleth is a reaction to "conventional" texts such as Proverbs (*Ecclesiastes*, 68). Murphy maintains that it is a misreading "to claim that Qoheleth jettisons wisdom per se" (*Tree of Life*, 55).

the dead is forgotten, leaving them with no reward (9:5).[63] Being a living dog is preferable to being a dead lion, since, whereas the living at least know that they will die, the dead do not know anything (9:5; although cf. 4:2–3; 7:1). Death obliterates one's love (אהבה / ἀγάπη), hate (שנאה / μῖσος), and zeal (קנאה / ζῆλος; 9:6), thus erasing some of the fundamental features that characterize what it means to be human (body, knowledge, memory, and emotions). There is, accordingly, no longer "a share for the dead forever in everything that happens under the sun" (9:6).

The nondiscriminating universality of death and its annihilation of a person's being lead Qoheleth to promote enjoyment and celebration (9:7–10). Such enjoyment consists in eating bread with gladness (שמחה / εὐφροσύνη) and drinking wine with a good heart. God's approval (רצה / εὐδοκέω) of such deeds buttresses their legitimacy (9:7).[64]

Wealth and possessions are integral to the enjoyment that Qoheleth recommends. Wealth is necessary, for instance, to procure bread, wine, oil, and white garments. This enjoyment is, moreover, relational in nature and not to be experienced in isolation (cf. 9:3a). Nor is enjoyment to be taken for granted, especially since it occurs in a world that is otherwise meaningless (הבל / ματαιότης; 9:9b). Experiences of enjoyment do not alter this fundamental view of life as meaningless. On the other hand, the fact that life is meaningless does not preclude the possibility of finding enjoyment (and good) in it. This equipoise underlies the paradox that typifies and distinguishes Qoheleth.

Qoheleth concludes his counsel to enjoy possessions by re-employing death's depriving nature as a warrant for enjoyment. People should do everything in their power to enjoy, since there is no work, reasoning, knowledge, or wisdom in Sheol/Hades (9:10). His direct address ("Sheol/Hades, where *you* are going there!") confronts readers/hearers with their mortality by forcibly reminding them that death is their inevitable and unavoidable destination (9:10). Qoheleth's admonition to enjoy life results directly from his belief in the inability to earn a reprieve from death and

63. It is unclear if Qoheleth refers to the living no longer remembering the dead (αὐτῶν as objective genitive) or to the dead no longer having a memory of their own (αὐτῶν as subjective genitive). The preceding verse, which speaks of the dead having no knowledge, might support the latter view.

64. The celebratory nature of this activity is indicated by the instruction to let one's garments always be white and to not let oil be lacking upon one's head (9:8).

the elimination of one's being after death.[65] Notwithstanding the two individuals who seem to avoid death (Gen 5:22; 2 Kgs 2:11), the Jewish Bible does not entertain the avoidance of death as a likely possibility. What distinguishes Qoheleth is his explicit and repeated insistence that avoiding death is impossible and the function of this belief as a basis for his ethos and ethic of enjoying possessions.

In Qoh 5 and 9, the specter of death's inevitability functions as the rhetorical warrant for admonitions to enjoy oneself.[66] Qoheleth responds to the uncontrollable facets of death by imploring people to find enjoyment in those things that lie within their control. This counsel to enjoy life (3:12–13; 5:17; 8:15; 9:7–10) signals a development from Qoheleth's initial rejection of his pursuit of pleasure (2:1–11; cf. 4:8a).

Qoheleth 11:7–12:8

It is fitting that in the book's original conclusion, death functions one last time as a warrant for enjoyment.[67] The advice on enjoyment (11:7–10) precedes a cryptic description (12:1–8) interpreted by many to refer to old age and/or death.[68] Old age is characterized as a period of deterioration

---

65. Murphy sees the command to enjoy life in 9:6, 9 as conditioned by 9:10: "One is to live life to the fullest in view of the total inertia that one will eventually experience in Sheol" (*Tree of Life*, 54–55).

66. On similarities here with the Epic of Gilgamesh, see, e.g., Lee, *Vitality of Enjoyment*, 64–65; William P. Brown, *Ecclesiastes* (IBC; Louisville: John Knox, 2000), 95.

67. Fox takes 11:7–12:8 as a single unit (*Qohelet and His Contradictions*, 277). That 12:9–14 is a later addition is one of the few points on which most Qoheleth scholars agree. See, e.g., Murphy, *Tree of Life*, 52, 59; Lohfink, *Qoheleth*, 142–43; Tremper Longman III, *The Book of Ecclesiastes* (Grand Rapids: Eerdmans, 1998), 37–38. On the conclusion as a warrant for enjoyment, see Lohfink, *Qoheleth*, 3; Fox, *Qohelet and His Contradictions*, 286.

68. For "old age," see Loretz, *Qohelet und der alte Orient*, 189–93; Maurice Gilbert, "La description de la vieillesse en Qohelet XII 1–7 est-elle allégorique?" in Emerton, *Congress Volume: Vienna, 1980*, 96–109. Fox rejects this view, since it does not agree with earlier emphases in the book (*Qohelet and His Contradictions*, 286–87). Arguments for "death" include Christian D. Ginsburg, *Coheleth* (London: Longman, Green & Roberts, 1861; repr., New York: Ktav, 1970); Charles Taylor, *The Dirge of Coheleth in Ecclesasites XII* (London: Williams & Norgate, 1874), iii–iv; von Rad, *Wisdom in Israel*, 45; Murphy, *Tree of Life*, 55; Lohfink, *Qoheleth*, 14–41; Fox, *Qohelet and His Contradictions*, 286–87. Burkes sees in 12:1–8 references to death and old age (*God, Self, and Death*, 77). Von Rad and some rabbinic interpreters (Qoheleth Rabbah; b. Šabb.

and lack.[69] Of the years spent there one will say: "I have no desire [חפץ / θέλημα] in them" (12:1). The body's decline is the principal feature of old age.[70] This period is also marked by fear (ירא),[71] terrors, and the failure of sexual desire (אביונה / κάππαρις; 12:5).[72]

Such deterioration foreshadows and parallels the destruction experienced in death. Everyone will go to an "eternal home" (בית עולם / οἶκος αἰῶνος), and "the mourners will go about the streets" (12:5). This transition to death ends with dust returning to earth and the breath returning to God who gave it (12:7). Qoheleth concludes this reflection, and the entire book, with a final reiteration that everything is meaningless (הכל הבל / πάντα ματαιότης; 12:8). Constructing an inclusio (הבל הבלים ... הכל הבל / ματαιότης ματαιοτήτων ... πάντα ματαιότης) with the opening line (1:2) highlights the centrality of the text's claim about the totality and pervasive scope of meaninglessness.

Qoheleth's somber depiction of old age and death functions as a warrant to enjoy the pleasures afforded in youth.[73] His funereal allusion both calls to mind and vividly illustrates the end of one's life.[74] By inviting readers/hearers to imagine their own deaths and funerals, Qoheleth provides a powerful rhetorical argument for his admonitions to enjoy life.[75] Situating oneself at, and envisioning, one's own funeral invites readers/hearers to

---

131b–132a) read each object in the poem as a reference to a (degenerating) body part (*Wisdom in Israel*, 45; cf. 228). For 12:1–8 as a cosmic deterioration, see Burkes, *God, Self, Death*, 77; Fox, *A Time to Tear Down*, 339–43; Lee, *Vitality of Enjoyment*, 29. Fox reads 12:1–8 as the death of an individual and the end of the universe (*A Time to Tear Down*, 342; cf. idem, *Qohelet and His Contradictions*, 290). It is not without reason that Fox calls 12:1–8 "the most difficult passage in a difficult book" (*Qohelet and His Contradictions*, 281).

69. So Burkes, *God, Self, and Death*, 77; Lavoie, *La penseé du Qohélet*, 99.

70. Von Rad understands the various components to refer to body parts (*Wisdom in Israel*, 45; cf. 228).

71. The Greek has ὄψονται, perhaps construing the Hebrew ירא for ראה or intentionally playing on the similarity between these words.

72. The last term is, literally, the "caper-berry" or "caper plant," an aphrodisiac.

73. So Fox, *Qohelet and His Contradictions*, 281.

74. On the funereal allusion, see Anat, "Lament on the Death of Humanity," 375–80; Fox, *Qohelet and His Contradictions*, 288–90, 299 Lee, *Vitality of Enjoyment*, 29; Lohfink, *Qoheleth*, 140–41. On the end of one's life, see Fox, *A Time to Tear Down*, 338.

75. On imagining one's own death or funeral, see Fox, *Qohelet and His Contradictions*, 289. Lee reads the poem as an eschatological treatment of the demise of all humanity (*Vitality of Enjoyment*, 29).

consider, from the perspective of death, one's life and how one has lived. Arguing that enjoying life and possessions is the appropriate response to such reflection, Qoheleth precedes the poem on old age and death with four exhortations, each of which concerns enjoyment:

> And sweet is the light, and good it is for the eyes to see the sun.
> For even if a person lives many years,
> one should enjoy [ישמח / εὐφρανθήσεται] them all;
> and one should remember the days of darkness,
> for they will be many;
> all that is coming is futile [הבל / ματαιότης]. (11:7–8)
>
> Enjoy [שמח / εὐφραίνου], young man, in your youth,
> and let your heart cheer [ייטיב / ἀγαθυνάτω] you in the days of your youth,
> and walk in the ways of your heart
> and in the sight of your eyes
> and know that for all these things God will bring you into judgment [משפט / κρίσει]. (11:9)
>
> And remove anger from your heart
> and lead away evil from your flesh [בשר / σαρκός],
> for youth and dark hair are fleeting [הבל / ματαιότης]. (11:10)[76]
>
> And remember your creator
> in the days of your youth,
> before the days of misery [רעה / κακίας] come,
> and years draw near, of which you will say,
> "I have no desire [חפץ / θέλημα] in them." (12:1)

These admonitions convey an ambivalent perspective on death and enjoyment. On the one hand, enjoying pleasure is commended regardless of one's age (11:8). The period of youth is especially singled out as an optimal time to take advantage of such enjoyment (11:9).[77] One should enjoy life before the "days of darkness" arrive (11:8).[78]

---

76. For הבל here as "ephemerality" or "fleetingness," see Fox, *Qohelet and His Contradictions*, 279.

77. *Papyrus Insinger* also speaks of old age (sixty years) as the time when enjoyment (of wine, food, and women) is severely limited (17.11–14).

78. Fox takes this line as a reference to death (*Qohelet and His Contradictions*, 279).

On the other hand, youth and folly are considered הבל / *ματαιότης* (11:10), and judgment ultimately awaits those who do enjoy themselves (11:9c).[79] Such future judgment may inform the discomfort in Vaticanus with the previous admonition to enjoy pleasure in one's youth, for rather than walking in the "ways of your heart" and "the sight of your eyes," as the Hebrew reads, a person is directed to "walk in the ways of your heart *blameless* [ἄμωμος] and *not* [μή] in the sight of your eyes" (11:9). The LXX similarly moralizes "blackness" (שחרות) in 11:10, likely connoting "prime of life" in the Hebrew, into "folly" (ἄνοια).[80] Even if one does not follow most commentators in taking 11:9 as an editorial gloss, its precise meaning remains uncertain.[81] Will a person be judged, as Vaticanus suggests, for enjoyment? Or (which seems more likely in light of Qoheleth's entire *oeuvre*) will one be judged for failing to enjoy and walk in the ways of one's heart?[82] What is clear is that death functions, yet again, as a rationale for enjoyment (11:8; 12:1).

Conclusion to Qoheleth

The following chart illustrates the relationships in Qoheleth between the perception of death and recommendations regarding the enjoyment of possessions.

---

79. Many, e.g., Lohfink, take the reference to "judgment" as a secondary gloss due to its apparent contradiction to other statements in the book (*Qoheleth*, 135, 139). Yet discarding such texts is methodologically tenuous given the uncertainty regarding the criteria employed in distinguishing between the "genuine" and "spurious" Qoheleth. (Another remark on judgment occurs in 3:17, and scholars are also divided on its authenticity). Fox takes 11:9 as genuine (*A Time to Tear Down*, 318). James L. Crenshaw is uncertain (*Ecclesiastes* [OTL; Louisville: Westminster John Knox, 1987], 184). Murphy thinks that Qoheleth affirms a divine judgment but remains ignorant regarding the *manner* of this judgment (*Tree of Life*, 57; cf. 59). Lohfink (*Qoheleth*, 139) thinks it unlikely that the author has in mind a "next-worldly judgment of the dead."

80. So Fox, *Qohelet and His Contradictions*, 280.

81. Some (e.g., Longman, *Ecclesiastes*, 259; Crenshaw, *Ecclesiastes*, 181, 184) take the *waw* in 11:9c as an adversative; others (e.g., Gordis, *Koheleth*, 335–36) take it as consecutive.

82. So Gordis, *Koheleth*, 336.

View of Death	Issues Related to Death	View/Role of God	Posses-sions
Uncertainty of Inheritance (2:18–21)	Meaninglessness of toil (2:18–19, 22–23)	Goods as divine gifts (2:24–26)	Enjoyment (2:24a)
		God's inscrutability (3:11); Goods as divine gifts (3:13)	Enjoyment (3:12)
In death, all return to dust (3:19–20)	Uncertainty of future (3:22b)		Enjoyment (3:22a)
Uncertainty of inheritance (5:12–13)	"Cannot take goods with you" (5:14–15)	Days and goods are a gift of God (5:17–18; 6:2)	Enjoyment (5:17)
Death is common fate of just and wicked (8:14)	One cannot control death (8:8, 13) or how one is remembered (8:10)	God is a giver (8:15)	Enjoyment (8:15)
Death is common fate of just and wicked (9:1–3)	Death destroys knowledge, memory, emotions (9:5–6, 10)	God has approved of enjoyment (9:7)	Enjoyment (9:7–10)
Death and dust are universal destiny (12:5, 7)	Inability to enjoy in old age (12:1–5) Days of darkness are coming (11:8)	God gave breath (12:7) God will bring into judgment (11:9)	Enjoyment (11:8–9)

Death and possessions are virtually inseparable in Qoheleth. Thinking about one invariably leads to considering the other. For Qoheleth, death is sovereign and omnipotent. One is impotent in its grasp, and this failure to control any facet of death results in an effort to exert a modicum of control over what one can: eating, drinking, and enjoyment in the present moment. Although death's uncontrollable nature renders life meaningless (הבל / ματαιότης), Qoheleth finds in these concrete acts the possibility of meaning. Qoheleth's consistent focus on enjoyment reflects an interest in meaningful living. The integral link between death and the enjoyment of goods suggests that Qoheleth considers meaningful living to be dependent on one's ability to face, and reflect on, one's mortality.

Many aspects of death and possessions lie outside a person's control: the recipient of one's inheritance, how the dead will be treated, and death's timing. It is impossible to lengthen one's life or to know what will happen after death. Death destroys every vestige of humanity. People cannot influence their death by the choices they make in life. Death is inevitable and unavoidable. In light of these myriad uncontrollable facets, Qoheleth prescribes enjoyment as one (and perhaps the only) way to exercise some modicum of control.

The fragility of this enjoyment is underscored, however, by the reminder that the ability to enjoy goods lies not in one's own power but in God's hands (2:24–26; 3:13; 5:17–18; 6:2). Because enjoyment is a divine gift, its occurrence or longevity (when it does occur) cannot be guaranteed. Like a vapor, it cannot be captured or contained. Efforts to manipulate it as a vehicle with a predetermined result are therefore futile (2:1–26). This ephemeral nature highlights the need to enjoy goods presently when they are received as a gift.

God is integral to Qoheleth's understanding of enjoyment. God's character functions as a warrant in six of the seven recommendations for enjoyment. Since God gives goods and the opportunity to enjoy them, enjoyment is one of the primary ways in and through which one can experience God. God, although uncontrollable, provides the opportunity, even if fleeting, to experience meaning in a world that is otherwise meaningless.

The Interplay of Death and Possessions in Ben Sira

Although not to the same extent as in Qoheleth, Ben Sira shows an interest in the interplay of death and possessions. After providing a brief overview of Ben Sira's respective attitudes toward death and possessions, I will explicate the two selections in Ben Sira (11:14–28 and 14:3–19) in which the interplay of death and possessions figures most prominently.

Death in Ben Sira

Death receives a significant amount of attention in Ben Sira.[83] With Qoheleth, Ben Sira insists that death is unavoidable: all must die (8:7;

83. So Collins, *Jewish Wisdom*, 78; Crenshaw, *Old Testament Wisdom*, 151; cf. Friedrich Reiterer, "Deutung und Wertung des Todes durch Ben Sira," in *Die alttestamentliche Botschaft als Wegweisung: Festschrist für Heinz Reinelt* (ed. Josef Zmijew-

38:22; 41:4). Death's timing is, moreover, uncertain (11:19; cf. 10:11). Ben Sira seeks to allay fear (9:13; 40:5) and anxiety (40:2–5) about death by stressing that death is in God's control (11:14; 41:4) and intimating, in sharp contrast to Qoheleth, that one can be remembered after death (41:3).[84]

Ben Sira provides scant information about what happens during and after death. One's spirit departs at death, and it is impossible to return from death (38:21, 23). Hades is the postmortem destination for everyone, and once there one cannot sing praise to God, give thanks, or ask questions (17:27; 41:4; cf. 21:10).[85] Aside from these brief comments, Ben Sira gives little description of a postmortem existence.[86] References to the afterlife are generally viewed as glosses in the Greek version, not reflective of the Hebrew *Vorlage*.[87] For Ben Sira, one who dies "inherits creeping things, wild beasts, and worms" (10:11).[88]

In contrast to Qoheleth, Ben Sira maintains that some can live on after death in other peoples' memories. Remembrance of the dead is possible through the ongoing life of one's reputation or name; whereas the days of a

---

ski; Stuttgart: Katholisches Bibelwerk, 1990), 204. For a recent analysis of Ben Sira's attempt to offer "symbolic modes of death transcendence" that "provide a buffer against death anxiety," see Williamson, "Death and Symbolic Immortality," 280–317.

84. Wisdom of Solomon rejects the notion that God made death (1:13; cf. 2:24). Collins highlights the stark contrast between Ben Sira and Wisdom of Solomon on this point (*Jewish Wisdom*, 187–90).

85. The Syriac version of Sir 41:4 ("Because this is the end of all sons of men before God") lacks the reference to the absence of "arguments about life" in Hades/Sheol. For the English translation, see Michael M. Winter, "Theological Alterations in the Syriac Translation of Ben Sira," *CBQ* 70 (2008): 300–312, here 306.

86. So Patrick W. Skehan and Alexander Di Lella, *The Wisdom of Ben Sira: A New Translation with Notes, Introduction, and Commentary* (AB 39; Garden City, N.Y.: Doubleday, 1987), 299. Some ancient manuscripts add: "The knowledge of the Lord's commandments is life-giving discipline; and those who do what is pleasing to him enjoy the fruit of the tree of immortality" (19:19).

87. So Skehan and Di Lella, *The Wisdom of Ben Sira*, 86; Burkes, *God, Self, Death*, 111 n. 58; Murphy thinks the original version lacks the eschatological thinking one finds in the longer version (*Tree of Life*, 68). Winter shows that some Syriac translations emphasize a postmortem salvation; he cites Sir 3:1; 14:6; 15:15; 41:4 ("Theological Alterations," 305–8). Collins maintains that the notion of a postmortem divine punishment was foreign to Proverbs, Qoheleth, and Ben Sira (*Jewish Wisdom*, 115).

88. The dead person is said to be "at rest" (22:11). The Hebrew reads "gnats" instead of "wild beasts."

good life are numbered, a "good name continues forever [ἀγαθὸν ὄνομα εἰς αἰῶνα διαμενεῖ]" (41:11–13).[89] Such is the case with the wise person (חכם / σοφός; 37:26),[90] the one who gives his life to reflect on the law of the Most High (39:1, 9–11), and merciful people (חסד / ἔλεος) whose acts of justice (δικαιοσύνη) are not forgotten (ἐπιλανθάνομαι; 44:10, 14).[91] The names of the latter live on through the detailed description of their wisdom and the proclamation of their praise by the assembly (44:15).[92] Not everyone, however, will be remembered equally after death.[93]

In another contrast to Qoheleth, Ben Sira maintains that a person's death *is* influenced by how one has lived. The person, for example, "who fears the Lord will be well at the time of the end, and on the day of death [ἡμέρᾳ τελευτῆς] he or she will be blessed" (1:13; cf. 33:1). Ben Sira accordingly admonishes his audience to cling to the Lord so that they may be exalted in their last days (2:3). Sinners, by contrast, will not be justified (δικαιόω) during life and will meet their end in the pit of Hades (9:11–12; 21:9–10; cf. 40:8–15). Evident in this outlook of Ben Sira is the law of

89. The verse numbers I cite refer to the critical Greek text in Joseph Ziegler, ed., *Sapientia Iesu Filii Sirach* (Septuaginta 12.2; Göttingen: Vandenhoeck & Ruprecht, 1965). My translation is based on this Greek text. For the translation in Ben Sira from Hebrew to Greek, see Benjamin G. Wright, "New Perspectives on Biblical Vocabulary and Translation Technique: Sirach in Relation to Its Presumed Hebrew 'Vorlage'" (Ph.D. diss., University of Pennsylvania, 1988).

90. For the Hebrew text of Ben Sira, I use the manuscripts in Pancratius C. Beentjes, *The Book of Ben Sira in Hebrew: A Text Edition of All Extant Manuscripts and a Synopsis of All Parallel Hebrew Ben Sira Texts* (VTSup 68; Leiden: Brill, 1997). For a synopsis of these extant versions, see Friedrich V. Reiterer, *Zählsynopse zum buch Ben Sira* (Fontes et Subsidia ad Bibliam pertientes 1; Berlin: de Gruyter, 2003). For other issues related to the Hebrew text, see Pancratius Beentjes, *"Happy the One Who Meditates on Wisdom" (Sir. 14,20): Collected Essays on the Book of Ben Sira* (CBET 43; Leuven: Peeters, 2006).

91. See 39:2–8 for a list of additional attributes describing the person whose name will endure forever.

92. So also will their wealth and inheritance be passed on to descendants (44:11); their offspring will continue forever (44:13).

93. Although some "have left behind a name," there are others of whom "there is no memory" (44:8–9a). The latter "have perished as though they had never existed; they have become as though they had never been born, they and their children after them" (44:9b). The Lord, in addition, is able to erase the memory of certain nations from the earth (10:17).

retribution,[94] and his view contradicts Qoheleth's claim that one's conduct has no bearing on one's death (cf. Qoh 8:14; 9:1–3).

Possessions in Ben Sira

Ben Sira's attitude toward possessions is ambiguous and not easily reducible to simplistic generalities.[95] He features the poor prominently, and his predominant attitude toward them is favorable.[96] Pervading his work are instructions to care for the poor (עני / πτωχός / πένης), needy (ἐπιδεής / προσδέομαι / δέομαι), and hungry (4:1–10; 29:8–9).[97] Aid is to be given to those who are wronged (ἀδικέω), orphans, and widows (4:9–10).[98] One who cares for such people is "like a son of the Most High" (cf. Luke 6:35–36). Echoing language from Deuteronomy, Ben Sira instructs, "stretch out your hand to the poor" (7:32; cf. 4:31; Deut 15:7–11).[99] Giving alms (ἐλεημοσύνη) is repeatedly presented as an ideal use of goods.[100] In caring for the poor, one enacts God's own kindness toward them (11:12–13).

94. So Hengel, *Judaism and Hellenism*, 1:142; Harrington, *Jesus Ben Sira*, 28.

95. So Crenshaw, *Old Testament Wisdom*, 147, 163 n. 19; Benjamin G. Wright III, "The Discourse of Riches and Poverty in the Book of Ben Sira," in *Society of Biblical Literature 1998 Seminar Papers* (2 vols.; Atlanta: Scholars Press, 1998), 2:559–578; Victor Morla Asensio, "Poverty and Wealth: Ben Sira's View of Possessions," in *Der Einzelne und seine Gemeinschaft bei Ben Sira* (ed. Renate Egger-Wenzel and Ingrid Krammer; BZAW 270; Berlin: de Gruyter, 1998), 150–78; Randal A. Argal, *1 Enoch and Sirach: A Comparative Literary and Conceptual Analysis of the Themes of Revelation, Creation and Judgment* (SBLEJL 8; Atlanta: Scholars Press, 1994), 252–54.

96. One need not, however, adopt the argument that he came from the poorer class, as in Victor Tcherikover, "Jerusalem on the Eve of the Hellenistic Reform," in *Hellenistic Civilization and the Jews* (ed. Victor Tcherikover; Philadelphia: Jewish Publication Society of America, 1961), 148; Friederich V. Reiterer, "Review of Recent Research on the Book of Ben Sira (1980–1996)," in *The Book of Ben Sira in Modern Research: Proceedings of the First International Ben Sira Conference 28–31 July 1996 Soesterberg, Netherlands* (ed. Pancratius C. Beentjes; Berlin: de Gruyter, 1997), 36.

97. On this theme, see Lutz Schrader, "Beruf, Arbeit und Mue als Sinnerfüllung bei Jesus Sirach," in Egger-Wenzel and Krammer, *Der Einzelne und seine Gemeinschaf*, 117–49.

98. Visiting the sick is also enjoined (Sir 7:35).

99. Generosity should also extend to one's neighbors (29:1–2).

100. Sir 3:14, 30; 7:10; 12:3; 16:14; 17:22, 29; 29:8, 12; 31:11; 25:2; 35:2; 40:17, 24. Asensio identifies alms as the "social aim of wealth in Ben Sira" ("Poverty and Wealth," 163).

Recalling Exod 22, Ben Sira intimates that God will hurt those who neglect the needy (δέομαι; 4:5–6; 35:17–23; cf. 21:5; Exod 22:21–27.). One is not to take bread from the poor, not even for the purpose of cultic sacrifice (34:24–26).

Ben Sira's prevailing attitude toward the rich (πλούσιος) is negative and cautionary (8:1–2; 13:2). The poor (πτωχός / πένης) are contrasted with the rich and are frequently preferred to the latter (13:2–7, 15–24; 21:4–5; 30:14–16; 31:3–4).[101] The rich exploit, abandon, exhaust, and deceive others (13:4–6). One should not lend to someone who is more powerful due to the likelihood of not being repaid (8:12–13).[102] Ben Sira critiques merchants (26:29; 37:11) and economic activities such as buying and selling (11:10b; 26:29–27:3; 31:5–11; 37:11).[103] He also condemns the vices of luxury (τρυφή) and gluttony (κοιλίας ὄρεξις / ἀπληστία; 18:30–33; 23:6; 31:12–17, 20–21; 37:27–31). The Syriac version of Ben Sira shows an increase in the number of positive statements on poverty and the number of negative statements on wealth.[104]

101. Jeremy Corley reads Sir 13:15–23 as an indication of a dichotomy between wealthy Hellenizers and poor Jews (*Ben Sira's Teaching on Friendship* [BJS 316; Providence, R.I.: Brown Judaic Studies, 2002]).

102. Hengel refers to Ben Sira's "impressive description of the power of the rich aristocracy" (*Judaism and Hellenism*, 1:136–37). He observes in Ben Sira an "unbridgeable opposition between poor and rich."

103. Skehan and Di Lella refer to such texts as "warnings … on the possible evils of the business world and the pursuit of wealth" (*The Wisdom of Ben Sira*, 238).

104. So Milward Douglas Nelson, *The Syriac Version of the Wisdom of Ben Sira Compared to the Greek and Hebrew Materials* (SBLDS 107; Atlanta: Scholars Press, 1988), 123–24. The Syriac version drops 40:9–10, and alters 40:8 to read: "with all the sons of flesh their anxiety is with them; *riches* disturb their sleep." The instruction not to live as a beggar is changed in the Syriac to an instruction to not *refuse* a beggar (40:28). Nelson claims, on this basis, that the Syriac translator "was suspicious of wealth and not averse to poverty. Perhaps, in dropping 40:10, he was afraid to identify the 'poor' with the 'wicked,' since, in his view, poverty was an accepted, if not recommended, state of being" (124). For the Syriac of Ben Sira, see Paul de Lagarde, *Libri Veteris Testamenti Apocryphi Syriace* (London: Williams & Norgate, 1861); Nelson, *Syriac Version*; Nuria Calduch-Benages, Joan Ferrer, and Jan Liesen, *La Sabiduría del Escriba: Edición diplomática de la versión siriaca del libro de Ben Sira según el Códice Ambrosiano, con traducción española e inglesa* (Biblioteca Midrásica 26; Estella, Navarra: Editorial Verbo Divino, 2003); W. Th. van Peursen, *Language and Interpretation in the Syriac Text of Ben Sira: A Comparative Linguistic and Literary Study* (Monographs of the Peshitta Institute: Studies in the Syriac Versions of the Bible and Their Cultural Contexts 16; Leiden: Brill, 2007).

Related to this critique of the rich is a (generally) negative view of wealth. A person's wrath (ὀργή), for instance, is linked to his or her level of wealth (πλοῦτος; 28:10b). The love of money is derided (10:9),[105] and depending on it can be dangerous (5:1; 11:18–19, 23–28). Anxiety (μέριμνα) and sleeplessness over wealth is self-destructive, as is pursuing it (31:1–2, 5–8); some sin in their pursuit of wealth (27:1). The wealth of the unjust (χρῆμα ἀδίκων), Ben Sira insists, will not last forever (40:13). He considers a kingdom to be conveyed from nation to nation by "injustice, insolence, and wealth" (χρῆμα; 10:8), and he criticizes those who take money (χρῆμα) from others (21:8). For Ben Sira, wealth and possessions are by no means a sign of divine approbation.[106]

Ben Sira can also write about wealth and those who have it in neutral terms, without any of the aforementioned criticism (40:18, 25–26).[107] Certain business practices, he notes, are not shameful (42:2–5).[108] He assumes people will engage in business matters such as making deposits and does not abjure this practice (42:7). He favors moderate eating (31:20, 22, 25–30) and speaks favorably of being cheerful and merry when one eats (30:25). He even writes of the potential goodness of riches, if they are not related to sin (13:24).[109] Most exceptional is the recognition that a rich person can be blameless, and Ben Sira intimates that this status can be achieved by giving alms (ἐλεημοσύνη; 31:8–11).[110] Nor are all of his statements about poverty favorable.[111]

Ben Sira establishes a causal relationship between the use of possessions and how one is treated by God. Giving alms is a primary means of secur-

105. At least according to some variants, for some manuscripts add here, or after verse 9a: "nothing is more wicked than one who loves money, for such a person puts his own soul up for sale."

106. Asensio sees in these kinds of statements an important "advance with regard to the ideas on wealth in the BHS" ("Poverty and Wealth," 159).

107. Such remarks have led some, such as Reiterer to claim that Ben Sira "views wealth positively" ("Review of Recent Research," 45).

108. These include keeping accounts with a partner, keeping accurate scales and weights, the acquisition (κτῆσις) of much or little, and profit from dealing with merchants.

109. Note, however, that, whereas riches have the potential to be "good," poverty is "evil only in the opinion of the ungodly" (13:24).

110. A caveat is provided that one must not pursue gold (31:8).

111. One should not beg, for instance, since death is preferable to begging (40:28–30).

ing one's future with the divine. Ben Sira likens almsgiving (ἐλεημοσύνη) to a "signet ring with the Lord," who will "preserve a person's kindness [χάριν]" (17:22). God will in fact "repay" (ἀνταποδίδωμι) those who give alms (17:23). The equation of alms with sacrificing a thank offering suggests that alms have an effectual power to secure divine power (35:2). This power of alms is also evident in Ben Sira's assertion that almsgiving (צדיקה / ἐλεημοσύνη) "atones for sin" (תכפר חטאת / ἐξιλάσεται ἁμαρτίας; 3:30).[112] Not surprisingly, Ben Sira exhorts readers not to neglect almsgiving (7:10). Failure to give alms brings an appropriate (negative) response: "There will be no good things for the one who continues in evil and the one who does not give alms willingly" (12:3).[113] By concluding a series of instructions on giving to others (7:32–35) with the reminder to "remember your *last things*" (אחרית / τὰ ἔσχατά; 7:36), Ben Sira suggests that contemplating death may lead to, or at least encourage, giving to the poor (7:32).[114] He also implies that generosity may benefit one on the day of death, for the person who gives to the poor will be blessed (7:32).

Ben Sira is equally insistent that wealth cannot protect one from divine judgment (5:1–8). His warnings against presumption, self-sufficiency, and relying on wealth (חיל / χρῆμα) conclude with an admonition to not "hold fast to dishonest wealth [נכסי שקר / χρήμασιν ἀδίκοις]," since it will not profit a person on the "day of distress" (5:1–8). Ben Sira's caution against the illusory sense of power that wealth provides (5:3) comports with other reminders that storing up riches does not guarantee security (11:10–11, 18–19, 20–21a, 23–24).[115]

In sum, although wealth is not intrinsically evil for Ben Sira, it does present a number of potential dangers for its owner and those who pursue it.[116] On the other hand, the emphasis on alms points to a potential benefit

112. The following verse ("Those who repay favors give thought to the future; when they fall they will find support," 3:31) raises the possibility that Ben Sira envisions alms as securing future divine favor. Almsgiving, he claims, is more helpful than "kindred and helpers" (40:24).

113. Alms, Ben Sira notes, are to be given to certain people (the "devout" and "humble") but not to others (the "sinner," "ungodly") (12:4–5a). One is not to give bread to the latter, since "by means of it they might subdue you; you will receive as much evil for all the good you have done to them" (12:5b). One should give alms "to the one who is good, but do not help the sinner" (12:7).

114. On the importance of remembering the end of one's life, cf. Sir 28:6.

115. So Harrington, *Jesus Ben Sira*, 39.

116. So Asensio, "Poverty and Wwalth," 163; cf. 158–63.

of wealth, if used properly. I turn now to explicate two selections from Ben Sira (11:14–28 and 14:3–19) in which the interplay of death and possessions figures prominently.

Ben Sira 11:14–28

Ben Sira 11:14–28 contains a reflection on the meaningful uses of possessions given death's inevitability and uncertain timing.[117] Interest in death and possessions is signaled in the introductory frame to the discussion that declares that the Lord is the source of "good things and evil things, life and death [מות / *θάνατος*], poverty and riches [ריש ועושר / *πτωχεία καὶ πλοῦτος*] (Sir 11:14).[118]

Ben Sira initially offers a rather conventional view of wealth in which God blesses with riches those who live rightly (11:17–18): "The Lord's gift [*δόσις*] remains with the righteous/godly [צדיק / *εὐσεβέσιν*], and [the Lord's] favor will last forever" (11:17). Furthermore, one becomes rich (עשיר / *πλουτέω*) through diligence (תענות / *προσοχή*) and restraint (*σφιγγία*; 11:18a).[119] This somewhat conventional view of wealth[120] also appears in Sir 11:15–16, a variant occurring in one-fourth to one-half of the manuscripts.[121] Such a view comports with a Deuteronomistic theology

117. Skehan and Di Lella see six "minipoems" in 11:7–28 (*The Wisdom of Ben Sira*, 238). I do not include the first of these (11:7–9), since it is the only one of the six that does not address death or wealth.

118. The third pairing (ריש ועושר / *πτωχεία καὶ πλοῦτος*) disrupts the previous parallelism in which the positive element precedes the negative one.

119. Ben Sira here echoes concerns in Qoheleth regarding industriousness (see, e.g., Qoh 11:6). Though Skehan and Di Lella note that the Hebrew may be translated literally as "There is a man who becomes rich *by afflicting himself*" (emphasis original), they see in 11:18 a description of a miser, perhaps due to reading this text through the lens of 14:3–10, 14, which they cite as a parallel (*The Wisdom of Ben Sira*, 239). The plans of this person to enjoy his goods (11:19ab) do not, however, comport with the figure of a miser.

120. Sanders classifies Proverbs and Ben Sira as "conventional wisdom" and Job, Qoheleth, and Wisdom of Solomon as "unconventional" wisdom (*Ben Sira*, 3).

121. *σοφία καὶ ἐπιστήμη καὶ γνῶσις νόμου παρὰ κυρίου, ἀγάπησις καὶ ὁδοὶ καλῶν ἔργων παρ' αὐτοῦ εἰσιν. πλάνη καὶ σκότος ἁμαρτωλοῖς συνέκτισται, τοῖς δὲ γαυριῶσιν ἐπὶ κακίᾳ συγγηρᾷ κακία*. This variant also appears in the Hebrew text of MS A:

[.] כמה ושכל / והביך דבר מייי הוא :
חטא ודרכים ישרים מייי הוא :
שכלות / וחו[..] לפשעים נוצרה ומרעים רעה ימם:

and is also attested in Proverbs.[122] A classic formulation is Prov 22:4: "The reward for humility and fear of Yhwh are riches [עשר / πλοῦτος], possessions [כבוד],[123] and life [חיים]."[124] Ben Sira's perspective represents a sharp divergence from Qoheleth's rejection of the act-consequence relationship.

Yet in 11:19c–d, Ben Sira quickly upends this conventional view of wealth. Referring to the rich person, the author declares, "And this is the share of his reward [שכרו / μισθοῦ]" (11:18b). In light of the positive connotation of "reward" (שכר / μισθός) and the preceding context of 11:14–18a, one expects the reward's share to be some sort of benefit.[125] Ben Sira maintains this expectation in the preliminary description of the rich person's "share of his reward": "When he says, 'I have found rest [נחת / ἀνάπαυσιν] and now I will eat from my good things [י[.]וב[..] אכל / φάγομαι ἐκ τῶν ἀγαθῶν μου]'" (11:19a–b).[126] The expectation of a benefit is increased by the threefold repetition of "and" (ו / καί) in 11:19b, c, d. Following the first two lines of 11:19, one expects that the second ו / καί will introduce a thought that parallels the first two lines of 11:19. However, the third line of 11:19 upsets this pattern: "but he does not know how much time will pass by [[.]חל [...] ולא ידע מה י / καὶ οὐκ οἶδεν τίς καιρὸς παραλεύσεται]." This disruption is continued, through synonymous parallelism, in 11:19d: "and he will leave [ע[.]ב / καταλείψει] them to others and die [מת / ἀποθανεῖται]."[127]

122. See, e.g., Prov 3:1–6; 10:22. Paul Volz treats Ben Sira and Proverbs together, without distinguishing between the two (*Hiob und Weisheit* [2nd ed.; Die Schriften des Alten Testaments 3.2; Göttingen: Vandenhoeck & Ruprecht, 1921]). Burkes cites Sir 11:17 as an example of "the type of instructional wisdom exemplified in Proverbs" (*God, Self, and Death*, 89). For similarities regarding views of God and the world in Proverbs and Ben Sira, see Gammie, "Sage in Sirach," 359.

123. For כבוד as "possessions," see William L. Holladay, ed., *A Concise Hebrew and Aramaic Lexicon of the Old Testament* (Leiden: Brill, 1988), 150–51. The Greek has δόξα.

124. Crenshaw sums up the view in Proverbs: "Those who please God escape Sheol and Abaddon's ravenous appetite, for God rewards them with riches and length of days" ("Shadow of Death," 211). Such statements lead Crenshaw to conclude that in Proverbs the "threat of death thus undergirds morality" (216 n. 43).

125. Perhaps the author is playing on the ambiguity of μισθός, which can also mean "requital" in a negative sense (LSJ, 1137). The Hebrew term (שכר) does not convey this same meaning.

126. He echoes Qoheleth's refrain regarding the appropriateness of enjoying and, in particular, eating the fruits of wealth.

127. This final line clarifies that the παραλεύσεται in 11:19 refers to the rich person's death.

There is hardly any hint, prior to 11:19c, of a dilemma associated with being wealthy, yet the shift in 11:19c introduces by way of illustration a quandary for those who have riches: death's uncertain timing makes it impossible to know how long one will be able to enjoy one's goods.

If we read Sir 11:19c-d as a crisis for the person with wealth, 11:20–28 can be understood as a response to this predicament. Ben Sira offers suggestions and proscriptions to the dilemma occasioned by death's uncertain timing and the consequent transfer of possessions to another. The precise meaning of his first proposal (στῆθι ἐν διαθήκῃ σου [בחוקך] καὶ ὁμίλει ἐν αὐτῇ) is ambiguous because of the various options for translating חוק / διαθήκη (11:20a). The NRSV renders διαθήκη as a general "agreement," to which one is enjoined to "stand by" and "attend."

However, διαθήκη can also refer more specifically to a "disposition of property by will" or a "testament." There are reasons to prefer this meaning for the term.[128] Reading διαθήκη as "testament" or "disposition of property" is compelling, given the preceding reference in Sir 11:19 to the uncertainty of when time will "pass away" and one "will leave" possessions to others and die. The multiple options for translating חוק (the Hebrew equivalent of διαθήκη) make a precise definition difficult. This difficulty is compounded with the (probable) shift(s) in meaning of חק from Biblical Hebrew to the time of Ben Sira in the second century B.C.E.[129] Benjamin G. Wright notes that διαθήκη in Ben Sira translates both ברית and חוק[130] and that, whereas ברית usually refers to a "covenant," חוק typically means

128. This is the first definition given in LSJ, 394, and BDAG, 228. The latter notes that in Hellenistic times it was exclusively understood in this way. For διαθήκη as will/testament, see Lucian, *Dial. mort.* 19.3; 21.1–2; *Nigr.* 30; *Demon.* 44; *Gall.* 12; *Ind.* 19; Heb 9:16, 17; cf. Gal 3:15, 17. The verb related to διαθήκη, διατίθημι, is also used to refer to the act of disposing of one's goods or making a will for such a purpose (LSJ, 415; BDAG, 238; cf. Josephus, *Ant.* 13.407; Oxyrynchus Papyri 104.4; 105.2; 489.3; Luke 22:29; Heb 9:16).

129. On the complex relationship between Classical Biblical Hebrew, Late Biblical Hebrew, and Qumranic Hebrew, see Menahem Kister, "Some Observations on Vocabulary and Style in the DSS," in *Diggers at the Well: Proceedings of a Third International Symposium on the Hebrew of the Dead Sea Scrolls and Ben Sira* (ed. T. Muraoka and J. F. Elwolde; Leiden: Brill, 2000).

130. Benjamin G. Wright notes that there are fifteen "non-problematic occurrences" of διαθήκη in Ben Sira; of these, seven translate ברית, and eight render חק (*No Small Difference: Sirach's Relationship to Its Hebrew Parent Text* [SBLSCS 26; Atlanta: Scholars Press, 1989], 179).

"decree" or "statute."[131] This difference in meaning obtains in the Hebrew Bible as well as Ben Sira.[132] Thus, the word חק "is used in a number of different ways in Sira, but not to mean 'covenant.'" Wright claims that in Sir 11:20 חק "probably means 'appointed task' as it does in Exod 5.14."[133]

Yet what kind of appointed task? It is significant, notwithstanding its later date, that חוק is used in the Talmud to refer to a "due share (a fixed living)" that a father will leave to his sons (b. 'Erub. 54a).[134] This usage may reflect a trajectory of this word's semantic domain that may also have had currency in Ben Sira's time. The close relationship between חק and the verbs חקה and חקק may also be suggestive, since both of these verbs are used in Middle and Qumranic Hebrew to refer to the act of carving, engraving, or inscribing, acts that can be associated with constructing a will or testament.[135]

If we render חוק / διαθήκη as "will" or "testament," then Sir 11:20a implies that one has composed a will that describes the distribution of property.[136] In this case, Ben Sira would be proposing that a proper response to the crisis outlined in 11:19b is to stand firm in the testament one has made

131. Ibid., 180; cf. BDB, 349.

132. For חק as "portion, term," "prescribed task," "appropriate portion," "due," "allotted portion," "appointed time," "limit," "law, regulation," "prescription, rule," see *HALOT* 1:346. Cf. *DCH* 3:299, where חק is defined as "statute, decree, law, rule, instruction" or an "expected allocation" of food or territory. In Qumranic Hebrew, the term is used as "statute" (4Q525 3.2,1) and "legal instruction" (4Q424 1,4).

133. Wright, *No Small Difference*, 181.

134. Marcus Jastrow, *Dictionary of the Targumim, the Tamud Babli and Yerushalmi, and the Midrashic Literature* (Peabody, Mass.: Hendrickson, 2005), 438. Jastrow renders חוק as "law, rule, custom; assigned share, mark."

135. In Middle Hebrew, חקק can mean "to hollow out, to engrave" or "to carve" (Isa 22:16); "to inscribe" (Isa 30:8; 49:16; Ezek 4:1; 23:14; Prov 8:27); "to enact, to decree" (Isa 10:1); "what is decreed" (Prov 31:5). In Phonecian, the term developed from "to carve" into "to stipulate in writing" (*HALOT* 1:347). In Qumranic Hebrew, חקק can mean "cut, engrave, decree" (4Q185 1.2,4; 1QpHab 7,13; 1QS 10,1; 4QD[e] 9.2,18) (*DCH* 3:303–4). In Aramaic, חקק means "to engrave" (Michael Sokoloff, *A Dictionary of Jewish Palestinian Aramaic of the Byzantine Period* [2nd ed.; Ramat-Gan: Bar Ilan University, 2002], 213). In the pual, חקה can mean "carved" or "engraved" (Ezek 8:10; 1 Kgs 6:35) (*HALOT* 1:347) or a "carved thing, engraving" (Ezek 23:14; 4QShirShabb[f] 15.2,4). It is used in the hithpael to mean "engrave for oneself" (Job 13:27) (*DCH* 3:302).

136. For Ben Sira's instructions regarding inheritance, see Sir 9:6; 22:23; 33:23; 42:3.

and "attend" (ὁμιλέω) to it (11:20a).[137] Because death's timing is uncertain, Ben Sira enjoins establishing a will and living in light of it.[138] By doing so, he would thus address one of Qoheleth's explicit complaints, namely, the uncertainty regarding who will receive one's inheritance. By establishing a testament that clearly provides for the transference of possessions after one dies, Ben Sira avoids the meaninglessness that Qoheleth finds in one's goods being given to either a fool or someone who did not labor for them (cf. Qoh 2:18–21).

Death's uncertain timing and the resulting transference of possessions to another do not, as in Qoheleth (2:18–19, 22–23), lead Ben Sira to eschew diligent toil nor to regard such toil as futile. To the suggestion that one stand in and attend to one's testament, Ben Sira adds that one is to "grow old" (παλαιόω) in one's work (ἔργον; 11:20). Ben Sira's admonition implicitly warns against those who might respond to death by abdicating work. It can therefore be understood as a rejoinder, if not to Qoheleth, then to the ideas he espouses (cf. Qoh 2:18–23). Ben Sira's exhortation not to abandon work continues after the first of three negative admonitions. After warning against marveling at the deeds (ἔργον) of the sinner, Ben Sira enjoins one to trust (רוץ[.] / πιστεύω) the Lord and remain (קוה / ἐμμένω) in one's toil (און / πόνος; 11:21).[139] This advice reveals none of the obsession one finds in Qoheleth with the countless problems associated with toil.[140] For Ben Sira, one should remain steadfast in one's toil because the Lord can quickly improve one's fortune (11:21b–22). At the same time, Ben Sira warns against the two extremes of want and self-sufficiency (11:23–25).

Ben Sira's perceptions of death shape his advice on possessions in significant ways. He views death (ἡμέρα τελευτῆς) as a judgment in which God repays (ἀποδίδωμι) a person according to one's conduct (ὁδός; 11:26).[141] Associating death with a divine judgment functions as a warrant for his

137. The verb ὁμιλέω can refer to "things or business which one has to do with" (LSJ, 1222).

138. As Ben Sira elsewhere utilizes the end of one's life as a rhetorical warrant for enjoining certain behaviors (cf. 7:32–36; 14:11–13; 28:6).

139. Instead of "your toil," MS A and some Latin manuscripts read "his light." Depending on the pointing, און can mean either "trouble, sorrow" or "vigor, wealth, strength."

140. See Qoh 2:18–19; 4:4, 6, 8; 5:13–16; cf. 2:22–23. For a hopeful portrayal of toil, cf. 5:17.

141. This verse is not extant in Hebrew.

parenesis regarding wealth.[142] One is to live and use possessions in the light of a future judgment. Construing death as a judgment is a sharp departure from Qoheleth, for whom judgment plays a minimal, if any, role in death.[143] Ben Sira rejects the notion in Qoheleth that one's behavior has no influence upon one's death.[144]

Since the revelation of one's deeds (יגיד עלין / ἀποκάλυψις ἔργων) does not occur until the end of one's life, one should not assess a person's character prior to his or her death (סוף / ἐν συντελείᾳ; 11:27b).[145] One should specifically not call anyone blessed prior to death (לפני מות / πρὸ τελευτῆς; 11:28a). Such untimely evaluations can be inaccurate because they are premature; one will rather be recognized or known (נכר / γινώσκω) by how one ends (באחריתו) life (11:28b).[146] Ben Sira here reflects a striking departure from Qoheleth, who witnessed no causal relationship between how one lived and the manner or timing of one's death.[147] Ben Sira differs by holding out hope that one's death might function as a vehicle of respective reward or retribution.[148]

The uncertain timing of death (11:19c) presents a potential dilemma for Qoheleth's recommendations regarding enjoyment.[149] Although Ben Sira and Qoheleth acknowledge death's uncertain timing, the motif appears only peripherally in the latter (cf. Qoh 9:11–12). The lack of an explicit endorsement in Ben Sira of the man's plans to enjoy his goods may indicate a key difference from Qoheleth. The latter consistently enjoins

142. Skehan and Di Lella point out that Ben Sira refers to "retribution in the present life, not in the afterlife" (*The Wisdom of Ben Sira*, 240).

143. But see Qoh 11:9.

144. See Qoh 2:14–15; 8:14; 9:2–3; cf. 3:19–20.

145. Skehan and Di Lella cite Qoh 7:2 as another instance where סוף is used "in the sense of '(death as) the end'" (*The Wisdom of Ben Sira*, 241).

146. According to the Hebrew. In the Greek version, a person will be known "by his children" (ἐν τέκνοις αὐτοῦ; Sir 11:28b). This difference represents a significant divergence in the vehicle by which one is known. One Greek minuscule (358) has ἔργοις instead of τέκνοις, comporting more with the Hebrew text by focusing upon one's deeds rather than children.

147. As Harrington points out, one need not read these lines as a reference to life after death (*Jesus Ben Sira*, 38). Ben Sira "may have been only referring to the person's reputation and physical descendants."

148. Burkes cites Sir 7:36; 18:24; and 28:6 as parallels to 11:28 (*God, Self, and Death*, 91).

149. Qoh 3:12–13; 5:17; 8:15; 9:7–10. Harrington sees parallels between Sir 11:19 and Qoh 2:21; 4:8; 5:12–14; and Luke 12:16–21 (*Jesus Ben Sira*, 39).

enjoyment in light of death (Qoh 3:12–13; 5:17; 8:15; 9:7–10) and does not recommend alternative uses of goods. The absence in Ben Sira of an overt approval of the man's plans to enjoy his goods might reflect ambivalence regarding the status of enjoyment as a meaningful act in light of death's uncertain timing.

Ben Sira and Qoheleth highlight wealth's fragility in the face of death. Qoheleth's recommendations to enjoy goods can be understood as an effort to secure a vestige of control, given the many uncontrollable aspects of death.[150] Yet Qoheleth qualifies the extent to which one can effectively control wealth, since it is given by God (and can therefore be removed). In Qoheleth and Ben Sira, wealth does not afford one control over one's plans. Death destroys any pretense of power over one's life that wealth might otherwise provide. For Ben Sira, it is the potential surprise of death's timing that causes an (unexpected) shift in tone regarding wealth. His contextualization of wealth within the purview of the uncertain timing of death reminds the wealthy that they can no more control the duration of their enjoyment than they can the moment of their death.

In regard to death and possessions, Ben Sira 11:14–28 shares many themes in common with Qoheleth. These include insatiability with wealth (Qoh 5:9–10; Sir 11:10),[151] death's uncertain timing (Qoh 9:11–12; Sir 11:19), plans (or recommendations) to enjoy one's goods (Qoh 3:12, 22; 5:17; 8:15; 9:7–10; Sir 11:19a, b), the inability to take one's goods beyond the grave (Qoh 5:14–15; Sir 11:19), the transfer of goods that coincides with death (Qoh 2:18–21; Sir 11:19d), toil (Qoh 2:18–19, 22–23; 4:4, 6, 8; 5:13–17; Sir 11:20, 21), and understanding possessions as a divine gift (Qoh 2:24–26; 3:13; 5:17–18; 6:2; Sir 11:14, 22; 32:13). Finally, Qoheleth and Ben Sira each treat possessions in a certain way because of their respective understanding of death.

The number of themes that Sir 11:14–28 and Qoheleth share in common suggest that Ben Sira was familiar, if not with Qoheleth, then with the same motifs regarding death and wealth that figure so prominently in Qoheleth.[152] Ben Sira's implied criticism of Qoheleth's recom-

---

150. See, e.g., Qoh 3:11–13; 5:9–6:2; 8:8–15; 9:1–10.

151. So Skehan and Di Lella, who understand Sir 11:10cd to mean that "one will never have enough wealth, no matter how energetically one chases after it" (*The Wisdom of Ben Sira*, 238). They also cite Qoh 5:9–11 as a parallel.

152. Blenkinsopp contends that Sir 11:18–19 shows that Ben Sira "seems to have been familiar" with Qoheleth (*Wisdom and Law*, 79). He cites this same text as an

mendation regarding enjoyment suggests that Ben Sira may be engaged in a contested dialogue concerning the relationship between death and possessions and the proper attitude toward each.[153]

The respective views of death and possessions in Qoheleth and Ben Sira differ in important respects. Both perceive goods as divine gifts, but Ben Sira employs this understanding to a different effect by situating it within a broader purview. Understanding possessions as divine gifts leads Qoheleth to recommend that they be enjoyed (2:24–25; 5:17–18). God, in Ben Sira's view, gives not only wealth but also poverty and death (11:14). The upending of the conventional view of wealth in Sir 11:19c does not contradict the declaration that "good things and evil things, life and death, poverty and riches are from the Lord" (11:14). Ben Sira's lack of lament and frustration (compared to Qoheleth) regarding death may be explained, in part, by his perception that God controls death. The greater willingness to accept death as a part of the human condition may be due to this premise that God is the source of life, death, poverty, and riches (Sir 11:14).

Ben Sira 14:3–19

Ben Sira 14:3–19 recommends specific uses of possessions in light of death's inevitability. After critiquing a miser for failing to use goods meaningfully (14:3–10),[154] Ben Sira offers alternative proposals for the use of possessions (14:11–19).

The miser is first faulted for failing to enjoy wealth (יקרה טובת / εὐφραίνω … χρῆμα; 14:5b). There is no purpose for a miser (רע עין / βάσκανος) to have riches (עושר / πλοῦτος) or wealth (חרוץ / χρῆμα; 14:3), since others will (eventually) live in luxury (יתבעבע / τρυφάω) on the miser's goods (טוב / ἀγαθός; 14:4). Like Qoheleth, Ben Sira recognizes the

---

instance in which Ben Sira "echoes [Qoheleth's] sentiments." He lists Sir 7:36 and 18:22–23 as other texts that reflect awareness of Qoheleth. For arguments that Ben Sira was familiar with Qoheleth, see Sanders, *Ben Sira*, 3–4, n. 2.

153. Evidence of Ben Sira's effort to engage in this ongoing dialogue is, as Skehan and Di Lella note, the dependence, "in thought and vocabulary," of Sir 11:10b on Prov 28:20 (*The Wisdom of Ben Sira*, 238). They note that Ben Sira has three of the four same words as Proverbs.

154. Skehan and Di Lella take βάσκανος as a reference to a miser (*The Wisdom of Ben Sira*, 259). One can also render this word as "envious one." LSJ Supplement (67) cites Sir 14:3 as an example of βάσκανος meaning "mean" or "niggardly." Cf. Sir 18:18; 37:11; Prov 23:6; 28:2.

tenuous nature of riches, given that death permanently ends one's ability to enjoy them. Unlike Qoheleth, Ben Sira does not make this observation with any patent sense of despondency. Death and the ensuing transfer of goods to another is not a source of meaninglessness but rather merely one of life's realities. Furthermore, Ben Sira blames the inability to enjoy one's goods not on death (as Qoheleth does) but on the choice of the owner.

The miser's failure to be generous is identified as his second fault. Being envious is manifest in turning away from (ἀποστρέφω) and disregarding (ὑπεροράω) others (14:8).[155] Two reasons explain this lack of generosity. First, one who is evil (רע / πονηρός) to oneself cannot be good (יטב / ἀγαθός) to another (14:5a).[156] Being envious[157] and jealous (תעיט / φθονερὸς) over bread leads, perhaps ironically, to a lack (מהומה / ἐλλιπὴς) at his own table (14:10). Misers become generous—and this involuntarily—only in death, when their goods are finally shared with others (14:4). Second, insatiability with wealth hinders generosity with others. Echoing Qoheleth's outlook and terminology, Ben Sira notes that a greedy person (כושל / πλεονέκτης) is not satisfied with a share (מעט חלק / ἐμπίπλημι μερίς; 14:9a; cf. Qoh 5:10; 4:7–8).[158] Concomitant with this insatiability is wicked injustice (ἀδικία πονηρὰ) that withers a person's life (14:9b).[159]

Ben Sira enjoins three constructive uses of possessions as alternatives to the miser's conduct (14:11–19). First, one is to treat oneself well. His advice ("Do well to yourself [היטיב לך / εὖ ποίει σεαυτὸν]," 14:11a) is an explicit contrast to the one who is evil to oneself (14:5a). Second, wealth is to be brought to the Lord in the form of worthy offerings (14:11b).[160]

---

155. This verse is not extant in Hebrew. *Contra* Lee, Qoheleth never complains about such illiberality toward others (*Vitality of Enjoyment*, 71). I do not see in Qoheleth the emphasis on generosity she finds, namely, that "one must also liberally share the means of enjoyment with those who may be in need" (cf. 133–35).

156. For a similar view, see Lucian, *Gall.* 14.

157. Literally, "an evil eye" (עין רע / ὀφθαλμὸς πονηρὸς).

158. Compare Qoh 4:8 (ὀφθαλμὸς αὐτοῦ οὐκ ἐμπίπλαται πλούτου. The Hebrew מעט conveys the sense of being diminished.

159. Ben Sira 14:9b is not extant in Hebrew.

160. Ben Sira later instructs worshipers of the Lord to be "generous" (ἐν ἀγαθῷ ὀφθαλμῷ), not restraining the fruits of their hands (35:7). "Give to the Most High as he has given to you," he commands, "and as generously [בטוב עין / ἐν ἀγαθῷ ὀφθαλμῷ] as your hand has found" (35:9 [Heb. 12]). As a motive for such generosity, Ben Sira adds that the Lord "is the one who repays, and he will repay you sevenfold" (35:10).

Third, one is to do good by stretching out (a hand), and giving to a friend (φίλος; 14:13; cf. 14:11a).

Ben Sira employs death's potential imminence and the inability to take possessions beyond the grave as warrants for these preferred uses of possessions. He instructs people to remember that "death will not delay [מות יתמהמה / θάνατος οὐ χρονιεῖ]" and that "the decree of Sheol/Hades is not declared to you [חוק לשאול לא הגד לך / διαθήκη ᾄδου οὐχ ὑπεδείχθη σοι]" (14:12). Ben Sira thereby seeks to prepare people for death's quick and unannounced arrival. Central to this preparation is the proper and meaningful use of goods. A reminder that life will eventually end ("before you die") is proposed as the rationale for being generous and giving to a friend (14:13; cf. 14:11a).[161] Ben Sira invokes the inability to take goods beyond death as the primary warrant for treating oneself well, recommending that one neither withhold (מנע / ἀφυστερέω) a good day from oneself nor allow a share of good desire (הלקה אח / μερὶς ἐπιθυμίας ἀγαθῆς) to pass one by (14:14).

As with Qoheleth, the transfer of one's goods to someone else figures prominently in Ben Sira's reflection on death. "Will you not leave behind your labors [תעזב חילך / καταλείψεις τοὺς πόνους σου] to another and your toils [יגיע / κόπους] for division by drawing lots?" (14:15). Death forever severs one's relationship with, and use of, possessions; one should therefore enjoy one's goods before death eliminates this possibility. Ben Sira differs from Qoheleth, however, by evincing no resentment or ennui, neither regarding this transfer nor the identity of the recipient. It appears as though the loss of control over one's possessions does not pose as acute a threat to Ben Sira as it does to Qoheleth.

Ben Sira nonetheless responds to the inevitable transfer of goods by proposing, as Qoheleth does, that one enjoy them in the interim: "Give and take and delight yourself [תין ופנ[..] נפשך / ἀπάτησον τὴν ψυχήν σου]" (14:16a).[162] He recommends such enjoyment precisely because of his conviction that one cannot enjoy goods in the afterlife: "There is no seeking luxury [תענוג / τρυφήν] in Sheol/Hades" (14:16a–b).[163] One is

---

161. Corley identifies the following as the significant treatments of friendship in the book: 6:5–17; 9:10–16; 13:15–23; 19:13–17; 22:19–26; 27:16–21; 37:1–6 (*Ben Sira's Teaching on Friendship*).

162. Israel Levi emends the Hebrew text by replacing the first two words (תן לאח) with וקח (*The Hebrew Text of the Book of Ecclesiasticus* [SSS 3; Leiden: Brill, 1904], 22).

163. This reason is absent in the Syriac version which reads: "Give and take and

to seize the opportunity to enjoy in the present before death terminates this possibility. Ben Sira's conclusion reiterates death's inevitability and unavoidability: "All flesh [בשר / σὰρξ] grows old like a garment, for the decree since the beginning is, 'By death you will die!' [גוע יגועו / θανάτῳ ἀποθανῇ]" (14:17). As in Qoheleth, the inevitability of death functions as the primary motive for enjoying possessions and (in Ben Sira's case) sharing them with others.

Conclusion to Ben Sira

Ben Sira envisions wealth as potentially beneficial for its owner, God, and other people. But this potentiality is only actualized in the concrete act of giving. Since the finality of one's death precludes future giving opportunities, one is to take advantage of such occasions before one dies. Because the timing of one's death is uncertain (Sir 11:19c–d), one has all the more reason for being generous with oneself, God, and others in the present moment.

The various uncontrollable facets of death lead Ben Sira to recommend enjoyment, generosity (with God, self, and others), and the giving of alms. These recommendations include more constructive options than in Qoheleth, despite the fact that the two texts hold similar perceptions of death. The following chart illustrates the manner in which Ben Sira's perceptions of death and recommendations regarding possessions relate to each other.

Death	Misc.	View/Role of God	Possessions
Remember the end of life (7:36)		One who blesses the poor will receive a blessing (7:32)	Give to poor (7:32)
… is preparing your own burial (21:8b)			Taking others' money … (21:8a)

nourish yourself, *and everything that is good to do, do it before God* [ܗܒ ܘܣܒ ܘܐܬܦܪܢܣ ܢܦܫܟ ܘܟܠ ܡܕܡ ܕܫܦܝܪ ܠܡܥܒܕ ܩܕܡ ܐܠܗܐ ܥܒܕ]" (emphasis added). For the Syriac and English translation, see Winter ("Syriac Translation," 305), who considers this specific change ("effectively a summary of Phil 4:8") a likely "alteration from mainstream Christianity."

Death is bitter … (41:1a)			to one at peace with goods and prosperous (41:1b)
Death's uncertain timing / transfer of goods to another / "can't take it with you" (11:19c–d)		Life, death, poverty, riches are from the Lord (11:14); Lord's gift is with righteous (11:17); Lord can quickly improve one's fortune / Lord's blessing is in the reward of the godly (11:21–22)	Limits enjoyment / Establish a testament / Remain in toil (11:20–21)
Death as a judgment with reward (11:26) / Revelation of deeds occurs at death (11:26)			Rejects desire for more goods and self-sufficiency (11:23–24)
Death's uncertain timing (14:12) / transfer of goods to another (14:4)	Inability to enjoy wealth (14:5)		Enjoyment / Generosity (14:8); greed leads to insatiability (14:9a)
Death's potential imminence, uncertain timing, inevitability (14:12b, 17) / Inability to take goods beyond death (14:15–16)			Enjoyment (14:11a, 14, 16a), Gifts to God (14:11b), Generosity with friends (14:13)
		The Lord repays an almsgiver (17:23) Alms atone for sin (3:30)	
			No good comes to one who doesn't give alms (12:3)

… on the day of calamity (5:8b)			Dishonest wealth will not benefit … (5:8a)
One builds one's own burial mound when … (21:8b)			building one's house with others' money (21:8a)

The following recommendations for the use of possessions emerge from our analysis of Qoheleth and Ben Sira:

1. Enjoyment:	Qoheleth	Ben Sira
2. Generosity with friends:		Ben Sira
3. Giving to God:		Ben Sira
4. Alms:		Ben Sira
5. Inheritance:		Ben Sira
6. Critique of Inheritance:	Qoheleth	

3
The Interplay of Death and Possessions in 1 Enoch and the Testament of Abraham

The previous chapter highlighted perspectives in two Hellenistic Jewish texts regarding the intersection of death and possessions. Specific proposals in these texts for the use of possessions include enjoyment (Qoheleth, Ben Sira), generosity (Ben Sira), giving to God (Ben Sira), alms (Ben Sira), and creating a will/testament for the disposition of one's goods (Ben Sira). Each of these recommendations, as I argued, is rooted in a particular perception of death. I suggest that these diverse views reflect the existence of a Second Temple conversation regarding death and possessions. Other texts participated in and contributed to this conversation, and I explicate a selection of these in this and the following chapter.

A primary function of chapters 2–4 is to frame and describe the type of conversation in which Luke 12:13–34 participates and to which it contributes. I accordingly seek to treat the texts in these chapters not as background material whose sole purpose is to illumine Luke's parable but rather as texts that frame a specific conversation within which Luke's parable is situated. I seek, in other words, to read these texts on their own terms and in their own voice. I now turn to analyze how the Epistle of 1 Enoch and Testament of Abraham participate in, and contribute to, this conversation on the interplay of death and possessions.

The Interplay of Death and Possessions in the Epistle of 1 Enoch

Notwithstanding its composition in an Aramaic milieu, its status as a Hellenistic Jewish text composed in the Second Temple period makes the Epistle of 1 Enoch a fitting text to consider in light of Luke-Acts.[1] The Epistle of 1 Enoch, like Qoheleth and Ben Sira, contains many sapiential features, leading some to classify it as wisdom literature.[2] Although 1 Enoch resists any rigid (and mutually exclusive) genre classification, wisdom elements are plentiful, especially in the epistolary section.[3] There is, moreover, evidence suggesting that Luke may have been familiar with the contents of 1 Enoch.[4] It is, however, the repeated interest in the interplay of death and

---

1. George W. E. Nickelsburg (*1 Enoch 1: A Commentary on the Book of 1 Enoch, Chapters 1–36, 81–108* [Hermeneia; Minneapolis: Fortress, 2001], 8) claims that the Epistle was included in the broader Enochic work between 175 and 150 B.C.E. (26); he thinks the Greek translation was in place by the end of the first century (14). He bases this on the *terminus ad quem* provided by the Epistle of Barnabas (135–138 C.E.), the citation of 1 En. 1:9 in Jude 14–15, and the Enochic material in Revelation. Loren Stuckenbruck (*1 Enoch 91–108* [CEJL; Berlin: de Gruyter, 2007], 1) also dates the Epistle to the second century B.C.E.

2. So John J. Collins, "Wisdom, Apocalypticism, and Generic Compatibility," in *In Search of Wisdom: Essays in Memory of John G. Gammie* (ed. Leo G. Perdue, Bernard Brendan Scott, and William Johnston Wiseman; Louisville: Westminster John Knox, 1993), 175–76; idem, *Jewish Wisdom*, 228; VanderKam, *An Introduction to Early Judaism*, 119–21. Patrick J. Hartin identifies several wisdom elements (e.g., woes, exhortations, judgment) that 1 Enoch and James share in common ("'Who Is Wise and Understanding Among You?' [James 3:13]: An Analysis of Wisdom, Eschatology, and Apocaypticism in the Letter of James," in Wright and Wills, *Conflicted Boundaries in Wisdom and Apocalypticism*, 167–68). Nickelsburg notes that the term "'wisdom' recurs at key points in the Enochic corpus as a designation for the corpus itself" and that Enoch [82:2–3] designates the books as "wisdom" (*1 Enoch 1*, 52).

3. So Robert A. Coughenour, "Enoch and Wisdom: A Study of the Wisdom Elements in the Book of Enoch" (Ph.D. diss., Case Western Reserve, 1972). He describes the "woes" in 1 Enoch as a wisdom element ("The Woe Oracles in Ethiopic Enoch," *JSJ* 9 [1978]: 192–97). Carol A. Newsom finds royal wisdom elements in Enoch's journey to the northwest ("The Development of 1 Enoch 6–19: Cosmology and Judgment," *CBQ* 42 [1980]: 310–29). Although sapiential features in 1 Enoch blend together with prophetic and apocalyptic materials, Nickelsburg considers the "mode of moral instruction in the corpus" to be "sapiential rather than set in the form of commandments and laws" (*1 Enoch 1*, 5; cf. 7).

4. So Aalen, "St. Luke's Gospel"; George W. E. Nickelsburg, "Revisiting the Rich and the Poor in 1 Enoch 92–105 and the Gospel according to Luke," *Society of Biblical Literature 1998 Seminar Papers* (Atlanta: Scholars Press, 1998), 579–605. There is, however, insufficient evidence for Aalen's suggestion that Luke may have been responsible for translating 1 Enoch into Greek (13).

possessions that makes the Epistle of Enoch (1 En. 92–105) most pertinent for Luke 12:13–34.[5]

Death and Divine Judgment in the Epistle of 1 Enoch[6]

Although both Qoheleth and the Epistle of 1 Enoch employ death as a warrant for their respective admonitions regarding possessions, each comes to conflicting, albeit overlapping, conclusions concerning the proper attitude toward possessions and their use. Whereas Qoheleth understands death as the end of one's being and Ben Sira intimates that death might represent some type of judgment, 1 Enoch insists that death is followed by a postmortem divine judgment.[7] The belief in a postmortem judgment pervades and undergirds the rhetoric of 1 Enoch and is especially prominent in the Epistle.

The Epistle's attitude toward possessions is rooted in and inseparable from this belief in a postmortem judgment.[8] The use of wealth functions

5. The testamentary nature of certain parts of 1 Enoch (in which a father transfers advice to his progeny before dying) may invoke the specter of death in the minds of readers/hearers (cf., e.g., 91:1–10, 18–19). Nickelsburg stresses the growth of the Enochic corpus from early works containing "testamentary material" to a "full blown Enochic testament" during the second century B.C.E. (*1 Enoch 1*, 22, 25, 132, 335–37). Although Stuckenbruck thinks Nickelsburg goes too far and cautions against identifying the genre of 1 Enoch as a testament, he does note that the Epistle's introduction and conclusion "retain the mood of the testamentary address" (*1 Enoch 91–108*, 15–16, 191; cf. 2).

6. My translation (of the Greek text) of 97:6–107:3 is from the Chester Beatty-Michigan Papyrus in Campbell Bonner, ed., *The Last Chapters of Enoch in Greek* (London: Christophers, 1937; repr., Stuttgart: Wissenshacftliche Buchgesellschaft, 1968). I rely primarily upon the Greek (when available), since it is widely agreed that this predates the Ethiopic. Many scholars (e.g., Nickelsburg) believe an Aramaic original was translated into Greek, which was then translated into Ethiopic. Nickelsburg considers the Greek version "quite reliable in the material it reproduces" (14). His translation is based on the Greek (when it is available and preserves a similar or better text than the Ethiopic). For concerns about the quality and reliability of the Chester Beatty Greek text, see Stuckenbruck, *1 Enoch 91–108*, 185–86. Where the Greek is not available, I rely on the translation in George W. E. Nickelsburg and James C. VanderKam, eds., *1 Enoch: A New Translation* (Minneapolis: Fortress, 2004).

7. This postmortem existence is not envisioned in Qoheleth or (the Hebrew text of) Ben Sira. The references in the latter to the afterlife in the Greek and Syriac translations are absent in the Hebrew manuscripts.

8. So Nickelsburg, *1 Enoch 1*, 7.

in the Epistle as a principal criterion upon which judgment is based. In a series of seven woes directed to those who "build iniquity and violence" and "build their houses with sin," 1 Enoch promises that all those who "acquire gold and silver in judgment[9] will quickly perish" (94:6–7). The third, and lengthiest, of the seven woes is aimed directly at the wealthy. Here a correlation is established between sins associated with wealth (blasphemy, iniquity, not remembering the Most High) and judgment:

> Woe to you, rich [*ʾabeʿlt*], for in your riches you have trusted; from your riches you will depart, because you have not remembered the Most High in the days of your riches. You have committed blasphemy and iniquity; and you have been prepared for the day of bloodshed and the day of darkness and the day of great judgment. (94:8–9)

Further, 1 Enoch associates the wealthy with sins against God and envisions God repaying them accordingly:[10] "He who created you will overturn you; and for your fall there will be no compassion, and your Creator will rejoice at your destruction" (94:10–11). The judgment will "find" these sinners who "practice hatred and evil" (95:2).

Two subsequent series of woes directed against the rich and powerful (96:4–97:10) further presuppose a causal relationship between judgment and wealth. Four of five woes in the first series are addressed to the wealthy and mighty (96:4–8). In a veiled critique of an ideology that associates wealth with divine blessing, 1 Enoch declares that sinners are convicted by their hearts, despite any veneer of righteousness that wealth provides (96:4a). This "word" will indeed testify against them as a "reminder of [their] evil deeds" (96:4b). Subsequent accusations leveled against the wealthy link their misappropriation of goods with their oppression of the weak.[11]

---

9. The precise meaning of this phrase is unclear. One manuscript (T[9]) reads: "and in *the* judgment (*wabakwennanē*)." On the woe oracles in the Epistle, see Nickelsburg, *1 Enoch 1*, 416–17; Stuckenbruck, *1 Enoch 91–108*, 193–95.

10. So Rodney A. Werline, "*The Psalms of Solomon* and the Ideology of Rule," in Wright and Wills, *Conflicted Boundaries in Wisdom and Apocalypticism*, 85.

11. "You devour (*balʿa*) the finest of the wheat, and quaff <wine from the mixing bowls>, while you tread on the lowly with your might" (96:5). See Nickelsburg for the difficulty involved in translating this phrase (*1 Enoch 1*, 468). Woes are also directed to those who drink water from every fountain (96:6a), commit iniquity, deceit (*gwehlut*) and blasphemy (96:7a), and the mighty who "oppress the righteous one" (96:8a). Nick-

The language and imagery of the Epistle contributes to the portrayal of the judgment as a legal proceeding in a courtroom.[12] Evidence adduced in the judgment against the sinners includes the prayer of the righteous (97:3, 5a) and a reading before God of the words of their "deeds partaking in lawlessness" (ἔργα τὰ μετασχόντα ἐν ἀνομίᾳ; 97:6; cf. 98:8). The indictment and judgment of sinners is a tacit reason for the righteous to take courage,[13] since the sinners will become "an object of contempt" and be "destroyed on the day of iniquity" (97:1). Implicit in God's remembrance of the "destruction" of the righteous (97:2) is that their ruin has not been in vain; those responsible for their devastation will be held responsible. The warning addressed to sinners, that they will not be able to flee on the day of judgment (97:3), functions as a comfort to those who have suffered at their hands.

The second set of woes explicitly links this judgment of the sinners to their unjust acquisition of wealth and the destructive self-sufficiency it engenders (97:7–10). To those who acquire (κτάομαι) gold and silver unjustly (οὐκ ἀπὸ δικαιοσύνης; 97:8a),[14] the Epistle attributes the following words:

> With wealth we have become wealthy [πλούτῳ πεπλουτήκαμεν], and we have acquired and procured possessions [τὰ ὑπάρχοντα ἐσχ<ήκ>αμεν καὶ κεκτήμεθα], and let us do whatever we wish,[15] for we have stored up [τεθησαυρίκαμεν] silver in our treasuries [θησαυροῖς], and many goods [ἀγαθὰ πολλά] in our houses, and as water they are poured out[ἐκκέχυται]. (97:8–9)

The excessive acquisition of abundant wealth, illustrated by the metaphor of gushing water, is linked to a presumption regarding doing whatever one

elsburg understands "the righteous one" as a reference to the previously mentioned "lowly" in 96:5b (*1 Enoch 1*, 427). A judgment is prescribed for each of these offenses: "for quickly you will be repaid, and cease and dry up" (96:6b); "it will be a reminder against you for evil" (96:7b); "for the day of your destruction will come. In those days, many good days will come for the righteous—in the day of your judgment" (96:8b).

12. Cf. Stuckenbruck, *1 Enoch 91–108*, 198.

13. In the Ethiopic, they are to "have faith" or "believe" (*ta'amanu*).

14. Nickelsburg suggests בלא קשטא is likely the underlying Aramaic (*1 Enoch 1*, 474).

15. The Ethiopic repeats the phrase "and we have done all that we have wished. And now let us do what we have wished." See Nickelsburg, *1 Enoch 1*, 469; Bonner, *Last Chapters of Enoch*, 33.

wishes.[16] The Epistle qualifies this unchecked desire by highlighting the temporary nature of unjustly acquired riches and the judgment that such riches will help bring about:

> You err [πεπλάνησθε]! For your wealth [πλοῦτος] will not remain [οὐ μὴ παραμείνῃ] but will quickly depart [ταχὺ <ἀπελεύσεται>] from you; for you have acquired everything unjustly [ἀδίκως πάντα κέκτησθε], and you will be handed over to a great curse [κατάραν μεγάλην παρα[δο]θήσεσθε]. (97:10)[17]

In a shift of address to the "wise" (98:1), the Epistle links wealth to excessive luxury, indulgence, and the transgression of gender boundaries (98:2–3a).[18] The severe judgment awaiting such people is depicted as the fitting result of their extravagance:

> So you will be destroyed [ἀπολεῖσθε] together with all your possessions [ὑπαρχόντων], [and] all glory [δόξης] and honor [τιμῆς]; and for dishonor [ἀτιμία] and slaughter and great destitution [πτωχεία], their spirits will be cast into the fiery furnace. (98:3b)[19]

The "unrighteous deeds" of these wealthy people are "written down day by day, until the day of your judgment" (98:8).[20] This second reference to the transcription of deeds (cf. 97:6) underscores the Epistle's claim

---

16. Nickelsburg sees in vv. 8–10 a twofold indictment against both the unjust acquisition of wealth and the purpose of this acquisition as "to secure their future." He asserts that the "frequent use of the first person plural and the double reference to 'all that we wish' indicate a self-centered point of view that excludes generosity to others" (*1 Enoch 1*, 474).

17. Nickelsburg notes that παραδίδωμι is often used in relation to human and divine judgment (*1 Enoch 1*, 474).

18. "For men will put on a beautiful work [κάλ[λος]] as women, [and] a beautiful color more than virgins, in kingship and greatness and in power. And they will have silver and gold as food [ἔσονται δὲ ἀργύριον καὶ χρυσίον [...] αὐτοις εἰς βρώματα], and in their houses these will be poured out [ἐκχυθήσονται] like water, because they have no knowledge or understanding [ἐπιστήμην αὐτοὺς μηδὲ φρό[ησιν μηδ]εμίαν <ἔχειν>]" (98:2–3a).

19. Most of this last phrase ("and for dishonor ... fiery furnace") is lacking in the Greek but extant in the Ethiopic version. Four lines in the Greek text are missing after 98:3. Cf. Bonner, *Last Chapters of Enoch*, 35.

20. One Ethiopic manuscript (m) reads: "until the day of your death and your judgment."

that the crimes of the wicked, left unchecked during life, will ultimately be punished. Such a claim would serve an important rhetorical purpose in responding to complaints or questions rooted in a Deuteronomistic understanding of retribution. The Epistle assures such complainants that, despite present appearances to the contrary, God will eventually punish the wicked for their crimes.

In 1 Enoch, the temporal consequences of the future judgment underscore the ephemeral nature of wealth. The Epistle repeatedly utilizes the future judgment as an illustrative warrant for shunning both wealth that is unjustly acquired and the sins that accompany such riches. The Epistle's judgment of the wealthy, although similar to Ben Sira's critique of the rich, is far more comprehensive in its castigation of all rich people.[21]

The depiction of judgment in 1 Enoch reassures those without wealth that whatever suffering they endure at the hands of the "rich and powerful" is not in vain and will not be forever neglected. Recompense will be given, but not in this present life.

Participating in a Conversation on Death and Possessions

The conception of a postmortem judgment contributes to a rejection in the Epistle of a number of ideas that are central to Qoheleth's worldview. The Epistle of 1 Enoch repudiates a number of prominent elements of Qoheleth's rhetoric: that the righteous and wicked experience death in the same manner; that one's conduct in life has no bearing on one's death; that death results in the destruction of one's being and memory; that the wicked are not punished for their deeds; that the labors of the just are not rewarded; and the use of death as a warrant for enjoyment. I am not asserting that the Epistle of 1 Enoch is replying directly to Qoheleth but rather that these texts participate in a broader Second Temple conversation concerning the meaningful use of possessions in light of death.[22] That

21. So Richard A. Horsley, "The Politics of Cultural Production in Second Temple Judea: Historical Context and Political-Religious Relations of the Scribes who Produced *1 Enoch*, Sirach, and Daniel," in Wright and Wills, *Conflicted Boundaries*, 139.

22. Two Qoheleth fragments found at Qumran allow for the possibility that 1 Enoch was aware of (at least some) the content of the latter. Frank Moore Cross ("The Oldest Manuscripts from Qumran," *JBL* 74 [1955]: 153, 162) dates 4QQoh[a] between 175 and 150 B.C.E., a date that matches the same twenty-five-year period that Nickelsburg (*1 Enoch 1*, 26) gives for the inclusion of 1 Enoch into the broader Enochic

the Epistle's participation in a broader cultural conversation regarding the interplay of death and possessions played a significant role is suggested by some of the similarities between 1 Enoch and Ben Sira.[23] It is possible, moreover, that Wis 2–5 functioned in this conversation as a mediating text between Qoheleth and 1 Enoch.[24]

Qoheleth and 1 Enoch represent antithetical responses to the incompatibility between their experience and a Deuteronomistic conception of divine retribution in the present life. Both texts recognize dissonance between the success of the wicked and the suffering of the just, on the one hand, and Deuteronomistic promises of divine retribution, on the other. But 1 Enoch and Qoheleth respond differently to this perceived dissonance. For Qoheleth, God does not exact justice in life but does provide opportunities, albeit fleeting, to enjoy life. The Epistle of 1 Enoch maintains a sense of divine retribution but postpones it from the present life to the hereafter. For this reason he can enjoin "the souls of the just who have died, the just and the pious [ψυχαὶ τῶν δικαίων τῶν ἀποθανόντων, τῶν

---

corpus. On this Qumranic fragment of Qoheleth, see James Muilenberg, "A Qoheleth Scroll from Qumran," *BASOR* 135 (1954): 20–28. Eugene Ulrich ("Ezra and Qoheleth Manuscripts from Qumran (4QEzra, 4QQoh$^{A, B}$)," in *Priests, Prophets and Scribes: Essays on the Formation and Heritage of Second Temple Judaism in Honour of Joseph Blenkinsopp* [ed. Eugene Ulrich et al.; JSOTSup 149; Sheffield: JSOT Press, 1992], 139–57) cites the first century B.C.E. as the earliest date for 4QQoh^{b}. C. L. Seow ("Linguistic Evidence and the Dating of Qoheleth," *JBL* 115 [1996]: 643–66) argues for dating Qoheleth to the Persian period: "between the second half of the fifth century and the first half of the fourth" (666). Kugel ("Qoheleth and Money," 45–47) also dates Qoheleth to the Persian period.

23. See Argal, *1 Enoch and Sirach*; Benjamin G. Wright III, "Putting the Puzzle Together: Suggestions Concerning the Social Location of the Wisdom of Ben Sira," in Wright and Wills, *Conflicted Boundaries*, 89–112. George W. E. Nickelsburg suggests that the Epistle of 1 Enoch may have been composed by the poor during Ben Sira's time ("Social Aspects of Palestinian Jewish Apocalypticism," in *Apocalypticism in the Mediterranean World and the Near East* [ed. D. Hellholm; 2nd ed.; Tübingen: Mohr Siebeck, 1989], 651).

24. It appears that Wisdom of Solomon responded to (and rejected) many of the central claims made in Job and Qoheleth. The "act-consequence" notion, repudiated in Job and Qoheleth, is embraced and defended in Wisdom of Solomon (1:8, 12; 2:18; 3:1, 10; 5:15; 19:13). On the attitude in Wisdom of Solomon toward death, see Michael Kolarcik, *The Ambiguity of Death in the Book of Wisdom 1–6* (AnBib 127; Rome: Pontifical Biblical Institute), 1991.

δικαίων καὶ τῶν εὐσεβῶν]"[25] not to lament their ill-treatment. Despite (and because of) such unjust suffering, he counsels them to:

> take courage [θαρσεῖτε] … and do not grieve [λυπεῖσθε] that your souls [ψυχαὶ] descended into Hades with grief [λύπης], and it did not turn out well [ἀπηντήθη] with your body of flesh [τῷ σώματι τῆς σαρκὸς] in your life according to your observance of divine law [κατὰ τὴν ὁσιότητα],[26] since the days that you lived (ἦτε)[27] were days of sinners and curses on the earth. (102:4–5)

The Epistle of 1 Enoch anticipates potential rejoinders to its argument by articulating conflicting perspectives that share a strong affinity with Qoheleth:

> When you die [ἀποθάνητε], then the sinners will say,[28] "The pious [εὐσεβεῖς] have died [ἀπεθάνοσαν] according to fate [εἱμαρμένην],[29] and what have they gained by [ἐπί] their deeds? They have even *died like us* [ὁμοίως ὑμῖν ἀπεθάνοσαν]. Look, therefore, *how they die* [ἀποθνήσκουσιν] *with grief and darkness, and what benefit* [περισσόν] *do they have?*"[30] (102:6–7)

This perspective of the "sinners" echoes observations and consequent claims at the heart of Qoheleth's program.[31] First is the observation that the godly and sinners are subject to the same fate (Qoh 8:14; 9:1–3; cf. 2:14–15). That this specific issue elicited debate among Second Temple

---

25. The Ethiopic reads: "Fear not, you souls of the righteous, and be hopeful, you who have died in righteousness." Nickelsburg thinks the original Greek read: μὴ φοβεῖσθε ψυχαὶ τῶν δικαίων, θαρσεῖτε οἱ ἀποθανόντες εὐσεβεῖς (*1 Enoch 1*, 513).

26. The Ethiopic reads "your goodness," which Nickelsburg notes is a normal equivalent in the Ethiopic of 1 Enoch (*1 Enoch 1*, 513).

27. Nickelsburg emends this to ζῆτε (*1 Enoch 1*, 513).

28. The Ethiopic has "about you [*lā'lēkemu*]," a phrase Nickelsburg believes was omitted from the Greek due to homoioteleuton (*1 Enoch 1*, 513).

29. The Ethiopic reads: "as we die" (*kama motna*), an idea present in the Greek version (102:7a).

30. Several Ethiopic manuscripts add "over us." Nickelsburg suggests that the absence of this phrase in the Greek and some Ethiopic manuscripts is due to the similarity with the words that follow (*1 Enoch 1*, 513).

31. Stuckenbruck identifies Qoh 2:14–16; 3:19–20; 11:7–12:7 as likely intertexts that may have "shaped the wording" of 1 En. 102:6b (*1 Enoch 91–108*, 205; cf. 204).

Jews is evident in the apparent rejection of Qoheleth's views in Wisdom of Solomon.[32] The parallels between 1 En. 102–104 and Wis 1:16–5:23 point to the likely disputed nature of this conversation in some circles of Second Temple Judaism.[33]

Second, the two questions posed by the Epistle's interlocutors imply that the godly (εὐσεβής) have gained nothing from their deeds and that there is no benefit (περισσός) for them.[34] Qoheleth raises this same question, and he advocates enjoyment in response to his observation that the just and wicked meet the same fate (Qoh 8:15; 9:7–10). The Epistle of 1 Enoch links the wicked to the very activity, enjoyment—and more specifically eating and drinking (ἐσθίω, πίνω)—that Qoheleth consistently espouses (Qoh 2:24; 3:13; 5:17; 8:15; 9:7):

> Henceforth let them arise and be saved [σωθήτωσαν], and they shall forever see you eating and drinking well [καλῶς ὑμᾶς φαγεῖν καὶ πιεῖν].[35] But, behold, they have died, and henceforth (and) forever they will not see the light.[36] Therefore indeed to plunder [ἁρπάσαι] and sin and steal and acquire possessions [ἐγκτᾶσθαι] in a foreign country and see good days.[37] (You) see therefore, the ones who justify themselves [οἱ δικαιοῦντες [ἑαυτ]ούς], of what sort their καταστ[ρο]φή was, for no righteousness [δικαιοσύνη] was found in them until they died [ἀπέθανον], and they per-

32. So Vittoria D'Alario, "La réflexion sur le sens de la vie en Sg 1–6: Une réponse aux questions de HJob et de Qohélet," in *Treasures of Wisdom: Studies in Ben Sira and the Book of Wisdom (Festschrift M. Gilbert)* (ed. N. Calduch-Benages and J. Vermeylen; Leuven: Leuven University Press, 1999), 329. Burkes asserts that Wisdom of Solomon "resoundingly answers the doubts of Job and Qoheleth" (*God, Self, and Death*, 161). Murphy does not think that Wis 2:1–9 is a rejoinder to Qoheleth (*Tree of Life*, 87).

33. Nickelsburg observes these parallels and finds them significant (*1 Enoch 1*, 59). Stuckenbruck claims that 1 En. 102:6b takes up and rejects the biblical motif that "after death those who inhabit Sheol are not distinguished from one another" (*1 Enoch 91–108*, 206).

34. This reference to "benefit" (περισσός) touches upon a chief interest and recurring theme in Qoheleth (Qoh 1:3; 2:11, 13, 15; 3:9; 5:8, 15; 6:8, 11; 7:11, 12; 10:10, 11; 12:9, 11).

35. The Ethiopic reads: "Henceforth we are equal, and how will they arise [two manuscripts have: 'what will they receive'] and what will they see forever?"

36. 102:8b is lacking in the Greek and present in the Ethiopic. Nickelsburg includes them because "they are logically related to the previous lines" and they "appear to have dropped … due to the similarity between 8a and 8d" (*1 Enoch 1*, 511, 513).

37. Bonner calls 102:9 "hopelessly corrupt" (*Last Chapters of Enoch*, 62).

> ished and became as those who are not [ἐγένοντο ὡς οὐκ ὄντες], and their souls [ψυχαί] descended with grief [ὀδύνης] into [Hades]. (102:8–11)

Whereas Qoheleth perceives a common destiny for all without regard for how one lives, 1 Enoch describes the respective fates of the righteous and wicked as starkly divergent.[38] In contrast to claims made by Qoheleth, 1 Enoch reveals that

> good things and joy and honor have been prepared and written down for the souls of the pious who have died [ταῖς ψ[υχαῖς] τῶν ἀποθανόντων εὐσεβῶν]; and much good will be given to you in the place of your labors, and your lot will exceed the lot of the living. The souls[39] of the pious who have died will come to life,[40] and they will rejoice; and their spirits [πνεύματα] will never perish [οὐ μὴ ἀπόλωνται], nor the memory [μνημόσυνον][41] from the presence of the Great One for all the generations of eternity. Therefore, do not fear their reproaches. (103:3–4)

In addition to rejecting claims that echo Qoheleth's view of the postmortem fate of the godly (εὐσεβής), the Epistle of 1 Enoch counters the allegation (also present in Qoheleth) that death destroys one's being and one's memory. The spirits (πνεῦμα) of the pious, he alleges, will "never perish" (103:4a), and their memory will persist for "all the generations of eternity" (103:4b). Their ongoing postmortem existence and perpetual continuation of their memory encourages the just to live righteously despite the lack of any perceived empirical benefit to doing so.

---

38. He buttresses this argument by swearing to the righteous that he "knows [ἐπίσταμαι] this mystery" (103:1). The Ethiopic text has: "And now I swear to you, the righteous, by the glory of the Great One, and by his splendid kingship and his majesty I swear to you that…" (translation from Nickelsburg and VanderKam, *1 Enoch*).

39. Although the Ethiopic is "your spirits" (*manfaskemu*), Nickelsburg presumes that the (missing) Greek text read ψυχαῖς (*1 Enoch 1*, 514).

40. Translation by Nickelsburg and VanderKam. This last phrase ("and much good … come to life") is absent in the Greek manuscripts but present in the Ethiopic; Bonner and Nickelsburg attribute its absence in the Greek to homoioteleuton (Bonner, *Last Chapters of Enoch*, 64; Nickelsburg, *1 Enoch 1*, 514).

41. Nickelsburg has "their memory" (*1 Enoch 1*, 514).

The Epistle of 1 Enoch both articulates and rejects the perception, attested in Qoheleth and Job,[42] that the wicked will avoid a divine judgment:[43]

> And you,[44] the dead of the sinners [οἱ νεκροὶ τῶν ἁμαρτωλῶν], when you die in your sinful wealth, those who are like you[45] will say about you, "Blessed are the sinners all their days, as many as they have seen in their life, and now they have died with goods and wealth, and affliction and murder they have not seen in their life.[46] They have died gloriously [ἐνδόξως ἀπεθάνοσαν], and judgment [κρίσις] did not befall them[47] in their life." (103:5–6)

Countering such a view, the Epistle insists instead that a severe judgment does await the wicked:

> You yourselves know [γινώσκετε][48] that into Hades they will lead [<κα>τάξουσιν] your souls; and there they will be in great violence [ἀνάγκῃ],[49] and in darkness and in a snare and in a burning blaze, and into great judgment [κρίσιν] your souls will enter[50] in all the generations of eternity [τοῦ αἰῶνος].[51] Woe to you, there is no joy for you.[52] (103:7–8)

42. Cf. Job 21:7–34, in which the ungodly (ἀσεβής) are said to reach old age with wealth (πλοῦτος), finish their lives with good things (ἀγαθός), and fall asleep in the rest of Hades (21:7, 13). The gluttonous and the hungry die in the same manner (21:23–26).

43. Though see Qoh 3:17; 11:9.

44. Following the Ethiopic *ʾalē lakemu*, Nickelsburg takes καὶ ὑμεις as a corruption of οὐαι ὑμεῖς, thus reading: "Woe to you..." (*1 Enoch 1*, 514).

45. The phrase "in your sinful wealth, those who are like you" is absent in the Greek and present in the Ethiopic.

46. The phrase "and now they have died ... they have not seen" is absent in the Greek text, explained by Bonner (*Last Chapters of Enoch*, 93) and Nickelsburg (*1 Enoch 1*, 514) as homoioteleuton.

47. "[T]hem" is absent in the Greek and present in the Ethiopic.

48. Nickelsburg notes that the Ethiopic (*taʾammerewwonu*) reflects either a second plural imperfect or a second plural imperative and that the "indicative is out of place" (*1 Enoch 1*, 514).

49. The Ethiopic reads: "and they will be wretched, their distress, great."

50. The Ethiopic here adds: "and the great judgment will be...."

51. Bonner translates αἰῶνος as "age" (*Last Chapters of Enoch*, 93).

52. The Ethiopic reads: "you will have no *peace*."

Rather than the great equalizer of the just and wicked (so Qoheleth), death is the beginning of an eternal, inseparable distinction between these two groups. Death thereby functions as a vehicle of justice in the Epistle rather than, as in Qoheleth, an example and reminder of injustice.

The future judgment functions as a warrant for the righteous not to despair about the conditions of their present lives and the perceived absence of any divine justice or intervention. In light of the divine justice that the Epistle associates with death, the author commands the righteous not to utter admonitions that resemble a lament:[53]

> For do not say, you who are just and devout [δίκ[αι]οι <καὶ> ὅσιοι] in life,[54] "During the days of the tribulation [θλίψεως],[55] we toiled laboriously [κόπους ἐκοπιάσαμεν]; and every tribulation we saw, and many evils we found,[56] and we were squandered [ἀνηλώμεθα] and we became few,[57] and we have not found any to help [ἀντιλήμπτορα];[58] we have been crushed [συν[τε]τριμμένοι <ἐσμὲν>] and utterly destroyed [ἀπλοώλαμεν], and we have been driven to despair [ἀπ[ηλ]πίσμεθα] even to no longer know salvation [σωτηρία[ν]] from day to day. We hoped to become a head, we became a tail;[59] we toiled [ἐκοπιάσαμεν] by laboring [ἐργαζόμενοι] and have not been master of the wages [[ὀ]ψωνίων];[60] we became food of sinners. The lawless loaded the yoke heavily upon us; the ones who lord over [us], our enemies, they goad us on and enclose us;[61] we sought where we might flee from them so that we might be revived [ἀναψύχ[ωμεν].[62] (103:9–13)

53. Compare, e.g., Ps 44.

54. The Ethiopic reads: "Do not say of the righteous and good who are in life...."

55. The Ethiopic has "*our* tribulation."

56. This phrase ("and every tribulation we saw, and many evils we found") is absent in the Greek.

57. The Ethiopic adds: "and our spirits, small; and we were destroyed."

58. Bonner (*Last Chapters of Enoch*, 93) translates: "we have found none to take our part."

59. Note the similarity in language with the blessings and curses in Deut 28:13, 44.

60. Based on the Ethiopic, Nickelsburg restores and emends the Greek to: καὶ το[ῦ κόπου] <ἡ>μῶν οὐ κεκυριεύκαμεν (*1 Enoch 1*, 514).

61. The Ethiopic adds: "and to our enemies we bowed our necks, and they had no mercy on us."

62. At this point three Greek lines are missing. Here the Ethiopic reads: "We complained to the rulers in our tribulation, and cried out against those who struck us down and oppressed us; but our complaints they did not receive, nor did they wish to give a hearing to our voice."

Conclusion to the Epistle of 1 Enoch

The preceding excerpts suggest that the Epistle of 1 Enoch was familiar with perspectives articulated in certain (sapiential) texts concerning death and possessions. Although it is possible that the Epistle represents a direct response to Qoheleth, it is more likely that the former is participating in a broader, contested conversation in which these motifs figure prominently. The positions defended in the Epistle of 1 Enoch are antithetical to several of the core tenets of Qoheleth. The righteous and the wicked, the Epistle avers, do not share the same fate after death (*contra* Qoh 8:14; 9:1–3). Nor does death represent an elimination of one's being (*contra* Qoh 9:5–6, 10). The spirits of the pious "do not perish" but will "come to life and rejoice and be glad." The righteous will experience "good things and joy and honor" (1 En. 103). Such rewards are "in place of their labors," intimating that those who labor do so not in vain and will, moreover, receive a reward for their toil (*contra* Qoh 2:11, 18–21; 5:14–15; cf. 1:3; 2:22–24; 4:4, 8). The memory of the righteous does not perish (*contra* Qoh 2:16; cf. 1:11). What happens to the righteous after death is, therefore, preferable to one's experience during life (cf. Qoh 9:5). Finally, the Epistle of 1 Enoch insists that death should *not* provide a warrant for enjoyment (*contra* Qoh 2:24–25; 3:12–13; 5:17; 9:7–10). The perception of death as a catalyst for a postmortem judgment shapes and undergirds the Epistle's chastisement of the greed of the wealthy and their enjoyment of goods.

Including the Epistle of 1 Enoch in our survey demonstrates the diverse and contested nature of the Second Temple conversation regarding death and possessions. The disparate and conflicting perspectives among these multiple voices highlight the numerous alternatives available for participants in this dialogue. The following chart illustrates the ways in which perceptions of death in the Epistle of 1 Enoch are related to views of possessions.

Death	View/Role of God	Possessions
Postmortem judgment with retribution (94:6–11)		Those who build houses with sin and acquire gold and silver in judgment will perish (94:6–7)

Postmortem judgment with retribution (94:6–11)		The rich forgot the Most High in the days of their riches, committed blasphemy and iniquity, and are prepared for a day of bloodshed/darkness and great judgment (94:8–9)
Postmortem judgment with retribution (95:2)	God rejoices at destruction of rich (95:2)	Judgment will find sinners who practice hatred and evil (95:2)
Postmortem judgment with retribution (97:1, 3)		Critique of unjust acquisition of wealth (97:8a, 10), which leads to judgment (97:10)
Postmortem judgment with retribution (98:3b, 8)		Destruction of wealthy with their possessions; their spirits will be cast into fiery furnace (98:3b)
Postmortem judgment with retribution (98:3b, 8)		Ephemeral nature of possessions/wealth (98:3b)
Just and wicked do not share same fate (102:6–7); souls of wicked descend with pain into Hades (102:11); pious will have joy, honor, and a reward for their labors; their souls will rejoice; their spirits and memory will never perish (103:3–4)	Wicked will be led into Hades, a place of violence, darkness, burning blaze for all eternity, and absence of joy (103:7–8)	Rejects suggestion that there is no benefit to the righteous (102:6–7) Rejects enjoyment (102:8), plunder, acquiring possessions in a foreign country (102:9–10)

By adding the Epistle of 1 Enoch to the conversation in which Qoheleth and Ben Sira participate, the following range of options for the use of possessions emerges:

1. Critique of Enjoyment:			1 Enoch
2. Enjoyment:	Qoheleth	Ben Sira	
3. Generosity:		Ben Sira	
4. Alms:		Ben Sira	
5. Inheritance:		Ben Sira	
6. Critique of Inheritance:	Qoheleth		

This range, outlined above, highlights a key difference between the Epistle of 1 Enoch and other texts I analyze, namely, the absence in the former of any constructive options for the use of possessions. The Epistle critiques the wealthy and certain uses of possessions—especially enjoyment; it offers no alternative option for how possessions might be used meaningfully. The lack of an alternative proposal is no doubt influenced by the worldview of the Epistle—and the socioeconomic status of the Enochic community—which assumes that those who have wealth are unjust and wicked.

The Interplay of Death and Possessions in the Testament of Abraham

The date (first–second century C.E.) of the Testament of Abraham, its Hellenistic Jewish character, and its obsession with death and possessions make it an apt comparative text, both with the other texts previously surveyed and Luke 12:13–34.[63] Moreover, the Testament of Abraham repre-

63. Most place the Testament of Abraham before 115–117 C.E.. So Mathias Delcor, *Le Testament d'Abraham* (SVTP 2; Leiden: Brill, 1973), 67–68; Dale C. Allison, *Testament of Abraham* (CEJL; Berlin: de Gruyter, 2003), 38–39. For a date of 100 C.E., see E. P. Sanders, "Testament of Abraham," in *The Old Testament Pseudepigrapha* (ed. James H. Charlesworth; 2 vols.; New York: Doubleday, 1983), 1:875. Allison (*Testament of Abraham*, 40) claims that the shorter recension (as it appears in MS E) likely appeared by the second century. For a fuller discussion of issues related to dating, see Allison,

sents a shift from propositional discourse to a story in which the interplay of death and wealth is presented through the narrative vehicles of plot and characterization. Of the four Hellenistic Jewish texts I examine, its form is therefore most similar to the narrative mode of Luke's parables.

Death as the Primary Plot Device

Death is the central obsession of the Testament of Abraham.[64] The plot revolves around, and is moved forward by, a conflict between God's numerous efforts to inform Abraham of his imminent death, and Abraham's myriad attempts to delay and avoid his own death.[65] The first line of the Testament alludes to Abraham's death,[66] and shortly thereafter the reader is warned of the fate awaiting Abraham:

> But even upon this one came the common and inevitable, bitter cup of death and the inscrutable[67] end of life.
>
> ἔφθασε δὲ καὶ ἐπὶ τοῦτον τὸ κοινὸν καὶ ἀπαραίτητον τοῦ θανάτου πικρὸν ποτήριον καὶ τὸ ἄδηλον τοῦ βίου πέρας. (1:3)[68]

Testament of Abraham, 34–40. On its Hellenistic Jewish traits, see Allison, *Testament of Abraham*, 30.

64. So Allison, *Testament of Abraham*, 50; John J. Collins, *Between Athens and Jerusalem: Jewish Identity in the Hellenistic Diaspora* (2nd ed.; Grand Rapids: Eerdmans, 2000), 250.

65. So George W. E. Nickelsburg, "Structure and Message in the Testament of Abraham," in *Studies on the Testament of Abraham* (ed. George W. E. Nickelsburg; SBLSCS 6; Missoula, Mont.: Scholars Press, 1972), 86.

66. "Abraham lived the span of his life [τὸ μέτρον τῆς ζωῆς αὐτοῦ], nine hundred and ninety-five years, and he lived the entire, complete state of his life in quietness and meekness and justice" (1:1). Reference to his death is more explicit in the opening line of the short recension: "when the days for Abraham to depart [παραστῆναι] drew near" (1:1).

67. On ἄδηλος as "inscrutable," see LSJ, 21; the word can also mean "unknown, obscure."

68. My translation is of the long recension in Francis Schmidt, *Le Testament grec d' Abraham: Introduction, édition critique des deux recensions grecques, traduction* (TSAJ 11; Tübingen: Mohr Siebeck, 1986). Cf. Michael E. Stone, trans., *The Testament of Abraham: The Greek Recensions* (SBLTT 2; Missoula, Mont.: Scholars Press, 1972). For arguments that the longer recension precedes the shorter recension, see Allison, *Testament of Abraham*, 12–27, esp. 14–15; Montague Rhodes James, *The Testament of Abraham: The Greek Text Now First Edited with an Introduction and Notes*

In the first action of the narrative, God instructs the archangel Michael to tell Abraham "about his death [θανάτου]" (1:4). God's concern that Abraham learn of his death is further evident both in repeating this instruction to Michael ("announce to him concerning his death [ἀνάγγειλον αὐτὸν περὶ τοῦ θανάτου]"; 1:6), and in telling Michael to confirm (πληροφορέω) to Abraham that he is about to die (1:6–7). This repetition and the detailed nature of the second instruction reflect God's intent that Abraham clearly understand the imminent approach of his death.

This intent to warn Abraham about his death is thwarted, however, when Michael fails to convey God's message clearly to Abraham. Rather than telling Abraham about his death (θάνατος), he ambiguously declares: "I was sent from the great king; I am carrying off with [ἀποκομίζομαι] a successor of his true friend, for the king is even summoning [προσκαλεῖται] him to himself" (2:6). After Michael confesses his inability to pronounce the death sentence upon Abraham, God decides, "I will cast the mention of Abraham's death [ῥίψω τὴν μνήμην τοῦ θανάτου]" into Isaac's heart, so that the latter will see his father's death in a dream (4:8). Michael is to interpret the dream, with the result that Abraham will "know his own end [γνώσεται τὸ τέλος αὐτοῦ]" (4:8). God underscores the importance of rightly interpreting the dream so that Abraham may indeed "know the sickle of death and the secret end of life [τὴν τοῦ θανάτου δρεπάνην καὶ τὸ τοῦ βίου ἄδηλον πέρας]" (4:11).[69]

(TS 2/2; Cambridge: Cambridge University Press, 1892), 49; G. H. Box, *The Testament of Abraham: Translated from the Greek Text with Introduction and Notes* (London: SPCK, 1927), xii–xv; Sanders, "Testament of Abraham," 872; cf. George W. E. Nickelsburg, "Eschatology in the Testament of Abraham: A Study of the Judgment Scene in the Two Recensions," in Nickelsburg, *Studies on the Testament of Abraham*, 23–64; idem, "Structure and Message," 85–93; Jared Warner Ludlow, *Abraham Meets Death: Narrative Humor in the Testament of Abraham* (JSPSup 41; Sheffield: Sheffield Academic Press, 2002), 152–80. For the chronological priority of the shorter recension, see Nigel Turner, "The Testament of Abraham: A Study of the Original Language, Place of Origin, Authorship, and Relevance" (Ph.D. diss., University of London, 1953), 48–100, 194–257; Francis Schmidt, "Le Testament d'Abraham: Introduction, edition de la recension courtre, traduction et notes" (2 vols.; Ph.D. diss., University of Strasbourg, 1971), 115–24. See Allison, *Testament of Abraham*, 12–27, for issues related to chronology.

69. God, in fact, redirects Michael's concern regarding eating food at Abraham's table to the more pressing issue of interpreting the dream correctly (4:9–11).

Michael's efforts to inform Abraham of his death are stymied by the latter's adamant unwillingess to comply with the divine summons to die. Although Michael interprets the dream as instructed, telling Abraham that he will take his soul from him and that he is "about to leave the worldly life and depart to God" (7:8–9), Abraham refuses, telling Michael: "I will never follow you [οὐ μή σε ἀκολουθήσω]"(7:12).[70] Abraham's noncompliance is the first of seven such refusals to acquiesce to death (7:12; 8:2, 12; 15:10; 16:16; 19:4).[71] The importance of Abraham's refusal is indicated by its verbatim repetition by Michael to God (8:2) and again by God who asks Abraham why he said it (8:12; cf. 15:10; 16:6; 19:4.). The focus of the subsequent conversation between God and Michael, moreover, is the latter's insistence that no one can escape death (8:9). The narrative pursues this allegation of death's inevitability by having God return Michael to complete the original task with which he was charged.

The remaining narrative of the Testament of Abraham consists primarily of Abraham's repeated efforts to delay—and thereby avoid—death. Although he admits he is mortal (θνητός) and not immortal (ἀθάνατος 9:5), Abraham attempts to delay his death by asking if he may see the entire inhabited world and all the creations (9:6a). His qualified willingness to depart after this tour ("*if* I now depart [ἐὰν μετέλθω] from this life...") reflects, however, his hope that he will somehow manage to avoid death (9:6b).[72]

Abraham's global tour delays his own death, but it also (not coincidentally) results in the deaths of countless others, for at Abraham's request the Lord destroys numerous wicked people.[73] The lengthiest reprieve Abraham earns in his attempt to delay death is this tour he takes of the entire world. Abraham's request for the Lord to punish sinners is likely yet another attempt to postpone and avoid his own death. [74] Others have noted the irony in Abraham's appeal for God to end the lives of sinners,

70. The intensity of Abraham's refusal is highlighted by the use of the aorist subjunctive with emphatic negation.

71. Abraham's refusals are absent, however, in the short recension.

72. The translation of Allison misses this nuance (*Testament of Abraham* 200: "when I depart from [this] life").

73. At Abraham's request, God sends wild beasts to devour thieves (10:4–7), opens up the earth to swallow a couple committing sexual immorality (10:8–9), and sends fire upon men who were trying to steal another man's possessions (10:10–12). In the short recension, those killed include adulterers, slanderers, and people about to commit murder (12:2–11).

74. Nicklesburg sees in the destruction of the sinners and Abraham's attempts to

given his own unwillingness to obey God's call to face death.[75] At any rate, the tour is eventually stopped lest Abraham destroy "the whole creation," and Abraham repents (μετανοέω) of his merciless treatment of sinners (10:15; 14:11).[76]

The global tour and many deaths caused by Abraham results in no change in Abraham's attitude toward death. After returning home,[77] Abraham refuses again to acquiesce to death, telling Michael a second time, "I will never follow you [οὐ μή σε ἀκολουθήσω]" (15:10). As before (cf. 7:12; 8:2, 12), this phrase is relayed by Michael to God (οὐκ ἀκολουθῶ σε) and in return by God to Michael (οὐκ ἀκολουθῶ σε; 15:12, 13).

Abraham's refusal to succumb to death is the catalyst for God summoning Death (ὁ θάνατος), who enters the narrative for the first time as a personified character.[78] The entrance of Death continues the narrative's ongoing conflict between the insistence that death is unavoidable and Abraham's efforts to evade this fate. Although God commands Death to take Abraham "and bring him to me" (16:1–5), Abraham remains vigilant in avoiding death, insisting to Death (as he did to Michael), "I will never follow you [οὐ μή σε ἀκολουθήσω]" (16:16).[79] Death rebuffs Abraham's command to depart from him, telling him that he will not depart until he takes Abraham's spirit (πνεῦμα; 17:3). After Abraham's second request for Death to leave, Death declares that he will not depart until he takes Abraham's soul/life (ψυχή; 19:3). Abraham refuses to follow him, saying he will only go with Michael. Death pleads with Abraham to "lay aside every desire and follow me" (20:3). Abraham resists, asking to be left "a little longer" so that he may rest in his bed (20:4). It is only after Isaac,

---

evade his own death a message about the inevitable nature of death ("Structure and Message," 295).

75. George W. E. Nickelsburg, "Summary and Prospects for Future Work," in Nickelsburg, *Studies on the Testament of Abraham*, 295.

76. The narrative never addresses the apparent conflict between Abraham's hospitality of "everyone" (1:2) with his merciless efforts at destroying the wicked.

77. Sarah dies at this point in the short recension (12:15).

78. Death is also personified in the Egyptian Stela of Taimhotep. For Jewish and Greco-Roman parallels to the personification of Death, see Allison, *Testament of Abraham*, 323–25. Burkes (*God, Self, and Death*, 57) notes an occasional personification or mythological treatment of death in Job (e.g., 28:22) and notes that Qoheleth never personifies death (79).

79. Allison takes Abraham's question regarding why Death has "come here" (16:14) as a stalling strategy (*Testament of Abraham*, 332).

Sarah, and male and female slaves enter the room and mourn that Abraham finally "entered into the faint [ὀλιγωρίαν] <of death>" (20:7).[80] Death invites Abraham to kiss his right hand, telling him, "cheerfulness and life and power will come to you" (20:8). The narrative concludes with Abraham finally encountering death.[81]

The Inevitability of Death

Chief among the points illustrated in the narrative is that death is inevitable and inescapable.[82] This chord is first struck at the story's inception: "But even upon [Abraham] came the common and inevitable [τὸ κοινὸν καὶ ἀπαραίτητον], bitter cup of death and the secret end of life" (1:3).[83] The primary conflict in the narrative, Abraham's repeated attempts to delay (and thereby avoid) the death God announces, addresses concerns related to the fear of death and the feasibility of avoiding it. The narrative insists that someone as virtuous as Abraham may delay death but that no one can avoid it. The impossibility of avoiding death is evident in Abraham's failed efforts to escape it. As in Qoheleth, death's grasp is all-encompassing, and it ensnares all with no regard for a person's righteousness or piety (cf. Qoh 8:14; 9:1–3).

The unavoidability of death is explicitly addressed and is the focal point in a discussion between God and Michael. After one of Abraham's many refusals to follow Michael into death, God instructs Michael to return and declare to Abraham:

> Or do you not know that *all* [πάντες] the ones from Adam <and Eve> have died [ἀπέθανον]? And neither have the kings been immortal [ἀθάνατοι]; no one <from the> ancestors has escaped [ἐξέφυγεν] the treasure of death [θανάτου κειμήλιον]; *all* [πάντες] have died [ἀπέθανον];[84] *all* [πάντες] have

80. Allison notes that the meaning of ὀλιγωρίαν θανάτου (cf. 17:19; 18:8) is uncertain (ibid., 357).

81. After his burial, the angels "escorted his precious soul" and ascended into the heavens (20:12).

82. Allison suggests that the language of the Testament of Abraham regarding death's unavoidability is reminiscent of that found on Jewish epitaphs (*Testament of Abraham*, 86).

83. Allison translates ἀπαραίτητον as "inexorable" (ibid., 63, 72). Cf. Wis 16:4, 16.

84. Allison notes the idea that "all have died" was often expressed on ancient Greek and Jewish epitaphs (ibid., 195).

> gone [καθείλοντο] to Hades; and *all* [πάντες] are gathered [συλλέγονται] by the sickle of death [θανάτου δρεπάνῃ]. (8:9)

The fourfold repetition of πάντες ("all") underscores the universality and all-encompassing nature of death. No one, not even righteous, hospitable Abraham, is exempt from its clutches. As Death itself notes, "For seven ages I destroy the world and lead *all* down to Hades: kings and rulers, rich and poor, slaves and free" (19:7).

Underscoring death's inevitability is the narrative's repeated depiction of Death's relentless pursuit of Abraham. Two encounters between Death and Abraham illustrate this unyielding chase:

> Abraham rose and went into his house, and Death *followed him there*. Abraham went up to his dining room. Death *also went up*. Abraham rested upon his couch. Then death *also came, and stood at his feet* (17:1).

The threefold repetition of Death's physical following after, and nearness to, Abraham illustrates the narrative's claim: Death will not relent (as Michael did) until Abraham succumbs to its grasp. Death expresses as much in his exchange with Abraham:

> Then Abraham said, "Go away from me, because I want to rest in my bed." But Death said, "I will not go away until I take your spirit from you." (17:2–3)

This example, in which Death follows his physical pursuit of Abraham with a verbal reiteration of his refusal to relent, is a pattern that is later repeated:

> And going up into his couch [Abraham] rested. Death also came, and he stood before him (19:1).

> Abraham said to [Death], "Go away from me, for I want to rest, for my spirit is enveloped by faintness." And Death said, "I will not withdraw from you until I take your soul." (19:2–3)[85]

Abraham's insistence on avoiding death is eventually (and only) overcome by Death's even greater persistence.

---

85. See the Stela of Taimhotep (*AEL* 3:63) for a similar characterization of death.

The Testament of Abraham thus illustrates the point made propositionally in Qoheleth and Ben Sira regarding the inevitable and unavoidable nature of death (cf. Qoh 2:14–17; 3:1–2a, 19–22; 9:1–6; Sir 14:17). Abraham's repeated attempts to avoid death reflect an inability to accept (much less embrace) death as a personal reality—an acceptance insisted upon in Qoheleth and Ben Sira. Abraham's elevated status in the eyes of God (and the narrator) buttresses the unavoidable nature of death. If righteous, hospitable Abraham, whom God so clearly favors, cannot escape death, what hope can there be for anyone else? This notion is introduced, albeit implicitly, in the introduction to the Testament of Abraham (cf. 1:2–3). Through Abraham the narrative illustrates two conflicting realities: the human propensity to avoid facing death and the (ultimately) futile nature of such an enterprise.

Death, Wealth, and Possessions

Wealth, after death, is the second most prevalent motif in the Testament of Abraham.[86] The narrative repeatedly highlights Abraham's vast amount of riches. His possessions include a field (χώρα), oxen, horses, and numerous servants (2:1, 7–9).[87] Michael pointedly asks Abraham about his wealth: "For was my king not rich in much trade [πλούσιος ἐν ἐμπορίᾳ πολλῇ], even having authority [ἐξουσίαν] over people and all sorts of cattle?" (2:11). Many of Abraham's goods are items that are regularly associated with wealth, such as linen, purple cloth, byssus, and "valuable and renowned incense" (4:2–3).[88]

The narrative consistently identifies Abraham's wealth as a divine gift. On three occasions God specifies the source of Abraham's wealth:

> For I blessed him as the stars of heaven and as the sand by the seashore, and he makes a good living, having many possessions, and is very rich. (1:5)

86. It is odd that Allison does not include the topic of wealth in his discussion of the "literary themes and leading ideas" of the work (*Testament of Abraham*, 48–52).

87. The number of his servants is given, alternatively, as "twelve" (2:1; cf. 15:5; 20:7) and "seven thousand" (17:18).

88. The same terms (πορφύραν καὶ βύσσον) appear in Luke 16:19 to emphasize the level of a rich man's wealth.

> ... for I have blessed him as the stars of heaven and as the sand by the seashore. (4:11)
>
> I blessed you above the sand of the sea and as the stars of heaven. (8:5)

Significant for our purposes is that each of these three statements occurs during a discussion over Abraham's death. In addition to explaining the source of the patriarch's abundant wealth,[89] they also function as a contributing reason (albeit somewhat unnecessary) for God summoning Abraham to death. The literary context of the third statement supports this contention; after Michael tells God of Abraham's first refusal to follow him to death (8:2), God instructs the archangel to remind Abraham *of all God has given him* (8:5–7). The divine blessings legitimate both God's right to call Abraham to death and the expectation that Abraham will dutifully follow this request. God's subsequent query (asking Abraham why he has resisted God and Michael) points to the perceived incongruity between God's material blessing of Abraham and the latter's refusal to submit to death (8:9). God's speech about the inevitability of death suggests that, blessing or not, Abraham has no choice but to follow death.

Emphasizing Abraham's wealth as a divine gift comports with the views of Qoheleth and Ben Sira (Qoh 2:24–26; 3:13; 5:17–18; 6:2; Sir 11:14). The Testament of Abraham also shares with Ben Sira (although to a much greater extent) an accent on God as the source of death and wealth (T. Ab. 8.9; cf. Sir 11:14).[90] Where the Testament of Abraham differs from Qoheleth is in suggesting that one should be as willing to embrace God's invitation to death as one is to receive God's provision of wealth.[91]

---

89. Allison rightly notes that, whereas in Gen 22:17 the "stars" and "sand" refer to the number of Abraham's descendants, here in the Testament of Abraham they refer to the amount of his wealth (*Testament of Abraham*, 78). He cites the following references to Abraham's vast wealth: 1QapGen 21:3; 22:29–32; Josephus, *Ant.* 1.165; *Sefer Ha-Yashar* 3:7–9. Genesis describes Abraham as "exceedingly rich" (πλούσιος σφόδρα; Gen 13:2; cf. Gen 24:1).

90. The repeated insistence that Abraham's wealth is a divine gift might reflect a concern to clarify that his wealth was not unjustly acquired. That wealth was not universally assumed to be a divine stamp of approval is clear in 1 En. 97:7–10. Unlike Qoheleth, Ben Sira, or 1 Enoch, the Testament of Abraham gives no indication that wealth poses a potential risk or danger to its owner. So Allison, *Testament of Abraham*, 79.

91. Qoheleth's primary interest is the ability (or lack thereof) to enjoy one's goods prior to death.

Making a Will/Testament

Integrally connected to death in the Testament of Abraham is the recurring motif of establishing a will or testament. God is determined not only that Abraham shall die but also that he shall be forewarned about his death. God can, presumably, end Abraham's life at any point, yet God chooses, repeatedly, to inform Abraham about his upcoming death. The primary reason given for these warnings is so that Abraham might make provision for his possessions. Furthermore, the only explicit reason provided for God's delay of Abraham's death is so that the latter can make plans for the distribution of his estate.[92] This reason is repeated no less than five times throughout the Testament of Abraham, and on each occasion God instructs Michael regarding Abraham:

> Speak to him about death [περὶ τοῦ θανάτου], *in order that he will make disposition concerning his affairs* [ἵνα διατάξεται περὶ τῶν πραγμάτων αὐτοῦ], for I blessed him as the stars of heaven and … he is exceedingly rich [πλούσιος πάνυ]; and above all he is just, good, and hospitable [δίκαιος, ἀγαθὸς καὶ φιλόξενος καὶ φιλόχρηστος μέχρι τέλους]. (1:4–5)[93]

> But only interpret well the dream so that Abraham might know the sickle [δρεπάνην] of death and the uncertain end of life [βίου ἄδηλον πέρας] and *in order that he might make disposition concerning all his possessions* [ἵνα ποιήσῃ διάταξιν περὶ πάντων τῶν ὑπαρχόντων αὐτοῦ], for I blessed him as the stars of heaven and as the sand by the edge of the sea. (4:11)

> God tells Michael to inform Abraham that Michael was sent "to you so that you might know the departure [μετάστασιν] from the world and *so that you might make disposition* [ποιήσῃς διάταξιν] *concerning your house and concerning all your possessions* [ὑπαρχόντων], and that you might bless your beloved Isaac. (8:11)[94]

---

92. Cf. Anitra Bingham Kolenkow, "The Genre Testament and the Testament of Abraham," in Nickelsburg, *Studies on the Testament of Abraham*, 140.

93. The short recension reads: "for your days have drawn near so that you might put your house in order [διοικήσεις], before you are removed [μεταχθῆναι] from the world" (1:3).

94. So that Abraham might bless Isaac is a second reason given for the advance warning given to Abraham. God concludes by asking, "Or do you not know that if I permit death to come to you, then I would be able to see whether you would come or

> For behold his end is near [ἤγγικεν] and the boundlessness of his life is complete [τελειοῦται] and *he might make disposition concerning his house and everything as much as he desires* [ποιήσει διάταξιν περὶ τοῦ οἴκου αὐτοῦ καὶ πάντα ὅσα βούλεται]. (15:1)

In the fifth instance Michael relays God's instruction (cf. 15:1) directly to Abraham in the form of a command:

> *Make disposition concerning everything that you desire* [ποίησον διάταξιν περὶ πάντων ὧν ἐὰν βούλῃ], for the day has come near [ἤγγισεν] in which you are about to depart from the body to come still once to the Lord. (15:7)[95]

A common linguistic pattern appears in these statements to convey the idea that Abraham is to make plans concerning the disposition of his estate. Four of the five announcements use the formula ποιέω + διάταξιν + περί + genitive, with the first announcement using the verbal form (διατάσσω). This particular construction (with the middle voice of διατάσσω) can mean "make testamentary dispositions" or "bequeath."[96] In the final announcement, the verb διατάσσω occurs in the imperative mood, signaling a shift in address both literarily (toward Abraham) and rhetorically (toward the reader). The reader joins Abraham in being directly commanded to prepare for one's own death by planning for the distribution of one's wealth and goods. Abraham's ultimate failure to make plans for the distribution of his estate thus constitutes direct disobedience of the divine will. In this way, Abraham is the antitype of the kind of person the reader is exhorted to become.

It is noteworthy that Abraham's specific refusal is not to die but to make disposition concerning his possessions. One wonders if Abraham refuses to make a testament because the act itself connotes too vividly the reality, unavoidability, and imminence of death.[97] Constructing a testament requires thinking of one's own mortality and reflects some level of acceptance that one will die. The making of a testament is thus one possible step in the process of facing—and coming to terms with—one's death.

---

not come? [<ἢ οὐκ οἶδας> ὅτι ἐὰν ἐάσω τὸν θάνατον ἀπελθεῖν σοι τότε ἂν εἶχον ἰδεῖν κἂν ἔρχῃ κἂν οὐκ ἔρχῃ;]" (8:12).

95. Michael neglects to mention "his house" (cf. 15:1).

96. LSJ, 414; cf. Allison, *Testament of Abraham*, 78.

97. So argues Nicklesburg, "Structure and Message," 88.

Hospitality and Death

Hospitality is preeminent among the many virtues attributed to Abraham. It is the primary way in which Abraham relates to and utilizes his possessions. The narrative's first description of Abraham highlights this specific attribute: he is a "righteous man [who] was extremely hospitable [πάνυ ὑπῆρχεν φιλόξενος ὁ δίκαιος]" (1:1).[98] His hospitality consists in the fact that he

> welcomed [ἐδέχετο] everyone, rich and poor [πλουσίους καὶ πένητας], kings and rulers, cripples and helpless, friends and strangers, neighbors and travelers—all alike did the devout, all-holy, righteous, hospitable [φιλόξενος] Abraham welcome [ὑπεδέχετο]. (1:2)[99]

Abraham's hospitality is on full display during his time with Michael. Abraham arose and "went to meet him, in the manner as was his habit to go and meet strangers and welcome [them] [ὑπηντήθη αὐτῷ καθότι ἔθος εἶχεν τοῖς ἐπιξένοις προσυπαντᾶν καὶ ἐπιδεχόμενος]" (2:2). Michael receives no special treatment from Abraham above and beyond what Abraham is said to extend to everyone.[100]

The frequent use of "stranger" to describe those for whom Abraham cares is one way of accenting the motif of hospitality. Abraham has two horses brought so that he and Michael, "this stranger" (ἐπίξενος), might sit on them (2:9). Abraham later washes the feet of Michael, "this stranger" (ἐπιξένος), and weeps over the "stranger" (ξένος; 3:7–9). In the short recension, Abraham describes this activity as "showing hospitality [ἐπιξενωθέντος]" (3:6).[101] The language of "entertaining" (ἐπιξενόομαι) is twice used to describe Abraham's care for Michael (4:1, 3).[102]

---

98. Abraham is also said to have "lived all the years of his life in quietness, gentleness, and righteousness [ἡσυχίᾳ καὶ πραότητι καὶ δικαιοσύνῃ]" (1:1).

99. Shortly thereafter God characterizes Abraham as one who "more than all is just [παρὰ πάντων δὲ δίκαιος]," "good and hospitable and loving goodness to the end of his life [ἀγαθὸς καὶ φιλόξενος καὶ φιλόχρηστος μέχρι τέλους]" (1:5).

100. In the short recension, Michael recalls Abraham's care for the visiting angels (2:10; cf. Gen 18).

101. Abraham acknowledges that this will be the last time he washes the feet "of a person receiving our hospitality [ξενιζομένου]" (3:7 [short recension]; cf. 3:9). Abraham refers to Michael as "this stranger [ξένῳ τούτῳ]" (4:2).

102. Isaac is to prepare for Abraham and Michael two couches and a table "with

In his exercise of hospitality, Abraham enacts the exhortations in Ben Sira to share generously with others. The act of hospitality represents a specific subset of generosity as well as a development from one view of sharing wealth (the giving of wealth or goods) to another (inviting someone to share one's goods through communal participation).

Central to the Testament of Abraham is the depiction of a causal relationship between Abraham's hospitality and his death. Abraham's hospitable treatment of Michael (initially) causes the angel to refuse to warn Abraham about his death. After experiencing Abraham's hospitality, Michael reports to God that he is unable to pronounce "the mention of death [τὴν μνήμην τοῦ θανάτου]" to Abraham, "that just [δίκαιον] man" (4:6; cf. 4:1–4). In explaining his difficulty, Michael highlights Abraham's hospitality, telling God that he has not seen the like (ὅμοιος) of Abraham upon the earth, one who is "merciful and hospitable, just, truthful, pious, abstaining from every evil matter [ἐλεήμονα καὶ φιλόξενον, δίκαιον, ἀληθινόν, θεοσεβῆ, ἀπεχόμενον ἀπὸ παντὸς πονηροῦ πράγματος]" (4:6).[103] In the short recension, Michael similarly tells God that he did not tell Abraham about his death, since "he is your friend and a just [δίκαιος] person who welcomes strangers [ξένους ὑποδεχόμενος]" (4:10). One can legitimately translate this participial phrase as: "he is a just person *because* he welcomes strangers." When Michael repeats a second time his inability to announce the "mention of death [τὴν μνήμην τοῦ θανάτου]," he implies that Abraham's virtues are the reason for this inability (4:6).[104]

Abraham's hospitality and generosity function as deterrents or mitigating factors in the planned announcement of his death. His hospitality may also be the reason for Michael's failure to relate to Abraham the precise message God gives him regarding the latter's death (2:3–6).[105] One can also read God's instruction to Michael to return to Abraham and "do

---

an abundance of every good thing" (4:1–2, 4). Abraham charges Isaac to beautify the chamber by spreading out linen, purple cloth, and byssus, to burn various valuable and renowned incense, to fill the house with sweet-smelling plants from the garden, and to light seven oil lamps (4:2–3).

103. This explanation only occurs in some manuscripts (EC DLM) and is lacking in others (A B I J Q).

104. This variant occurs in MSS EC DLM.

105. Instead of telling Abraham about his imminent death, per God's instructions, Michael cryptically tells him: "I was sent from the great king; I am carrying off with a successor of his true friend, for the king is even summoning him to him" (2:6).

whatever he says to you" as an allowance of flexibility that is in response to, and a consequence of, Abraham's hospitality (4:7).

Abraham's hospitality also influences the manner in which the character Death appears to him. Death appears in a beautiful form to Abraham because of the man's "just deeds [δικαιοσύναι]," his "boundless hospitality [ἄμετρον τῆς φιλοξενίας]," and the greatness of his love for God (17:7).[106] Death clarifies that his own appearance differs depending on whether the person to whom he appears is just (δίκαιος) or a sinner (ἁμαρτωλός; 17:7–8). This explanation marks an explicit contrast with Qoheleth, who insists there is no qualitative difference between the death of the δίκαιος and the ἁμαρτωλός (Qoh 8:14; 9:1–3).[107] This view in the Testament of Abraham does comport, however, with the belief in 1 Enoch that the just and wicked will experience antithetical treatment in the judgment.

In the Testament of Abraham, hospitality influences not only one's death but also one's postmortem experience. The narrative concludes with a paraenetic aside ("let us emulate the hospitality of Abraham [τὴν φιλοξενίαν ζηλώσωμεν])," directly inviting its readers/hearers to mimic the patriarch's hospitality, so that "we might be worthy of eternal life" (20:15). This conclusion reflects the concern, evident throughout the narrative, with the causal relationship between hospitality and death.[108] One can read this conclusion as an inclusio with the opening description of Abraham (cf. 1:1–2). The hortatory shift in the narrative's conclusion makes one of the consistent plot threads explicit. As Abraham's hospitality endeared him to God, readers are encouraged to likewise be hospitable in the hope (and expectation) that by doing so they will similarly influ-

---

106. Death's affirmation of Abraham's hospitality is noteworthy in that Abraham does not offer Death the hospitality he provides to Michael. Allison notes that in chapter 16 Abraham "offers his guest nothing and shuns his company" (*Testament of Abraham*, 86).

107. Qoheleth claims that both the δίκαιος and the "ungodly" (ἀσεβής) share the same fate in death and that the "good" (ἀγαθός) share the same fate as "the one who sins" (ἁμαρτάνω) (Qoh 9:2).

108. *Contra* Allison (*Testament of Abraham*, 409), who maintains that this exhortation "cannot be original, *for it misses the central concerns of the story*" (emphasis mine). He claims that T. Ab. "does not, despite chap. 1, focus on Abraham's 'hospitality' … ." Yet descriptions of Abraham's hospitality occur throughout the narrative (cf. 1:1–2; 2:2; 3:7–9; 4:1, 3, 6, 10; 17:7; cf. 2:9). I am not arguing that 20:15 is original to T. Ab., but that it does reflect an emphasis germane to the narrative.

ence their future deaths.[109] One cannot cheat death, but there are strategies available for influencing both the manner of one's death and one's experience after death. As with constructing a will or testament, the narrative offers hospitality, a practice one can control, as a strategy for coping with the uncontrollable nature of death.

Conclusion to the Testament of Abraham

In light of death's inevitability and unavoidability, the Testament of Abraham argues narratively that two specific uses of possessions can be potentially meaningful. Qoheleth responds to the uncontrollable vagaries of death by finding meaning in eating, drinking, and enjoying life and toil; for Ben Sira, meaningful uses of possessions in light of death's inevitability include using wealth to give to oneself, God, and one's friends and remaining committed to one's will or testament. The Testament of Abraham illustrates that a person can, given the threat of death's inescapability, find meaning both in hospitality and determining who will receive one's goods as an inheritance. The latter proposal, although conflicting with Qoheleth's evaluation of an inheritance as meaningless, resonates with Ben Sira's recommendation of the practice (cf. Qoh 2:18–21; 5:13; Sir 11:20–21). The following chart shows the relationships between death and possessions in the Testament of Abraham.

Death	View/Role of God	Possessions
		Abraham is rich and hospitable (1:1–5)
Death is inevitable (19:7; cf. 17:1–3; 19:2–3)		

109. The Romanian version expands this hortatory conclusion: "Likewise should we, my beloved brothers, receive travelers, strangers, the poor, and everyone, that we may give them rest and hospitality in our houses; that we, too, might be found worthy of the gift of eternal life … ." (Nicolae Roddy, ed., *The Romanian Version of the Testament of Abraham: Text, Translation, and Cultural Context* [SBLEJL 19; Atlanta: Society of Biblical Literature, 2001], 52).

	Wealth is a divine gift (8:5)	Abraham should welcome death (8:2–9)
Death can be delayed if …		one practices hospitality (4:1–7)
Death appears in a beautiful form …		to one who is hospitable (17:7)
Eternal life is available …		to one who practices hospitality (20:15)
Death is inevitable (1:4–5; 4:11; 8:9, 11; 15:1, 7)	Wealth is a divine gift (1:5; 4:11; 8:5)	Making a will/testament to dispose of possessions (1:4–5; 4:11; 8:11; 15:1, 7)
Postmortem judgment (11:1–12; 12:1–15; 13:4–11; 14:2–3)		

The following shows the respective proposals on possessions in the four texts we have analyzed.

1. Inheritance:		Ben Sira		T. Ab.
2. Enjoyment:	Qoheleth	Ben Sira		
3. Generosity:		Ben Sira		
4. Hospitality:				T. Ab.
5. Alms:		Ben Sira		
6. Giving to God:		Ben Sira		
7. Critique of Inheritance:	Qoheleth	Ben Sira		
8. Critique of Enjoyment:	Qoheleth		1 Enoch	

Conclusion to Chapters 2 and 3

The examination of Qoheleth, Ben Sira, 1 Enoch, and the Testament of Abraham shows that the Second Temple conversation regarding the interplay of death and possessions consists of diverse and often conflicting perspectives. This spectrum of conflicting points of view reflects the existence of a lively contested conversation over the use of possessions, given death's unavoidability and inevitability. These texts evince a concern for how possessions can be used meaningfully, given one's inevitable departure from life. In each text, the specific recommendation for the use of possessions corresponds to a particular understanding of death. This does not mean, however, that different authors with the same view of death propose using possessions in the same way. On the contrary, the same perception of death often results (in different authors) with disparate recommendations regarding the use of possessions. The chart on the opposite page indicates the respective ways in which specific understandings of death contribute to concrete proposals for the meaningful use of possessions.

The interplay of death and possessions entails a spectrum of options for understanding death and corresponding options for attitudes regarding possessions and their use. Options for understanding death include whether death entails a postmortem judgment (Testament of Abraham, 1 Enoch) or whether the just and unjust experience equal treatment in death (Qoheleth).[110] Each author wrestles with the uncertain (and potentially unknowable) timing of death. Closely related is the question raised in the Testament of Abraham regarding whether death is timely or untimely. Each author also acknowledges, to a greater or lesser extent, the inability to take one's goods beyond the grave.

A recurring theme around which many of the perceptions of death and wealth revolve is control. For each of these authors, death represents the ultimate loss of control. This lack of control includes and extends to the timing of one's death, the identity of the recipient of one's goods after death, ensuring how (and if) one will be remembered after death, and what (if anything) one will experience after death. Many of the perspectives concerning the use of possessions reflect attempts to find ways of exerting control given the lack of control associated with death. Each author's advice regarding possessions can be understood, in part, as a coping strat-

110. Ben Sira is more ambivalent on this point.

Death	Enjoyment	Generosity	Gifts to God	Alms	Hospitality	Will/ Inheritance
Uncertain aspects of inheritance	Qoh					
Death is inevitable	Ben Sira	Ben Sira	Ben Sira			T. Ab.
All return to dust	Qoh					
"Can't take it with you"	Qoh; Ben Sira	Ben Sira	Ben Sira			Ben Sira
Common fate of just and wicked	Qoh					
Death destroys all	Qoh					
Death's uncertain timing	Ben Sira	Ben Sira	Ben Sira			Ben Sira
Possibility of delaying death					T. Ab.	
Death as judgment				Ben Sira		
Postmortem judgment / different fate for just/wicked					T. Ab.	

egy in the face of the loss of control posed by death. Enjoyment, generosity, hospitality, making a will, and giving to God are disparate uses of wealth, but each represents an effort to establish control over an area of one's life. In light of this, it is significant that Ben Sira and the Testament of Abraham establish a causal relationship between a person's use of possessions and one's subsequent treatment in death. Using possessions becomes a specific vehicle whereby one can exert some control over and through death.

The intersection of death and possessions in the Testament of Abraham shows that interest in this twinned motif was not exclusively restricted to sapiential or wisdom texts.[111] Although apocalyptic features do not preclude the presence of sapiential motifs,[112] the Testament of Abraham does not fit as neatly into the designation of wisdom as Qoheleth, Ben Sira, or (even) the Epistle of 1 Enoch. Nor was the concern for death and possessions limited to Jewish texts. In the following chapter I broaden my examination of texts focused on death and possessions by incorporating two Greco-Roman authors: Lucian and Seneca. Analyzing a selection of

111. I am less interested in wisdom as a literary genre and more interested in how it represents a way of thinking about reality. As Collins points out, wisdom literature is a "macro-genre that embraces several literary forms," and in the Hebrew Bible, wisdom "is characterized by a particular view of the world or theological perspective" (*Jewish Wisdom*, 1). Blenkinsopp designates "sapiential literature" as a subset of wisdom, thus not requiring that a text belong to a narrowly established set of genres to be classified as sapiential (*Wisdom and Law*, 2). He cites Song of Songs and the Eden narrative in Genesis as examples of literature that are "sapiential" but whose genres would, prima facie, preclude them from being classified as "wisdom" (2, 4, 6–9; cf. 42). Katherine Dell distinguishes between wisdom as an attribute and as a genre (*'Get Wisdom, Get Insight': An Introduction to Israel's Wisdom Literature* [Macon, Ga.: Smyth & Helwys, 2000], 4). André Caquot speaks of *ḥokmâ* as "a human and divine capacity and not as a current of thought or a literary genre" ("Israelite Perceptions of Wisdom and Strength in the Light of the Ras Shamra Texts," in Gammie et al., *Israelite Wisdom*, 25). The Testament of Abraham illustrates many of the difficulties with assigning texts to a single genre; like 1 Enoch, the Testament consists of disparate literary forms and therefore resists being classified into one genre.

112. So Collins, *Between Athens and Jerusalem*, 248, 251. As he demonstrates elsewhere, sapiential and apocalyptic characteristics frequently occur together ("Wisdom, Apocalypticism, and Generic Compatibility," 165–85). Blenkinsopp uses the label "apocalyptic wisdom" to refer to texts that evince aspects of both these traditions (*Wisdom and Law*, 173–78). For problems involved with constructing an artificially rigid boundary between wisdom and apocalyptic literature, see the collection of essays in Wright and Wills, *Conflicted Boundaries*.

their works will not only expand and diversify the range of perspectives regarding the interplay of death and possessions but will also deepen and give nuance to my analysis of Luke 12:13–34 (chs. 5–8).

4
The Interplay of Death and Possessions in Lucian and Seneca

There is ample Greco-Roman material on the separate motifs of death and possessions.[1] Compared to Hellenistic Jewish (or ancient Egyptian) literature, however, Greco-Roman texts display less interest in the intersection of these two themes. Texts that focus explicitly on possessions often have negligible treatment of death. Plutarch's *De cupiditate divitiarum*, for example, rarely mentions death.[2] Similarly, although several Greco-Roman

1. Martha C. Nussbaum identifies the "fear of death" as a focal issue in Hellenistic philosophical schools (*The Therapy of Desire: Theory and Practice in Hellenistic Ethics* [Princeton: Princeton University Press, 1994], 3). For Greco-Roman attitudes toward death, see Richmond Lattimore, *Themes in Greek and Latin Epitaphs* (Illinois Studies in Language and Literature 28; Urbana: University of Illinois Press, 1942); Donna C. Kurtz and John Boardman, *Greek Burial Customs* (Aspects of Greek and Roman Life; London: Thames & Hudson, 1971); Robert Garland, *The Greek Way of Death* (London: Duckworth, 1985); Elizabeth A. Meyer, "Explaining the Epigraphic Habit in the Roman Empire: The Evidence of Epitaphs," *JRS* 80 (1990): 74–96; Gabriel Sanders, *Lapides memores: Païens et chrétiens face à la mort: Le térmoignage de l'épigraphie funéraire latine* (ed. Angela Donati, Dorothy Pikhuis, and Marc van Uytfanghe; Epigrafia e antichità 11; Faenza: Fratelli Lega, 1991); Jan Maarten Bremer, "Death and Immortality in Some Greek Poems," in *Hidden Futures: Death and Immortality in Ancient Egypt, Anatolia, the Classical, Biblical and Arabic-Islamic World* (ed. Jan Maarten Bremer and Theo P. J. van den Hout; Amsterdam: Amsterdam University Press, 1994): 109–24; idem, "The Soul, Death, and the Afterlife in Early and Classical Greece," in Bremer and van den Hout, *Hidden Futures*, 91–106; Bartel Poortman, "Death and Immortality in Greek Philosophy: From the Presocratics to the Hellenistic Era," in Bremer and van den Hout, *Hidden Futures*, 197–220; Sarah Iles Johnston, *Restless Dead: Encounters between the Living and the Dead in Ancient Greece* (Berkeley: University of California Press, 1999).

2. Plutarch refers to death twice (*Cupid. divit.* 7), and neither reference bears

authors excoriate greed[3] and identify avarice (πλεονεξία / *avaritia*) or the love of money (φιλαργυρία) as the source of all evil,[4] such critique is usually neither informed by nor framed within a discussion of death. This relative lack of attention to the intersection of death and possessions shows that it was possible to discuss one motif (death or possessions) without reference to the other. The interplay of death and possessions, in other words, was a possible conversation but not a necessary or required one.

In Greco-Roman literature, the interplay of death and possessions most frequently occurs in moral discourse. In this chapter I analyze Lucian's *Dialogues of the Dead* and Seneca's *Epistulae morales*. I do not argue that these works either sum up or are representative of Greco-Roman thought on death and possessions. These two texts merit analysis in part because they demonstrate that the interplay of death and possessions was important to some Greco-Roman authors. These two texts also exhibit perspectives on death and possessions that are significant in light of attitudes toward these two motifs in the four Hellenistic Jewish texts previously surveyed as well as Luke's parable of the Rich Fool. Perspectives on death and possessions in Lucian and Seneca resonate with certain views in Hellenistic Jewish texts but also offer distinct perceptions not present in them. Including Lucian and Seneca in our analysis thereby highlights the cross-cultural character of the conversation on death and possessions and demonstrates the variegated nature of this conversation. Finally, elements of Greco-Roman culture shaped significantly the milieu in which Luke-Acts was composed.

Death and Possessions in Lucian's *Dialogues of the Dead*

Lucian of Samosata was one of several Greco-Roman satirists in the Hellenistic period. Although his lifespan (ca. 120–ca. 180) postdates the composition of Luke-Acts, his writings exhibit a number of salient parallels

---

directly upon his critique of avarice or his recommendations regarding the use of possessions.

3. See, e.g., Virgil, *Aen.* 3.56; cf. Propertius, *Elegiae* 3.13.48; Horace, *Sat.* 2.3.94; Ovid, *Metam.* 1.128–131.

4. Diogenes, *Ep.* 50.22–23; Diodorus Siculus, *Library of History* 21.1.4a; Dio Chrysostom, *Avar.* 17.6; Apollodorus Comicus, *Philadelph. Frag.* 4; *Ceb. Tab.* 19.5; Diogenes Laertius, *Lives of the Philosophers* 6.50; *De Gnomologio Vaticano inedito* 265; Claudianus, *De laudibus Stilichonis* 2.3; Stobaeus, *Ecl.* 3.417, 5 H; cf. Plato, *Leg.* 9.870a, c; Hippocrates, *Ep.* 17, 43. For an early Christian parallel, see Polycarp, *Phil.* 2.4.1; cf. Ambrose, *Ep.* 15; *Duties of the Clergy* 2.17.89.

with the New Testament in general and with Luke's Gospel in particular.[5] The satirical nature of Lucian's works is noteworthy, given the similar literary function that some observe between the genres of satire and parable.[6] Lucian's *Dialogues of the Dead* provides an extended satire of attitudes toward death and possessions. Because death is the backdrop of each dialogue, all statements on possessions and wealth are framed within this context of the end of one's life and the transition to an afterlife. Although my primary focus is the *Dialogues of the Dead*, I will also consider Lucian's other works that reveal perspectives on death and possessions.[7] Before analyzing the interplay of death and possessions in the *Dialogues*, I will briefly survey the depiction of and attitude toward death in these stories.

The Unavoidability, Irreversibility, and Universal Fear of Death

Death functions in Lucian's *Dialogues* as a revelatory judgment, a moment that lays bare one's life and deeds for others to see.[8] Menippus describes the

5. See Hans Dieter Betz, *Lukian von Samosata und das Neue Testament: Religiongeschichtliche und paränetische Parallelen* (Ein Beitrag zum Corpus Hellenisticum Novi Testamenti; TUGAL 76; Berlin: Akademie, 1961).

6. Sheldon Sacks proposes the following literary continuum: myth / apologue / action / satire / parable (*Fiction and the Shape of Belief* [Berkeley: University of California Press, 1966], 7, 24–26). Commenting on this scale, John R. May claims that myth "establishes world … parable subverts it, apologue defends world, action investigates or describes it, and satire attacks it" ("Visual Story and the Religious Interpretation of Film," in *Religion in Film* [ed. John R. May and Michael Bird; Knoxville: University of Tennessee Press, 1982]). May is influenced here by the work on parables by John Dominic Crossan, *The Dark Interval: Towards a Theology of Story* (Niles, Ill.: Argus Communications, 1975), 53. Niall Rudd identifies attack, entertainment, and preaching as the three elements of satire (*Themes in Roman Satire* [London: Duckworth, 1986], 1–39).

7. My analysis excludes works whose Lucianic authorship is considered spurious (e.g., *Lucius, Amores*). On the disputed nature of Lucian's works, see M. D. Macleod, *Lucian* (LCL; Cambridge: Harvard University Press, 1967), 8:ix–x, 1–2, 47–51, 147–48, 237, 303–5, 319–23, 379, 413–14, 469, 505–7, 523.

8. Death functions as an extensive judgment in Lucian's *Cataplus* (13, 23–29). The judgment is akin to a judicial proceeding, complete with a court (δικαστήριον), a sentence (δίκη), accusation (κατηγορέω), accusers (κατήγορος), witnesses (μάρτυς), and testifying (μαρτυρέω, καταμαρτυρέω). Lucian employs the analogy of a courtroom to describe the afterlife in *Menippus* (11–14) and *Zeus Catechized* (17–18). In the latter, Zeus insists that the afterlife consists of punishments and rewards (κόλασις καὶ τιμή) and that each person's life is scrutinized (ἐξετάζω) in a court (δικαστήριον) (*Jupp. conf.*

experience awaiting all who die: "We must be judged [δικασθῆναι δεήσει], and they say the judgments are oppressive, wheels and stones and vultures; *and the life* [βίος] *of each person will be revealed* [δειχθήσεται]" (*Dial. mort.* 20.13).[9] In this manner, the *Dialogues* illustrate Ben Sira's maxim that "revelation of deeds occurs at the end" of a person's life (Sir 11:27b; cf. 11:26).[10] As in Ben Sira, one should not be judged blessed (εὐδαίμων) until death and the end of one's life (*Char.* 10–11). Like 1 Enoch and the Testament of Abraham, however, the *Dialogues* explicitly situate this judgment experience in an afterlife. I am interested not in whether Lucian personally believes in his portrayals of the afterlife but in assessing how such depictions function rhetorically in his arguments regarding the meaningful use of possessions.[11]

---

18). The good, pious, and those who have lived virtuously join the heroes in the Elysian fields (*Jupp. conf.* 17–18; *Luct.* 7). Lucian elsewhere notes that the common belief is that most people are neither punished nor rewarded but instead wander through Hades (*Luct.* 8).

9. Emphasis added. Translations of Lucian are my own. For the Greek text, see vol. 7 of Lucian, *Dialogi mortuorum* (trans and ed. M.D. MacLeod; LCL; Cambridge: Harvard University Press, 1961). References follow the order in LCL. In *Menippus*, punishments include flogging, roasting on fire, stretching on the rack, pillories, and wheels of torture (*Men.* 14). Some are devoured by vultures (*Luct.* 8).

10. In *Cataplus*, people are prosecuted for the wicked things (πονηρός) they commit during their life (23). Every wicked deed committed in life leaves "an invisible mark on the soul [ἀφανῆ στίγματα ἐπὶ ψυχῆς]" (24). In *Menippus*, Minos examines and punishes people in proportion to their crimes and sends them to the place of the wicked (ἀσεβής) (*Men.* 12). All types of people are punished: kings, slaves, satraps, poor (πένης), rich (πλούσιος), and beggars (πτώχος) (*Men.* 14). However, the rich are punished twice as much as the poor, and the latter are allowed to rest between punishments. The ones punished most severely are those prideful in their wealth and offices (*Men.* 12). The rich likely receive a greater punishment, since they commit many "unlawful deeds [παράνομα]," including plundering, oppressing, and despising the poor (*Men.* 20; cf. *Sat.* 10, 12). On account of this, those in Hades pass a resolution condemning the souls of the rich to enter and remain in donkeys for 250,000 years, after which they will be allowed to die (*Men.* 20). Lucian elsewhere depicts the afterlife as a time when the wicked are punished and the good (χρήστος) abide in good fortune (εὐδαιμονία) (*Jupp. conf.* 17; *Luct.* 7–9). The latter text also refers to the postmortem punishments associated with Tityus and Tantalus (cf. *Bis acc.* 21; *Sacr.* 9; *Men.* 14; cf. *Philops.* 25; *Luct.* 8).

11. In *De luctu*, Lucian notes that the mass of people (πολὺς ὅμιλος) and the common people (ἰδιώτης) hold beliefs such as the existence and nature of Hades, the punishment of the wicked, and reward for the good and just (*Luct.* 2–9). In *Zeus Rants*, Damis and Timocles debate whether the gods punish people during their lifetimes

Death and the postmortem experience elicit fear from many characters in the *Dialogues*. Such is the case with the philosopher to whom Hermes pointedly asks: "Playing the coward with death [πρὸς θάνατον ἀποδειλιᾷς]?" (*Dial. mort.* 20.9). Some people enter death "weeping and some begging to be set free and some coming down with pain" (*Dial. mort.* 22.1). Reluctance to enter death is evident in resistance (ἀντιβαίνω), lying on their backs, and setting themselves firmly against (ἀντερείδω) Hermes, who must push them in by their heads (*Dial. mort.* 22.1). Lucian depicts refusals to submit to death in other texts.[12] Diogenes notes that everyone except children and infants weeps (δακρύω) and wails aloud (οἰμώζω) as they anticipate entering the afterlife (*Dial. mort.* 22:6).[13] The reluctance to enter the afterlife is reflected in Menippus's query to the philosopher, "So why are you still hesitating [μέλλω]?" (*Dial. mort.* 20.13). Even Socrates, although "seeming not to fear [δείδω] death at all," changed his tone once he faced death and "shrieked [κωκύω] like newborn babes and cried for his children and became all out of sorts" (*Dial. mort.* 4.1).[14]

The tacit assumption is that, if the noble Socrates succumbed to the fear of death, then there is little hope that anyone else will fare differently. Socrates' experience is presented as emblematic of "everyone: until the entrance, they are bold and courageous, but the precise testing [ἔλεγχος ἀκριβής] are the things inside" (*Dial. mort.* 4.2). The reluctance to enter death that characterized Abraham in the Testament of Abraham is depicted in the *Dialogues* as a nearly universal trait.[15] As is shown below,

---

(*Jupp. trag.* 36–37). Damis later argues that the twin failure of the good to be rewarded and the wicked to be punished is evidence that the gods do not exercise providence (*Jupp. trag.* 48–49).

12. Lucian depicts a similar scene using a same verb in *Cataplus*. When taken to death, the tyrant "was straining and holding back the entire way, and because he set his feet firmly against [ἀντερείδω] the ground, he was by no means easily led" (4). The tyrant also seeks to escape death by begging, entreating, asking to be released for a short while, and promising a bribe (4).

13. On the universal wailing (οἰμώζω) expressed by those entering Hades, see Lucian, *Char.* 1, 8.

14. Cerberus remarks that, since Socrates "saw [death] was inevitable [ἀναγκαῖον], he became emboldened, as he pretended to comply willingly with what by all means he must suffer [ἔδει παθεῖν], so the spectators would marvel" (*Dial. mort.* 4.2).

15. This universal fear of death and attempt to avoid its fate is also a common experience in Lucian's other depictions of postmortem scenes (*Cat.* 3, 4, 8–10, 13–14). For a rare instance in which one seeks to die before one's time, see *Cat.* 7. Another

Lucian envisions a direct proportion between a person's amount of possessions and one's fear of death.

Like Socrates, other characters whom one might not expect to fear death do so. Diogenes is surprised to learn that an elderly man who weeps (δακρύω) upon entering death was not rich (πλουτέω) but a beggar (πτώχος; *Dial. mort.* 22.9).[16] He was not only poor but also childless, lame, and could scarcely see. Even such a person as this was reluctant to enter death: "Yes, for the light was sweet, and death was fearful and to be avoided [τὸ τεθνάναι δεινὸν καὶ φευκτέον]" (22.9). Diogenes chastises the old man for "acting like a boy in the face of that which must be [πρὸς τὸ χρεών]," noting that the man's old age should have led him to pursue death (22.9).[17] Implicit in Diogenes's comment is that people who fear death, or mourn over those who have died, fail to recognize death's potential benefits.[18]

The *Dialogues* depict death as inescapable (ἀναγκαῖον) and inevitable (ἔδει παθεῖν; *Dial. mort.* 4.2).[19] In the words of Antilochus:

> For these things were decreed by nature: certainly everyone dies; one must therefore abide by her law and not be distressed with her instructions.
>
> ταῦτα γὰρ ἔδοξε τῇ φύσει, πάντως ἀποθνήσκειν ἅπαντας, ὥστε χρὴ ἐμμένειν τῷ νόμῳ καὶ μὴ ἀνιᾶσθαι τοῖς διατεταγμένοις. (*Dial. mort.* 26.3)[20]

---

exception to this general rule are Christians, most of whom despise (καταφρονέω) death and are willing to face it due to their belief that they will be immortal (ἀθάνατος) and live forever (*Pereg.* 13; cf. 23, 33).

16. The man's name is listed as "Beggar" (πτώχος). The term πτώχος originally referred to someone who "crouches or cringes." As a substantive it refers to a "beggar," and it later came to mean "poor" (LSJ, 1550).

17. As a reason, Diogenes cites the ability of death to remove the evils of old age (*Dial. mort.* 22.9).

18. Death is preferable at times, since the absence of a need (thirst, hunger, warmth) is better than having such a need met (*Luct.* 16–17). People are thus mistaken to consider death "the greatest of evils" (*Luct.* 24).

19. Lucian elsewhere refers to the inevitability of death. No one, claims the philosopher Demonax, is unacquainted with mourning (πένθος) someone who has died (*Demon.* 25). Lucian notes that the line from Homer that Demonax most frequently quoted was: "Idler or toiler, 'tis all one to Death [κάτθαν']'" (*Demon.* 60; cf. *Il.* 9.320). People die at different ages, but all must perish (*Char.* 19). An "infinite number of roads" lead to the god Death (*Tox.* 38).

20. Antilochus is responding to Achilles' disappointment with the equality in Hades and his desire to return to earth as a living thrall.

It is especially impossible to extend one's own lifespan. In *Cataplus* a tyrant is called "vain" (μάταιος) for thinking he could live longer (ἐπιβιόω) "when the thread assigned to him had already expired" (*Cat.* 3).[21] Delaying death is, in short, "impossible [ἀδύνατος]" (*Cat.* 4).[22]

The unavoidability of death is illustrated through not only the deaths of many but also the deaths of semidivine figures such as Heracles and Alexander (*Dial. mort.* 11, 12). Diogenes' surprise at seeing Heracles in Hades illustrates the point:

> "Is not this one Heracles? It is not another, by Heracles! The bow, the club, the lionskin, the stature; it is all Heracles! *Has he died, then, even though he is a son of Zeus?* Tell me, glorious victor, are you dead [νεκρός]? For above on earth, I used to sacrifice to you as [though you were] a god. (*Dial. mort.* 11.1, emphasis added)

Diogenes is likewise shocked to encounter Alexander in Hades: "What is this, Alexander? *Have you also died* [τέθνηκας], *just like all of us?*" (*Dial. mort.* 13.1, emphasis added).[23] The deaths of Heracles and Alexander reinforce death as an inevitable and unavoidable destiny to which all succumb. Hades is also depicted as inescapable; once a person arrives there, it is impossible to depart (*Dial. mort.* 7.2; 8.2; *Cat.* 4, 8). Diogenes disabuses Alexander of any hope that he may escape from Hades: "For it is not lawful for anyone who has once sailed across the lake and passed into the inside of the entrance to go home again [ἀνέρχομαι]" (*Dial. mort.* 13.3).[24]

---

21. Lucian elsewhere uses "thread" (νῆμα) to refer to the lifespan apportioned to a person (*Cat.* 7; *Philops.* 25). The terms λίνον and νῆμα (both "thread") appear to be interchangeable for Lucian (cf. *Jupp. conf.* 2, 7).

22. This despite the many attempts of the tyrant to escape Hades and return to earth (*Cat.* 8–14).

23. Upon meeting Alexander in Hades, Philip remarks: "For now that you're already dead, don't you suppose there are many who mock that pretension, since they see the corpse of the god lying outstretched, already clammy and swollen, according to the law of all the bodies?" (*Dial. mort.* 12.5).

24. One exception to this rule occurs. Despite telling Protesilaus that he cannot return to earth ("This is a love … [among] all the dead, but it will happen to none of them"), Pluto eventually relents, giving him "one day" to return to be with his love (*Dial. mort.* 28.1–3).

Death as a Reassessment of Possessions

As with some ancient Egyptian texts, Lucian's *Dialogues* consistently refer to the impossibility of bringing one's possessions across death's divide.[25] The inability to take goods into the afterlife has direct consequences upon the nature of the afterlife experience and also influences the attitudes in the *Dialogues* toward possessions.

The lengthiest of the dialogues describes in great detail what people must leave behind after death. In his first instruction to those who have died, Charon tells them that before crossing the river it "is necessary to proceed naked [γυμνοὺς ἐπιβαίνειν χρή], leaving behind all these useless things" (*Dial. mort.* 20.1). Such stripping is mandatory preparation for the afterlife; its importance is further indicated when Charon insists that Hermes not take anyone across the river who is not "bare" (ψιλός) or who has not "thrown off" (ἀποβάλλω) their things. Charon repeats his insistence, this time to Hermes, that he make everyone "proceed naked [γυμνοὺς ἐπιβαίνειν]."[26] Although what precisely must be stripped off is not entirely clear, the evaluation of the things that are stripped off is unambiguous. They are all deemed "useless" (περισσός; 20.1). Many subsequent dialogues not only clarify the specific content of what must be stripped of but also illustrate the "useless" nature of the things that people cherish.

The primary consequence of this inability to bring goods into the afterlife is an elimination of virtually every distinction among people in their postmortem existence, contributing to a state of equality among inhabitants of the afterlife.[27] The commitment to an afterlife *sans* socioeconomic differences prevents individuals from bringing anything with them that might mark themselves as superior to others. Charmoleos, for

25. See, e.g., the inscription of Petosiris and the Song from the tomb of King Intef. The inability to take one's goods into the afterlife is also a motif in Lucian's other works (*Cat.* 8; *Char.* 14, 20). In Clotho's words, the time of ownership (κτῆσις) expires (ἐξήκω) at death (*Cat.* 8).

26. The titular character of Lucian's *Charon* also refers to people being naked prior to the voyage on his boat (*Char.* 14). In *Menippus*, those in Hades must also strip naked (*Men.* 12).

27. In *Dialogues of the Dead*, all persons arrive at the same postmortem destination. In *Cataplus*, Hades is the destination for almost everyone, but at least one person goes to the Isles of the Blessed, where "the good" (ἄριστος) live (*Cat.* 24; *Jupp. conf.* 17). In *Sacrifices*, people are forbidden to enter heaven (ὁ οὐρανός) (*Sacr.* 9).

example, must leave his beauty, lips, kisses, thick hair, the redness of his cheeks, and all his skin (*Dial. mort.* 20.3). The tyrant Lampichus is forced to leave his purple robe, diadem, and wealth (πλοῦτος; 20.4).[28] Hermes' refusal to grant Lampichus's subsequent request to keep his diadem and mantle underscores the impossibility of transferring to the afterlife any previous symbols of dominance over others.[29] Accordingly, after the athlete Damasias asks to be let in since he is naked, Hermes tells him that he must also strip off all his flesh (σάρξ) and throw away (ἀπορρίπτω) his wreaths and proclamations (20.5).[30] Hermes tells a philosopher to discard his "falsehood, too, and conceit, and *the opinion that you are better* [ἀμείνων] *than others*" (20.8, emphasis added). The postmortem erasure of distinctions cannot allow for the kind of superiority Hermes perceives in the philosopher.[31]

People are thus forced to discard items that not only distinguish them from others but that also, to a significant degree, define their identity. A rhetorician must discard his "endless talking, antitheses, balanced clauses, well-rounded sentences, barbarisms, and the other burdens of words" (*Dial. mort.* 20.10). A general wishes to bring armor and a trophy into the afterlife "because I was victorious … and *gained the highest distinction* [ἀριστεύω], and the city honored me" (20.7). In keeping with the removal of distinctions (and the preservation of peace), Hermes directs him to leave his trophy on earth above, "for in Hades there is peace [εἰρήνη], and there will not be a need for any weapons" (20.7).[32] The transition to the afterlife thus requires a certain destruction of those aspects of one's iden-

28. When he asks if a tyrant should come naked, Hermes replies, "A tyrant, by no means, but a corpse [νεκρόν] most certainly! Therefore lay aside these things!" (*Dial. mort.* 20.4). Hermes tells him he must also do away with his vanity (τῦφον) and pride (ὑπεροψίαν; 20.4).

29. There is a tacit accusation that wealth and possessions might contribute to certain vices. When Lampichus thinks he has discarded everything, Hermes tells him that his "cruelty [ὠμότητα], folly [ἄνοιαν], insolence [ὕβρις], and temper [ὀργήν]" remain. "Leave these also," Hermes instructs (*Dial. mort.* 20.4). Lampichus finally declares that he is stripped (ψιλός).

30. The verb ἀπορρίπτω can also mean "disown" or "renounce."

31. The tyrant Megapenthes is shocked to discover that the afterlife has no regard for the elevated social position he enjoyed during his life (*Cat.* 13).

32. Lucian elsewhere depicts the afterlife as a place where all people are at peace (εἰρήνη; *Cat.* 15). The peaceful nature of the afterlife is in stark contrast to the world, in which people die fighting with one another *over possessions* (*Cat.* 21).

tity that one cherishes the most. It just so happens that these are the very aspects that mark people as socially or economically privileged.[33]

The elimination of distinctions in the afterlife is the central concern of the penultimate dialogue, between Diogenes and Mausolus. Noting that he not only was a king and ruler but also that he subdued and subjected lands, Mausolus cites his royal position on earth as the reason that he is proud and worthy to be honored more than others (*Dial. mort.* 29.1). After referring to being handsome, tall, and mighty in war, Mausolus cites the chief reason for his pride: the vast memorial (μνῆμα) that lies over him in Halicarnassus. He boasts that no other memorial is as great as his own, nor as beautifully adorned. "Don't you think it is right to be so proud [φρονεῖν] of these things?" (*Dial. mort.* 29.1). After clarifying that "these things" refer to Mausolus's kingdom, his beauty, and the weight of his tomb, Diogenes articulates the reigning law of the afterlife: "But, O handsome Mausolus, neither the strength nor that beautiful form are still with you" (29.2).

The postmortem ethos of eliminating distinctions, coupled with the equality it engenders, enables Lucian to reassess the value ascribed to those things that serve during life to distinguish people from one another. Diogenes points out, for example, that there is little or no difference between the skull of Mausolus and his own. Diogenes also highlights the uselessness of Mausolus's memorial. Although his tomb and its costly marble might give cause for the people of Halicarnassus to boast, Diogenes cannot see what benefit it provides to Mausolus (*Dial. mort.* 29.2). The absence of distinctions in the afterlife not only prohibits bringing certain traits into death but also portrays such traits as useless. Mausolus articulates the chief concern underlying this and other dialogues: "Will all those things, therefore, be useless [ἀνόνητα] to me? And will Mausolus and Diogenes be held in equal honor [ἰσότιμος]?" (29.3). Menippus succinctly encapsulates a central tenet of the afterlife and of Lucian's *Dialogues*, declaring in the penultimate line of the *Dialogues*: "For in Hades all are of equal privilege [ἰσοτιμία] and alike [ὅμοιοι]" (30.2). By demonstrating the uselessness of distinguishing characteristics in the afterlife, Lucian encourages people to reassess the worth people ascribe during their lifetime to such traits.

33. Such is the case for those in Hades who must strip off their wealth, lineage, and power (*Men.* 12).

The elimination of distinguishing features results in an afterlife that is primarily characterized by its equality.[34] Chiron describes the "equal privilege" (ἰσοτιμία) he observes in the afterlife as "entirely democratic" (δημοτική; *Dial. mort.* 8.2).[35] The erasure of physical and physiological traits makes it impossible to distinguish between people's appearances. Diogenes notes the absence of differentiating traits (golden hair, light-blue or dark eyes, rosy face, vigorous sinews, strong shoulders) and declares that "all with us is one dust … skulls stripped of beauty" (1.3). Leaving behind physical characteristics at death leads Menippus to declare, in the final dialogue, his inability to judge whether one person is more handsome than another (30.2).[36]

The chief difference removed in the afterlife is an economic one. Disparities between the poor and the wealthy are erased in Lucian's vision of the postmortem experience. Included in the many items that Hermes forbids a philosopher to bring into the afterlife are gold, pleasure-filled living (ἡδυπάθεια), and luxury (τρυφή; *Dial mort.* 20.8).[37] Craton must likewise remove those items such as wealth (πλοῦτος) and luxury (τρυφή) that would mark him as economically superior to others (20.6).[38] Hermes further charges him not to bring

34. This equality also characterizes the afterlife in Lucian's other works (*Cat.* 15; *Char.* 22).

35. For an example of what this might look like during life, see Strabo (*Geogr.* 7.3.9).

36. In *Cataplus*, the afterlife is also characterized by the inability to distinguish whether someone is more beautiful (κάλος) than another (22; cf. *Men.* 15).

37. Hermes also forbids the philosopher from bringing his shamelessness (ἀναισχυντία), temper (ὀργή), and effeminacy (μαλακία). The "heaviest" item carried by the philosopher is his flattery (κολακεία) (*Dial. mort.* 20.9). The lengthiest and most vicious attack in the *Dialogues* is directed toward this philosopher. Lucian elsewhere critiques those who "cultivate philosophy for hire and put virtue on sale over a counter" (*Nigr.* 25). A philosopher "who intends to teach contempt for wealth should first of all show that he is himself above gain" (*Nigr.* 25–26). Lucian accuses philosophers of being greedy, hypocritical (they rail against wealth and pleasure but indulge in luxury), and failing to contribute anything to the world (*Symp.* 36; *Icar.* 29–31; *Vit. auct.* 12; *Pisc.* 34–36; *Par.* 52; *Men.* 5).

38. Lucian elsewhere notes that the Athenians look down upon anyone who seeks to introduce luxury (τρυφή) among them (*Nigr.* 12). Cf. *Nigr.* 13 for an illustration of how the Athenians educate a luxurious visitor regarding his erroneous ways. Athens is suited for one who despises wealth (πλοῦτος καταφρονέω) (*Nigr.* 14). The decadence

> obsequies nor the ancestors' honors, but leave behind even family and fame (even if the city publicly proclaimed you), and the inscriptions on the statues, and do not speak of the great tomb they keep over you. For even mentioning these things is weary. (*Dial. mort.* 20.6)

Craton's acquiescence to these instructions dramatizes the unfeasibility of breaking this proscription of postmortem socioeconomic distinctions. The elimination of such disparities also exists in other works of Lucian; Micyllus finds that in the afterlife there is no demanding back of debtors' debts and no payment of taxes (*Cat.* 15).

The parity experienced in the afterlife causes some people to reevaluate the perspectives and values they held prior to death. While living, Achilles preferred a glorious death to living a lengthy life in obscurity. Achilles is quickly disillusioned, however, with the afterlife because of its egalitarian nature. He discovers in the afterlife that glory is useless (ἀνωφελής), despite the praise it elicits from the living. Achilles observes that there is

> equal honor with the dead, and neither beauty nor strength remain, but we all are lying dead under the same nether darkness, *are all alike, and differing in no way from one another*, and neither the Trojan dead fear me nor do the Greek dead serve me, but there is *a strict equality of speech, and one dead person is like* [*another*]. (*Dial. mort.* 26.2, emphasis added)

This equality grieves Achilles and leads him to prefer living as a servant to existing without any social hierarchy.

This elimination of distinctions and consequent equality in the afterlife provides an opportunity for characters in the dialogues to reframe their understanding of possessions. A primary consequence of the establishment of equality in the afterlife is a reorientation toward possessions in which greed and the hoarding of wealth is critiqued as a bankrupt enterprise.[39] Diogenes instructs Pollux to announce to the rich (πλούσιος),

---

of Rome is reflected in its welcoming of one who "loves wealth" (πλούτος ἐράω) and whose soul (ψυχή) is committed to pleasure (ἡδονή) (*Nigr.* 15–17).

39. In Lucian's *Icaromenippus,* Menippus articulates this notion, one that is also similar to conclusions drawn in Qoheleth: "For ever since I examined the things of life closely, I began to find all human things (I mean riches and offices and powers) to be ridiculous and of poor quality and uncertain, despising them and supposing the earnest effort concerning these things was an obstacle to things truly worth effort" (*Icar.* 4; cf. 18).

"Why, O fools, do you guard [φυλάττετε] gold? And why do you torment yourselves by counting the interest, and adding together talents on talents, since you must come here shortly needing (only) one obol?' (*Dial. mort.* 1.3).[40] With such dialogue, Lucian presents readers with the opportunity to reconsider their own attitudes toward, and use of, possessions.[41] The potential imminence of death invites one to reassess, in particular, the futility of expending energy amassing riches. Lucian reorients one's perception of the value of gold by juxtaposing its uselessness in the afterlife ("a yellow, heavy substance") with the violence it provokes among those who fight for it (*Char.* 11–12). Effort spent collecting wealth is deemed wasteful, given that the fruit of one's labor is unable to accompany one beyond death.[42]

Death and its aftermath provide a perspective that highlights the fragility of wealth. This view informs various questions Diogenes puts to Alexander; after asking how the latter is able to cope with leaving behind his wealth and its various accoutrements, Diogenes concludes: "Don't these things grieve you since they are passing beyond[43] memory? Why are you weeping, O vain [μάταιος] one? Didn't the wise Aristotle teach you these things, not to deem the things from fortune to be secure [βέβαιος]?" (*Dial. mort.* 13.4).[44] One of the ways that death thus relativizes the value of possessions is by exposing their promise to provide security as an illusion.[45] Lucian elsewhere suggests that true philosophy will lead a person from

40. The obol is a coin that a person places in a corpse's mouth in order to pay Charon's fare.

41. *Cataplus* includes just such a reassessment. While alive, Micyllus perceived the tyrant as a superhuman and thrice blessed because of his wealth. This perception changes after death, and Micyllus admits laughing at himself because he used to marvel at such a worthless creature (*Cat.* 16–17).

42. Clotho faults the tyrant Megapenthes for (mistakenly) thinking that his gold and talents might be useful in the afterlife (*Cat.* 9).

43. One variant (β) reads ὑπό instead of ὑπέρ.

44. The inability to bring goods into the afterlife is the reason that once there, the poor laugh (οἱ πένητες γελῶμεν), while the rich grieve (ἀνιάω) and wail (οἰμώζω) (*Cat.* 15; cf. 17, 20). Note the parallel to Luke 6:20–21, 24–25. In *Cataplus*, the dead lament the loss of their wealth, fields, and house (*Cat.* 20; cf. *Men.* 18).

45. Alexander acknowledges that the one thing he gained from Aristotle's wisdom is "grief over those greatest goods, which I reckoned little before" (*Dial. mort.* 13.5). For Lucian, one does not "own" one's goods so much as one is a "proprietor" of them for a given period of time. After death, "another takes them over and enjoys the title" (*Nigr.* 26).

desiring wealth (πλοῦτος) and considering it a blessing to ridiculing and criticizing it (*Nigr.* 4). Such scorn is fitting, given the futility of yearning after wealth (*Nigr.* 20).[46] The pursuit of riches, claims Lucian, is due in part to an inability to perceive their true nature.[47]

The absence and useless nature of possessions in the afterlife prompts further questions for those who spend their life pursuing them. In his response to Mausolus's query regarding whether he and Diogenes will be equal in the afterlife, Diogenes underscores the negative consequences of being overly attached to goods during one's life:

> For Mausolus will lament when he remembers the things above on earth, in which he used to think he was happy [εὐδαιμονέω], but Diogenes will laugh at him. And he will speak of the tomb built for himself in Halicarnassus … but Diogenes has not known if he even has some tomb for his body; for he did not care about this; but he has left behind a report for the best people concerning this, that *he has lived a life of a man … that is more lofty than your memorial, and is built on a firmer place.* (*Dial. mort.* 29.3, emphasis added)

This statement suggests that *living well* is preferable to establishing monuments and that the former is a more helpful and meaningful preparation for death than the latter. Both the *Dialogues* and the Egyptian Immortality of the Writers critique the establishment of monuments, with the latter proposing instead the profession of a scribe as the optimal way to secure one's memory. *The Dialogues* are less concerned with preserving memory and more intent on preparing for death by living well.[48]

---

46. On the ridiculousness of the rich, see Lucian, *Nigr.* 21–23. The futility of pursuing wealth is underscored by understanding that possessions are brief, imaginary blessings (*Demon.* 8).

47. Riches (personified) intimates that ignorance and deceit prevent people from seeing that she is lame and blind. This difficulty in accurately perceiving wealth is compounded by the "very lovely mask" that she wears. People thus become enamored with Riches, not knowing they are "falling in love with things hateful and ugly" (*Tim.* 27). People remain deluded even after becoming rich since Riches comes with a host of vices (conceit, folly, boasting, effeminacy, hubris, and deceit). Such vices cause one to admire that which one should shun (*Tim.* 28; cf. 32). In contrast, Lucian associates poverty (πενία) with toil, patient endurance, wisdom (σοφία), and manliness (*Tim.* 31; cf. 32–33).

48. Lucian elsewhere critiques the building and inscribing of monuments (*Cat.* 9;

Lucian's *Dialogues* constitute a rhetorical argument that living well requires a willingness to contemplate death and to confront one's own mortality.[49] After pleading guilty to mocking the dead who lament their loss of wealth, Menippus acknowledges enjoying tormenting them since they were not only content "*to live badly* [κακῶς], but also in death they still have remembered and cling to the things above" (*Dial. mort.* 3.1).[50] The outrageous behavior (ὕβρις) of such people consists partly in their failure to "not at all remember about death." Menippus identifies this forgetfulness of death as the reason (τοιγαροῦν) that Croesus will "lament [οἰμώξεσθε] all those things that have been taken away" (3.2). The subsequent lament by Croesus,[51] Midas, and Sardanapalus of their respective goods (many and great possessions, gold, luxury) confirms Menippus's indictment.

Their wailing is a reminder that a person's behavior in death illumines how well (or not) one has lived. Lucian, through Menippus, thus suggests that living well is incumbent upon, and enhanced by, contemplating one's own death.[52] Like Qoheleth, Lucian insists that "to live always with death before their eyes" will enable people to cease their "vain [ματαίων] toil" (*Char.* 20).[53] By contrast, a failure to remember one's mortality results in becoming possessed (τυγχάνω) by one's mortal goods (*Men.* 12). Facing

---

Men. 17). Like the Egyptian Immortality of the Writers, Lucian underscores the fragility of monuments (*Cat.* 11).

49. Lucian's interest in living well is articulated in Menippus's quest to learn "what the best life is and what life someone especially wise would choose" (*Men.* 6). Given the salient perspective that death provides on living well, it is no coincidence that Menippus's quest leads him to Hades.

50. "Whenever we lament and moan [about] those memories above, Midas his gold, Sardanapalus [Asurbanipal] his great luxury [πολλῆς τρυφῆς], and I, Croesus, my treasures [θησαυρῶν], he [Menippus] laughs and reproaches us, calling us slaves and refuse" (*Dial. mort.* 3.1). Pluto also faults Menippus for mocking these people on account that they "mourn [λυποῦνται] great losses" (3.1).

51. "Many indeed, O gods, and great were the possessions [κτημάτων]!" (*Dial. mort.* 3.2).

52. This point is explicit in Lucian's *Charon*: "If they had realized at the very beginning that they were mortal and that after this brief sojourn in the world they would go away as from a dream, taking leave of everything above ground, *they would live more sanely and would be less unhappy after death*" (*Char.* 17, emphasis added).

53. For Lucian, one should cease toiling, since life does not endure forever, nothing people hold in honor is eternal, and one cannot take one's goods into death. At death, one's possessions are given to another (*Char.* 20).

one's mortality, in other words, has the potential to free a person from being enslaved to one's possessions.

Essential to living well is some type of detachment from one's possessions and a relinquishment of avarice. Menippus himself models this disinterest in material goods. Upon entering death he voluntarily offers his bag and stick[54] to Hermes and notes that he did not even bring his cloak (*Dial. mort.* 20.2). This readiness to leave behind his goods is the probable reason that Hermes calls him "best [ἄριστε] of men," invites him to take the privileged front seat near the helmsman, and to examine everyone entering the boat (20.2).[55]

His willingness to depart from his goods is, moreover, the chief cause of his ability to enter death and the afterlife without any of the weeping that characterizes others who die.[56] He is one of the few who actively welcomes death. When asked if he is "grieved to die [ἄχθῃ ἀποθανών]," he replies: "How so, when I was eagerly seeking [σπεύδω] death, even though no one invited [me]?" (*Dial. mort.* 20.11). Menippus and Diogenes are the only characters who enter death willingly, "not having to be forced or pushed" (4.2).

Lucian elsewhere proposes that the unwillingness to enter death is rooted in an attachment to one's possessions (*Cat.* 8, 14–15). The soul (ψυχή), maintains Micyllus, attaches itself (προσέχω) to gold, silver, clothing, and dinners and becomes unwilling to depart from them at death. The tie that binds people to such things is like an "unbreakable fetter" (ἄρρηκτός … δεσμός). In the journey to Hades, such people lament, are fearful, and seek to turn back (*Cat.* 14). Micyllus's willingness to enter death is due to not owning a farm, a communal house, gold, or furniture. For Lucian, death requires a parting from one's possessions, and the willingness to enter death is partially rooted in a detachment from one's goods. The *Dialogues* suggest that such detachment enables one not only to enter death willingly but also to live meaningfully.[57]

---

54. These two items are typical Cynic garb.

55. Menippus is the only person allowed to keep anything in death; Hermes tells him he may keep his independence, plain speaking, cheerfulness, noble bearing, and laughter (*Dial. mort.* 20.9).

56. Similarly, in *Cataplus*, poverty stricken Micyllus is one of the only ones with no need to lament during his transition to death (*Cat.* 20). Micyllus does offer a satirical lament over the loss of his scraps of leather, old shoes, and rotten sandals (*Cat.* 20).

57. Lucian elsewhere suggests that the rich, in comparison to the poor, "live a much more miserable [ἄθλιος] life than we" (*Gall.* 15; cf. 21).

The postmortem elimination of socioeconomic distinctions also has implications for the self-perception of the poor. Diogenes instructs Pollux:

> And to the poor [πένησιν] … who are many and grieved with their circumstance and are sorry for their poverty [ἀπορίαν], tell [them] neither to weep nor lament; describe in detail the equality of privilege [ἰσοτιμίαν] here, and that they will see the rich ones there no better than they are themselves. (*Dial. mort.* 1.4)[58]

As in 1 Enoch, reevaluating wealth from the perspective of the grave draws attention to its ephemeral nature. The transitory (and therefore limited) power of wealth is contrasted by Crates with the true "wealth" (κτῆμα) of wisdom[59] that lasts beyond the grave: "We therefore will possess wealth [πλοῦτον] even here, but they will have come carrying an obol" (*Dial. mort.* 21.4). Wealth is not only fleeting and transitory, but it fails to provide meaning for those who have it during their lives.[60] This failure to serve as a source of existential meaning is evident in the myriad problems wealth poses for its owners.[61]

An important implication of this reassessment of the value of possessions is that the absence of distinctions in the afterlife more accurately reflects reality than the presence of distinctions during one's life. Menippus hints at this very point in his refusal to ask Homer to describe what Nireus was like when he fought in the Greek army: "You speak to me of

58. Similarly, those who bewail their poverty (πενία) fail to see that after dying (which will come shortly), they will no longer worry (*Demon.* 8).

59. Diogenes and Crates inherit "wisdom [σοφίαν], independence [αὐτάρκειαν], truth, plain speaking [παρρησίαν], freedom" (*Dial. mort.* 21.3). "But the others didn't care about wealth such as this," laments Crates, "and no one attended to us, expecting to inherit [κληρονομήσειν] from us; but all were looking at gold" (21.4). Diogenes registers no surprise: "For having wasted away by luxury [διερρυηκότες ὑπὸ τρυφῆς], they were just like rotten purses; so that even if at some time someone put into them wisdom or plain speech or truth, it fell out immediately and wasted away, since the bottom couldn't contain it. … But the gold they would guard with teeth and nails and every instrument" (21.4).

60. On the ephemerality and fragility of wealth, see Lucian, *Tim.* 29, 36; *Char.* 18.

61. This point is a central motif in Lucian's *Gallus*. See especially *Gall.* 14–15, 20–25. Wealth is a source of worry (φροντίζω) for its owners (*Gall.* 20; cf. 21–22, 29, 31; *Tim.* 36). Riches corrupt one with luxury, and cause one to be envied (*Tim.* 36, 56). Wealth is, in short, a "source of irreparable misfortunes" (*Tim.* 56; cf. *Par.* 12). For a self-defense by the personification of Riches, see *Tim.* 38.

dreams, but I of the things I see and you now have" (*Dial. mort.* 30.2). Implicit in Menippus's quip is the suggestion that the present life is akin to a dream, whereas the postmortem existence is more real than the dream-like existence upon earth.[62] Lucian elsewhere characterizes life as a procession (πομπή) or play (δρᾶμα) in which Fortune (Τύχη) assigns people various roles (*Men.* 16). Death marks the end of the procession, and one must return one's costume to Fortune. One thereby returns to one's state before birth, and no one is different from his or her neighbor. This metaphor underscores both the brevity of life (compared with the afterlife) and the gifted nature of one's goods.[63] At any rate, Lucian's *Dialogues* proposes that to live in light of a perspective informed by death is to live without regard for the temporal (socioeconomic) distinctions that characterize life on earth.[64]

The reorientation provided by death also has implications for one's evaluation of greed. Avarice is the most common attitude that characters in the *Dialogues* display toward wealth.[65] Hermes complains to Charon that, in contrast to those who died long ago, many people dying now come "with their bellies and legs swollen with luxury" (τρυφή; *Dial. mort.* 14.2). Most of these people die on account of their wealth, apparently conspiring against each other (*Dial. mort.* 14.2). Wealth is considered by Charon to be "exceedingly much beloved" (14.2). Lucian disparages such greed, and his depiction of the afterlife reinforces this critique.[66]

Lucian's critique of avarice and his proposal of a detachment (both attitudinal and practical) from possessions diverge from Qoheleth's recommendation of enjoyment as a meaningful use of goods in light of death.[67] Both instructions, however, are rooted in the perception of the inability to

62. In *Charon*, Hermes likens life before death to a dream (*Char.* 17). In *Menippus*, the wealthy dead who are punished in Hades review their life "as if it were some dream" (*Men.* 12).

63. At death one "returns" (ἀποδίδωμι) what one was given (*Men.* 16).

64. The laws for behavior at banquets seek to enact this type of equality by erasing distinctions between the poor and rich (*Sat.* 17–18).

65. Lucian elsewhere criticizes barbarians by calling them "money-lovers" (φιλόπλουτος; *Dom.* 6). In *Saturnalia*, the rich are associated with "pettiness, love of money, greed," and other vices (*Sat.* 14).

66. The folly of those who pursue luxury is evident in their desire that their clothing be burned at their future gravesite and that servants adorn their gravesite with wreaths of flowers (*Nigr.* 30).

67. This critique of greed is a common trope among Cynics.

use goods after death. Lucian and Qoheleth thus illustrate how a similar perception of death can result in conflicting attitudes toward possessions and their use.

The Instability of Inheritance and the Distribution of Possessions

The creation of a will or testament is a potentially fruitful area to examine, since it is an act that stands at the intersection of death and possessions. An inheritance plays, moreover, a pivotal role in Luke 12:13–15 (the passage preceding the parable of the Rich Fool) and in two other Lukan parables (15:11–32; 20:9–16).

The construction of a will or testament and the closely related issue of inheritance receive considerable attention in discussions about death and possessions in ancient Egyptian, Greco-Roman, and Second Temple Jewish texts. These texts evince a range of diverse and conflicting views regarding, in light of death, the potential viability and meaningfulness of such a practice. The Testament of Abraham presents the construction of a will and distribution of one's possessions as an ideal use of goods, given death's potential imminence (1:4–5; 4:11; 8:11; 15:1, 7). Qoheleth, in contrast, highlights potential problems and uncertainties of inheritances in light of death (2:18–21; 5:12–13). Ben Sira offers advice on issuing an inheritance (9:6; 22:23; 33:23; 42:3) and, as I argued, proposes the commitment to one's will and testament as a productive use of possessions in light of death. In ancient Egyptian literature, transferring an inheritance was considered to be an appropriate means of handling one's possessions.[68] The only potential dilemma in Egyptian texts regarding an inheritance concerns riches that might be procured through dishonest means.[69]

---

68. Inheritances were typically passed along to sons, sometimes only to the firstborn (cf. the Memphite Theology, an Old Kingdom Pyramid text; the Story of Sinuhe, a Middle Kingdom prose tale [*AEL* 1:52–53, 231]). The Instruction of Prince Hardjedef, a didactic text, notes the importance of providing for the funerary priest, even noting that one "prefer him even to your [heir]" (*AEL* 1:59). The transmission of one's possessions often occurred when one was in "old age and near his death" (*AEL* 1:231). Ben Sira also recommends this as the time when one should distribute one's inheritance (Sir 33:23).

69. Heirs were not expected to be able to inherit wealth or possessions that had been acquired unjustly. Whereas the "brave bestows wealth on the just," the "cheat cannot retain his plunder." This royal inscription on the poetical stela of Merneptah is

In contrast to Ben Sira and the Testament of Abraham, Lucian's *Dialogues* highlights numerous problems and uncertainties associated with an inheritance. Frequent references are made to people scheming to inherit the property and riches of wealthy individuals. Such schemers, described on one occasion as "the ones who contemplate the estate" (*Dial. mort.* 15.1), are the central preoccupation of four successive dialogues (15–18). Lucian consistently identifies greed as the primary motive of those who pursue the inheritances of others (*Dial. mort.* 16.3), calling such greedy pursuit as "vain gaping [μάτην ἐπιχαίνω]" (15.1). Among the numerous examples he cites is the case of two rich (πλούσιος) cousins who "flatter one another for the property [κλήρος]" (21.1).[70]

Myriad examples illustrate the intrigues and conspiracies surrounding attempts to procure inheritances. The greed of heirs results, at times, in failed murder plots (*Dial. mort.* 17.1). Cnemon laments the fact that he died before he could inherit the possessions of Hermolaus and that Hermolaus instead inherited Cnemon's property upon the latter's death (18). Diogenes and Crates, by contrast, take pride in never having wished for someone's death in order that they might inherit possessions (21.3).

Death is understood to be a fitting (and hoped for) consequence for greedy pursuers of inheritances (*Dial. mort.* 16.1).[71] Pluto wishes that the young men who plot to divide up an older man's inheritance would meet an early death and that the old man would return to youth. Of the young men, he declares: "Let the wicked come now, dying wickedly, leaving behind, from the midst of their hopes, their dreamed of wealth" (15.2).[72]

In some instances the anxiety-filled quest for inheritances is itself identified as the cause of some deaths. Such is the case with Terpison who recounts: "and I would often lie sleepless with worry [φροντίς], because I was counting each one, and getting things arranged. To me, these things

followed by the explicit remark: "What a man has of ill-gotten wealth / Falls to others, not <his> children" (*AEL* 2:76; there is doubt about these last two lines).

70. In *Cataplus*, the tyrant Megapenthes is accused of killing Cydimachus and his children and taking their property (*Cat.* 8).

71. Pluto tells Terpison that his death (at the young age of thirty) is just since Terpison spent all his time plotting against Thucritus, an older man, "and waiting for his piece of land [περιμένων τὸν κλῆρον]" (*Dial. mort.* 16.1).

72. Pluto hopes that all young men who with eagerness anticipate the deaths of older men in order to come into their wealth will die before the older men do (*Dial. mort.* 17.5).

at any rate have also become the cause of death—sleeplessness and worry [φροντίς]" (*Dial. mort.* 16.4).[73]

Those who scheme to inherit wealth do not, however, hold a monopoly on greed. Avarice is also cited as the primary reason why some refuse to leave their property or wealth to heirs. Diogenes claims that the poisoning of Damis by his son was "not unjust" (ἄδικα), since Damis, though he had a thousand talents "and lived luxuriously" (τρυφάω) at ninety, would not even give his son four obols (*Dial. mort.* 22.7). Diogenes notes that the money-lender Blepsias "was first in accusing himself of much folly [ἄνοια], since he was guarding the money [χρῆμα] for heirs who were not at all related, the vain one [μάταιος] thinking he would live forever [ἀεὶ βιώσεσθαι]" (22.7).

In the *Dialogues*, those who develop wills intentionally mislead people into thinking that they will be named as heirs of their estate. Polystratus admits, for example, that he maintained a public façade of making each of his admirers an heir, "but the true wills [ἀληθεῖς διαθήκας]" were different (*Dial. mort.* 19.3).[74] Even when there is congruity between what is promised and the contents of a will, death might prevent one's intended heir from inheriting one's fortune. The two rich (πλούσιος) cousins Moerichus and Aristeas named each other as their respective heir. Yet after both died on the same day, their properties (κλῆρος) passed to two relatives who had no idea they would receive such things (21.2).

Conflicting views exist in the Second Temple period concerning whether establishing a will (and providing an inheritance) is meaningful, given death's inevitability.[75] In Ben Sira and the Testament of Abraham, constructing a will/testament (and specifying the recipients of one's inheritance) reflects an attempt to secure control in the face of death; providing an inheritance can also function meaningfully as a potential vehicle of remembrance. Lucian's stories illustrate, on the other hand, the inability to

73. Lucian often identifies wealth as a source of worry (*Gall.* 20; cf. 21–22, 29, 31; *Tim.* 36).

74. People had lavished affection on the elderly Polystratus because he was rich and childless (*Dial. mort.* 19.3). His true heir (κληρονόμος) was not anyone from his family (γένος) but rather a "pretty boy" that Polystratus had bought. Simylus is glad to learn that none of the others inherited anything from Polystratus (*Dial. mort.* 19.4).

75. I acknowledge the problematic use of the term "Second Temple" when speaking of an author like Lucian who technically postdates this period. I use the term only because I find it more helpful than others in referring to the period during which most of the texts I analyze in this project were composed.

predict with any certainty how someone will distribute one's inheritance. It is only with the reading of the will (διαθήκη) that one can be certain of one's true intentions regarding the identity of someone's heir(s).[76] Both Qoheleth and Lucian highlight the fragile and undependable aspects of an inheritance. Whereas Qoheleth focused upon the inability to control who would inherit one's goods, Lucian draws attention to the uncontrollable aspects faced by the potential heirs of an inheritance.[77]

Death and Possessions in Seneca's *Moral Epistles*

The numerous missives comprising Seneca's *Epistulae Morales* are apt comparative texts for Luke's parable of the Rich Fool.[78] Seneca's lifespan (4 B.C.E.–65 C.E.) and the date of his epistles (63–65 C.E.) place them in the same social milieu as Luke-Acts.[79] Luke's second volume even mentions Seneca's brother Gallio (Acts 18:12, 14, 17). As examples of moral discourse, the epistles come close to the type of wisdom literature we explored in chapters 2 and 3. The sapiential tenor of Seneca's letters is evident in the ubiquity of terms such as *philosophia*, *philosophus*, *sapientia*, and *sapiens*.[80] Seneca considers wisdom (*sapientia*) to be chief among the

76. Lucian elsewhere notes that the only time the sons of Rome speak the truth is in their wills (*Nigr.* 30). This they do, he asserts, so that they will not have to face the consequences of their truth-telling.

77. In *Cataplus*, the tyrant Megapenthes is unhappy to discover in Hades that his failure to leave instructions for his gold results in his enemy inheriting it (*Cat.* 8). Instead of enjoying his wealth or sharing it with others, Megapenthes kept his treasure (θησαυρός) buried. An anonymous person in Hades laments the fact that his heir will "squander" the talents left to him; another person questions who will inherit his vines (*Cat.* 20).

78. Bovon (*L'Évangile Selon Saint Luc*, 256) notes the existence of numerous parallels between Luke's parable of the Rich Fool and Seneca, but he does not cite any specific texts from Seneca.

79. After being banished in 41 C.E., Seneca returned in 49 as the appointed tutor of Nero. He committed suicide in 65.

80. For *philosophia*, see *Ep.* 4.2; 5.2, 4, 5; 8.7, 9; 14.11, 12; 15.1; 16.3, 4, 5; 17:2, 5, 6; 20.2; 21.9; 24:26; 29.12; 30.3; 37.9; 38.1; 40.7; 45.1, 2, 3; 48.10, 12; 50.9; 52.9; 53.10, 12; 55.4; 58.26; 71.7; 72.3; 73.1, 9; 78.3; 82.5, 7; 88.24, 25; 89.1, 4, 6, 8–11, 16–17; 90.1–2, 20, 35; 94.1, 2, 4, 13, 24, 31, 39, 47; 95.10, 12, 37, 61, 64; 98.17; 99.14; 102.20; 103.4; 106.12; 108.1, 17, 22, 23, 25, 30, 36; 111.4; 115.18; 117.33; 123.17. For *philosophus*, see *Ep.* 16.5; 39.2; 40.2; 52.13; 94.9; 95.23; 100.1; 108.6, 9. For *sapientia*, see *Ep.* 6.4; 9.1, 14, 22; 11.1, 6, 7; 14.10, 13; 16.1; 17.8, 10; 20.5; 22.16; 26.3; 29.3; 52.6; 59.16; 67.14; 71.7,

virtues, and the person who possesses it has "attained … the most important goal" (*Ep.* 93.8).[81] Most relevant to this study is the attention Seneca's letters give to death, possessions, and the integral relationship between these two themes.[82]

Perceptions of Death

Death is a recurrent theme in Seneca's epistles, leading him at one point to refer to "all my deadly talk about death" (*Ep.* 58.37).[83] His letters express many of the same attitudes toward death that I have pointed out in other texts, including the unavoidability and inevitability of death, death as the ultimate equalizer, and the universal fear of death.

Seneca repeatedly mentions and emphasizes the unavoidability and inevitability of death.[84] Death is the one certainty amid a life that is otherwise filled with uncertainties.[85] He concurs with Cato's statement that the entire human race, "both that which is and that which is to be, is condemned to die" (*Ep.* 71.15). In short, everyone must suffer loss and death:

19, 30; 72.6; 75.9, 10; 79.8; 81.23; 85.32; 88.33; 89.4, 5, 6; 90.26; 93.8; 94.50; 95.1, 7, 13, 60; 98.9; 104.19; 117.1, 25, 31, 33. For *sapiens*, see *Ep.* 9.3, 8, 13, 15, 16; 11.1; 14.8, 14, 16; 17.9; 29.7; 30.8; 31.2; 59.8; 66.18; 70.4, 14; 71.30; 72.8; 73.13; 81.14; 85.38; 87.18; 88.26; 92.14, 24; 93.10; 94.52; 109.2–3; 117.8.

81. Seneca distinguishes between wisdom (the "perfect good of the human mind") and philosophy (the "love of wisdom and the endeavor to attain it") (*Ep.* 89.4).

82. For an introduction to Seneca, see Anna Lydia Motto, *Seneca Sourcebook: Guide to the Thought of Lucius Annaeus Seneca in the Extant Prose Works—Epistulae Morales, the Dialogi, De Beneficiis, De Clementia, and Quaestiones Naturale* (Amsterdam: Hakkert, 1970). Cf. Susanna E. Fischer, *Seneca als Theologe: Studien zum Verhaltnis von Philosophie und Tragödiendichtung* (Beiträge zur Altertumskunde 259. Berlin: de Gruyter, 2008); Shadi Bartsch and David Wray, eds., *Seneca and the Self* (Cambridge: Cambridge University Press, 2009).

83. I follow the English translations in Seneca, *Epistulae Morales* (trans. Richard M. Gummere; LCL; 3 vols.; Cambridge: Harvard University Press, 1925).

84. *Ep.* 4.9; 70.27; 71.15; 77.11–13; 78.6; 91.19; 93.12; 99.7–9, 22; 101.14–15; 117.21. Death is the "ultimate and inevitable end" (*ultimum ac necessarium*; *Ep.* 117.21).

85. "The period which lies between our first day and our last is shifting and uncertain. … Everything is slippery, treacherous, and more shifting than any weather. All things are tossed about and shift into their opposites at the bidding of Fortune; amid such a turmoil of mortal affairs *nothing but death is surely in store for anyone*" (*Ep.* 99.9, emphasis added).

"You will die, not because you are ill, but because you are alive" (78.6; cf. 91.19). Death strikes people at all different ages (70.3–4) and in myriad different ways (66.42–43), but it does strike all. None can escape from its grasp, since death is an integral aspect of being human (99.8).[86] One cannot be born and not die.[87] People die differently, but they all succumb to the experience of death: "The methods of ending life are different, but the end is one and the same. Death has no degrees of greater or less, for it has the same limit in all instances: the finishing of life [*finesse vitam*]" (66.13).

The brevity and fragility of life underscore the potential imminence of death. The time a person has to live is scant, and time passes more quickly as a person ages (*Ep.* 48.12; 49.4; 58.23). The fragility of life is further evident in the multiple and unpredictable opportunities to die unexpectedly (4.8). Fortune is capable of ending life just as she indulged a person's life (4.7).[88]

Although not all people experience death equally, death does make all people equal. As in Lucian's *Dialogues*, death functions as an ultimate equalizer in its elimination of any and all distinctions between people. Death is "the point where the prosperous man is upset, and the point where the unfortunate is set free" (*Ep.* 110.4). People who are "unequal at birth" become "equal in death [*pares morimur*]" (91.16). Death levels everyone (99.8–9).

Despite the universality of death, most people, in Seneca's view, fear death and are unwilling to face their own mortality.[89] There is no place, he claims, where one can be free from the fear of death (*Ep.* 82.4). This fear, often manifest in the hope or attempt to prolong one's life, makes a peaceful or contented life impossible (4.4–5), for people who fear death "are unwilling to live, and yet they do not know how to die" (4.5).

---

86. "Whoever complains about the death of anyone, is complaining that he was a man. Everyone is bound by the same terms" (*Ep.* 99:7).

87. "He who is privileged to be born, is destined to die" (*Ep.* 99.8).

88. "Do not trust her seeming calm; in a moment the sea is moved to its depths. The very day the ships have made a brave show in the games, they are engulfed. Reflect that a highwayman or an enemy may cut your throat; and, though he is not your master, every slave wields the power of life and death over you" (*Ep.* 4.7–8).

89. *Ep.* 4.9; 58.23; 77:11, 16–20; 82.16, 23; 85.26–27; 91.19–21; 102.26; 104.25, 33. Diogenes also speaks of the fear of death hanging over everyone (*Ep.* 28.5).

Seneca consistently stresses the need for everyone, both young and old (*Ep.* 12.6), to face death and one's own mortality.[90] Confronting death entails both a willing readiness to die and contemplation of one's mortality throughout life. Seneca insists that one must, throughout life, prepare to meet death (82.8).[91] Each day should be regarded as one's last (12.8; 93.6). He cites the example of Pacuvius, who, he claims, held a regular burial sacrifice for himself in which he was "carried out to burial every day," while eunuchs sang: "He has lived his life, he has lived his life!" (12.8–9).

The proper attitude toward death is not fear, Seneca avers, but scorn (*contemno*; *Ep.* 75.14). He accordingly counsels Lucilius: "Despise death [*contemne mortem*]. There is no sorrow in the world, when we have escaped from the fear of death" (*Ep.* 78.5–6). Elsewhere he writes, "Death ought to be despised [*contemni*] more than it is wont to be despised" (82:16).[92] In addition to despising death, one is to consider and meditate upon it. One's heart "is never more divine than when it reflects upon its mortality" (120.14). Contemplating one's inevitable death can allow one to be calm in the face of its ever-present possibility (4.9).[93]

In addition to contemplating death, one must not fearfully flee its arrival. People such as Socrates model how to face death honorably (*Ep.* 70.9).[94] Socrates not only confronted his own death nobly but also remained in prison to free humankind from "the fear of two most grievous things, death and imprisonment" (24.4–5).[95] The brave endurance of

90. *Ep.* 4.3–6, 9; 24; 58.23; 63.16; 67.8–10; 69.6; 70.9; 74.30; 76.28–29; 77.14–15, 19; 78.5–6; 80.5–6; 92.35; 93.12; 104.25, 33; 117.21; 120.14–15.

91. So, too, does Diogenes, who emphasizes the need to practice (μελετάω) how to die (Diogenes, *Ep.* 39.3, 13).

92. One should not fear death precisely because it inspires us with fear (*Ep.* 4.3).

93. "Why do you voluntarily deceive yourself and require to be told now for the first time what fate it is that you have long been laboring under? Take my word for it: since the day you were born you are being led thither. We must ponder this thought, and thoughts of the like nature, if we desire to be calm as we await the last hour, the fear of which makes all previous hours uneasy" (*Ep.* 4.9).

94. Though see Lucian for a portrait of Socrates as a coward before death (*Dial. mort.* 4.1).

95. Facing death honorably may, at times, require suicide. He discusses whether one should commit suicide if one is awaiting certain death or being tortured (*Ep.* 70.7–15). Suicide is honorable in some cases ("the foulest death is preferable to the cleanest slavery," 70.21) but not in all (70.20–26). Seneca's own suicide (in 65 C.E.) shows that these discussions were not esoteric reflections of adiaphora.

death is a glorious feat, ranking "among the greatest accomplishments of the human mind" (82.17). Examples of those who have "despised death" (*contempores mortis*) are many (24.11).[96] The greatest proof of a lofty soul is that it is not afraid to depart the body at death (120.15). Ideally, one will not only face death but also welcome its arrival.[97]

Seneca maintains that facing and overcoming fear of death is possible if a person can perceive death accurately. Fools, for example, fear death because they believe that the transition to it is a "dangerous reef" (*Ep.* 70.2). Knowing that death is not evil, however, enables one to face it and not be fearful (82.13–14, 23; 85.26–27). In fact, the only evil aspect of death is the fear that precedes its arrival (104.10). The natural inevitability of death is another reason adduced for facing its arrival calmly. Since death "visits each and all … what does it matter for how long a time you avoid that which you cannot escape?" (93.12). By highlighting the naturalness of death, Seneca underscores the irrationality involved with fearing it. The fear of a disease is understandable, yet the fear of death "is not fear of a disease but of nature" (78.6).

Seneca is uncertain with regard to what happens to a person after death and ambivalent about the existence of an afterlife. On the one hand, he suggests the possibility that death utterly annihilates (*consumo*) one, after which "nothing mortal remains" (*Ep.* 24.18; 93.10). In this scenario death is a return to what one was before birth.[98] Although he does not fear such "nonexistence [*non esse*]," he does admit that it is death's greatest disadvantage (54.4–5; 65.24; 99.30.). His own lack of fear of this state of nonbeing is due to a dual recognition that nonexistence is merely a return to what one was before birth (65.24) and that there is no suffering after

96. In addition to Socrates, he mentions Scipio, Mucius, and Cato. The latter "had the will to die" (*Ep.* 24.6, 10). Seneca states that he cites these examples "for the purpose of encouraging you to face that which is thought to be most terrible" (24.9).

97. On the other hand, Seneca warns against pursuing death (*Ep.* 117.21–24). He cites Epicurus approvingly: "It is absurd to run towards death because you are tired of life, when it is your manner of life that has made you run towards death." Seneca understands this quote to be a critique of "those who crave, as much as those who shrink from, death" (24.22). "Nothing is baser," he claims, "than to pray for death" (117.22). One who prays for death, he contends, does not really wish to die, since one is capable of taking one's own life at any time (117.24). One does not seek out death, but one is to be prepared and welcome its advent.

98. "It is all the same; you will not be, and you were not" (*Ep.* 77.11; cf. 54.4–5).

death (54.5).[99] "If we are annihilated," he writes, "nothing remains; good and bad are alike removed" (24.18).

On the other hand, Seneca entertains the possibility that death does not annihilate but rather "strips us bare [*exuit*]. If we are then released, there remains the better part, after the burden has been withdrawn" (*Ep.* 24.18). In this scenario one can enjoy a postmortem existence with the gods (102.22). This experience exceeds that lived on earth: "These delays of mortal existence are a prelude to the longer and better life" (102.22–23). A person's mortal life is a preparation for "another birth" (102.23). In short, death is for Seneca "either the end, or a process of change" (65.24).

One thing of which Seneca is certain is that the soul departs the body at the moment of death.[100] The soul, furthermore, cannot perish (*Ep.* 71.16).[101] Precisely whither the soul goes is, however, not clear. One possibility is that the soul enters a "better life, destined to dwell with deity amid greater radiance and calm" (71.16). An alternative possibility is that the soul "without suffering any harm to itself, [is] mingled with nature again, and will return to the universe" (71.16).[102]

Wealth and Possessions

Most of Seneca's comments on wealth appear in the form of criticisms of greed, pleasures, and luxury.[103] He frequently derides greed (*aviditas*) and avarice (*avaritia*),[104] identifying these twin "chronic" vices with an insatiable hunger for more wealth and possessions. He considers the following to be an especially "effective" proverb: "The greedy mind is satisfied by no gains" (*Ep.* 94.43). "Having much" indeed leads one to desire more, "but he who has enough has attained that which never fell to the rich man's lot—a stopping-point" (119.6). Some people "crave [*concupisceret*] something

---

99. Before and after death there is "a deep peace," and one's experience after death will be the same as that before death (*Ep.* 54.5).

100. *Ep.* 70.12; 82.12; cf. 76.25; 86.1; 92.33; 102.22–23; 120.15. Diogenes describes death as the departure of the soul (ψυχή) from the body (σῶμα) (39.3, 8–9, 28–29).

101. For an extended treatment of the soul, see *Ep.* 113.

102. He also recognizes the possibility that the soul might enter the body of another person or animal (*Ep.* 108.18–21).

103. On the public display of luxury in Rome, see Karl-Wilhelm Weeber, *Luxus im alten Rom: Die öffentliche Pracht* (Darmstadt: Primus, 2006).

104. *Ep.* 7.7; 19.7; 75.11, 14; 76.4; 90.36, 38–39; 94.23; 95.33; 104.20; 108.9–11; 110.9; 115.16.

more after obtaining everything" (119.8). Yet instead of making people rich, money "always smites men with a greater craving for itself. ... He who possesses more begins to be able to possess still more" (119.9).[105] One is thus never content, living instead as a "slave to greed" (110.9).[106] Such slavery makes greed a hindrance to meaningful living.

Seneca frequently castigates luxury,[107] often associating this vice with greed.[108] Like avarice, luxury only teaches one to "crave more [*maiora cupere*]" (*Ep.* 16.8). Avarice and luxury are both relationally disruptive, breaking "the bonds that hold mortals together" (90.36). Greed and luxury are, in addition, contagious; a luxurious friend augments one's own covetousness (7.7).[109] A recurring target of Seneca's ire is gluttony (95.24–25; 108.14–16), the luxurious indulgence of food (18.11–12; 94.22; 110.11–18; 119.13–14). He contrasts those who live in luxury with those who toil (96.5), indicating a preference to live among the latter (82.2).[110]

Closely related to Seneca's repudiation of luxury is his denunciation of pleasure (*voluptas*) and those who submit to it (*Ep.* 114.23; cf. 51.8; 74.14–15; 110.10). He identifies the service of pleasure as the "source of all evil" (110.10). He accuses people of seeking "pleasure from every source" (95.33) and hopes that "minds [will] instead be removed from allurements of pleasure [*voluptatem*]" (51.5). Pleasure presents the same trap as luxury: those who sink themselves into it find that "what was once superfluous to

---

105. "Suppose that the property of many millionaires is heaped up in your possession. Assume that fortune carries you far beyond the limits of a private income, decks you with gold, clothes you in purple, and brings you to such a degree of luxury and wealth that you can bury the earth under your marble floors; that you may not only possess, but tread upon, riches. Add statues, paintings, and whatever any art has devised for the satisfaction of luxury; you will only learn from such things to crave still greater" (*Ep.* 16.8).

106. Plutarch also identifies greed (πλεονεξία) as a source of an insatiable hunger for more wealth (*Cupid. divit.* 2–3).

107. *Ep.* 7.7; 16.8; 71.15; 73.23–25; 74.18–19; 82.2, 10; 90.18–19, 36; 94.23; 95.16–18, 33, 42; 96.5; 97.1; 112.4; 114.3, 9, 25; 115.8–18; 119.15; 122.3–14; 124.3.

108. "Luxury," he maintains, "is precipitated into greed" (*Ep.* 95.33).

109. Seneca here identifies luxury with "the world," telling Lucilius that he "must either imitate or loathe the world" (*Ep.* 7.7).

110. For a positive evaluation of toil, see *Ep.* 95.18. On one occasion he describes toil negatively: "Work is not a good [*Labor bonum non est*]. Then what is a good? I say, the scorning [*contemptio*] of work. That is why I should rebuke men who toil to no purpose [*in vanum*]" (*Ep.* 31.4; cf. Qoh 2:19).

them has become indispensable" (39.6).[111] People thereby become "slaves of their pleasures [*voluptatibus*] instead of enjoying [*fruuntur*] them" (39.6).

As he does with life itself, Seneca accentuates the fragile nature of wealth and possessions. Their ephemeral nature, he points out, is rooted in their status as (divine) gifts.[112] At one point Seneca identifies "God, who is the Father of us all," as the source of these gifts (*Ep.* 110.10).[113] The status of goods as divine gifts has implications for the identity of the true owner of such goods. As Seneca avers, "what Chance has made yours is not really yours" (8.10). A consequence, therefore, of viewing possessions as divine gifts is that they are able to be removed as easily as they are given (8.9–10). Although Seneca shares Qoheleth's understanding of possessions as divine gifts, the former does not join the latter in responding to this perception with explicit recommendations to enjoy possessions (see Qoh 2:24–26; 3:13; 5:17–18; 6:2).[114]

Seneca, like Lucian, establishes a close relationship between luxury and anxiety. Luxury cannot be obtained, he maintains, "except with wretchedness and anxiety" (*Ep.* 119.15). This path is in sharp contrast to the "laws of life" that are laid down by the "Builder of the universe" and that provide "well-being" (119.15). The craving for riches leads instead to "daily worry" and fear (14.18; 115.16). Such "daily worry" is, furthermore, in direct proportion to the measure of possessions a person gains (115.16).

---

111. See his citation of Epicurus: "Whoever does not regard what he has as most ample wealth, is unhappy, though he be master of the whole world" (*Ep.* 9.20). Seneca contrasts needs (provided by nature) with the superfluous (*supervacuus*). "It is the superfluous things for which men sweat, —the superfluous things that wear out togas threadbare, that force us to grow old in camp, that dash us upon foreign shores. That which is enough is ready to our hands. He who has made a fair compact with poverty is rich" (*Ep.* 4.10–11).

112. Seneca alternately refers to the source of such gifts as "God," "Jupiter," "Fortune," or "Chance."

113. God is said to have "placed ready to our hands those things which he intended for our own good; he did not wait for any search on our part, and he gave them to us voluntarily" (*Ep.* 110.10).

114. In his *Dialogues* Lucian also writes of possessions as divine gifts. In *Timon*, Hermes claims that divine gifts are not to be thrown away (*Tim.* 37). Zeus, the "Wealth Giver," distributes (διαδίδωμι) gifts such as wealth and gold to whomever he desires (*Sat.* 2, 14). Like Qoheleth, Lucian highlights the indiscrimate nature of such giving. Zeus sometimes sends away those who are good and wise and pours out wealth on the all-wicked and foolish men (Lucian, *Sat.* 3; cf. 11).

This fearful anxiety stymies the enjoyment of a person's goods, since one is perpetually trying to accrue more (14.18). Anxiety over wealth, the product of the pursuit of goods, renders a person incapable of enjoyment.[115] Possessing riches, Seneca argues, "means even greater agony of spirit than the acquisition of riches" (115.16). The price one pays (anxiety, danger, lost honor, personal freedom, and time) in pursuing certain objects indicates that some people regard themselves as the cheapest of all (42.7).

Seneca proposes moderation, simplicity, and contentment as alternatives and solutions to the vices of avarice and indulgence. He enjoins moderation as an ideal practice (*Ep.* 5.5–6; cf. 14.15.), particularly in the treatment of one's own body (8.5; 14.1–2).[116] One should even be willing to sacrifice one's body if reason, self-respect, and duty so demand (14.2).

Simplicity, a step beyond moderation but not yet at the point of poverty, is also recommended as a proper and healthy use of possessions (*Ep.* 8.5; 25.4). A person can be simple in eating, drinking, dressing, and furnishing one's home.[117] A lifestyle of simplicity is predicated upon an understanding that nature provides for a person's basic needs (bread and water); riches differ from basic needs in that they are not "essential." Seneca calls for a "return to the law of nature; for then riches are laid up for us. The things which we actually need are free for all, or else cheap" (25.4).

Seneca proposes contentment as the ideal attitude to have toward one's possessions and economic status. A person is to be content if one is poor.[118] True poverty, he asserts, is craving more than one has (*Ep.* 2.5).[119] He cites

---

115. "While he puzzles over increasing his wealth, he forgets how to use it. He collects his accounts, he wears out the pavement in the forum, he turns over his ledger, —in short, he ceases to be master and becomes a steward" (*Ep.* 14.18).

116. The body is only to be indulged for the purpose of good health (*Ep.* 8.5; cf. 14.1).

117. "Eat merely to relive your hunger; drink merely to quench your thirst; dress merely to keep out the cold; house yourself merely as a protection against personal discomfort. It matters little whether the house be built of turf, or of variously colored imported marble; understand that a man is sheltered just as well by a thatch as by a roof of gold. Despise everything that useless toil creates as an ornament and an object of beauty. And reflect that nothing except the soul is worthy of wonder; for to the soul, if it be great, naught is great" (*Ep.* 8.5).

118. He cites Epicurus approvingly: "Contented poverty is an honorable estate" (*Ep.* 2.5).

119. "What does it matter how much a man has laid up in his safe, or in his warehouse, how large are his flocks and how fat his dividends, if he covets his neighbor's

approvingly a saying of Epicurus, who identifies the road to riches not as the accumulation of money but as the subtraction of one's desires (21.7).[120] Seneca grants that riches are acceptable to possess if one possesses the proper attitude toward them. He enjoins a kind of mental detachment from one's possessions: "I would have you reach the point at which you possess it dauntlessly; this can be accomplished only by persuading yourself that you can live happily without it as well as with it, and by regarding riches always as likely to elude you" (*Ep.* 18.13). One can live amidst riches and be "truly great" if one is not spoiled by them (*Ep.* 20.10).

The Interplay of Death and Possessions

The interplay of death and possessions in the *Epistles* is to be understood within Seneca's broader concern, emphasized repeatedly, for the quality rather than the quantity of a person's life. A person should be concerned, he maintains, not with how long one lives but with how well one lives (*Ep.* 70.4–6).[121] Employing the analogy of a play, he notes that "it matters not how long the action is spun out, but how good the acting is" (77.20). In addition, a long life is not tantamount to a life well lived. Indeed, living nobly is often incompatible with living a long life (101.15). Seneca worries more about failing to live well than he does about death. In fact, "dying well means escape from the danger of living ill" (70.6). For Seneca, an essential component of living well is a person's attitude toward, and use of, possessions.

Pleasures, Luxury, and the Fear of Death

Seneca associates the fear of death with luxury (e.g., *Ep.* 122.3) and attributes this universal fear with the (equally universal) attachment to possessions. People fear death because it "seems to rob us of many goods and to withdraw us from the abundance to which we have become accustomed" (82.15). Pleasures and luxury are identified as two specific causes of the

---

property, and reckons, not his past gains, but his hopes of gains to come? Do you ask what is the proper limit to wealth? It is, first, to have what is necessary, and, second, to have what is enough" (*Ep.* 2.5–6).

120. Seneca imagines a garden whose pleasure (*voluptas*) is not the whetting of one's appetite but rather its quenching and slaking of one's thirst (*Ep.* 21.10).

121. "The point is, not how long you live, but how nobly you live" (*Ep.* 101.15).

fear of death (77.16–20). The reluctance to relinquish one's possessions makes people unwilling to depart from a life in which their possessions will remain. Seneca implies that developing a detachment from one's goods is a *sine qua non* of facing death. He stresses this point by insisting that rejecting pleasures (*voluptas*) and spurning wealth (*opes*) are necessary steps if one is to embrace and welcome death (104.25, 33–34). Even someone who is given over to luxury can endure suffering or want if one "ceases to shudder at death" (78.25).

Seneca links folly with greed and the attempt to prolong one's death. In addition to not being satisfied with their income, such people "grasp at the utmost space of time to which the life of man can be extended" (*Ep.* 120.17). He insists, however, that "we stand daily nearer the brink, and every hour of time thrusts us on towards the precipice over which we must fall" (120.17–18).[122] Seneca intimates that the reluctance to separate from one's possessions is integrally related to one's desperate attempts at prolonging life. It is as though one's life is inextricably bound up with one's possessions, and one's own death necessitates the death of the other. Freedom requires that a person is delivered from the twin fears of death and poverty (*paupertas*; 80.5–6).

The inseparability of a person's attachment to life and possessions is explicit in Seneca's hope that accurately perceiving death will enable people to let go of both of these. Understanding death rightly entails knowing that "whatever is will cease to be, and yet it will not perish, but will be resolved into its elements" (*Ep.* 71.13). A person who comprehends death in this way "would endure with greater courage its own ending and that of its possessions" (71.13–14).[123]

---

122. He continues, noting that death is not only in the future but "is happening at this minute, and a large portion of it has already happened; for it consists of our past lives. But we are mistaken in fearing the last day, seeing that each day, as it passes, counts just as much to the credit of death. The failing step does not produce, it merely announces, weariness. The last hour reaches, but every hour approaches, death. Death wears us away, but does not whirl us away" (*Ep.* 120.18).

123. Seneca notes that the process of everything being broken up and put together again is done by "the eternal craftsmanship of God, who controls all things" (*Ep.* 71.13–14).

Ingratitude, Insatiability, and the Fear of Death

Seneca identifies the fear of death as a source of despair for most individuals. People are driven to anguish by the ubiquitous and omnipresent threat of death (*Ep.* 74.3).[124] People also respond to death by passing "unfavorable judgment on Providence because life is short" (74.10). Seneca understands such comments as the source of ingratitude for divinely gifted possessions: "It is a result of complaints like these that we are unappreciative in our comments upon the gifts of heaven; we complain because they are not always granted to us, because they are few and unsure and fleeting" (74.11). Seneca links such ingratitude to a fear of death, and he associates both with apathy toward life and death (74.11). He characterizes this type of person as insatiable, since "no amount of prosperity can satisfy us" (74.11). The unending craving for the gifts of Fortune impedes a person's ability to be grateful for such gifts (74.7–8).[125] So also does craving after possessions stymie the capacity to reflect upon one's own mortality: "But how will a person take thought of his own end, if he craves all things without end? And yet there is nothing so essential for us to consider" (70.17–18).

Luxury and the Living Dead

Seneca understands death not as a single event but as a lengthy process that continues throughout one's entire life. He calls it a commonplace that "we do not suddenly fall on death, but advance towards it by slight degrees; we die every day" (*Ep.* 24.20).

> For every day a little of our life is taken from us; even when we are growing, our life is on the wane. We love our childhood, then our boyhood, and then our youth. Counting even yesterday, all past time is lost time; the very day which we are now spending is shared between ourselves and death. It is not the last drop that empties the water-clock, but all that which previously has flowed out; similarly, the final hour when we cease to exist does not of itself bring death; it merely of itself completes the

124. "For there is no quarter from which death may not approach" (*Ep.* 74.3).

125. Seneca contrasts this ingratitude with "virtue," which needs nothing, since "it is pleased with what it has, and does not lust after that which it has not. Whatever is enough is abundant in the eyes of virtue" (*Ep.* 74.12).

> death-process. We reach death at that moment, but we have been a long time on the way. (*Ep.* 24.20; cf. 120.18)

Seneca cites this drawn-out process of death as a reason for not needing to fear death.[126] One need not be afraid of mortality, since the death "of which we are afraid, is the last but not the only death" (*Ep.* 24.21).[127]

Although this slow death occurs in everyone, it is accelerated at an advanced pace in particular individuals, for Seneca considers certain people to already be dead despite the fact that they are technically alive. One who spends his life in idleness, for example, "has not lived; he has merely tarried awhile in life. Nor has he died late in life; he has simply been a long time dying" (*Ep.* 93.3–4). Such a person has not lived (in this case, eighty years) but merely "existed eighty years, unless perchance you mean by 'he has lived' what we mean when we say that a tree 'lives'" (93.4).

Those who live in luxury are singled out as the primary example of the living dead. In addition to causing some people to die (*Ep.* 71.15), luxury also facilitates, and contributes to, a living death. After noting that people who fear death are also given to luxurious banqueting, Seneca reflects that they are "not really banqueting; they are conducting their own funeral services" (122.3). Although still alive, they are carrion (122.4). These types, Seneca declares, are "as good as dead" (122.10). The person who, for instance, lies on a perfumed couch "is no less dead than he who is dragged along by the executioner's hook" (82.3). Even leisure, if it is without study, is a "tomb for the living man" (82.3–4).

Whereas living in luxury leads to a premature psychic death, living well enables one to live after death. The living dead stand in sharp contrast to the person who "dies before one's time but whose life has been complete" (*Ep.* 93.4). Such a person not only succeeds in living during his life but "exists even after his death" (93.4). Nor does one need to ask regarding such a person how long he lived, since "He still lives! At one bound he has

126. "Still, we mortals are also carried past in no less speedy a course; and this prompts me to marvel at our madness in cleaving with great affection to such a fleeting thing as the body, and in fearing lest some day we may die, when every instant means the death of our previous condition. Will you not stop fearing lest that may happen once which really happens every day?" (*Ep.* 58.23).

127. Elsewhere he notes: "For we are not suddenly smitten and laid low; we are worn away, and every day reduces our powers to a certain extent" (*Ep.* 26.4).

passed over into posterity and has consigned himself to the guardianship of memory" (93.5).

Lucian and Seneca

Jewish and Greco-Roman texts evince a contested conversation in which conflicting perspectives are offered regarding the proper use of possessions in light of the finality and inevitability of death. Each of these options for how one might employ possessions is shaped and influenced by a particular perspective of death.

The threat posed by the uncontrollable nature of death results in various attempts to secure some element of control and meaning. Many such efforts involve the use of wealth and possessions. Enjoyment, generosity, toil, inheritance, and remembering the dead are not merely disparate motifs but interrelated vehicles whereby people seek to find control (and thereby locate and negotiate meaning). In Lucian and Seneca, death frequently functions as an opportunity to reframe (and thereby reevaluate) how possessions are understood, valued, and used. As a reframing perspective, death functions rhetorically as a warrant for meaningful living.

This conversation on death and possessions is a possible but not a required or necessary one. As previously noted, it was possible to write about death apart from possessions and vice versa. Authors were not obligated to consider either motif in light of the other. To think of each in light of the other reflects, therefore, a choice to engage in a specific kind of conversation. In the following three chapters, I situate Luke 12:13–34 within this contested conversation on the interplay of death and possessions.

5
Luke 12:13–34: Participating in a Second Temple Conversation on the Interplay of Death and Possessions

Chapters 2–4 outlined a spectrum of diverse and often conflicting perspectives in Greco-Roman and Hellenistic Jewish texts regarding the intersection of death and possessions. The demonstration in these chapters of the highly variegated and contested nature of the conversation regarding death and possessions is important, given the tendency of scholarship on the Rich Fool parable to neglect this diversity.[1] The primary aims of chapters 5–7 are to situate Luke's parable of the Rich Fool and its immediate literary context within this Second Temple (primarily sapiential) conversation and to show the insights into the parable that such a reading strategy engenders.

Situating the parable within a Second Temple (primarily sapiential) conversation marks a methodological departure from most readers who interpret Luke's parable through a "prophetic" lens. Such readers, as noted in chapter 1, conclude that the story is a simple critique of avarice.[2] These

1. This trend does not appear to be decreasing, as is evident in Snodgrass, *Stories with Intent*, 390–93. He prefaces his analysis of Luke's parable with a section entitled "Helpful Primary Source Material," which includes no less than forty-four primary texts (biblical, Jewish, Greco-Roman, and early Christian). His classification of all these texts under the heading "Denunciations of Misuse of Wealth" implies that Second Temple texts only considered wealth in these terms. Most curious is the inclusion of Qoh 8:15 among these texts that denounce the misuse of wealth.

2. So, e.g., Cyprian, *De dominica oratione* 4.20; Cassian, *Institutes*, 7.30; Cyril of Alexandria, *The Gospel of Saint Luke*, 360; Talbert, *Reading Luke*, 141; Crossan, *In Parables*, 83; John R. Donahue, *The Gospel in Parable: Metaphor, Narrative and Theology in the Synoptic Gospels* (Philadelphia: Fortress, 1988), 177, 79; Malherbe, "The Christianization of a *Topos*," 132.

readings neglect, however, the similarities, allusions, echoes, and resonances between Luke's parable and Second Temple sapiential texts. I do not suggest that reading the parable as a sapiential narrative precludes other (e.g., prophetic) interpretations.[3] Indeed, prophetic and sapiential readings of the parable can be compatible and need not be mutually exclusive.[4] My aim is to show how reading Luke's parable in concert with sapiential discussions on death and possessions yields different insights than when the parable is read through the primary lens of prophetic texts. Reading the parable as a sapiential narrative draws attention, for example, not only to avarice but also to issues such as the meaningful use of possessions given the fragility of life and the uncontrollable aspects of death.

In chapters 5–7 I argue that Luke's parable and its immediate literary context illustrates, participates in, and reconfigures this Second Temple conversation regarding the intersection of death and possessions.[5] It participates in this conversation by evaluating the relative meaningfulness of six sapiential recommendations for utilizing possessions. Such evaluation is not explicit but rather occurs in Luke's positioning of the parable as a text in dialogue with sapiential traditions and within its current literary context. The parable and its immediate literary context reconfigures this

---

3. *Contra* Metzger, who supposes that one's understanding of the parable "depends entirely upon whether one is working primarily from within Israel's wisdom tradition or the prophetic or later apocalyptic traditions" (*Consumption and Wealth*, 76; cf. 72–73, 79). Metzger cites Sir 11:1–28 as the primary representative of Israel's wisdom tradition. He assigns the Epistle of Enoch to the prophetic/apocalyptic traditions and not to wisdom (76).

4. On the presence of sapiential motifs in prophetic literature, see Blenkinsopp, *Wisdom and Law*, 99; Johannes Fichtner, "Jesaja unter den Weisen," *TLZ* 74 (1949): 75–80; Johannes Lindblom, "Wisdom in the Old Testament Prophets," in *Wisdom in Israel and the Ancient Near East* (ed. Martin Noth and D. W. Thomas; VTSup 3; Leiden: Brill, 1955): 192–204; J. William Whedbee, *Isaiah and Wisdom* (Nashville: Abingdon, 1971); James M. Ward, "The Servant's Knowledge in Isaiah 40–55," in Gammie et al., *Israelite Wisdom*, 121–36; Samuel Terrien, "Amos and Chokmah," in *Israel's Prophetic Heritage* (ed. B. W. Anderson and W. Harrelson; New York: Harper & Bros., 1962): 108–15; William McKane, *Prophets and Wise Men* (SBT 44; London: SCM, 1965); Hans Walter Wolff, *Amos the Prophet* (Philadelphia: Fortress, 1973); R. N. Whybray, "Prophecy and Wisdom," in *Israel's Prophetic Tradition* (ed. R. Coggins et al.; Cambridge: Cambridge University Press, 1982), 181–99.

5. By focusing on *how* Luke engages these texts, I seek to avoid the perils described in Samuel Sandmel, "Parallelomania," *JBL* 81 (1962): 1–13; cf. Terence L. Donaldson, "Parallels: Use, Misuse, and Limitations," *EvQ* 55 (1983): 193–210.

conversation by appropriating certain motifs, such as the unjust acquisition of goods and the attempt to exert control in the face of death, and adapting these themes to Luke's particular existential, ethical, and theological concerns. It illustrates this conversation by virtue of its form as a narrative and, in particular, as a parable. As a narrative, Luke's parable is markedly different from the more common sapiential forms of propositional discourse. Notable differences accompany this shift in literary form, and one such difference will be explored in chapter 8 and the conclusion.

I am not arguing that Luke was familiar with every text surveyed in the previous three chapters,[6] but I do propose that he was cognizant of the conversation on death and possessions out of which these texts emerged and with which they are engaged. That Luke is familiar with this conversation is suggested by the number of shared motifs and specific lexical similarities that many of his parables have in common with texts whose focus is the intersection of death and possessions. Nor should Luke's familiarity be surprising since, as was demonstrated in chapters 2–4, this conversation transcended different Mediterranean cultures, occurring in Greco-Roman, Hellenistic Jewish, and even ancient Egyptian texts.[7]

Chapters 5–8 will proceed as follows. After highlighting the prominence of the twin motifs of death and possessions in Luke 12:13–34, I will demonstrate that Luke uses sapiential language to treat these motifs. He illustrates the interplay of death and possessions in sapiential terms and with tropes from Jewish wisdom traditions. Second, I will argue that Luke 12:13–34 evaluates the relative meaning of six specific sapiential recommendations for using possessions by framing their use within a broader context of death's inevitability, uncertain timing, and potential imminence. Third, I will demonstrate the ways in which Luke 12:13–15 and 12:21 interpret the parable. Fourth, I will show that reading Luke's parable in concert with sapiential texts (as opposed, for example, to prophetic texts) is a heuristic strategy for understanding why the rich man is called a fool. Finally, a comparison of Luke's parable with its parallel version in Thomas (Gos. Thom. 63) will, in addition to highlighting

6. I use "Luke" to refer to the text of the Third Gospel, not the historical author(s) of this text.

7. Luke's familiarity with this conversation may, furthermore, be due to the occurrence of sapiential motifs in various Jewish texts. Murphy points out that "the wisdom tradition formed part of the general cultural mix of Israel" and therefore "found expression, even unconsciously, in many works" (*Tree of Life*, 221).

Thomas's interests, further underscore the distinctive features of Luke's parable. Due to the overlap in some of the aforementioned topics, the same exegetical data will at times serve related motifs. We now turn to adduce reasons for reading Luke 12:13–34 as a sapiential discourse.[8]

Possessions and the Inevitability and Uncertain Timing of Death

Possessions and the inevitability of death are prominent features in Luke's parable of the Rich Fool. Possessions are referred to throughout the parable, first appearing in the opening line, whose subject is "the land" (ἀνθρώπου τινὸς πλουσίου εὐφόρησεν ἡ χώρα; 12:16).[9] As noted previously, this is the only parable unique to Luke whose subject in the parable's introduction is a "possession" and not a person.[10] Depicting the land as the subject makes clear its prominent role in the parable, but it also positions the man and his possessions as beholden to the land. The relationship between the man and his possessions dominates and drives the parable's plot. The first action in the parable (εὐφορέω) is that of the land (12:16), and all of the rich man's plans (12:17–19) are subsequent responses to the land's abundant production.

Each line of the parable highlights in some way the man's relationship to his possessions.[11] The land's abundant production (12:16) results in the man's declaration that he has nowhere to store his crops (καρπός; 12:17b). The lack of adequate storage space is the basis for his query regarding what he should do (12:17a), a question whose response constitutes his subsequent plans (12:18–19). He proposes to "pull down his barns [καθελῶ μου τὰς ἀποθήκας]" and build larger ones (12:18a). These larger barns will be sufficient, he imagines, to store "all my grain and goods [πάντα τὸν σῖτον καὶ

---

8. On Luke 12:13–34 as a unit, see Dupont, *Les béatitudes*, 183.

9. Translations obscure this nuance when they (mis)render the opening line of the parable as follows: "There was a rich man…." See, e.g., Linnemann, *Parables of Jesus*, 16; Luther's 1545 version; and the NAB English translation.

10. The subject of four parables is ἄνθρωπός τις (10:30; 15:11; 16:1, 19). Other subjects of the "L" parables include τίς γυνὴ (15:8); τίς κριτής (18:2); τίς ἐξ ὑμῶν (11:5); and ἄνθρωποι δύο (18:10).

11. Bailey sees goods as the point around which the parable is organized: "In the first stanza goods are *given*. In the central stanza they are *stored*. In the last stanza these same goods are *left*" (*Through Peasant Eyes*, 58, emphasis original).

τὰ ἀγαθά μου]" (12:18b).[12] The imagined "many goods [πολλὰ ἀγαθά]"[13] that he will have stored up for "many years [ἔτη πολλά]" (12:19a) is the reason for advising his soul to "rest, eat, drink, be merry" (12:19b). The man's possessions additionally serve as the means by which he will engage in these planned activities of enjoyment and rest.[14]

God's announcement both alludes to the man's possessions (ἅ δὲ ἡτοίμασας) and questions to whom they will belong (τίνι ἔσται; 12:20b).[15] God's speech comprises two halves: the first concerns the rich man's imminent demise ("Fool, on this night they are demanding your life from you"; 12:20a), and the second focuses upon the future of the man's goods ("and the things you prepared, to whom will they belong?"; 12:20b). Finally, it is possible that the unspecified subject of ἀπαιτοῦσιν ("they are demanding [back]"; 12:20a) are the "many good things" (πολλὰ ἀγαθά) of 12:19a.[16]

The man's possessions are consistently depicted in terms that evoke images of abundance. The verb used to describe the land's production, εὐφορέω, connotes an abundant yield.[17] The term χώρα can similarly refer to a vast area such as a "country, region," or "open country."[18] The land's

12. Several variants read "fruits" (γενήματα) instead of grain (A, F, M, N, Q, U, W, Γ, Δ, Θ, Λ, Ψ, minuscules 2, 28, 33, 565, 700, 1071, 1424).

13. A few variants read "fruits" (γενήματα) instead of "goods" (*, D, Π). One minuscule (1346) reads "my fruits and my good things."

14. A more subtle reference to possessions is the use of τί ποιήσω, a phrase Luke links on seven occasions to the use of possessions (3:10, 12, 14; 10:25; 12:17; 16:3; 18:18).

15. The referent of the relative pronoun ἅ are the "many goods" (πολλὰ ἀγαθά) in 12:19.

16. So Frank Stagg, *Studies in Luke's Gospel* (Nashville: Convention, 1965), 90–91; R. Wayne Stacy, "Luke 12:13–21: The Parable of the Rich Fool," *RevExp* 94 (1997), 288. The strongest evidence (it seems to me) for this argument is that πολλὰ ἀγαθά (12:19) is the nearest antecedent to ἀπαιτοῦσιν (12:20). Other possibilities that have been proposed for the identification of the referent of ἀπαιτοῦσιν include God (Fitzmyer, *The Gospel according to Luke*, 1:974, who reads it as a divine passive), angels (Metzger, *Consumption and Wealth*, 79), and a horde of disgruntled peasants (Mary Ann Beavis, "The Foolish Landowner: Luke 12:16b-20)," in *Jesus and His Parables: Interpreting the Parables of Jesus Today* [ed. V. George Shillington; Edinburgh: T&T Clark, 1997], 64–66).

17. LSJ, 737. Some variants read ηὐφόρησεν (A, D, G, K, L*, W, Γ, Θ, Λ, Π, Ψ, f^{13}, minuscules 28, 33, 579, 1071) or ἐφόρησεν (minuscule 700). The word is absent in one ninth-century uncial (M). The Vulgate renders εὐφορέω here with *uberes fructus*.

18. LSJ, 2015; cf. BDAG, 1093–94. Luke uses this same term to refer to the region

yield is so immense that the man decides to build larger (μέγας) barns to contain it (12:18). He envisions his goods as "many" (πολλά) and as lasting for the same amount (πολλά) of years (12:19). These details corroborate the description of the man as πλούσιος (12:16).[19]

Death's unpredictable timing and potential imminence play a significant role in the parable. Many scholars have observed the prominent role of possessions in the parable, and this emphasis is reflected in the common classification of the parable under the category of "wealth" or "possessions."[20] Relatively minimal attention, however, has been given to the important role in the parable of death's inevitability and uncertain timing.[21] Death is the focus of the first half of God's speech:

---

of Ituraea and Trachonitis governed by Philip (Luke 3:1) and the "country" of the Gerasenes (8:26). Charles Hedrick refers to the rich man's χώρα as a "large country estate" (*Parables as Poetic Fictions: The Creative Voice of Jesus* [Peabody, Mass.: Hendrickson, 1994], 154).

19. There is insufficient evidence, however, for the suggestion, so Beavis, "The Foolish Landowner," 64, that the man is an urban-dwelling absentee landlord.

20. So Cyprian; Bultmann, *History of the Synoptic Tradition*, 328; Jeremias, *The Parables of Jesus*, 128; David Wenham, "The Purpose of Luke-Acts: Israel's Story in the Context of the Roman Empire," in *Reading Luke: Interpretation, Reflection, Formation* (ed. Craig G. Bartholomew, Joel B. Green, and Anthony C. Thiselton; Scripture and Hermeneutics Series 6; Grand Rapids: Zondervan, 2005) 79–103; Eichholz, "Vom Reichen Kornbauern," 180–81. For classifications of the parable under "wealth" or "possessions," see, e.g., Halvor Moxnes, *The Economy of the Kingdom: Social Conflict and Economic Relations in Luke's Gospel* (Eugene, Ore.: Wipf & Stock, 1988), 146; Snodgrass, *Stories with Intent*, 389; Talbert, *Reading Luke*, 140; Christopher M. Tuckett, *Luke* (NTG; Sheffield: Sheffield Academic Press, 1996), 96; John Nolland, "The Role of Money and Possessions in the Parable of the Prodigal Son (Luke 15:11–32): A Test Case," in Bartholomew, Green, and Thiselton, *Reading Luke*, 190.

21. Those who mention the motif of death's inevitability and uncertain timing include Chrysostom, *In Eutropium* 2.5; Athanasius, *Apologia de fuga sua* 15; Calvin, *Commentary on a Harmony*, 148–49; Marshall, *Luke*, 146 n. 2. Those who identify death's inevitability as an important element in the parable include Jeremias, who contends that the parable's original eschatological warning (directed to a "fool obsessed by his possessions and unconscious of the sword of Damocles hanging over his head") was transformed "into a warning against the wrong use of possessions" (*The Parables of Jesus*, 106; cf. 165). Bornkamm suggests the man failed to know "that he must die" and that he did not "understand the folly of his cares, which devour body and soul instead of serving life" (*Jesus of Nazareth*, 88). Cf. Bovon, *L'Évangile selon Saint Luc*, 257; Dupont, *Les béatitudes*, 183.

ἄφρων, ταύτῃ τῇ νυκτὴ τὴν ψυχήν σου ἀπαιτοῦσιν ἀπὸ σοῦ.

Fool! On this night they are demanding (back) your life from you. (12:20a)[22]

Luke elsewhere uses ψυχή to refer to someone's life (Luke 6:9; 9:24; 17:33; Acts 7:14; 15:26; 27:10, 22, 37). Nor is it uncommon for Second Temple Jewish literature to employ ἀπαιτέω + ψυχή to refer to the phenomena of death. The Testament of Abraham uses the language of taking Abraham's ψυχή as a circumlocution for death.[23] Wisdom of Solomon uses ἀπαιτέω + ψυχή in its description of death as "the debt demanded of the life [τὸ τῆς ψυχῆς ἀπαιτηθεὶς χρέος]" (Wis 15:8). Diogenes describes death as the departure of the soul (ψυχή) from the body (σῶμα; *Ep.* 39.3, 8–9, 28–29).[24] For Philo, death is the point at which the soul becomes separate from the body (*Leg.* 1.105–108). When Seneca refers to death, the image he employs most frequently is this departure of the soul from the body.[25] Heraclitus similarly describes death as the ascent of the soul (ψυχή) from the body into heaven (*Ep.* 5.2, 3).

The imminent death of the rich man in Luke's parable is also implied in the second half of God's speech: "And the things you prepared, to whom will they belong? [ἃ δὲ ἡτοίμασας τίνι ἔσται]" (12:20b). The divine announcement of the man's imminent demise is a stark contrast to his previously stated intentions of living for "many years" (12:18–19). God's speech reveals these plans to be illusory pretensions of control.

---

22. Some variants read αἰτοῦσιν (p^{75}, B, L, Q, minuscules 33, 579) in place of ἀπαιτοῦσιν. Most interpreters read the speech as a reference to the man's death. See, e.g., Seng, "Der Reiche Tor"; Fitzmyer, *The Gospel according to Luke*, 2:971; Snodgrass, *Stories with Intent*, 398. Some dissent and see the speech as a reference to an eschatological judgment. So Jeremias, *The Parables of Jesus*, 165; David Peter Seccombe, *Possessions and the Poor in Luke-Acts* (Linz: Fuchs, 1983), 143; Madeleine I. Boucher, *The Parables* (Wilmington, Del.: Glazier, 1981), 127.

23. See, e.g., T. Ab. 7:8–9; 19:2–3; cf. 20:12. On one occasion, reference is made to taking Abraham's πνεῦμα (17:2–3).

24. Cited in Abraham H. Malherbe, *The Cynic Epistles: A Study Edition* (SBLSBS 12; Missoula, Mont.: Scholars Press, 1977), 165.

25. *Ep.* 70.12; 82.12; cf. 76.25; 86.1; 92.33; 102.22–23; 120.15.

Death and Possessions in the Parable's Broader Literary Context (Luke 12:4–34)

The importance of reading the parable in light of its immediate literary context is suggested by the numerous lexical and thematic similarities between the two. Extricating the parable from its literary context (12:13–34) obfuscates literary connections such as the motifs of death's inevitability and possessions.[26] A consequence of reading the parable in light of texts that focus on the interplay of death and possessions is drawing attention to the importance of the parable's literary context as a locus of meaning for the parable.[27]

Death and anxiety provide an introductory frame for Luke 12:4–34. The specter of death, ubiquitous in Luke-Acts,[28] appears in Jesus' warning

26. Scott is an example of treating the parable apart from its literary context (*Hear Then the Parable*, 127–40). Jeremias calls 12:13–15 a secondary addition but one that is nonetheless "necessary for the understanding of the parable" (*The Parables of Jesus*, 164–65; cf. 100). He does not, however, treat the subsequent discourse on anxiety. On the advantages of studying parables in their literary context, see Birger Gerhardsson, "If We Do Not Cut the Parables Out of Their Frames," *NTS* 37 (1991): 321–35.

27. Bultmann claims that Luke brought the parable, the preceding saying about inheritance, and the following sayings about anxiety together into one unified section (12:13–34) (*History of the Synoptic Tradition*, 324). "It cannot be doubted," he writes, "that Luke uses the apophthegm in 12:13f as an introduction to the parable" (193; cf. 335). He sees 12:13–14 as a unitary composition, since "Jesus' saying is intelligible only in reference to the question" (23). He classifies 12:13–14 as a scholastic dialogue (54). The dominical saying in 12:15 is formed as a transition from 12:13–14 to the parable (335; cf. 192–93, 23). The parable's application, beginning with οὕτως, is secondary, possibly does not occur in Luke's original text, and "is typical of secondary interpretation of similitude and parable" (178). The absence of this application in Codex Bezae and other manuscripts suggests to Bultmann that it may have been lacking in Luke's original text. Cf. Jülicher, *Die Gleichnisreden Jesu*, 2:614. Jeremias cites Luke 12:21 as the primary example of the parable's shift from the "eschatological" to the "hortatory," claiming that 12:21 moralizes the parable, blunting the "sharp edge of its warning" (*The Parables of Jesus*, 48). He avers that the absence of 12:21 in Thomas's version is further evidence of its secondary status in Luke's Gospel (106).

28. The shadow of death pervades Luke-Acts. Fourteen characters die (7:12, 15; 8:42, 49; 9:9; 23:32, 33; Acts 1:16–20; 5:5, 10; 7:57–60; 9:37; 12:2, 23; 20:9), as do several others in parables (12:20; 16:22; 19:27; 20:14–16; cf. 16:28). References are made to the deaths of Jesus (Acts 2:23, 36; 3:15; 4:10; 5:30; 7:52c, 10:39; 13:28; 25:19; cf. 1:3; 4:27; 5:28; 17:3; 26:23), Stephen (Acts 8:1a; 22:20), many others (Luke 2:26, 29, 36–37, 9:59; 11:47–51; 13:1, 4; 17:22; Acts 2:29; 5:36, 37; 7:4, 15, 19, 24, 28, 52b; 13:26), and

to fear not those who can only kill (ἀποκτείνω) the body but rather the one who is able to kill (ἀποκτείνω) and cast into hell (12:4–5).[29] The motif of fear (φοβέομαι), closely linked to anxiety, is mentioned four times in this opening statement (12:4–5) and plays an important role throughout Luke 12:4–34. The prospect of death is one of the potential consequences of being brought before the synagogues, rulers, and authorities (12:11). The death of a family member is the presumed catalyst for the inheritance at the center of the dispute preceding the parable (12:13–15). Death is later alluded to in the statement regarding the impossibility of extending one's life (12:25–26a). The brief lifespan of the grass in the field is also stressed: it is alive today and tomorrow cast into the oven (12:28).

Death is thus a significant motif in the episodes preceding and following Luke's parable. This prevalence of language about death in the immediate literary context of the parable suggests that the parable might also concern itself with this motif. God's speech confirms that this is the case (12:20).

How Luke speaks about death is just as important as the prominent attention he gives it. In Luke 12:4–34, death is understood as a given reality facing Jesus' audience. The latter are aware, and seem to be afraid, that they might be killed (12:4). The type of death envisioned here is an uncontrollable event, determined by the will—and violence—of another. Moreover, both people and God are capable of killing (12:4–5). It is this violent,

---

even animals (Luke 2:24; 8:33). Death is a danger for many characters (Luke 4:28–30; 7:2; 8:23; 13:31; 19:47; 20:19; 22:1–2, 33; cf. 9:22; 17:25; 18:31–34; Acts 5:33; 9:23–24, 29; 12:19; 14:5–6, 19; 16:27–28; 21:31; 22:4, 22; 23:12–15, 21, 27; 25:3; 26:10, 21; 27:10, 42; 28:3–4, 6; cf. Luke 4:34; Acts 28:4). Much of Jesus' teaching focuses on aspects of death (Luke 9:27; 10:19; 12:4–5; 13:3, 5; 20:28–32, 35–38; 21:18, 32), and his ministry consists of delivering people from death or its potential (Luke 7:2, 22; 9:38–42; cf. 4:40; 5:12–15, 18–26; 6:18; 7:21–22; 8:43; 9:11; 17:12). Luke employs myriad images to illustrate death (Luke 1:79; 2:34b–35; 3:9, 17; 9:23–24, 60; 11:44; 13:34; 17:2, 37; 20:18; 22:20; 23:33). His vocabulary for death includes six verbs: ἀποθνήσκω (8:42; 52, 53; 16:22; 20:28, 29, 31, 32, 36; Acts 7:4; 9:37; 21:13; 25:11); θνήσκω (7:12; 8:49; Acts 14:19; 25:19); τελευτάω (7:2; Acts 2:29) ἐκψύχω (Acts 5:5, 10; 12:23); κοιμάομαι (Acts 7:60; 13:36); ἀπολύω (Luke 2:29); the adjective νεκρός (7:15, 22; 9:7, 60; 15:24, 32; 16:30, 31; 20:35, 37, 38; 24:5, 46; Acts 3:15; 4:2, 10; 5:10; 10:41, 42; 13:30, 34; 17:3, 31, 32; 20:9; 23:6; 24:21; 26:8, 23; 28:6.), and the noun θάνατος (1:79; 2:26; 9:27; 22:33; 23:15, 22; 24:20; Acts 2:24; 13:28; 22:4; 23:29; 25:11, 25; 26:31; 28:18).

29. Dupont summarizes 12:2–12 as an "appeal not to fear human hostility" (*Les béatitudes*, 183).

unpredictable, and uncontrollable nature that likely underlies the fear to which Jesus repeatedly refers (12:4–5). The inability to prolong one's life further underscores death's uncontrollable nature. One is powerless in the snare of death's sovereignty. Death shatters any pretensions of control, as God's declaration to the rich man makes clear (12:20a). Death can function, furthermore, as a catalyst of family discord, as it does in the fraternal dispute about the inheritance (12:13–15).

The motif of possessions is also featured prominently in the parable's immediate literary context. It appears immediately preceding the parable in an inquiry regarding dividing a family inheritance (12:13–15). The transition between Jesus' response to this question and the parable is the admonition that life (ζωή) does not consist in the abundance of possessions (ὑπάρχω; 12:15b). Specific possessions such as food (τροφή) and clothing (ἔνδυμα) are both explicitly addressed (12:23; cf. 12:22) and alluded to (12:27, 28, 29, 30, 31) in the discourse following the parable (12:22–34). The ravens model the possibility of not hoarding possessions (12:24). The discourse concludes by recommending an alternative use of possessions (selling and giving to the poor), describing this act as an everlasting treasure, and arguing that one's heart will be set upon the kingdom if a person sells one's goods and gives them to the poor (12:33–34).

Other elements point to an important connection between Luke's parable and its immediate literary context. Five of the words that appear in the parable (12:16–21) are repeated in Luke 12:22–29.[30] Furthermore, Luke concludes the parable with a reference to θησαυρίζων (12:21), and both θησαυρόν (12:33) and θησαυρός (12:34) appear in the discourse's conclusion (12:22–34). Finally, διὰ τοῦτο ("on this account") in 12:22 indicates a sequential and dependent relationship between the parable and the subsequent discourse (12:22–34). Luke seems to intend that the parable be understood within this broader literary context, and this context deepens the parable's sapiential elements and its potential meanings.

30. These include φάγε (12:19) / φάγητε (12:22, 29); πίε (12:19) / πιήτε (12:29); ψυχή, ψυχήν (12:19, 20) / ψυχῇ, ψυχή (12:22–23); ἀποθήκας (12:18) / ἀποθήκη (12:24); and θεός (12:20; cf. 21) / θεός (12:24, 28).

Sapiential Elements in Luke's Parable

Reading the parable in light of wisdom texts is further warranted by the presence of sapiential motifs in the parable and its immediate literary context.[31] Several sapiential elements are present in Luke's parable, justifying Bornkamm's description of it as a text "in the style of the wisdom literature."[32] These sapiential characteristics include, in addition to the intersection of death and possessions, the use of the term παραβολή ("parable"; 12:16a), the man's soliloquy (12:17–19), and the use of the epithet ἄφρων ("fool"; 12:20a).

In the Greek Bible, παραβολή appears more frequently in wisdom texts than in any other type of literature.[33] The term is associated with other sapiential terms[34] and with Solomon, who is said to have written three thousand παραβολαί (1 Kgs 5:12, LXX). For these and other reasons, παραβολή has been classified as one of four types of wisdom literature.[35]

31. See Christopher M. Hays (*Luke's Wealth Ethics: A Study in Their Coherence and Character* [WUNT 275; Tübingen: Mohr Siebeck, 2010], 126–27) for a recent treatment that recognizes the important role of wisdom in understanding Luke 12.

32. Bornkamm finds it significant that Jesus speaks this parable without referring to apocalyptic images (*Jesus of Nazareth*, 88). Bovon identifies a list of specific elements in the parable that have an "equivalent" in Hebrew and Jewish wisdom (*L'Évangile selon Saint Luc*, 252).

33. Seventeen of the forty-five uses of παραβολή in the LXX occur in texts commonly assigned to the wisdom corpus (Psalms, Proverbs, Qoheleth, Ben Sira, and Wisdom). The term also appears in the prophets (12x), the Pentateuch (8x), historical books (5x), Tobit (2x), and Daniel (1x).

34. A wise person (σοφός) can understand a παραβολή (Prov 1:5–6); Qoheleth associates παραβολαί with σοφία, γνῶσις ("knowledge"), and ἐπιστήμη ("skill") (1:17; cf. 12:9); Ben Sira links παραβολαί both with σοφία and the intelligent (συνετός) person (1:25; 3:29).

35. Maurice Gilbert, *Les cinq livres des Sages: Les Proverbes de Salomon, Le livre de Job, Qohélet ou l'Écclésiaste, Le livre de ben Sira, La Sagesse de Salomon* (Paris: Cerf, 2003). In every case save one, παραβολή in the LXX is a translation of the Hebrew משל. For the classification of παραβολή as a subset of *mashal* see, e.g., Scott, *Hear Then the Parable*, 8–19, 35; cf. Snodgrass, *Stories with Intent*, 8; Alastair Hunter, *Wisdom Literature* (London: SCM, 2006), 33. Arland J. Hultgren classifies a parable as a subset of the rabbinic *meshalim* (*The Parables of Jesus: A Commentary* [Grand Rapids: Eerdmans, 2000], 6). For the Hebrew term , see George M. Landes, "Jonah: A *Māšāl?*" in Gammie et al., *Israelite Wisdom*, 138–46, 151 n. 8. Landes also discusses the relationship between "parable" and "mashal" (137, 145–46). On the use of the term παραβολή in Greco-Roman authors, see Marsh H. McCall, *Ancient Rhetorical Theories of Simile*

Furthermore, the "Jewish wisdom tradition" is recognized as one of the key components of Jesus' parables.[36]

Speaking to oneself is a motif that is frequently utilized in sapiential texts.[37] Although not distinctive to wisdom literature, this literary device is more prevalent in sapiential texts than other modes of writing. The monologue, for instance, is employed repeatedly in Qoheleth,[38] leading one scholar to call the book "the longest sustained monologue in the First Testament"[39] and another to call it the "nearest the Hebrew Bible gets to pure monologue."[40] Relevant to Luke's parable is Eunny Lee's observation that Qoheleth "repeatedly speaks of conversing *with his own heart* (1:16; 2:1; 3:17, 18; cf. 16)."[41] This literary device, the interior dialogue, appears also in nonbiblical wisdom literature, and Lee notes that Egyptian sapiential sources offer "the most pertinent parallels."[42] The soliloquy device appears also in Sir 11:19, a text that has not only an explicit focus on the intersection of death and possessions but also striking parallels with

---

and Comparison (Cambridge: Harvard University Press, 1969), 6–7, 18, 27, 147–55; George A. Kennedy, *Aristotle on Rhetoric: A Theory of Civic Discourse* (New York: Oxford University Press, 1991), 180. Cf. Hultgren, *The Parables of Jesus*, 9; Scott, *Hear Then the Parable*, 19–20.

36. So Hultgren, who considers eschatology the second major element (*The Parables of Jesus*, 10–11). Cf. Scott, *Hear Then the Parable*, 68. At the same time, it is important to keep in mind the point made by Katherine Dell, that some elements of Jesus' parables distinguished them from Israelite wisdom traditions (*'Get Wisdom, Get Insight': An Introduction to Israel's Wisdom Literature* [Macon, Ga.: Smith & Helwys, 2000], 164–65).

37. Michael Wolter highlights some of the parallels in Jewish wisdom literature (*Das Lukasevangelium* [HNT 5; Tübingen: Mohr Siebeck, 2008], 449).

38. See, e.g., Roland E. Murphy, who notes the presence of this activity in Qoh 1:16–17; 2:1, 15; 3:17 ("The Sage in Ecclesiastes and Qoheleth the Sage," in Gammie and Perdue, *The Sage in Israel*, 266).

39. Gary D. Salyer, *Vain Rhetoric: Private Insight and Public Debate in Ecclesiastes* (JSOTSup 327; Sheffield: Sheffield Academic Press, 2001), 176.

40. Harold Fisch, *Poetry with a Purpose* (Bloomington: Indiana University Press, 1988), 158.

41. Lee, *Vitality of Enjoyment*, 24. See also Jan Assman, "A Dialogue between Self and Soul: Papyrus Berlin 3024," in *Self, Soul and Body in Religious Experience* (ed. A.I. Baumgarten et al.; SHR 78; Leiden: Brill, 1998).

42. Lee makes specific reference to The Dispute Between a Man and His Ba and The Complaints of Khakheppere-Sonb: "Reflective wisdom literature of other ancient Near Eastern cultures likewise exploits dialogues (including internal dialogues) to explore contradictory realities and viewpoints" (*Vitality of Enjoyment*, 24 n. 46).

Luke's parable in 12:16–20. This literary device, although not distinctive to wisdom literature, is a characteristic feature of it.

In the Greek Bible, the term ἄφρων is frequently employed in sapiential literature, occurring almost exclusively in wisdom texts. Only four of its 133 uses in the Greek Bible appear in "nonwisdom" texts.[43] God's (θεός) only direct speech in Luke-Acts is sapiential in tone.

The discourse following the parable (12:22–34) also incorporates sapiential motifs, and it is not without reason that its content has been called "wisdom sayings."[44] The use of nature (birds and flowers) both as a source of theological insight and as a warrant for behavior is characteristic of "nature wisdom," one particular type of sapiential discourse.[45] One learns, in this discourse about God's benevolence for people, not from divine revelation but by observing the natural environment.[46]

Luke presents Jesus in 12:22–34 as the preeminent teacher of wisdom. The reference to Solomon (12:27) recalls both the most dominant figure in Jewish wisdom and the presumed author of Qoheleth and other wisdom texts.[47] It is relevant that early rabbinic and early Christian sources asso-

---

43. The term ἄφρων appears in Psalms, Proverbs, Qoheleth, Job, Wisdom of Solomon, Ben Sira, and Psalms of Solomon. The four "nonwisdom" texts in which it occurs are 2 Sam 13:13; Isa 59:7; Jer 4:22; 17:11.

44. So Bultmann, *History of the Synoptic Tradition*, 102–3.

45. On "nature wisdom" as one of the five types of sapiential material, see Collins, "Wisdom, Apocalypticism, and Generic Compatibility," 168. James L. Crenshaw describes "nature wisdom" as one of three types of wisdom material ("Method in Determining Wisdom Influence Upon 'Historical' Literature," *JBL* 88 [1969]: 132). Cf. John G. Gammie, "From Prudentialism to Apocalypticism: The Houses of the Sages amid the Varying Forms of Wisdom," in Gammie and Perdue, *The Sage in Israel*, 481. Origen describes Solomon's contemplation of nature as an example of his wisdom (*Princ.* 4.3.14).

46. So Seow, *Ecclesiastes*, 66.

47. God is said to have put wisdom (σοφία) in Solomon's heart (2 Chr 9:23). The king is said to have exceeded all other kings in riches and wisdom (πλούτῳ καὶ σοφίᾳ; 2 Chr 9:22). For links between Solomon and wisdom (σοφία), see 1 Kgs 2:35; 5:9, 14, 34; 5:14; 2 Chr 1:10–11; 9:3, 5–7, 22–23; 2 Macc 2:9. Solomon is also linked to φρόνησις (1 Kgs 2:35; 5:9; 10:4, 23, 24; 11:41) and is called φρόνιμος and σόφος (1 Kgs 2:46). The tradition attributes both proverbs (Prov 1:1; 10:1; 25:1) and psalms (72:1; 127:1) to Solomon. He is credited with speaking three thousand proverbs and five thousand songs (1 Kgs 5:12). Rabbinic sources that attribute Qoheleth to Solomon include Rabbah Leviticus (28.1, Soncino), Song of Songs Rabbah (1.6), and R. Simeon b. Menasia (b. Meg. 7a). The latter also assigns three thousand proverbs to Solomon.

ciate Solomon with parables.[48] The attitude in Luke 12 toward Solomon is thoroughly critical, comporting with Luke's critiques of Solomon elsewhere (11:31; Acts 7:47).[49] Jesus unfavorably compares Solomon's luxurious dress to the beautiful attire of the lilies (12:27).[50] In the discourse preceding the parable, Jesus calls himself a "greater" (πλεῖον) figure than Solomon (Luke 11:31). His greatness consists specifically in having "more" (πλεῖον) wisdom than Solomon (cf. 11:32).

The comparison of Jesus to Solomon serves an important rhetorical function in 12:22–24. Luke's presentation of Jesus as the preeminent teacher of wisdom gives the latter credibility to speak authoritatively on existential issues such as how one is to live meaningfully. At the heart of 12:13–34 is the interplay of death and possessions, a motif eliciting conflicting perspectives within Hellenistic Jewish texts. By presenting Jesus as superior to Solomon *in wisdom*, Luke establishes Jesus' perspective on death and possessions to be superior to that of Israel's former king. Because Solomon was traditionally cited as the author of many wisdom books, the supremacy of Jesus' wisdom is simultaneously a superiority of Luke's view of death and possessions over the views in works attributed to Solomon (e.g., Qoheleth).

Origen and Melito of Sardis attribute Proverbs to Solomon (Eusebius, *Hist. eccl.* 4.26; 6.25; cf. *Princ.* 4.2.4). In Codices Vaticanus, Sinaiticus, and Alexandrinus, Song of Songs is entitled "Song of Solomon." For attributions of Proverbs, Song of Songs, and Ecclesiastes to Solomon, see Song of Songs Rabbah 1.6; Augustine, *Doct. chr.* 2.8.13; Jerome, *Preface to Samuel and Kings*; Cassiodorus, *Divine Letters* 12. Origen assigns Ecclesiastes and the book of Wisdom to Solomon (*Princ.* 4.3.14; 4.4.6), but in the Muratorian Fragment, Ecclesiastes is attributed to Solomon's friends. Song of Songs Rabbah considers Solomon to be one of the ten authors of the Psalms (4.5). Solomon was also considered the author of Ecclesiastes in the medieval period (e.g., Peter Lombard, prologue to his *Commentary on the Psalter*).

48. 'Abot de Rabbi Nathan 1; Jerome, *Preface to Samuel and Kings*.

49. In Stephen's speech, Solomon is identified (and therefore critiqued) as the one who built a house for God (Acts 7:47). Solomon's decision to build the temple is denounced in Acts 7:48. The absence of Solomon in Luke's genealogy may be another slight toward the Israelite king.

50. References to Solomon's luxury abound in the Hebrew Bible (1 Kgs 10:10, 14, 21, 26; 1 Chr 29:28; 2 Chr 9:4, 9–10, 13–15, 20, 25–28). On the textual variants in 12:27, see Bruce Metzger, *A Textual Commentary on the Greek New Testament: A Companion Volume to the United Bible Societies' Greek New Testament* (4th ed.; Stuttgart: Deutsche Bibelgesellschaft/United Bible Societies, 1994), 136.

Sapiential language frames the discussion and illustration of death and possessions in 12:13–34. The multiple sapiential features provide further reason for reading Luke's parable in concert with wisdom texts. These sapiential elements invite us, furthermore, to read Luke's parable as a sapiential narrative and to read Luke 12:13–34 as a sapiential discourse.[51] Reading the parable in this manner engenders insights that do not result from other (e.g., prophetic) readings. It is to these insights that we now turn.

Appropriating and Reconfiguring Qoheleth and Ben Sira

Luke's parable resonates in multiple ways with the Second Temple (primarily sapiential) conversation regarding the intersection of death and possessions. The two most explicit of these resonances is the citation of Qoh 8:15 and the allusion to Sir 11:14–19. Three of the four specific intentions of the rich man (ἀναπαύου, φάγε, πίε, εὐφραίνου; 12:19) involve the same three Greek verbs used in Qoh 8:15 (φαγεῖν, πιεῖν, εὐφρανθῆναι).[52] This lexical similarity suggests a possible familiarity on the part of Luke with this saying in Qoheleth.[53] Luke's probable awareness of Qoheleth is buttressed by the likely knowledge of other Second Temple Jewish texts (e.g., 1 Enoch, Wisdom of Solomon) with Qoheleth.[54] The multiple parallels between Luke's parable and Sir 11:14–28 invite consideration of the ways in which the parable illustrates and reconfigures this text.[55] Specific similarities exist between Luke's parable and Sir 11:14–19.[56] Both texts share a

51. Walter T. Wilson suggests that texts "that are not primarily sapiential in character may be understood to take advantage of sapiential themes or conventions" (*Love without Pretense*, 2).

52. Codex Bezae retains only the first of these four imperatives from Luke 12:19, omitting "eat, drink, enjoy." Some combination of these words occurs in Epic of Gilgamesh 10.3; Tob 7:10; 1 En. 97:8–9; Euripides, *Alc.* 788–789; and Menander, *Frag.* 301.

53. *Contra* John Jarick, who maintains that, with the possible exception of Rom 8:20, no New Testament writer "ever betrays any familiarity with Ecclesiastes at all" (trans. *Gregory Thaumaturgos' Paraphrase of Ecclesiastes* [SBLSCS 29; Atlanta: Scholars Press, 1990], 2).

54. Interest in Qoheleth among Second Temple Jews is also evident in its appearance in Qumran scrolls (4Q109, 4Q110, 4Q468l).

55. So Bailey, *Through Peasant Eyes*, 63. Harrington (*Jesus Ben Sira*, 38) cites Luke's parable as a parallel to Sir 11:19.

56. So Skehan and Di Lella, *The Wisdom of Ben Sira*, 239; George W. E. Nick-

similar plot outline and four specific lexical parallels: a rich person with many goods (ἀγαθά) speaks in the first person about resting (ἀναπαύω) and feasting (φάγομαι) yet is unaware of the time of his death, an event that will separate him from his goods.

There are also notable distinctions between Luke's parable and Sir 11:14–19. The latter specifies that the rich man leaves his goods "to others" when he dies (Sir 11:19). The fate of the man's goods in Luke's parable, however, is uncertain and is the focus of the final question posed by God (Luke 12:20b). The parable does not assume what is a given in Ben Sira and Qoheleth, that death automatically results in the transfer of one's possessions to another.[57] Nor is the precise intimation of God's question at the close of the parable clear (12:20b). Absent in Luke 12:13–34 is the kind of lament that characterizes Qoheleth's response to the inherently uncontrollable nature of the transference of one's goods to another (Qoh 2:18–21; 5:12–13). One can, as I will argue below, read God's question to the rich man (12:20b) as a tacit judgment of the man's failure to adopt any of the sapiential recommendations regarding the use of possessions given death's inevitability.

The dilemma of Ben Sira's rich man is his ignorance regarding the length of his life and, therefore, how much time remains for him to feast on his goods. The possible imminence of his death might serve as a motive for wasting no time in enjoying his goods. As such, the potential lesson would be akin to the frequent recommendations in Qoheleth to enjoy one's goods before death ends this opportunity. The announcement of the man's imminent death in Luke's parable may similarly demonstrate the need to enjoy one's goods before dying (and not merely planning to enjoy them). Such would be the parable's function if it occurred in Qoheleth, namely, as an illustration of the need to enjoy one's goods in the present moment before death forever terminates such a possibility. But this is not the point of the parable in Luke's context. God's question concerning the future of the man's goods provides an opportunity to reflect upon the merits of the man's response to the land's production. Luke's parable provides the

---

elsburg, "Riches, the Rich and God's Judgment in 1 Enoch 92–105 and the Gospel according to Luke," *NTS* 25 (1978–1979): 324–344; Fitzmyer, *The Gospel according to Luke*, 2:973; Wright, "Parables on Poverty and Riches," 222. Hultgren suggests that Luke's parable might be "inspired" by Sir 11:18–19 (*The Parables of Jesus*, 105).

57. *Contra* Scott, who imagines that the man's goods will be inherited by the villagers (*Re-imagine the World*, 95, 131).

opportunity to consider and evaluate, in light of death's inevitability, the relative meaning of the rich man's choices regarding the use of his goods. More important, the parable's conclusion makes clear that the rich man's plans constitute a failure vis-à-vis his relationship with God (12:21). The parable thus also raises questions concerning the precise manner in which the man failed to be rich toward God.

The instructions issued in Sir 11:22–28, although not explicitly cited in Luke, are nonetheless relevant to his parable.[58] The abundant production of the land, viewed in light of Sir 11:22, can be understood as a divine blessing. God's appearance and query concerning the future fate of these fruits might support this view. Is God asking the rich man about the goods *because* they are a divine gift? At any rate, the view expressed in Sir 11:22 would suggest that Luke's rich man is pious (εὐσεβής), since he has (presumably) received a divine blessing.

The two sets of negative prohibitions (Sir 11:23–24) are also pertinent to Luke's parable. Ben Sira warns the one who receives a divine blessing against the twin dangers of greed (11:23) and self-sufficiency (11:24):

> *μὴ εἴπῃς τίς ἐστίν μου χρεία καὶ τίνα ἀπὸ τοῦ νῦν ἔσται μου τὰ ἀγαθά*
> *μὴ εἴπῃς αὐτάρκη μοί ἐστιν καὶ τί ἄπο τοῦ νῦν κακωθήσομαι*

> Do not say, "What is my need?" and "From this point on what goods will be mine?"

58. The considerable time I spend on the broader context of Qoh 8:15 and Sir 11:14–19 is due to my conviction that these two allusions in the parable are examples of metalepsis. John Hollander describes metalepsis as a literary reference to a "precursor text," the understanding of which is dependent upon the reader's knowledge of the broader literary context in which the precursor text appears (*The Figure of Echo: A Mode of Allusion in Milton and After* [Berkeley: University of California Press, 1981]). Richard Hays defines metalepsis as "a rhetorical and poetic device in which one text alludes to an earlier text in a way that evokes resonances of the earlier text *beyond those explicitly cited*" (*The Conversion of the Imagination: Paul as Interpreter of Israel's Scripture* [Grand Rapids: Eerdmans, 2005], 2, emphasis original). Cf. idem, *Echoes of Scripture in the Letters of Paul* (New Haven: Yale University Press, 1989), 14–21. David W. Pao uses the term "evocation" to emphasize "the fact that the scriptural tradition recalled in the use of certain key words may be more profound than the content explicitly noted in the quotations and allusions" (*Acts and the Isaianic New Exodus* [Tübingen: Mohr Siebeck, 2000], 7 n. 26).

> Do not say, "There is enough for me" and "From this point on will I be harmed at all?"[59]

Both sets of prohibitions seem applicable to Luke's rich man, whose initial response to the land's production reflects the attitude articulated in the first prohibition. The man, in other words, identifies a need (the lack of adequate storage) related to having more goods in the future. Of central concern in his monologue is the role of his goods and his anticipated enjoyment of them. His expectation that he will have enough goods "laid up for many years" mirrors the attitude in Ben Sira's second pair of prohibitions. The man exhibits no awareness of the possibility that he might be harmed, much less of the ultimate harm that so shortly awaits him.

These (and other) echoes and parallels suggest the likelihood that Luke's parable is influenced by sapiential texts.[60] This and the following chapters indicate *how* the intertextual relationships between these (and other sapiential) texts and Luke's parable invite one to read the latter as a sapiential narrative.[61]

Evaluating Sapiential Recommendations Regarding Possessions

Luke's parable and its immediate literary context participate in a Second Temple conversation on death and possessions by evaluating the relative merits (and meaningfulness) of six sapiential options for the use of possessions. Four of the sapiential recommendations regarding the use of

---

59. For the neuter τί as an adverb, see LSJ, 1798.

60. Benjamin D. Sommer defines "influence" as the way in which a text "evokes its antecedents, how one author is affected by another" (*A Prophet Reads Scripture: Allusion in Isaiah 40–66* [Stanford, Calif.: Stanford University Press, 1998], 6–7).

61. On the term "intertextuality," see Julia Kristeva, *Semiotiké: Recherches pour une sémanalyse* (Collections Tel Quel; Paris: Le Seuil, 1969), 113. Sommer understands intertextuality to refer to the "manifold connections between a text … and other texts" (*A Prophet Reads Scripture*, 6–7). Such connections may exist "whether the authors of the texts knew each other or not." Richard B. Hays and Joel B. Green define intertextuality as "the notion that every text embodies the interplay of other texts and so exists as a node within a larger literary and interpretive network" ("The Use of the Old Testament by New Testament Writers," in *Hearing the New Testament: Strategies for Interpretation* [ed. Joel B. Green; Grand Rapids: Eerdmans, 1995], 228). For the idea that every text is engaged in an interplay with other texts, see Michel Foucault, *The Archaeology of Knowledge* (London: Routledge, 1972), 23. Robbins claims that "every text is a rewriting of other texts" (*The Tapestry of Early Christian Discourse*, 30).

possessions in light of death appear in Luke's parable and its immediate literary context. Enjoyment (12:19), recommended throughout Qoheleth and in Ben Sira (11:19a–b), is the chief goal envisioned by the rich man in the parable (12:19).[62] The motif of inheritance is explicitly raised in the dispute preceding the parable (12:13–15) and is alluded to in God's question to the rich man regarding the future ownership of the man's goods (12:20b).[63] The giving of alms, frequently recommended in Ben Sira, is enjoined in Luke's discourse following the parable (12:33). The option of giving to God is framed in the language of "being rich toward God [εἰς θεὸν πλουτῶν]" (12:21) and creating "an unfailing treasure in heaven" (12:33). The two other sapiential options for the use of goods, generosity and hospitality, are not explicitly addressed in 12:13–34. Yet the man's failure to enact, let alone consider, generosity, alms, or hospitality is noteworthy, given their prominence both in sapiential texts and in Luke-Acts.[64]

Luke evaluates these six options regarding the use of possessions by framing them within a broader purview of life's fragility and death's inevitability, uncertain timing, and potential imminence. These motifs (enjoyment, inheritance, giving to God, generosity, hospitality, alms) thus play an important rhetorical function in Luke's parable and its immediate literary context, for Luke 12:13–34 illustrates whether, and how, possessions can be employed meaningfully within the specific purview of death's uncertain timing and potential imminence. Since the potential meaning of Luke 12:13–34 is related to its broader literary context, I will also attend to the ways in which these sapiential recommendations are treated in Luke-Acts.

Enjoyment

The legitimacy of enjoyment as a meaningful enterprise is a contested issue in discussions of the interplay of death and possessions. On the one hand, enjoyment is recommended as a fitting response to the uncertainties associated with death. Enjoyment is Qoheleth's primary recommendation in

62. See Qoh 2:24–26; 3:12–13, 22; 5:17–19; 7:14; 8:15; 9:7–10; 11:7–12:7.

63. Cf. J. D. Derrett, "The Rich Fool: A Parable of Jesus Concerning Inheritance," *HeyJ* 18 (1977): 131–51.

64. I consider alms and hospitality two specific types of generosity; alms refers to the giving or sharing with the poor; hospitality consists of providing help (whether in the form of goods, money, or provisions) to someone, usually a traveler. This latter act often occurs in one's own home.

response to the uncontrollable aspects of death.[65] Syriac Menander joins Qoheleth in proposing enjoyment because of the inability to use goods after death (Sy. Men. 368–376).[66] Egyptian texts, like Qoheleth, recommend enjoying possessions in light of death's inevitability, its uncertain timing, negative depictions of the afterlife, and the inability to enjoy goods after death.[67] Lucian is able to speak approvingly of eating (ἐσθίω) and drinking (πίνω), and he associates such activity with the happiest of deaths (*Par.* 57). He faults those who fail to enjoy their goods (*Char.* 17; *Cat.* 8, 17; *Tim.* 13–14). Other texts, however, critique enjoyment, frequently associating it with luxury, indulgence, or gluttony.[68] For instance, 1 Enoch associates "eating and drinking" with sinners (102:8–11); Seneca and Diogenes critique enjoyment, especially in its extreme forms.[69]

Luke joins such texts in evaluating the relative merit and meaning of enjoyment. A primary intent of the rich man is to utilize his possessions for the purpose of enjoyment (12:19), a plan articulated with an allusion to Qoh 8:15.[70] One can speak even more precisely about how Qoh 8:15 functions in Luke's parable. The rich man's stated intention (12:19) appears to endorse Qoheleth's specific recommendation to eat, drink, and be merry (Qoh 8:15; cf. 5:17). The man's plan (12:19) also echoes the general admonitions regarding enjoyment that both pervade Qoheleth (2:24–25; 3:12, 22a; 5:17; 8:15; 9:7–10; 11:8–9) and appear in Ben Sira (14:14–17). As such recommendations propose enjoying one's possessions, the man's plans to do likewise represent an effort to actualize these recommendations.

---

65. Qoh 2:24a; 3:12, 22a; 5:17; 8:15; 9:7–10; 11:8–9.

66. Tjitze Baarda, trans., "The Sentences of the Syriac Menander," in Charlesworth, *The Old Testament Pseudepigrapha*, 2:583–606.

67. On death's inevitability, see The Dispute between a Man and His Ba (*AEL* 1:165, 168); Statue of Nebneteru (*AEL* 3:18–22); Instruction of Ankhsheshonq 8.7–8, 13–14; on death's uncertain timing, see Admonitions of Ipuwer (*AEL* 1:157, 160); on negative depictions of the afterlife, see Stela of Taimhotep (*AEL* 3:62); on not being able to enjoy goods after death, see Petosiris (inscription 127; *AEL* 3:52); Tomb of King Intef (*AEL* 1:196–97).

68. The Harper's song from the tomb of Neferhotep explicitly repudiates the exhortation to enjoy life (*AEL* 3:115–16).

69. Diogenes, *Ep.* 39; Seneca. *Ep.* 9.20; 51.5, 8; 74.14–15; 95.33; 110.10; 114.23.

70. I am not persuaded by Eichholz, who insists that Qoheleth's statements on enjoyment are not apt parallels to the parable, due to the difference in their respective understandings of death (*Gleichnisse der Evangelien*, 187).

However, the relationship in the parable between death's inevitability and the enjoyment of possessions is fundamentally different than that in Qoheleth and Ben Sira. In these latter two texts, death functions as the principal warrant for enjoying one's possessions.[71] Qoheleth and Ben Sira recommend enjoyment *because of* their respective understandings of death (e.g., its inevitability, uncertain timing, and destruction of a person's being). Egyptian texts likewise recommend enjoying possessions because of the numerous uncertain and uncontrollable aspects of death.[72]

The plans of Luke's rich man, however, are not (ostensibly) rooted in any particular perception of death. On the contrary, he intends to enjoy life despite any regard or acknowledgement of his own mortality. Recommendations regarding the use of possessions in texts surveyed in chapters 2–4 result from specific perceptions of death. The rich man in Luke 12 evinces no awareness of his inevitable death, and this lack of consciousness regarding his mortality constitutes a sharp contrast both with sapiential texts such as Qoheleth and Ben Sira and the declaration of his death in the divine address (12:20a). In drawing the man's attention to his imminent demise, God's voice functions as a reminder of the insistence throughout sapiential texts on death's inevitability.

Furthermore, the character in Luke's parable only anticipates an enjoyable future. That this future never materializes demonstrates his *investment* (both economically and psychically) in the future. His focus on the future is evident in the use of seven verbs in the future tense: ποιήσω,[73] συνάξω,[74] ποιήσω,[75] καθελῶ,[76] οἰκοδομήσω, συνάξω, ἐρῶ. Only one of the eight verbs he uses is not in the future tense.[77] These verbs highlight the imagined and anticipatory nature of the man's acts. The energy he expends dwelling

71. So Crenshaw, *Old Testament Wisdom*, 144.

72. P. Ins. 17.4–7, 11–15; Dispute between a Man and His Ba (*AEL* 1:165, 168); Statue of Nebneteru (*AEL* 3:18–22); Instruction of Ankhsheshonq 8.7–8, 13–14; Admonitions of Ipuwer (*AEL* 1:157, 160); Stela of Taimhotep (*AEL* 3:62); Petosiris (inscription 127; *AEL* 3:52); Song from the Tomb of King Intef (*AEL* 1:196–97).

73. It is possible to consider this first use of ποιήσω as, alternatively, an aorist subjunctive.

74. Some variants have instead the aorist active infinitive συνάξαι (W*, Λ, f^{13}).

75. This word, along with much of 12:18 (including οἰκοδομήσω), is absent in p^{45}. Minuscule 33 only has the first letter (π) of this word.

76. P^{45} lacks the first four letters of this word.

77. The one exception is ἔχω (12:17). The five verbs in 12:19 are not in the present tense, but all of these words occur in the man's imagined future.

upon the future necessitates some level of detachment from his present. The focus in God's speech on the imminent present is a stark contrast to the man's imagined future existence.

Two elements in God's speech underscore the present imminence of the man's death. The demanding of the man's life (ἀπαιτοῦσιν), in contrast to the man's imagined actions, is a present activity. Moreover, this act will occur (or is already occurring) "on *this* [ταύτῃ] night" (12:20a).[78] God's speech not only shatters the man's assumption that he wields control over his destiny but also pulls him out of his imaginary future into the reality of the present.[79]

The man's removal from acting in the present marks a significant departure from Qoheleth, for whom one's present is one of the few (if only) guarantees one is given. The man's plans indicate a failure to heed the warning, pervasive in sapiential texts, that the future lies outside the sphere of a person's control.[80] The uncertain nature of the future is one of the reasons Qoheleth recommends enjoying goods in the present (Qoh 3:22). The man's plans to enjoy his goods in the future also diverge from the plans of Ben Sira's rich man, who intends to eat from his goods "now" (νῦν / עתה), rather than in a distant, imagined future (Sir 11:19a–b). Qoheleth advises enjoying goods in one's youth, since old age curtails one's ability to do so (11:8–9; 12:1–5). The divine announcement of the man's death illustrates this sapiential emphasis on the inability to predict the future with any degree of certainty.

The man's focus on the future highlights another difference between his actions and Qoheleth's advice. Although the man plans to enjoy his goods, he never is able to do so. The closest he comes to enjoying his goods is to plan such enjoyment. This is not a trivial distinction, since sapiential texts regularly impugn those who spend time planning for a future that they cannot control or may never experience. Seneca describes people for whom "the search for the superfluous means a great outlay of time" and who "have gone through life merely accumulating the instruments of life."

78. Jülicher cites the present tense of ἀπαιτοῦσιν as evidence for the "picture [*Vorstellung*] of the immediate execution [*Vollzuges*]" of the rich man (*Die Gleichnisreden Jesu*, 2:612).

79. For Dupont the man's *erreur fatale* is his failure to have reckoned with the "present life" (*Les béatitudes*, 185). Dupont connects the man's failure to give alms with this detachment from his present.

80. See, e.g., Jas 4:13–16; Seneca, *Ep.* 99.9.

Of these people "there is none whose life does not look forward to the morrow. … such persons do not live, but are preparing to live. They postpone everything." Seneca's reflection can be applied to the rich man in Luke's parable: "Even if we paid strict attention, life would soon get ahead of us; but as we are now, life finds us lingering and passes us by as if it belonged to another, and though it ends on the final day, it perishes every day" (*Ep.* 45.12–13).

Especially relevant to Luke's parable is Seneca's claim that the person who delays life in this manner "cannot stand prepared for the approach of death if he has just begun to live" (*Ep.* 23.10–11). The rich man embodies Seneca's observation that some people "only begin to live when it is time for them to leave off living" (*Ep.* 23.10–11). Lucian critiques those who fail to enjoy their wealth or goods. He faults the tyrant Megapenthes, who buries his treasure (θησαυρός) rather than enjoying or sharing it with others (*Cat.* 8). The personification of riches complains that her owners, instead of enjoying (ἀπολαύω) her, lock her up with bolts, keys, and seals (*Tim.* 13–14). Lucian especially targets those who die before they can enjoy their possessions. Some people collect (συναγείρω) riches but die before being able to enjoy (ἀπολαύω) them (*Char.* 17). One man groans because he regrets his failure to enjoy (ἀπολαύω) his money before dying (*Cat.* 17).

Interpreters who identify the man as a hedonist often overlook that he does not actually engage in any of his planned acts of enjoyment.[81] The

81. To regard the man's plans as a reflection of Qoheleth's recommendation is to call into question the identification, by Malherbe ("The Christianization of a *Topos*," 133, etc.) of the man as a hedonist. Others had also labeled the man a hedonist (e.g., Schlatter, *The History of the Christ*, 166–70), but Malherbe has been influential, and many (Wright, "Parables on Poverty and Riches," 222; Hock, "The Parable of the Foolish Rich Man," 181; Tannehill, *Luke*, 206; James A. Metzger, *Consumption and Wealth in Luke's Travel Narrative* (Biblical Interpretation Series 88; Leiden: Brill, 2007), 83; Hays, *Luke's Wealth Ethics*, 126) have followed his lead in viewing the man in like manner. Scott, on a variation of this theme, sees the man's speech as a sign that he is an Epicurean (*Re-imagine the World*, 130). Metzger roots his argument for hedonism in the fact that two of the four verbs in 12:19 are in the present tense (ἀναπαύου, εὐφραίνου) and therefore "hint not at sporadic but ongoing festivity" (*Consumption and Wealth*, 77–78). He reads too much into the tense of these verbs, as he does when he avers, on the basis of the use of aorist verbs in Qoh 8:15, that there is "no indication that Qoheleth recommends such celebration with regularity" (77). Metzger also sees the verb ἀναπαύου as a sign of hedonism, especially since this word is absent in Qoh 8:15 and Tob 7:10. For a rejection of characterizations of the rich man as a hedonist,

man only *intends* to enjoy his goods, and he thus fails to apply this specific counsel of Qoheleth and Ben Sira.[82] The inability to enjoy his goods (apart from his imagination) is a failure to adopt Qoheleth's most consistent advice regarding the meaningful use of possessions in light of death.[83]

The strongest argument against those who identify the man as a hedonist is the absence of any explicit critique of the man's intent to "rest, eat, drink, enjoy" within the parable itself. God's speech (12:20) critiques the man's assumption about having many years to live, but there is no overt rejection of the man's plans to *enjoy* his goods: ἄφρων, ταύτῃ τῇ νυκτὶ τὴν ψυχήν σου ἀπαιτοῦσιν ἀπο σοῦ· ἃ δὲ ἡτοίμασας, τίνι ἔσται; ("Fool! On this night they are demanding your life from you; and the things you prepared—to whom will they belong?").[84] Moreover, if Luke intended to depict the man as a hedonist, he would have likely used specific terms (e.g., ἥδομαι, ἡδονή) associated with such activity.[85] Luke does use the latter word pejoratively to critique a lifestyle ("the worries and riches and pleasures of life"; 8:14) that is more congruent with hedonism than the plans of the rich fool.[86]

---

see Jülicher, *Die Gleichnisreden Jesu*, 2:611; Hedrick, *Parables as Poetic Fictions*, 150; Dupont, *Les béatitudes*, 185.

82. Metzger thinks it likely that the man *does* enact his plan of enjoyment (*Consumption and Wealth*, 80). In order to read the parable this way, Metzger imagines that an interval of several months occurs between the man's plans (12:19) and God's announcement (12:20). Metzger's primary motive in reading the parable in this manner appears to be his desire to make sense of 12:20, which he reads as God's punishment of the rich man.

83. The rich man also fails to abide by the talmudic instruction: "Everyone must give an account before God of all good things one saw in life and did not enjoy" (y. Qidd. 4:12).

84. So Metzger, *Consumption and Wealth*, 83. Cadoux argues that the man's failure consists not in enjoyment but in toil: "The result of his systematic selfishness is that all his life has been not enjoyment but toil, and that all the results of his toil will be enjoyed by those for whom he cares nothing" (*Parables of Jesus*, 205).

85. The use of the term to describe eating and drinking in certain contexts (e.g., Tob 7:10) suggests that these activities could be hedonistic depending on how one engaged in them. Metzger contends that this Tobit reference does not connote hedonism, since it is "spoken in the context of a special celebration before marriage and not offered as a way of life to be pursued with regularity" (*Consumption and Wealth*, 77). For pejorative uses of the noun in the New Testament (the verb does not occur), see Jas 4:1, 3; Tit 3:3; 2 Pet 2:13.

86. Jülicher notes that φάγε and πιέ (12:19) occur in Luke 7:34 and Job 1:18, where they denote a feast "without an adjoining evil sense" (*Die Gleichnisreden Jesu*, 2:611). He understands εὐφραίνου as a "low level hedonism [*niedriger Genusssucht*],"

A further difficulty posed for those who maintain the rich man is a hedonist whose plans to enjoy his goods are indicted in the parable is the acceptance (tacit and explicit) Luke elsewhere shows of Qoheleth's recommendation to eat, drink, and enjoy. Luke depicts much of Jesus' teaching within a symposia setting, and not once does Jesus critique the feasting and drinking that accompanies such activities (Luke 5:29–39; 7:36–50; 11:37–54; 14:1–15:32). Jesus is rather depicted as partaking in the eating and drinking at these events.

Luke more broadly endorses enjoyment (15:23, 24, 29, 32) and the activities of eating and drinking.[87] Jesus describes his Father's kingdom as one in which people will eat and drink (22:29–30). Much of the critique leveled at Jesus' disciples concerns their eating (ἐσθίω) and drinking (πίνω; 5:30, 33). Jesus defends the disciples' eating (ἐσθίω) on one occasion by citing the precedent of David, who ate (ἐσθίω) the bread in the temple and gave the same to his companions (6:1–4). Jesus, in contrast to John, came "eating and drinking [ἐσθίων καὶ πίνων]" (7:34a). Jesus acknowledges that this behavior resulted in accusations that he was a "glutton and drunkard" (7:34b). The disciples are to "eat and drink [ἐσθίοντες καὶ πίνοντες]" what is given to them when in others' homes and to "eat [ἐσθίετε] the things set before" them whenever they are received into a town (10:7–8). A reader of the Rich Fool parable has not been prepared by the narrative to think negatively of eating and drinking. On the contrary, the primary critique of eating and drinking in Luke is offered by Jesus' opponents.[88]

In light of sapiential texts, the man's planned enjoyment is deficient for two reasons: it is postponed and not actualized, and it is not a response to any apparent awareness of his own mortality. As I will later show, his enjoyment is deemed additionally inadequate in light of Luke's gospel because it is envisioned as a solitary act apart from community.

---

a "genuine serenity [*echte Heiterkeit*]." The rich man, he avers, did not engage in continual eating and drinking for years on end.

87. Luke is the only New Testament Gospel that reflects an interest in the activity of enjoyment (εὐφραίνω). The term does not appear in Matthew, Mark, or John. Eight of its fourteen uses in the New Testament are in Luke-Acts.

88. Jesus' sole critiques are aimed at those who are "full now" (ἐμπεπλησμένοι νῦν) (6:25) and those who are anxious about what they will eat (12:22, 29). Cf. Luke 12:45, where Jesus faults those who eat, drink, get drunk, and beat other slaves. I take 17:27–28 not as a critique of eating, drinking, marriage, buying, selling, planting, and building but as a general description of human activity.

Inheritance

Luke's parable and its immediate literary context participate in a contested Second Temple (primarily sapiential) conversation regarding the legitimacy and meaningfulness of an inheritance. On the one hand, many texts endorse the development of a will or testament for the purpose of ensuring the transfer of one's goods to another. Proverbs considers leaving an inheritance to one's heirs to be the act of a good person (Prov 13:22).[89] The Testament of Abraham presents the construction of a will, and distribution of one's possessions as a meaningful act, given the potential imminence of death (T. Ab. 1:4–5; 4:11; 8:11; 15:1, 7). Ben Sira offers advice on issuing an inheritance (Sir 9:6; 22:23; 33:23; 42:3) and, so I argued, proposes commitment to one's testament as a meaningful act in the face of death's uncertain timing (Sir 11:20). Giving an inheritance is likewise considered a proper use of possessions in many ancient Egyptian texts.[90]

Qoheleth and Lucian, on the other hand, highlight the fragile and undependable aspects of an inheritance. Whereas Qoheleth focuses upon the inability to control who would inherit one's goods (Qoh 2:18–21; 5:12–13.), Lucian's *Dialogues* draw attention to the uncontrollable aspects faced by potential heirs of an inheritance. Greed causes characters in the *Dialogues* to scheme to inherit the property and riches of wealthy individuals. Such greed leads to the deaths of those schemed against and the schemers themselves.[91] Plutarch inveighs against the practice of misers providing inheritances to heirs because such wealth, rather than being enjoyed, is perpetually preserved (φυλάσσω; *Cupid. divit.* 7).[92] Plutarch also, echoing a similar concern in Qoheleth, mentions the likelihood of one's inheritance being taken by "some outsider, an informer or tyrant" (*Cupid. divit.* 7).

Luke's interest in this contested Second Temple conversation regarding an inheritance is evident not only in chapter 12 but also in two parables (15:11–32; 20:9–16). Luke 12 juxtaposes an individual seeking his share

---

89. According to the MT. The LXX reads: "A good person will inherit sons of sons."

90. See, e.g., the Memphite Theology (*AEL* 1:52–53); the Story of Sinuhe (*AEL* 1:231).

91. *Dial. mort.* 15.1–2; 16.1, 3–4; 17.1; 18; 21.1, 3. Scheming to acquire an inheritance is the central preoccupation of four successive dialogues (*Dial. mort.* 15, 16, 17, 18).

92. Plutarch likens such people to "earthen pipes," since they convey wealth to others and take nothing for themselves (*Cupid. divit.* 7).

of an inheritance (12:13) with a man about to die who (apparently) has not left an inheritance to anyone (12:20). The former episode (12:13–15) does not appear to identify any potential benefit of an inheritance.[93] As in Lucian's *Dialogues*, Luke depicts a case in which an inheritance engenders a familial conflict (cf. *Dial. mort.* 21.1; 22.7).[94] The fraternal dispute in Luke 12 over the inheritance reflects a concern that appears elsewhere in Luke. Conflict over an inheritance is a chief source of the elder brother's disdain regarding the father's treatment of his younger brother (Luke 15:11–32). In another parable, the desire for an inheritance is the primary motive for the murder of the intended recipient of the inheritance (Luke 20:9–16).[95]

Jesus' response to the brother's request to divide the inheritance signals a reluctance to participate in the fraternal dispute (12:14).[96] Implicit in Jesus' rejoinder is a lack of enthusiasm for pursuing one's share of inheritance as a meaningful enterprise. Like Lucian's *Dialogues*, Luke appears to identify greed (πλεονεξία) as the motive for the brother's question for his share of the inheritance (12:15; cf. *Dial. mort.* 15.1; 16.3; 21.1).

Luke's parable depicts a man who apparently has not prepared a testament or will. This neglect is implied in the question God puts to the rich man: "the things you prepared—whose will they be?" (12:20c).[97] Like Abraham in the Testament of Abraham, Luke's rich man demonstrates no acknowledgement of the potential imminence of his death, nor does he enact any plans for his demise such as constructing a testament or will. If, as in the Testament of Abraham, establishing a testament necessitates

---

93. For a thorough analysis of the textual transmission of this episode, see Tjitze Baarda, "Luke 12, 13–14: Text and Transmission from Marcion to Augustine," in *Judaism, Christianity and other Greco-Roman Cults: Studies for Morton Smith at Sixty* (ed. Jacob Neusner; 4 vols.; Leiden: Brill, 1975), 1:107–62; repr. in *Early Transmission of Words of Jesus: Thomas, Tatian, and the Text of the New Testament* (ed. Tjitze Baarda; Amsterdam: Boekhandel/Utgeverij, 1983), 117–72.

94. Hock situates the brother's question within Jewish inheritance laws ("The Parable of the Foolish Rich Man," 183).

95. Lucian speaks of the greed of heirs resulting in failed murder plots (*Dial. mort.* 17.4; cf. 21.3).

96. μεριστήν is a hapax legomenon in the New Testament. For textual variants related to this term, see Metzger, *Textual Commentary*, 135.

97. So Donahue, who sees God's final question (12:20b) as an inclusio with the question posed to Jesus in 12:13 (*The Gospel in Parable*, 178). The rich man's greed has prevented him, Donahue contends, from providing for his heirs. As a result, the man dies leaving "what will be a bitter dispute over the inheritance (cf. 12:13)."

facing one's mortality, then the rich man's apparent lack of one might suggest that he has neglected to reflect upon—and therefore face—the inevitability and uncertain timing of his own death.

Wills and testaments held an important function in the Greco-Roman society that formed part of the matrix out of which Luke's Gospel emerged.[98] John T. Fitzgerald contends that a will or testament revealed the true content of a person's character.[99] He cites a statement from Pliny the Younger, who remarks that people believed a will to be a mirror (*speculum*) of a person's character (*morum*; *Ep.* 8.18.1).[100] Hellenistic moralists and Roman jurists understood the making of a will to be a "moral obligation."[101] If this were the case, then to die without making a will would constitute a significant breach of a sociocultural moray. Transgressing this cultural expectation might be especially egregious if it were done by someone with the (apparent) quantity of possessions held by Luke's rich man.

Luke 12:13–34 represents one of many (sapiential) views regarding the legitimacy of establishing an inheritance as a meaningful act, given death's inevitability. Luke appears to view the transference of an inheritance through a will as a potentially meaningless use of possessions. It is bankrupt in its ability to provide meaning because the amassing of goods fails to enhance life (12:15). Luke joins Lucian in highlighting the conflict inheritances produce. It leads to fraternal strife (12:13; cf. 15:11–32) and, in a later parable, to both the conspiracy and committing of a murder (20:14). Luke thus differs from the Testament of Abraham, in which the making of a testament was presented, in addition to hospitality, as a primary way of finding meaning within the context of the uncontrollable facets of death. Luke will propose alternative uses of possessions as more meaningful in light of death's inevitability and potential imminence.

98. See John T. Fitzgerald, "Last Wills and Testaments in Graeco-Roman Perspective," in Fitzgerald, Olbricht, and White, *Early Christianity and Classical Culture*, 637–72; Edward Champlin, *Final Judgments: Duty and Emotion in Romans Wills, 200 B.C.—A.D. 250* (Berkeley: University of California Press, 1991).

99. Fitzgerald, "Last Wills and Testaments," 643.

100. Ibid., 640.

101. Ibid., 644.

GENEROSITY

The rich man's failure to share his goods with others is striking, given the recommendations in sapiential texts and Luke-Acts to be generous in sharing one's possessions.[102] Ben Sira recommends generosity because of death's uncertain timing and the impossibility of enjoying possessions after death (Sir 14:8–13). Egyptian texts also adduce the uncertain timing of death as a reason for sharing possessions generously with others.[103] Pseudo-Phocylides, a first-century Hellenistic Jewish wisdom text, cites both a person's mortality and the inability to take goods into the afterlife as warrants for being generous: "If you are rich, do not be sparing; remember that you are mortal [θνητός]. One cannot bring one obol or money into Hades" (109–110).[104]

Generosity with others is consistently recommended and practiced throughout Luke-Acts. Generosity with one's possessions is modeled by literary characters, both in the narrative of Luke-Acts (8:1–3) and in Lukan parables such as the Samaritan (10:30–37). For John the Baptist, repentance entails the generous sharing of clothing and food, and he claims these acts will enable a person to avoid judgment (3:11). The book of Acts depicts the community of believers engaged in various aspects of generosity. Among these is the daily distribution (τῇ διακονίᾳ τῇ καθημερινῇ) to widows (Acts 6:1–7), sending relief (διακονίαν πέμψαι) to believers in Judea in anticipation of a famine (Acts 11:28–30), and the supplying of Paul and his companion(s) with provisions by island natives (Acts 28:10).

When read within the twin context of sapiential texts and Luke-Acts, the man's lack of generosity appears as a stark failure.[105] The lack of generosity is especially significant, given both the claim that the man's storage

---

102. In light of the broader context of Luke's statements on wealth, Fitzmyer faults the man for failing to share his goods with others (*The Gospel according to Luke*, 2:972).

103. See, e.g., Instruction of Ankhsheshonq (12.5, 17–18; *AEL* 3:168–69).

104. For a first-century date for Pseudo-Phocylides, see Pieter W. van der Horst, "Pseudo-Phocylides Revisited," *JSP* 3 (1988): 15; Collins, *Jewish Wisdom*, 158. Walter T. Wilson places it between 100 B.C.E. and 100 C.E. (*The Sentences of Pseudo-Phocylides* [CEJL; Berlin: de Gruyter, 2005], 7). On the sapiential nature of Pseudo-Phocylides, see idem, *Mysteries of Righteousness: The Literary Composition and Genre of the Sentences of Pseudo-Phocylides* (TSAJ 40; Tübingen: Mohr Siebeck, 1994), 4–5. He classifies the work as a "gnomic poem" (*The Sentences of Pseudo-Phocylides*, 10).

105. Tannehill contends that the man fails because he could have shared his abundant crops as a "generous benefactor" (*Luke*, 206). Referring to the contrast in Sir

of goods was "for himself [ἑαυτῷ]" (12:21) and the subsequent proposal to give alms (12:33).

Giving to God

Neither does the rich man give his goods to God, a potential use of goods that Ben Sira enjoins in the face of death's uncertain timing (Sir 14:11b). Luke explicitly addresses this possibility of giving possessions to God in the parable's conclusion: although rich (πλούσιος), the man has failed to be "rich toward God" (εἰς θεὸν πλουτῶν; 12:16, 21). What, however, does being rich toward God entail? One clue is provided by the link between the man's poverty toward God with his act of "storing up for himself" (12:21). I will argue below that the man's failure to be rich toward God consists not only in the selfish orientation of his storage of goods but also in not abiding by Luke's proposal of alms as the optimal alternative for how one might give to, and be rich toward, God (12:21, 33; cf. 18:22).

Hospitality

Hospitality, another specific type of generosity, is also neglected by the rich man.[106] The absence of hospitality (or its intention), coupled with the man's lack of generosity, corroborates the claim in 12:21 that his storage of goods was "for himself." The lack of hospitality is significant in light of the emphasis sapiential texts and Luke-Acts give to this practice. Hospitality is, for instance, the chief virtue exemplified by Abraham in the Testament of Abraham (1:1–2; 2:2; 3:7–9; 4:1, 3, 6, 10; 17:7; 20:15; cf. 2:9).

Offering hospitality to others is a frequent occurrence in Luke-Acts. Luke does not employ the technical term for hospitality (φιλοξενία), but he depicts several episodes in which it is practiced.[107] Characters enact

---

31:5–11 between the "fool" who is "taken captive by gold" and the "rich man who is blessed," he notes that the latter "is generous."

106. Andrew Arterbury defines hospitality in the ancient Mediterranean as "the act of assisting one or more travelers for a limited amount of time. This assistance essentially consisted of provisions and protection" (*Entertaining Angels: Early Christian Hospitality in Its Mediterranean Setting* [NTM 8; Sheffield: Sheffield Phoneix, 2005], 6).

107. See, e.g., Luke 10:38–42; 11:5–8; 19:1–10 (cf. Luke 10:7); Acts 16:34; 17:7; 28:14, 30. For situations where people neglect to show hospitality, see Luke 9:35; 10:10.

hospitality by welcoming others into their homes and providing food for them.[108] It is not insignificant that the final sentence of Acts describes Paul as being in the habit of practicing hospitality by welcoming (ἀπεδέχετο) all who came to him (Acts 28:30).

Relevant to the claim in 12:21 that the rich man is not "rich toward God" is the function of hospitality (or its neglect) in Luke as a criterion by which people will be judged.[109] Jesus' instructions on banquet behavior includes the promise of a divine reward for those who show hospitality to the marginalized (14:12–14). Inviting the poor, crippled, lame, and blind to a banquet will result in being blessed (μακάριος) and repaid (ἀνταποδίδωμι) at the resurrection of the just (δίκαιος; Luke 14:12–14).[110] A person is repaid at the resurrection precisely because the invitees are incapable of repayment. An alternative social community is envisioned here, one based not on reciprocity but rather on the principle of mercy articulated in Luke 6:32–36. The man's storage of goods "for himself" is incriminating, given Luke's

108. Levi's first act as a follower of Jesus, after rising and leaving everything, is to provide a great banquet for him (5:29). Jesus is also invited into the home of a Pharisee, where he reclines (κατακλίνω) at table (7:36). Jesus later accuses this Pharisee of showing him a lack of hospitality, compared to that shown by the woman who anoints him (7:44–46). Another Pharisee invites Jesus to dine with him, and Jesus also reclines (ἀναπίπτω) at his table (11:37). Characters who welcome (ὑποδέχομαι) others include Martha, Mary, and Zacchaeus (10:38–42; 19:1–10). Hospitality also figures prominently in the parable of the Friend at Midnight (11:5–8). Hospitality is also practiced by characters in Acts: the jailer brings Paul and Silas into his home and feeds them (Acts 16:34); Jason entertains (ὑποδέχομαι) Paul and Silas (Acts 17:6–7); Publius welcomes (ἀναδέχομαι) and hospitably entertains (φιλοφρόνως ἐξένισεν) Paul for three days (Acts 28:7); and believers in Rome invite Paul to stay with them for a week (Acts 28:14).

109. The disciples are instructed to shake the dust off their feet as testimony against a town that does not welcome (δέχομαι) them (9:5; 10:10–11). The refusal of the Samaritans to welcome (δέχομαι) Jesus does not bode well for them, given this context of judgment (9:53). One metaphor employed to describe a postmortem fate is being welcomed into people's homes (16:9). Specific attention is given to welcoming and providing for people who are socially and economically vulnerable or marginalized. Welcoming (δέχομαι) a child in Jesus' name is tantamount to welcoming (δέχομαι) him and the one who sent him (9:48).

110. Jesus suggests that one will be repaid regardless of whom one invites. Inviting friends, relatives, or rich neighbors will result in being repaid by them (Luke 14:12). A similar point is later illustrated in the parable of Lazarus and the Rich Man (16:25).

understanding of the meal as a social event, one providing an opportunity to welcome and include the marginalized.

The rich man's lack of hospitality is noteworthy, given the parallels between the respective descriptions of this man and Abraham in the Testament of Abraham. Both men are "rich" (πλούσιος; T. Ab. 1:5; 2:11; Luke 12:16), each owns a "field" (χώρα; T. Ab. 2:1, 7–8; Luke 12:16), and to each death intrudes. Yet key differences obtain between the two men in regard to their use of possessions, for Abraham is consistently portrayed as one who "welcomed [ἐδέχετο] everyone" (T. Ab. 1:2; cf. 2:2). His welcoming of the "cripples and helpless" is significant in light of Jesus' instructions to invite such people to banquets (T. Ab. 1:2; Luke 14:12–14). Moreover, God and Michael give Abraham special treatment because of his hospitality; this virtue is a reason for his death being delayed (T. Ab. 4:1–7). The conclusion to the Testament of Abraham implies that his hospitality was also the chief reason for the eternal life that Abraham experiences (T. Ab. 20:15). Unlike Luke's rich man, Abraham does end up being rich toward God, and this status is due in part to the patriarch's hospitality.

Alms

The parable's immediate literary context indicates that Luke was aware of options for utilizing possessions that the rich man did not adopt. Chief among these is alms, the sharing of one's goods with the poor, and a third specific type of generosity. In Ben Sira, the giving of alms (ἐλεήμοσυνη) is repeatedly presented as an ideal use of possessions and a proper response to the poor.[111] In the literary context of the parable, alms are also Luke's primary recommendation for how a person is to use possessions in light of death's inevitability (12:33). One is first enjoined to sell one's possessions (πωλήσατε τὰ ὑπάρχοντα) and then to give alms (δότε ἐλεημοσύνην).[112] This proposal to sell one's goods and give alms has an important literary function in that it represents a constructive alternative to the rich man's failure to act in the parable.[113] He intends to collect, gather, and save instead of selling and sharing. Moreover, these planned acts are understood to be

111. Sir 3:14, 30; 7:10; 12:3; 16:14; 17:22, 29; 29:8, 12; 25:2; 31:11; 35:2; 40:17, 24.

112. Leaving (ἀποτάσσομαι) all one's possessions becomes a requirement for anyone who wishes to become a disciple of Jesus (Luke 14:33).

113. So Dupont, *Les béatitudes*, 183.

"for himself" and not for anyone else (12:21). He gives to no one else, and he does not (apparently) plan on doing so.

Luke's awareness of alms as an ideal use of possessions is evident elsewhere in Luke-Acts (Luke 11:41; Acts 9:36; 10:2, 4, 31; 24:17). The Gospel uses the technical term for alms only twice (ἐλεήμοσυνη; 11:41; 12:33), but there are important links between these two instances.[114] Jesus prescribes alms as the antidote to the greed (ἁρπαγή) and wickedness (πονηρία) of the Pharisees (Luke 11:41; cf. 11:39). This proposal is a precedent for Luke's subsequent recommendation of alms (12:33) as an alternative to greed (12:15). These parallels reflect and reinforce, furthermore, a specific belief that one's greed can be overcome by the act of giving alms.

The recommendation regarding alms in Luke 11:41 may also be intended as an antidote to the deadness of the Pharisees' lives, an accusation implicit in Jesus' description of them as unmarked graves (τὰ μνημεῖα τὰ ἄδηλα; 11:44).[115] In the statement that precedes the parable, Jesus notes that one's life (ζωή) does not consist in the abundance of one's possessions (ὑπαρχόντων; 12:15). Luke's use of ζωή and not βίος is significant here, given that every use of ζωή in Luke is linked with the use of possessions (10:25; 12:15; 16:25; 18:18, 30).[116] In the parable of the Samaritan, for example, the abundance of (eternal) life is connected to sharing one's possessions with someone in desperate need (and to showing hospitality; 10:25–37).

---

114. The technical term for alms is also used to describe the consistent practice of characters in Acts such as Dorcas/Tabitha (Acts 9:36) and Cornelius (10:1–31). The use of the imperfect ἐποίει in 9:36 suggests that giving of alms was an ongoing practice of Dorcas. It is possible that the tunics and clothing that Dorcas made were given away in the form of alms (9:39).

115. Their "unseen deadness" is evident in the fact that people walk over them without knowing it (Luke 11:44).

116. The first occurrence of the term highlights how hospitality and generosity are integral ingredients in loving neighbor and, therefore, in inheriting eternal life and living (10:25). Immediately preceding the parable of the Rich Fool, Jesus declares that one's life does not consist in the abundance of possessions (12:15). In the parable of Lazarus and the Rich Man, the latter is told by Abraham that he received his "good things" during his life and that Lazarus did not (16:25). Jesus' answer to the rich ruler's question of what must be done to inherit eternal life is that he must sell everything and give to the poor (18:18, 22). Those who have left homes or families for the kingdom of God will receive much more, both in this age and in "eternal life" (18:30). It is perhaps equally significant that none of the occurrences of the term ζωή in Acts are linked to the use of possessions (Acts 2:28; 3:15; 5:20; 8:33; 11:18; 13:46, 48; 17:25).

These direct associations between life and the use of possessions invite us to consider that Luke depicts his rich man as having begun to die long before the announcement of his imminent biological death. God announces the end of his βίος (12:20), but there is a sense in which his ζωή had already begun to die. An unspoken implication of 12:15 is that the abundance of one's possessions might lead to a living death. This reading is compelling, given the link between the rapacity of the Pharisees (11:41) and the description of them as "unmarked graves" (11:44). As noted previously, the man in the parable is depicted as less alive than his possessions, the latter of which engage in more activity than the former. Seneca's frequent reference to the "living dead" is relevant here, as is his attribution of such a premature death to luxury (*Ep.* 122.3, 4, 10; 82.3–4). It is significant, moreover, that Jesus instructs a person to sell the very thing (ὑπάρχοντα, "possessions") in which the abundance of life does not consist (12:15, 33). Whereas an abundance of possessions does not lead to life (and can even contribute to a living death), giving alms functions as a potential vehicle of life, both for the recipient and the giver.[117]

Selling one's possessions and giving alms is understood as an act that not only influences one's degree of life in the present but also has lasting consequences in the future. Selling goods and giving alms is likened to an "unfailing treasure" (θησαυρὸν ἀνέκλειπτον) in heaven, one that cannot be stolen or destroyed (12:33).[118] This impregnable investment, closely related to the view of alms in Ben Sira, stands in sharp contrast to the ease with which the rich man was separated from his goods (12:20). The counterintuitive implication is that the selling and giving away of goods produces a lasting investment that will not be stolen or destroyed. A similar principle is articulated in Jesus' later remark to the rich ruler, that selling one's goods and distributing to the poor provides one with treasure in heaven (ἕξεις θησαυρὸν ἐν τοῖς οὐρανοῖς; 18:22).

Jesus reiterates that relinquishing control over one's possessions (by selling and giving them away) results in a secured investment. A similar point is made in the conclusion to the discourse on anxiety (12:33), where alms are offered as an alternative to the greed and anxiety of the man in the

117. In Luke-Acts a causal relationship exists between giving alms and how one is treated by God. See esp. Acts 10:2, 4, 31; cf. 9:37–42.

118. Lucian also refers to riches that cannot be taken away, whether it be from a blackmailer, mob, or tyrant. Such riches are not found, however, in giving them to the poor but rather in a self-reliance born from poverty (*Tim.* 36–37).

parable.[119] The rich man's endeavor to control his goods (by storing and saving them) is ultimately shown to be impotent in protecting them—and himself—from life's vicissitudes. Moreover, Jesus' remark to the rich ruler hints that the secure treasure in heaven is one's own (ἕξεις, "you will have"), implying that selling possessions and giving to the poor somehow secures one's own future with God. In this regard, Luke echoes Ben Sira's promise that storing up almsgiving in one's treasury will provide a person with divine favor and enable one's sins to be forgiven (Sir 3:14, 30; 17:22; 29:12).

Second Temple texts whose focus is the interplay of death and possessions propose various uses of goods in light of the uncontrollable facets of death. Luke participates in this conversation by recommending alms as a meaningful use of goods in light of death's inevitability and life's fragility. Alms, Luke proposes, is a vehicle of meaning and life, both for the giver and the recipient. This recommendation of alms is significant, for with it Luke aligns himself with the favorable attitude toward alms in Ben Sira (and other Jewish works such as Tobit).[120]

The proposal of alms as a meaningful use of possessions is a notable difference from Lucian or Seneca. Seneca does not advise this activity, and giving to the needy appears in Lucian only peripherally.[121] The absence of alms in these two authors is indicative of the relative dearth of material on alms in Greco-Roman texts.[122] This discrepancy in attention to alms reflects a broader and more fundamental divergence among texts whose focus is the interplay of death and possessions. In contrast to Qoheleth, Ben Sira, the Testament of Abraham, and Luke, neither Lucian nor Seneca display an avid interest in constructive uses of possessions; they focus instead on the inherent destructive potential of wealth and goods. Underlying this difference regarding how texts speak about and conceive possessions are two disparate premises regarding their nature. Whereas Lucian

---

119. So Richard B. Hays, *The Moral Vision of the New Testament* (San Francisco: Harper SanFrancisco, 1996), 124.

120. Sir 3:14, 30; 7:10; 12:3; 16:14; 17:22, 29; 29:8, 12; 25:2; 31:11; 35:2; 40:17, 24; Tob 1:3, 16; 4:7–11, 16; 12:8–9; 14:2, 11.

121. Lucian twice refers to using goods in this way, although on neither occasion is it related to death. Thrasycles suggests that Timon, if he is unwilling to throw his goods into the sea, distribute (διαδίδωμι) them "to all the needy" (δέω) (*Tim.* 57; cf. *Tim.* 8; *Vit. auct.* 9).

122. So Harrington, *Jesus Ben Sira*, 33. While Luke is influenced by both Jewish and Greco-Roman literature, his focus on alms as an ideal use of possessions indicates the important influence of *Jewish* sapiential literature.

and Seneca highlight the dangers of wealth and possessions, Hellenistic Jewish texts speak not only of their dangers but also their beneficial possibilities.[123]

Conclusion

Luke's parable and its immediate literary context is situated within a contested Second Temple conversation regarding the meaningful use of possessions, given uncontrollable facets of death. A spectrum of six specific proposals are offered in texts for how a person might use possessions meaningfully, in view of death's inevitability, uncertain timing, and potential imminence. Luke's rich man, however, enacts none of these suggestions. The closest he comes to doing so is to *plan* on enjoying his goods. When read in light of the broader conversation on the intersection of death and possessions, the neglect to practice any of these recommendations constitutes an egregious fault. The rich man fails to use his goods meaningfully, given death's inevitability, uncertain timing, and potential imminence. For his failure to enact any of these sapiential recommendations regarding the use of possessions in light of his mortality, the rich man earns the epithet "fool." His folly, in light of these sapiential texts, consists in having a limited imagination. In light of the parable's immediate literary context, however, the man's folly only partially consists in failing to adopt these specific sapiential recommendations. The following chapter explores the multiple reasons for why Luke might regard the rich man as a fool.

123. Statements about the dangers of goods are not absent in the latter texts, but they are not at the forefront. Among Jewish texts, 1 Enoch is a notable exception. It differs from Lucian and Seneca, however, for it views possessions not as inherently dangerous but as a sign of someone who is unjust and wicked.

6
The Rich Man's Folly in Light of Sapiential Texts and the Parable's Immediate Literary Context

In light of Second Temple (sapiential) texts in which the interplay of death and possessions figures prominently, the folly of Luke's rich man consists partially in his failure, given death's uncertain timing and potential imminence, to enact any of the six sapiential recommendations for the use of possessions. There are, however, additional reasons for the man's folly, and two of these are highlighted in the parable's immediate literary context (12:13–15, 21).

Luke 12:21 functions literarily and theologically as an interpretive lens for the parable: "So is the one who stores up for oneself and is not rich toward God [οὕτως ὁ θησαυρίζων ἑαυτῷ καὶ μὴ εἰς θεὸν πλουτῶν]."[1] This

---

1. Jülicher anticipates Bultmann and others by questioning whether 12:21 was original to the parable (*Die Gleichnisreden Jesu*, 2:614). Of significance is his presupposition that 12:21, if shown not to be original, should not be used to illumine the parable. Although he cannot find a "clear motive for cancelling" 12:21 from Luke, he finds it unhelpful in understanding the parable; he considers it a "vague and quite unnecessary" saying that one could omit easily and "with pleasure." Martin Dibelius also focuses (almost exclusively) on the parable's tradition history, and he follows Bultmann in regarding 12:21 as a secondary addition (*From Tradition to Gospel* [trans. Bertram Lee Woolf; 2nd ed.; New York: Charles Scribner's Sons, 1935], 258). The parable only becomes "moral" or parenetic if one adds 12:21. The message in 12:21 is not inherent to the parable itself, he claims, since "nothing was said in the parable about lack towards God." Dupont considers 12:21 "Luke's personal point of view" (*Les béatitudes*, 115). This verse does not, of course, function as an interpretive key for those few Lukan manuscripts that lack 12:21 (Codex Bezae and three Old Latin mss [it^{a,b,d}]). Luke 12:21 is absent in Thomas's version. Cadoux does not see a significant connection between the parable and 12:15 (*The Parables of Jesus*, 205). He takes 12:21 as an "editorial comment" that expresses a "favorite idea of Luke's and takes attention away from the question in which the parable culminates."

assessment of the rich man faults him on two related counts: he treasures up for himself (12:21a) and is not rich toward God (12:21b). This conclusion (12:21) interprets the parable by suggesting these specific shortcomings as reasons for the man's folly. The charge of treasuring for oneself echoes the critique of avarice that prefaces the parable (12:15). In addition, the first half of 12:21 confirms what was presaged in 12:15, namely, that the rich man's plans are to be primarily understood in terms of greed.

In what follows I analyze the parable in light of these two issues raised in 12:13–15 and 12:21, namely, the critique of greed and the failure to be rich toward God.[2] These two issues are related, since Luke 12:21 theologically evaluates the rich man's plans by equating his "storing up for himself" as a failure to be rich toward God. In addition to showing how 12:13–15 and 12:21 interpret the parable, I will also explore how the parable reads and interprets these texts.[3]

My analysis will also situate both of these issues (the critique of greed and being rich toward God) vis-à-vis the Second Temple (sapiential) conversation regarding death and possessions. Luke 12:13–15 and 12:21 raise as many questions as they answer. Why is greed, for example, tantamount to folly? What is it about the man's greed that causes him to be evaluated as foolish? What does it mean, moreover, to be rich toward God? How precisely do the man's plans reflect a "poverty" toward God? The matrix of the Second Temple sapiential conversation on death and possessions will prove to be a fruitful source of answers to these and other questions.

The Critique and Analysis of Greed in 12:13–21

Luke's critique of greed is explicit in the warning against avarice (πλεονεξία) that precedes the parable (12:15).[4] The import of this admonition is indi-

---

2. In chapter 7 I analyze 12:22–34.

3. See chapter 5 for arguments that the parable should be read in light of its literary context. The justification for doing so includes the lexical and thematic links between 12:13–15, 16–20, 21, and 22–34. θησαυρίζων occurs in 12:21, and both θησαυρόν (12:33) and θησαυρός (12:34) appear in the conclusion to the discourse (12:22–34). The man, although "rich" (πλούσιος) (12:16), is not rich toward God (εἰς θεὸν πλουτῶν). ἑαυτῷ is used in both 12:17 and 12:21 to highlight the man's solitary nature. Metzger suggests that the comparative function of παραβολή would lead readers to see in 12:16 a "comparison between the man from the crowd and the rich man" in the parable (*Consumption and Wealth*, 71 n. 33).

4. Although this is the sole occurrence of πλεονεξία in Luke-Acts, Luke's concern

cated by the use, unattested elsewhere in Luke, of a double imperative: "Beware and guard yourselves [ὁρᾶτε καὶ φυλάσσεσθε]."[5] The warning against avarice frames Luke 12:16–21 and functions literarily as an interpretive lens through which Luke (at least) understands the parable. In light of 12:13–15, the parable illustrates someone whose plans are characterized by greed.[6] Like the brother seeking his share of the inheritance, the rich man pursues a sapiential option regarding possessions that Luke deems meaningless and futile. Moreover, the rich man in the parable has an abundance of possessions (12:15), but his life (ζωή) does not consist in them. His goods do not enhance or contribute to the flourishing of his ζωή.

The conclusion of the parable (12:21) evaluates the man's plans in a similar manner by interpreting them as a selfish treasuring up of goods. Like the comment immediately preceding the parable (12:15), 12:21 understands the man's plans as a greedy endeavor.[7] But Luke contributes two insights in 12:21 that are not made explicit in 12:13–15.[8] First, in light of the man's imminent death, his plans are found to be inadequate because they evince no awareness of anyone else. His treasure is stored up *for himself* (ἑαυτῷ) and himself alone (12:21a). Second, the man's plans, although ostensibly concerned with the use of possessions, are interpreted in 12:21b theologically and construed as a *theological* act. Accordingly, the man's ostensibly economic plans do not have theological implications but rather constitute a theological endeavor. One who stores treasure for oneself, as

---

for greed is by no means limited to this episode. Judas (Luke 22:2–6; Acts 1:16–20), Ananias, and Sapphira (Acts 5:1–11) illustrate the deadly consequences of greed.

5. So Metzger, *Consumption and Wealth*, 67; Seccombe, *Possessions and the Poor in Luke-Acts*, 139; Herman Hendrickx, *The Parables of Jesus* (rev. ed.; Studies in the Synoptic Gospels; San Francisco: Harper & Row, 1986), 98–99. This use of φυλάσσω is ironic, given its association with protecting, guarding, or hoarding possessions (Qoh 5:12; Lucian, *Dial. mort.* 1.3; *Tim.* 13–14; *Men.* 2; Plutarch, *Cupid. divit.* 7). Luke is aware of this association and elsewhere uses φυλάσσω in a similar manner (11:21). In 12:15, Luke plays on this typical usage by applying the verb to *avarice*. Rather than guarding wealth, one is to guard against every form of seeking and accumulating a superfluous share of it.

6. Many understand the parable as an illustration of the principle in 12:15. See, e.g., Wolter, *Das Lukasevangelium*, 447.

7. Tannehill understands 12:21 to refer to the "proper use of possessions," namely, "not being greedy" (*Luke*, 206).

8. *Contra* Snodgrass, who sees no difference between 12:15 and 12:21 (*Stories with Intent*, 716 n. 32). The second insight has to do with the reference to "not being rich toward God" (12:21b) and is treated below.

the rich man does in the parable, lives in a state of poverty vis-à-vis God.[9] The principle underlying this theological evaluation of the man's plans is that an inverse relationship exists between one's relationship with God and one's selfish accumulation of goods. As one increases treasure for oneself, one simultaneously becomes poorer in relation to God.

The parable corroborates the interpretation in 12:21a regarding the selfish nature of the envisioned storage of goods. The man in the parable is depicted as solitary and socially isolated.[10] His life, in this way, bears some resemblance to the pervasive focus in Qoheleth on life as a solitary endeavor, one almost entirely void of community and relationships.[11] Seven of the eleven verbs in the rich man's monologue are in the first-person singular (*ποιήσω*, *συνάξω*, *ποιήσω*, *καθελῶ*, *οἰκοδομήσω*, *συνάξω*, *ἐρῶ*).[12] This use of the first person also resembles Qoheleth.[13] When the man does reason or speak, he converses not with others but only himself, establishing himself as his sole interlocutor. His first act is "reasoning to himself [διαλογίζετο ἐν ἑαυτῷ]" (12:17), and he later envisions speaking to his self (ψυχή; 12:19). The repetition of ἑαυτῷ in 12:21 recalls the previous use of the term in the parable, further suggesting a link between the solitary nature of "treasuring" and the solitary plans of the rich man.[14] An

---

9. This illustrates Johnson's insight that the "disposition of possessions is a sign of the response of the heart to God" (*Literary Function*, 155).

10. Bovon describes the rich man as being "enclosed in himself [*enfermé en soi*]" (*L'Évangile selon Saint Luc*, 245). Donahue emphasizes here how wealth can socially isolate someone from others and God (*The Gospel in Parable*, 179). Rembrandt's painting of this parable conveys this solitary and socially isolated nature of the rich man.

11. Fox (*A Time to Tear Down*, 343) sees in Qoheleth "no awareness of himself as part of a nation or a community. His values are solitary, all his judgments gauged by benefit or harm to the individual." See also Burkes, *God, Self, and Death*, 80, 84; James G. Williams, "What Does It Profit a Man? The Wisdom of Koheleth," in *Studies in Ancient Israelite Wisdom* (ed. James L. Crenshaw; New York: Ktav, 1976), 376.

12. On the use of the monologue in Luke, see Philip Sellew, "Interior Monologue as a Narrative Device in the Parables of Luke," *CBQ* 54 (1992): 239–53.

13. Burkes notes that in Qoheleth the "use of the first person pronoun is unusually frequent in comparison to other biblical books" (*God, Self, Death*, 71). See also R. N. Whybray, *Ecclesiastes* (NCBC; Grand Rapids: Eerdmans, 1989), 6; Eric S. Christianson, *A Time to Tell: Narrative Strategies in Ecclesiastes* (Sheffield: Sheffield Academic Press, 1998), 41.

14. Interpreting the man's plans as ones that only involve himself is significant, given the emphasis throughout Luke on experiencing enjoyment, eating, and drinking in a communal context (5:29–39; 7:36–50; 11:37–54; 14:1–15:32).

important narrative function of the divine announcement (12:20) is the provision of a perspective distinct from that of the rich man.

The man's solitary nature is noteworthy, given the causal relationship Lucian envisions between wealth and a solitary lifestyle. Lucian contends that a rich man (πλούσιος ἀνήρ) is actually poor (πένης) if he eats alone (*Par.* 58). The role of death in Lucian's following dialogue makes the parallel especially pertinent. After choosing once again to be rich, the character Timon declares: "For myself, I purpose now to buy the whole farm, build a tower over the treasure just large enough for me to live in, and have it for my tomb when I am dead" (*Tim.* 42). Timon's solitary existence, implied here, becomes explicit in his continuing description. Relevant for Luke's parable and the subsequent proposal of alms is the effect of wealth upon Timon's attitude and (lack of) actions toward others:

> Let these things be resolved and made into law for my remaining life: *no mixing with anyone, ignorance of all, and contempt for everyone.* A friend, stranger, companion, or Altar of Mercy will be much nonsense; and to pity one who weeps or to help one in need will be a transgression against the law and a dissolution of customs. *And my mode of life will be solitary*, just as wolves; *and Timon will be my only friend. … And let Timon become rich alone, despise everyone, and live luxuriously alone by himself*, apart from flattery and wearisome praise. And let [Timon] sacrifice to the gods and feast sumptuously *alone, a neighbor and borderer to himself, shaking off [all] others.* And once for all let it be resolved [that] *he will welcome himself when he must die, and lay the crown upon himself.* (*Tim.* 42–43)

Timon's lack of compassion for others is plain in the new, favorite name he chooses for himself: "the Misanthrope." He will not help people, he declares, whether someone is perishing in a fire or drowning (*Tim.* 44).

Lucian's characterization of Timon underscores the social consequences of greed. Avarice is a vice whose tentacles not only ensnare its primary victim but also isolate him or her socially. Such is the fate of the rich man in Luke's parable. He envisions himself as the sole recipient and beneficiary of his "many goods things" (12:19a).[15] This social dimension of greed is evident in the term πλεονεξία, one denotation of which is "one's

15. Metzger sees in 12:19 evidence for the completely selfish orientation of the man (*Consumption and Wealth*, 75).

own advantage" over others.[16] Luke is eager to immunize his implied audience against these social dangers of greed. His proposal of alms envisions an alternative relational structure, integral to which is the strengthening of social bonds.

The rich man's attitude toward his possessions further buttresses the interpretation in 12:21 that his plans exclude consideration of others. He consistently employs the possessive pronoun "my" (μου) to refer to possessions. The crops (καρπός; 12:17), the barns (12:18),[17] the goods (ἀγαθός; 12:18), and the self (ψυχή; 12:19)[18] are all considered "mine" (μου). This view is in stark contrast to the insistence in Qoheleth and the claim in Seneca concerning the status of goods as divine gifts (Qoh 2:24–26; 3:13; 5:17–6:2; 8:15; *Ep.* 110.10; 8.9–10). The irony regarding the rich man's perception as an owner of these four things is revealed most clearly when each one of them is removed by the parable's end. An unspecified "they" are demanding (ἀπαιτοῦσιν) his life (ψυχή; 12:20a). God's concluding question reminds the man that his "ownership" of his goods has come to an abrupt end (12:20b). This announcement of his imminent death reveals that he is no longer (and perhaps never was) possessor and controller of these items. He is rather subject to the control of another (or others).

Tacit in this divine announcement are two realities, both of which Qoheleth also discovers: attempts to control possessions so as to obtain a specific manageable outcome are futile and doomed to fail (Qoh 2), and the status of goods as divine gifts precludes the possibility of human ownership. For Qoheleth, this failure meant, on the one hand, an inability to secure meaning in his quest to seize and possess wisdom, wealth, and pleasure. On the other hand, it led him to abandon his quest to control possessions with a predetermined outcome and to enjoy them instead. The rich man does not appear to be given any second chances, since his imminent

16. LSJ, 1416. A πλεονέκτης is one who "has or claims more than one's due," implying (in a limited-goods economy) that others suffer as a result of such greed (LSJ, 1416). Metzger notes: "πλεονεξία was also associated with an aggressive, ruthless and sometimes violent grasping for power or honor *at the expense of others*" (*Consumption and Wealth*, 68, emphasis original). Dupont (*Les béatitudes*, 184) similarly understands πλεονεξία as "*d'avoir advantage*." Eichholz ("Vom reichen Kornbauern," 180) defines the term as "*Mehr-haben-wollen* (*als man hat*)." Cf. Wolter, *Das Lukasevangelium*, 447–48. For a list of sources that attest this social aspect of πλεονεξία, see Metzger, *Consumption and Wealth*, 68; Wolter, *Das Lukasevangelium*, 448.

17. Uncial W lacks the word μου before ἀποθήκας (12:18).

18. Uncial F lacks τῇ ψυχῇ μου.

death is a part of God's announcement.[19] The man's failure and folly thus serve as a potential instructive lesson to the hearers of the parable and to readers/hearers of Luke.

The rich man's assumption regarding the control he wields over his goods is ironic, given the parable's description of the man and his goods, for the man is described only in terms of his relationship to his possessions.[20] Apart from ἄφρων ("fool"), the parable uses only one word to describe the man: "rich" (πλούσιος; 12:16).[21] By producing abundantly, the land accomplishes more than the man whose agency is restricted throughout the parable to speaking (or thinking) his intentions. Apart from planning, the man does not do anything. This failure to act is significant in light of the emphasis in other Lukan parables on the importance of action.[22] To fail to act is for Luke an act of failure.

19. Luke does, however, have a penchant to conclude stories before a character makes an important choice (Luke 15:11–32; 16:19–31; 18:18–25). Ending the story before revealing what the character will do has a rhetorical function of inviting readers/hearers to identify with the character and thereby make his choice their own. It may be that Luke employs this same device here in the Rich Fool parable. Perhaps the rich man has some time between the divine announcement and his death during which he can choose to use his possessions in meaningful ways, and perhaps a potential effect of the story is to encourage readers/hearers to consider how they might use possessions given the possibility of their own imminent death.

20. Metzger notes that the man is "indeed *defined* exclusively by his wealth" (*Consumption and Wealth,* 70, emphasis original).

21. Apart from τινός (12:16). This is the first of three ἄνθρωπός τις πλούσιος parables (16:1–8; 16:19–31) and the second of seven or eight ἄνθρωπός τις parables in Luke (10:30–36; 14:16–24; 15:11–32; 16:1–8, 19–31; 19:12–27; 20:9–15 [many manuscripts omit τις in 20:9]). κριτής τις is the subject of one parable (18:2). Luke 14:2 is the only occurrence of ἄνθρωπός τις outside of a parable. The phrase ἄνθρωπός τις does not occur in Acts.

22. In the parable of the Samaritan (10:30–36), action is the only thing that distinguishes the latter character from the priest and the Levite. The fourfold repetition of the verb "to do" (ποιέω) in the dialogue between Jesus and the lawyer (10:25–37) also underscores the importance of action. The conclusions to both mini-dialogues between Jesus and the lawyer include commands that the lawyer "do" something (τοῦτο ποίει), in the first instance to love God and neighbor (10:28), in the second to do mercy (ποίει ὁμοίως) like the Samaritan (10:37). Jesus' first answer to the lawyer (10:28) provides an important caveat to the lawyer's answer (10:27) by stressing the insufficiency of cognitive knowledge. *Doing* the commandments, not merely knowing them, leads to inheriting eternal life and living (10:28). Similarly, *doing* mercy, like the

Because each of the rich man's plans is a response to his goods, there is, moreover, a sense in which the man is owned by what he owns.[23] He is, as it were, possessed by his possessions. The ownership exerted by the possessions over the man is illustrated most graphically, if one understands the man's goods as the referent of ἀπαιτοῦσιν,[24] in their taking away of the man's ψυχή (12:20). The man exemplifies Seneca's description of the "owners of great estates: they are only accessories and incidentals to their possessions" (*Ep.* 82.18). Pertinent also to Luke's parable is Lucian's assertion that being possessed by one's goods is a consequence of failing to face one's own mortality (*Men.* 12).

The instruction to give alms (12:33) serves an important function, for it is an explicit alternative and corrective to the avarice of 12:15 and the "treasuring up for oneself" in 12:21.[25] Luke presents a constructive option as a counter to the rich man's greed. Problematic for the man's plans is Jesus' declaration, immediately preceding the parable, that one's life (ζωή) does not consist in the abundance of one's possessions (12:15). This remark frames the parable by raising an expectation that the parable will address this claim. The parable accomplishes this by illustrating that the man's plans fail to engender life (ζωή), either for him or for others.

The parable's conclusion, that the man is storing "for himself" (12:21a), additionally suggests that relationality might be one aspect of the "life" mentioned in 12:15. The rich man's plans certainly illustrate this claim, for he lives alone, dreams alone, and will (apparently) die alone. Life (ζωή) for this man does not consist in the abundance of possessions, since the pursuit and protection of goods involves insularity from others. One's life consists rather in the selling and giving of one's goods (12:33), since this act requires some type of relational interaction, central to which is the extension of life to another.

The critique of greed, a central component of Luke's interpretation of the parable (12:13–15, 21), is a leitmotif in many sapiential discussions

---

Samaritan, leads to eternal life. The lawyer is exhorted to imitate this *doing* of mercy (10:37b).

23. Cf. Chuck Palahniuk, *Fight Club* (New York: W. W. Norton, 1996), 44.

24. So Stagg, *Studies in Luke's Gospel*, 90–91; Stacy, "Luke 12:13–21," 288.

25. Dupont views 12:21 as an anticipation (albeit an abridged form) of 12:33 and the recommendation in Matt 6:19–20 (*Les béatitudes*, 117). Tannehill reads 12:33 in light of 12:21, taking the former as a rejection of the man's attempt to lay up treasure for himself (*The Narrative Unity of Luke-Acts*, 1:246–47).

of death and possessions.[26] Plutarch's *De Cupiditate*, although not giving extensive attention to the motif of death, exemplifies the rejection by Greco-Roman moralists of greed as a meaningful enterprise. Several of the texts explored in chapters 2–4 situate a critique of greed within a discussion about death.[27] Proverbs, for instance, warns that death is the ultimate consequence for those who are "greedy for gain" and that greed for gain "takes away the life of its possessors [τὴν ἑαυτῶν ψυχὴν ἀφαιροῦνται]" (1:19). Relevant to Luke 12 is Lucian's description of a person who refused to leave property to heirs because of his greed (*Dial. mort.* 22.7).[28]

Alms as Divine Wealth in 12:20, 21b, 22–34

Another important way in which Luke's conclusion (12:21) interprets the parable is by evaluating the man's plans in theological terms. Luke equates the act of storing up for oneself with "not being rich toward God [μὴ εἰς θεὸν πλουτῶν]" (12:21b).[29] This interpretation is potentially significant, since the man's plans (12:17–19) exhibit no patent reference to God. But despite this (or because of it?), his plans are deemed to reflect and constitute a poverty vis-à-vis God. This theological poverty is an overt contrast to his previously described economic wealth (πλουσίος; 12:16). The man, although rich, is poor in relation to God.

By theologically construing plans that are ostensibly concerned with the use of goods, Luke reconfigures an existential aspect of the sapiential conversation for his own theological purposes. Yet Luke 12:21 does not explicitly clarify what it means to be rich toward God. Such elucidation is provided in the subsequent discourse (12:22–34),[30] for the negatively phrased statement (μὴ εἰς θεὸν πλουτῶν; 12:21b) invites reflection upon its positive corollary. If the man in the parable illustrates one who is not rich toward God, what does being rich toward God entail? The positive alternative appears in the penultimate line of the discourse (12:33). As in 12:21, there is in 12:33 both a reference to "treasure" (θησαυρός) and a

26. For Seneca's critiques of greed, see *Ep.* 94.43; 110.9; 119.6, 8, 9; cf. 16.8.

27. Sir 11:23–26; 14:9a; 1 En. 94:6–7; 97:8a–10; Lucian, *Dial. mort.* 1.3; 14.2; 16.1; Seneca, *Ep.* 120.17.

28. Egyptian texts also critique greed in the context of broader discussions about death. See, e.g., the Instruction of Ptahhotep (11, 14, 19–22; *AEL* 1:66–67).

29. So Bovon, *L'Évangile selon Saint Luc*, 258.

30. I also treat this discourse in chapter 7.

reflexive pronoun (ἑαυτοῖς). Selling one's possessions (πωλέω) and giving alms (δίδωμι ἐλεημοσύνη) is the counterexample both to greed (12:15) and to treasuring goods for oneself (12:21). Instead of storing "for oneself" (12:21), one gives away to others (12:33). Whereas storing treasure for oneself constitutes poverty toward God, selling possessions and giving alms is likened to purses that do not become obsolete and an "unfailing treasure" (θησαυρὸν ἀνέκλειπτον) in heaven. It is unassailable by thief or moth and cannot be stolen or destroyed (διαφθείρει). Its impregnability speaks to its "eternal" quality and is a sharp contrast to the treasure from which the rich man was so quickly and easily separated (12:20). Luke later makes a similar point, indicating that selling all one has (πωλέω) and giving to the poor (διαδίδωμι πτώχος) provides one with treasure (θησαυρός) in heaven (18:22).

Luke's theological reading of the interplay of death and possessions is evident in three ways: God's appearance in the parable (12:20), the comment regarding the man's failure to be rich toward God (12:21), and the important function of God in the subsequent discourse (12:22–34). Luke's parable of the Rich Fool is unique in being the only canonical parable in which God appears as a character in the narrative. Although God's time on stage is relatively brief, God's announcement in 12:20 is a crucial element in the plot, providing both the peripeteia and anagnorisis.[31] God evaluates the man as a fool, informs him of his imminent demise, and questions him regarding the future ownership of his goods. The importance of God's appearance in the parable is underscored by the subsequent references to God in 12:21 and the subsequent discourse (12:22–34), in which characterizations of God figure prominently in the discourse's rhetoric.

Luke 12:22–34 constitutes an argument that God's character has implications for the meaningful use of possessions. The character of God functions in Luke's argument (12:22–34) as a warrant both for admonitions not to worry (12:22, 25, 26, 29) and for the instruction regarding giving alms (12:33). In this extended argument, God is primarily depicted as a father (πατήρ; 12:30, 32) who cares for animals and the grass (12:24,

31. The peripeteia is a moment of reversal, and the anagnorisis is a moment of recognition or discovery. In Greek tragedy, the former usually preceded the latter. The first half of God's announcement regarding the man's death (12:20a) functions as a peripeteia, and the question concerning the future status of the possessions (12:20b) functions as the anagnorisis.

28) and (even more so) for people (12:24, 28, 31–32).[32] God's care for the former, evident by observing nature, is adduced as evidence of care for the latter. God's fatherhood is manifest in knowing (οἶδα) that people need (χρῄζω) food and drink (12:30). A corollary of such knowledge is that one need not pursue food and drink as the "nations of the world" do (12:30a). Not seeking after these elements can free people to seek instead the father's βασιλεία ("kingdom"), which the father is pleased to give them (12:31a, 32). Freedom to seek this kingdom is predicated upon trusting that God their father will meet their basic needs for survival (12:31b).

The exhortation to seek the kingdom and give alms is thus rooted in a specific understanding of God as one who cares for people and provides their basic necessities. Luke has previously established that God's character as a caring father has implications for how one uses possessions. In light of the fact that God is a merciful father, for instance, one is to lend "expecting nothing in return" (Luke 6:35–36).

This Lukan depiction of God is both consonant with and divergent from portrayals of the deity in Second Temple sapiential texts. Luke joins Qoheleth and other wisdom texts in stressing the need to fear God (Luke 12:4–5).[33] Luke also shares with Qoheleth a perception of God as one whose primary activity consists of giving (Qoh 2:24–26; 3:13; 5:17–18; 6:2; 8:15; Luke 12:24, 28, 31–32). Yet whereas the gifted nature of possessions leads Qoheleth to recommend enjoyment, God's status as a giver in Luke functions as a warrant to share one's goods in the form of alms (Qoh 2:24a; 3:12; 5:17; 8:15; Luke 12:33).[34] For Luke, God's propensity to give is grounds for an *imitatio dei* in which people become givers themselves.[35]

Luke's depiction of God as a caring father comports with some sapiential texts and diverges from others. On the one hand, this portrayal echoes Ben Sira's representation of God as a merciful, compassionate father.[36]

32. Diane G. Chen (*God as Father in Luke-Acts* [SBLit 92; New York: Lang, 2006]) argues that the depiction of "God as Father" is central to Luke's theology.

33. See, e.g., Qoh 3:14; 5:7; 7:18; cf. Prov 1:7, 29; 2:5; 8:13; 9:10; 10:27; 14:26, 27; 15:16, 33; 16:16; 19:23; 22:4; 23:17; Sir 2:1–18.

34. As noted above, Luke's emphasis on alms comports with Ben Sira's view of this as an ideal use of possessions.

35. Similarly, loving one's enemies and doing good to them results in becoming "children of the Most High," precisely because these actions embody God's treatment of people (Luke 6:35).

36. Cf. James L. Crenshaw, "The Concept of God in Old Testament Wisdom," in Perdue, Scott, and Wiseman, *In Search of Wisdom*, 4–5, 8–9; Jeremy Corley, "God as

Both Ben Sira and Luke employ the familial term "father" (πατήρ) to refer to God (Sir 23:1, 4; cf. Sir 51:10; Luke 12:30, 32).[37] Nor is this notion unique to Jewish texts; Seneca also speaks of God as a father "of us all" and ties the notion of divine fatherhood to God's giving nature (*Ep.* 110.10). On the other hand, Luke's paternal term for God is a sharp departure from Qoheleth, who refrains from using the term "father" and the divine personal name.[38]

In light of Luke 12:22–34, the rich man is poor toward God because his plans represent a failure to trust in the character of the God depicted in this discourse. Saving for the future is inappropriate and foolish, given the characterization of God as one who cares for birds and grass and who values people more than these (12:24, 27–28, 30b, 31b–32). The man's monologue effectively violates the prohibition in the discourse against seeking what one might eat or drink (12:29). His plan to store his surplus of goods for future use indicates that he views himself, and not God, as the provider of his goods. An unspoken premise of the man's plans is that, if he does not take care for himself by treasuring his goods for future use, then no one else will.

The invitation to give alms (12:33) is, by contrast, predicated on an understanding of God as a beneficent being. One can give alms if one trusts in the accuracy of Luke's rendering of God as a magnanimous giver. The act of giving alms demonstrates trust in the kind of God described in

---

Merciful Father in Ben Sira and the New Testament," in *Ben Sira's God: Proceedings of the International Ben Sira Conference Durham–Ushaw College 2001* (ed. Renate Egger-Wenzel; BZAW 321; Berlin: de Gruyter, 2002), 33–38; Pancratius C. Beentjes, "God's Mercy: 'Racham' (pi.), 'Rachum', and 'Rachamim' in the Book of Ben Sira," in idem, *'Happy the One Who Meditates on Wisdom' (Sir 14.20): Collected Essays on the Book of Ben Sira* (Biblical Exegesis and Theology 43; Leuven: Peeters, 2006), 231–48; cf. Harrington, *Jesus Ben Sira*, 32–33.

37. Luke refers to God as "father" elsewhere (Luke 6:36; 10:21–22; 11:13; 22:29; Acts 1:7). In each of these cases it is Jesus who uses the term πατήρ. Peter also refers to God as "father" (Acts 2:33).

38. Qoheleth never uses YHWH. He either uses אלהים (1:13; 3:10, 13; 5:18; 7:18; 8:2, 13) or, far more frequently, האלהים (2:24, 26; 3:11, 14, 17–18; 4:17; 5:1–2, 5–6, 17–19; 6:2; 7:13–14, 26, 29; 8:12, 15, 17; 9:1, 7; 11:5, 9; 12:7, 13, 14). The characterization of God in Qoheleth is complex, and the portrayal of God as a giver is only one aspect of a more rounded treatment. God has been understood to be depicted in Qoheleth, for example, as a despot "whose decrees cannot be altered by human response" (Perdue, "Cosmology and the Social Order," 471–72).

12:22–34. The man in the parable displays no such trust, marking him as one who has "little faith" (ὀλιγόπιστος; 12:28).

The man's poverty toward God is indicated, secondly, in his neglect to use goods in the same manner that God uses them: as gifts to others. Jesus' instruction to give alms is presented as a consequence of his understanding of God as a giver. One imitates God by giving alms. The rich man's plan to use his goods for his own benefit (and not for anyone else) represents the antithesis of alms, the preferred use of goods. This sharp contrast explains Luke's equation between the man's storage of goods for himself and his failure to be rich toward God (12:21). The latter failure refers not to literal gifts of tithes or sacrifices but rather to the man's storage of a surplus of goods for his own (ἑαυτῷ) personal benefit.[39]

A third aspect of the man's failure to be rich toward God consists in his lack of recognition that his goods are divine gifts. This neglect is especially pronounced, in view of the focus on goods as divine gifts in sapiential texts. Nor is it a coincidence that Luke 12:22–34 underscores God's nature as one who gives (12:24, 28, 31–32). A corollary of this depiction of God as a giver is a perception that one's own goods are indeed gifts from God. This is Qoheleth's perception, and it regularly informs his frequent recommendations to enjoy goods (Qoh 3:12–13; 5:17–18; 6:2; 8:15). Ben Sira 11:14, an intertext for Luke's parable, identifies good things (ἀγαθά) and wealth (πλοῦτος) as two things that are "from the Lord." Yet the rich man consistently views his *ἀγαθά* as his own, evidenced by his fourfold repetition of *μου* (12:17–19). Luke 12:22–34 contrasts the rich man's perspective as owner of his goods with a reminder that they are given by God. In light of this contrast, God's statement (ἡτοίμασας, "*you* prepared") may indeed be ironic (12:20a).[40]

Planning to store goods for one's own benefit is a failure to be rich toward God because it demonstrates a lack of trust in God's care and is the antithesis of giving alms, an act replicating God's own pattern of giving. Furthermore, being rich toward God entails giving alms because this act is akin to storing treasure with God (12:33–34; cf. 18:22).[41] The discourse

39. Luke periodically critiques the giving of sacrifices or tithes (see 11:42; 18:12; 20:47; 21:1–6).

40. So Bovon, *L'Évangile selon Saint Luc*, 256.

41. For Dupont, the man's folly, when viewed in light of Luke's redaction, consists in the failure to consider the "immediate advantages" of his riches and their ability to provide happiness for him in "another life" (*Les béatitudes*, 114). Fitzmyer finds the

following the parable (12:22–34) characterizes God in specific terms in order to counter a destructive mindset (anxiety) and engender a specific use of goods (alms). The admonition to give alms concludes the broader sapiential discourse in 12:13–34, providing a counterbalance to attempts to secure meaning through the pursuit of an inheritance (12:13–14) and solitary enjoyment (12:16–21).

It is not surprising that the God Luke depicts in 12:22–34 would not only have a vested interest in the man's use of goods but would also consider the man's plans as foolish. God's announcement invites the hearers of the parable and readers/hearers of Luke to evaluate the use of possessions in light of death's inevitability and potential imminence. Ben Sira and Lucian employ this rhetorical strategy, using death's inevitability and uncertain timing as an opportunity to assess one's use of possessions. God's question ("And the things you prepared—whose will they be?") reveals an interest not only with the end of the man's life but also with the life of the man's possessions after his death. Unlike 1 Enoch, the possessions in this story have a life of their own, one whose end does not coincide with the death of the rich man (cf. 1 En. 98:3b.). God's query invites reflection upon the ongoing life of the rich man's possessions: What kind of life will the rich man's possessions have after he dies? More to the point, whose life will the rich man's possessions enhance once he dies?

The man's strategy is foolish since its realized outcome depends upon two undependable factors: the fragility of goods and precariousness of plans for the future. In contrast to the ephemerality and unreliability of goods and plans for the future, giving alms ("an unfailing treasure in heaven") is an act of love that can never be destroyed. Luke assumes that all else can be taken away from someone, whether it be possessions or (in the extreme case) life. This everlasting nature of the act of love through alms underscores all the more the meaninglessness of a solitary lifestyle. The life lived alone is guaranteed not to produce lasting significance or meaning since such lasting meaning requires some element of relationality.

Luke's reading of the parable (12:21) thus reveals an interest in utilizing sapiential motifs for theological ends. At the same time, Luke employs theological motifs (e.g., the character of God) to serve his existential and ethical purposes. By characterizing the man's plans as a failure to be rich

parable (and other places in Luke) showing "the use of wealth on behalf of others as the way to become 'rich with God' " (*The Gospel according to Luke*, 2:972).

toward God, Luke redefines a theological world of which wisdom is an integral part. Appropriating sapiential motifs contributes to his interest in meaningful living.

In Luke's "theological wisdom,"[42] the use of possessions is an integral aspect and central ingredient to living meaningfully. Furthermore, the likelihood of living and using possessions meaningfully is enhanced when one considers and contemplates various facets of death (its inevitability, uncertain timing, and potential imminence). These potential threats of death and the uncertain vicissitudes of life provide a lens through which one can more easily discern if one's use of goods is meaningful.

To sum up, the parable's immediate literary context interprets the parable in three significant ways. Both Luke 12:15 and 21 highlight the man's greed as a reason for his folly. Luke 12:21 understands the man's plans as entirely selfish and construes these plans theologically. The parable simultaneously interprets its immediate literary context by illustrating the socially isolating nature of greed. I turn now to explore two additional ways in which reading the parable in concert with sapiential texts whose focus is the interplay of death and possessions elucidates the nature of the rich man's folly.

The Folly of Saving for the Future

Second Temple (sapiential) texts highlight two additional aspects of the rich man's folly: his plans to store up his goods for future use and his neglect of his own mortality. The first of these is directly related to the man's greed, further buttressing the importance of reading the parable in light of 12:15 and 12:21. Similarly, the man's neglect of his mortality is both a sapiential motif and a concern of the parable's broader literary context.

In addition to his plans for enjoyment, the rich man's primary (intended) use of his possessions consists of storing them up for the future. The small size of his barns, relative to the land's abundant yield (12:16), leads to his decision to tear them down and build larger ones. His limited imagination is revealed in not even considering sharing his goods with others as a valid option. The purpose, at any rate, in building larger barns is so that he can store his goods for future use (12:18). He envisions his enjoyment as a *consequence* of this storage, but this enjoyment is not stated

42. On this term, see Gammie, "From Prudentialism to Apocalypticism," 482.

as the *reason* for storing his goods (12:18–19). His plans to store the land's yield can be read as an attempt to abide by sapiential instructions that extol the virtues of saving one's goods for the future.[43] In light of such advice, the man's plans are indeed a prudent effort to prepare for the future.

This decision to store his goods for future use is, however, deficient in light of sapiential texts that feature the interplay of death and possessions. Such texts do not propose saving for the future as a legitimate use of possessions. Saving one's goods for future use does not even appear as a possibility in the sapiential texts we have surveyed. Some of these texts explicitly criticize saving goods for the future. Lucian, for example, disparages those who "guard" (φυλάσσω) their gold, since money is not needed in the afterlife (*Dial. mort.* 1.3). He also faults those who guard (φυλάσσω) their wealth instead of enjoying (ἀπολαύω) it (*Tim.* 13–14). He tells of a resolution passed in Hades against the rich who both guard (φυλάσσω) their fortunes and keep them locked up (κατάκλειστος; *Men.* 2). Papyrus Insinger favors enjoying goods over saving them: "The life of one who saves is one that passes without its having been known" (17.20). Not being "known" recalls the emphasis, both in sapiential texts and Luke 12:16–21, on the social isolation of those who are greedy. In sum, recommendations to save one's goods appear in sapiential texts, but not as proposals in response to the uncontrollable nature of death and life's vicissitudes.

Most wisdom texts do not advocate saving as a meaningful counterbalance to death. Even texts with conflicting or antithetical views of death and its aftermath agree in not proposing the saving of goods as a meaningful option. Qoheleth recommends enjoyment because death irreversibly ends this possibility (3:19–22a; 5:14–17). This same reason leads Ben Sira to recommend enjoyment and generosity (11:19c-21; 14:11a-16). The Testament of Abraham recommends hospitality as a means of securing divine favor after death (20:15). Producing a testament is also meaningful in that it provides one with the (potential) confidence of knowing who will receive one's goods.

Each of these options for utilizing possessions has the potential to provide meaning (even in light of death) because of the *gift* that is given to oneself, God, or another. Goods that are saved are not gifts. They are *potential* gifts, but as long as they remain in storage, this potential remains

43. See, e.g., Syriac Menander 380–381; P. Ins. 5.15; 6.23–24; 7.1–6.

unrealized. In contrast, Luke repeatedly illustrates the actualization of wealth's potential in the concrete act of giving or sharing it with others.[44]

As noted previously, Luke provides a negative assessment of the man's storage of goods in 12:21. It is possible, on the one hand, to read 12:21 as a critique of the selfish nature of the man's storage of goods and not necessarily as a denunciation of the act of saving or storage. The instruction to give alms does, however, offer an explicit contrast to the act of saving up for the future. The parable illustrates that the storage of goods is a meaningless enterprise by framing such activity within the announcement of the man's imminent death. It is in light of death's inevitability, uncertain timing, and potential imminence that the storage of goods is shown to be a worthless enterprise. Such is one of the tacit lessons of God's question to the rich man (12:20b). Death reveals the man's relationship with his possessions to be inadequate, futile, and, therefore, meaningless. The parable and its conclusion suggest that death's inevitability and potential imminence make adages extolling the virtue of saving to be futile.

In sapiential texts, saving is an inadequate use of goods in light of death because one cannot be certain of what the future holds.[45] The uncertain nature of the future influences Qoheleth's admonition to enjoy goods (Qoh 3:22). Papyrus Insinger recommends enjoyment in the present moment, since one does not know what tomorrow holds:

> Death and the life of tomorrow, we do not know their <nature>. (17.6)
> Today with its livelihood is what the wise man asks for. (17.7)
> He who loves to hoard wealth will die robbed of it. (17.8)

This last line (P. Ins. 17.8) is illustrated in Luke's parable and God's question to the man about the future status of his goods (12:20b). The man's plans, of course, exhibit no awareness of this inability to know what the future holds.

Sapiential texts emphasize in particular that one cannot predict the timing of one's death.[46] One should accordingly be prepared for death, since one cannot know its precise time of arrival.[47] In Egyptian texts, the

44. See, e.g., Luke 8:1–3; 10:25–37; 14:12–14; 15:20–32; 18:22; 19:1–10.
45. See, e.g., the ancient Egyptian text The Eloquent Peasant (*AEL* 1:177).
46. Seneca, *Ep.* 4.7–8.
47. Instruction of Any (*AEL* 2:138).

uncertain timing of death is a warrant for enjoyment[48] and generosity,[49] but never for saving goods for the future. For Seneca, the brevity and fragility of life underscore death's potential imminence. Life is brief and passes quickly (*Ep.* 48.12; 49.4; 58.23). Opportunities to die unexpectedly are many (*Ep.* 4.8). The Epistle of James, an early Jewish-Christian text imbued with sapiential features, chastises people whose plans for the future include doing business and making money (Jas 4:13).[50] James calls such boasting evil, and he critiques their plans since the future is uncertain (4:14a), and one does not know if death is imminent (4:14b). The proper perspective is to recognize and affirm that one lives and enacts plans only if the Lord wills it (4:15).

In light of such texts, the rich man's plans in the parable, both to store his goods and later to enjoy them, are foolish because they reflect an assumption that the future will unfold according to his plans. The man's level of certainty is reflected in the declarative statements he makes about the future (12:18–19). He does not express desires but assumes that the future will progress precisely as he imagines. He evinces no awareness of a possibility that the future might have different plans than he does. The man's plans suggest, on the contrary, that he envisions his future as a manageable vessel, with himself captaining the helm. This illusion, dismissed in sapiential texts as incompatible with experience, is shattered by God's announcement (12:20a).[51] The man appears to be on the brink of experiencing the same fate prescribed for the rich person (πλούσιος) in James,

48. Admonitions of Ipuwer (*AEL* 1:157, 160).

49. Instruction of Ankhsheshonq (12.5, 17–18; *AEL* 3:168–69).

50. Luke Timothy Johnson comments: "James mediates to the Christian community the wisdom traditions both of the Greco-Roman and Jewish cultures" (*The Letter of James: A New Translation with Introduction and Commentary* [AB 37A; New York: Doubleday, 1995], 164). On the sapiential character of James, see Johnson, *The Letter of James*, 33–34; Louis Simon, *Une Ethique de la Sagesse: Commentaire de l'epitre de Jacques* (Geneve: Labor et Fides, 1961); Rudolf Hoppe, *Der theologische Hintergrund des Jakobusbriefes* (FzB 28; Wurzburg: Echter, 1977); Hubert Frankemölle, "Zum Thema des Jakobusbriefes im Kontext der Rezeption von Sir 2, 1–18 und 15, 11–20," *BN* 48 (1989): 21–49; Hermann von Lips, *Weisheitliche Traditionen im Neuen Testament* (WUNT 64; Neukirchen-Vluyn: Neukirchener, 1990).

51. Dupont sees this contrast (between the man's envisioned future and God's announcement of his death) as a primary manifestation of the man's folly (*Les béatitudes*, 113).

who will pass away like a flower of the grass and fade away in the mist of his pursuits (Jas 1:10, 11).[52]

The man's assumption that his goods will last for "many years" is incongruous with the sapiential insistence upon the ephemeral nature of possessions.[53] The rich man's miscomprehension of the future resembles Qoheleth's (mis)perception during his initial program of enjoyment (Qoh 2). In Qoheleth, moreover, the perception of goods as divine gifts underscores their fragile and ephemeral nature. In light of Qoheleth, the rich man's neglect regarding the precarious nature of goods may be a direct consequence of failing to recognize them as a divine gift.

Ignoring Death's Inevitability, Uncertain Timing, and Potential Imminence

The rich man's storage of goods, in light of sapiential texts, indicates no cognizance of the possible imminence of his own death. If this is the case, he differs sharply from the insistence in sapiential texts on the need to face one's mortality and prepare for death. Diogenes stresses the need to practice (μελετάω) how to die (*Ep.* 39.3, 13). Pervading Seneca's epistles is an insistence on facing one's inevitable death.[54] A person, he maintains, must throughout life prepare to meet death (*Ep.* 82.8); each day is to be regarded as one's last (*Ep.* 12.8–9; 93.6). Adopting this perspective would seem to preclude saving goods for the future. Lucian also finds fault with those who fail to contemplate their mortality and inevitable death (*Dial. mort.* 3.2; *Char.* 17, 24; *Men.* 12). Reflecting upon one's future death is reasonable, given life's brevity and the innumerable opportunities to die (*Char.* 17).

Sapiential texts also insist that an awareness of death's inevitability should inform how a person uses possessions. For Syriac Menander, riches are used properly when done so in the consideration of the end of one's life (322–327). Ben Sira intimates that remembering the end of life will encourage giving to the poor and being generous with others (7:32–36). For Lucian, reflecting upon one's mortality would lead people to alter

52. Johnson cites Luke 12:16–21 as a parallel to the focus in Jas 1:9–12 on the transience and fragility of life (*The Letter of James*, 186–87).

53. See, e.g., Lucian, *Tim.* 29; *Dial mort.* 21.4.

54. *Ep.* 4.3–6, 9; 24; 58.23; 63.16; 67.8–10; 69.6; 70.9; 74.30; 76.28–29; 77.14–15, 19; 78.5–6; 80.5–6; 92.35; 93.12; 104.25, 33; 117.21; 120.14–15.

certain behaviors regarding their possessions.[55] Thinking of one's inevitable death, and the impossibility of bringing possessions into the afterlife, enables people to cease their "vain toil" for possessions (*Char.* 20). Such texts draw attention to a likely causal relationship between the man's plans in Luke's parable to store up his goods and his (apparent) neglect of his future demise.

Conversely, ignoring one's mortality prevents a person from using possessions meaningfully. Lucian identifies the belief that one will live forever as the reason that some hoard money rather than giving it to their heirs (*Dial. mort.* 22.7). He further contends that failing to face the reality of one's future death results in people being possessed by their possessions (*Men.* 12). Luke's rich man is indeed owned by what he owns, and his slavery to his goods may be due to his failure to contemplate his mortality.

Sapiential texts also identify having wealth as a cause of mortality avoidance. People who are doing well (εὖ πράττωσιν), for instance, do not take into account the myriad ways that death might meet them (*Char.* 17). Such people mistakenly think that their goods will be theirs forever (*Char.* 17). Seneca also maintains that an insatiable hunger for wealth makes it difficult for one to contemplate one's eventual death (*Ep.* 70.17–18). Craving wealth leads people to attempt (unsuccessfully) to prolong their life (*Ep.* 120.17).

Some of the specific uses of possessions recommended in sapiential texts can facilitate the process by which a person faces one's own mortality. Producing a testament, for example, is a task that requires some level of consideration of one's morality. By contrast, there is nothing inherent in the act of saving that requires a person to consider one's inevitable death. Saving might entail facing a number of other possible contingencies or events, but not death's inevitability. Indeed, storing up one's goods might be the quintessential act of enabling people to deny death.

The discourse following the parable (Luke 12:22–34) points to a possible link between one's anxiety over possessions and an attempt to extend one's life (12:22–26). This discourse, too, insists on the inevitability and unavoidability of death. Flowers and grass perish (12:28), and one cannot prolong the length of one's days (12:25). Moreover, this discourse concludes a section that begins with the reminder of death (12:4–5).

55. A person building a house would not continue if he knew that he would die as soon as the roof was complete (*Char.* 17).

In light of such texts, the man's foolish use of goods is a consequence of his failure to reckon with his inevitable death. In contrast to the neglect of his mortality, the parable insists through God's speech that death is an inevitable and unavoidable event, the timing of which is frequently unpredictable.[56] Luke's insistence on the inevitability and unpredictable timing of death comports with the views of many sapiential texts.

The importance of being willing to face death is an important motif in Luke's broader literary context. The parable and the discourse that both precedes and follows it are spoken during the journey narrative in which Jesus is on his way to Jerusalem (9:51, 53), a destination synonymous with death in general (13:33–34) and with Jesus' death in particular. The one who intimates that facing death is a prerequisite to living well is himself voluntarily walking a road whose ultimate end is his own death.[57]

In Luke 12, meaningful living entails rejecting certain options for the use of possessions and adopting others. One is to reject the storage of a surplus of goods for the future, planning for the future, the pursuit of an inheritance, and solitary enjoyment. These uses of possessions are deemed meaningless in light of death's uncertain timing and potential imminence. A primary reason for their meaninglessness is their failure to enhance life (ζωή), either for themselves or others (12:15). In their inability to produce an unfailing treasure, these options also constitute a failure to be rich toward God (12:21).

---

56. Bovon understands the parable as an invitation to "remember that you must die" (*L'Évangile selon Saint Luc*, 257). Dupont identifies the man's ignorance (*oublier*) of death as one reason for his folly (*Les béatitudes*, 113). Eichholz understands the man's refusal to face death as his "crucial error" ("Vom reichen Kornbauern," 187). Johnson notes that the man's fault is due in part to his failure to consider the possibility of his imminent death (*Literary Function*, 153).

57. On Jesus' willingness to face death, especially within the Greco-Roman context, see Gregory E. Sterling, "*Mors Philosophi:* The Death of Jesus in Luke," *HTR* (2001): 383–402; Peter J. Scaer, *The Lukan Passion and the Praiseworthy Death* (NTM 10; Sheffield: Sheffield Phoenix, 2005).

7
Luke 12:13–34: Reconfiguring Second Temple Conversations on Death and Possessions

I have shown that Luke 12:13–34 rejects specific uses of possessions as meaningless in light of death's inevitability and uncertain timing. Luke's parable is prefaced with the twin motifs of inheritance and avarice, each of which figures prominently in sapiential discussions of death and possessions. In Luke 12, both of these options are rejected as meaningless: a person's life does not consist in the abundance of possessions (12:15). Luke's rejection of these options, and his espousal of one specific alternative (alms), represents his participation in this Second Temple conversation regarding death and possessions.

Still, Luke not only participates in this conversation but also reconfigures (and illustrates) it by appropriating certain motifs and adapting them to his own theological, existential, and ethical concerns.[1] I turn now to analyze two such examples: the dilemma of an appropriately acquired surplus and the role of anxiety in the interplay of death and possessions.

The Dilemma of an Appropriately Acquired Surplus

Many sapiential texts criticize the unjust acquisition of wealth.[2] Although such texts differ on many points, they find common ground on castigating those who procure wealth unjustly.[3] In the Epistle of 1 Enoch, God pun-

1. For another example of analyzing how a biblical text appropriates and reconfigures perspectives from a diverse and contested Second Temple conversation, see Matthew S. Rindge, "Jewish Identity under Foreign Rule: Daniel 2 as a Reconfiguration of Genesis 41," *JBL* 129 (2010): 85–104.

2. See, e.g., 1 En. 97:8–10; Prov 15:27; Ps 49; Jer 17:11; The Instruction of Amenemope (6–7); stela of Merneptah (*AEL* 2:76); Pseudo-Phocylides, *Sentences* 5–6.

3. Wilson identifies this motif (the "theme of wealth unfairly acquired") as one

ishes such people (97:8–10). The evaluation of wealth in such texts is often dependent, as it is in Ben Sira, upon whether it was acquired justly or not.[4] Riches are good, he avers, if they are free from sin (Sir 13:24a).

Luke's parable provides no explicit indication that the rich man procured his goods through unjust means.[5] On the contrary, the parable specifies that the man's goods are produced naturally from the land (12:16).[6] Neglecting to attribute the man's wealth to unjust acquisition is significant, given the prevalence of this motif in sapiential texts. It is therefore possible that Luke's parable addresses a distinct, albeit related, question. If wisdom texts generally agree that the unjust acquisition of goods is abhorrent, what about the *proper* acquisition of goods? How is one to utilize goods and possessions that have not been procured unjustly? Luke reconfigures this sapiential motif regarding the unjust appropriation of goods by displaying a concern instead with what to do with possessions that are *appropriately* or *justly* acquired.

The specific dilemma that faces the man in the parable is that of an appropriately acquired *surplus*.[7] Unlike characters in parables that lack something,[8] the quandary facing this rich man in Luke 12 is what to do with an abundance of goods.[9] How does someone handle a surplus of

---

that "belongs principally" to wisdom texts (*The Sentences of Pseudo-Phocylides*, 80). As examples he cites Job 20:15; Prov 11:28; 13:11, 22; 28:8, 21–22; Wis 5:8; Sir 5:8; 13:24; 14:9; 21:4; 40:13.

4. So Wright, "Discourse of Riches and Poverty," 564; cf. Crenshaw, *Old Testament Wisdom*, 147.

5. So Martin Luther King Jr., "The Man Who Was a Fool," in idem, *Strength to Love* (Philadelphia: Fortress, 1981), 69–76; Eichholz, *Gleichnisse der Evangelien*, 183; Bovon, *L'Évangile selon Saint Luc*, 253; Moxnes, *The Economy of the Kingdom*, 88; Verhey, *Remembering Jesus*, 270.

6. So Moxnes, *The Economy of the Kingdom*, 83.

7. Observations regarding the man's surplus frequently involve tendentious speculation. Mary Ann Beavis maintains, for instance, that the rich man plans to store the goods in order to drive up the price of grain ("The Foolish Landowner," 64). Joel Green thinks that the man keeps his surplus so as to avoid saturating the market and to receive a "higher price when the market is not glutted" (*The Gospel of Luke* [NICNT; Grand Rapids: Eerdmans, 1997], 490–91). For a similar view, see Charles Hedrick, *Parables as Poetic Fictions*, 156–57.

8. See, e.g., the parables of the Widow and the Unjust Judge (18:1–8) or the Friend at Midnight (11:5–8).

9. John R. Donahue sees in the parable a warning against greed and superfluous possessions (*The Gospel in Parable*, 179).

goods, possessions, or wealth? In particular, how does one respond to a surplus of goods in view of the inevitability and uncertain timing of death? In Luke's parable, God is shown to demonstrate an interest in the man's use of a surplus of goods that he receives as a gift (12:20–21). Luke displays his interest in the issue of a surplus with his use of πλεονεξία (12:15), a term that denotes pursuit of a superfluous quantity.[10]

The extravagance of the man's surplus is indicated by his need to tear down his existing barns because they cannot adequately contain the produce of his field (12:16–17). The concern regarding a surplus also appears in Jesus' contention immediately preceding the parable that one's life does not consist in the abundance (περισσεύω) of possessions (12:15). The subsequent reference to Solomon (12:27) would also likely evoke in Luke's implied audience various associations with the king's luxurious lifestyle.

The implication of Jesus' statement (12:15) is that a person's life consists in something other than a surplus of goods. The discourse following the parable contends that one's life consists not in maintaining a surplus but in selling one's goods and giving them in the form of alms (12:33). One is to sell possessions (ὑπάρχοντα), the very thing in which one's life does not consist (12:15), and give the proceeds to others. One's own surplus can thereby be transformed into that which meets life's basic necessities for the needy.

The parable's conclusion (12:21) draws attention to the motif of a surplus by likening (οὕτως) the rich man to one who "stores up for oneself [θησαυρίζων ἑαυτῷ] and is not rich [πλουτῶν] toward God" (12:21). An implication of this theological assessment in 12:21 is that the question of what to do with a surplus of goods represents an existential, ethical, and theological dilemma.[11] The existential nature of this quandary is a consequence of drawing attention to the sapiential texture of 12:13–34. The surplus provides an opportunity for the man to consider how to use his goods meaningfully, especially in light of death's inevitability and uncertain timing.

10. See LSJ, 1415–16; Gerhard Delling, "πλεονέκτης, πλεονεκτέω, πλεονεχία," *TDNT* 6:266–74.

11. *Contra* Sellew, who avers that the man merely faces a practical (not even a moral) dilemma ("Interior Monologue," 244). This view, though perhaps representing the perspective of the rich man at the outset of the parable, is at odds with the assessment Luke provides at the parable's conclusion.

The ethical opportunity that the surplus represents becomes explicit with the proposal of alms as a constructive alternative to the socially destructive consequences of πλεονεξία. Finally, the failure to (plan to) share his goods with others is understood as a theological choice (12:21). To be rich toward God is to share one's goods in the form of alms with those most in need.[12] The God with and to whom one is rich is the God described in the subsequent discourse, one whose care and provision enables one to give alms without worrying or being anxious.

God, Anxiety, and the (Illusory) Control of Life and Possessions (12:22–34)

Luke reconfigures the sapiential conversation on death and possessions by identifying anxiety as an integral component in the intersection of possessions and death's inevitability and uncertain timing. Anxiety receives significant attention in the discourse addressed to the disciples (Luke 12:22–34).[13] The term μεριμνάω ("worry, be anxious") occurs three times (12:22, 25, 26), and μετεωρίζομαι ("be anxious about") appears once (12:29).

However, the importance of anxiety is indicated more pointedly by the way in which it governs the entire discourse (12:22–34). The concept appears in the discourse's initial instruction ("Do not worry..."; 12:22), and the proceeding section (12:23–28) consists of warrants to buttress this command (12:22). This pattern is repeated a second time: an order not to worry (12:29) is followed by a rationale supporting the command

12. So Johnson, *Literary Function*, 155; idem, *Gospel of Luke*, 202.

13. Luke Timothy Johnson notes the importance of recognizing the audience whom Jesus addresses ("The Lukan Kingship Parable," *NovT* 24 [1982]: 145). See also A. W. Mosley, "Jesus' Audiences in the Gospels of St. Mark and St. Luke," *NTS* 10 (1963): 139–49. Jesus' audience in 12:13–34 shifts, and Luke is not entirely clear about its makeup. In 12:1–12 Jesus speaks to the disciples (12:1), although it is clear that a crowd is also listening (12:1, 13). In 12:14 Jesus addresses the brother, but in 12:15 he speaks to a larger group (αὐτούς), either the crowd or the crowd and the disciples. The parable (12:16–21) is also told to this larger group (αὐτούς). The discourse in 12:22–34 is directed to the disciples (12:22). The ambiguity in identifying the precise audience is expressed by Peter, who later asks if Jesus is speaking "this parable" (referent unspecified) to the disciples or to everyone (12:41). The parable and discourse on anxiety occur within a broader literary context (12:4–34) in which anxiety is of primary concern. This section begins with Jesus teaching about whom one should not fear (φοβέομαι) and whom one should fear (12:4–5).

(12:30). Proceeding these two sets of commands/warrants are alternatives to pursue instead of worry (12:31–34).

The importance of anxiety for Luke 12:4–34 is indicated, furthermore, by the attention given at the outset of this discourse to the fear (φοβέομαι) of being killed (12:4–5). In his attempt to alleviate such fear (12:6–7), Jesus employs a similar *qal wahomer* strategy utilized later in the discourse on anxiety (12:24, 27, 28, 30). In both instances Jesus contends that God cares for birds (sparrows/ravens) and that people surpass (διαφέρω) birds (in value to God; 12:7, 24). Implicit in this comparison is that God's care for people will surpass that shown to the birds.

Each subsection in the discourse on anxiety concludes with reminders not to worry (12:25, 29). Among the reasons not to be anxious is the inability of anxiety to prolong life (12:25) or to effect change in other areas of one's life (12:26). One should not worry (about eating and drinking), since God ("the Father") is aware of such needs (12:29–30). The striving of nations after such things indicates ignorance about God's awareness of their needs (12:30).

An alternative to anxiety is offered in the twin forms of pursuing God's kingdom and selling one's possessions and giving alms (12:31, 33). The pursuit of the former will result in being given the very things one needs and about which one worries (food, drink, clothing; 12:31). The Father is not only aware of needs; it is also his "good pleasure to give" the kingdom (12:32b). This claim is offered as a reason for the command not to fear (μὴ φοβοῦ; 12:32a), a prohibition echoing Jesus' previous instruction (μὴ φοβηθῆτε; 12:4). The latter imperative (12:32) functions as a prerequisite to selling one's goods and giving alms (12:33).

The discourse on anxiety can be read as a rhetorical argument[14] culminating in the recommendation to sell one's goods and give alms. Most of this argument consists of warrants for the giving of alms, an act that is possible if one trusts that the Father will care for one's needs.[15] One can trust God to provide because of the divine care bestowed on nature and the even greater value that people have to God (12:24, 28). The tacit assumption is that an absence of fear regarding daily provision of food and drink (itself made possible by trusting that God's good pleasure is to give

---

14. So Sondra Ely Wheeler, *Wealth as Peril and Obligation: The New Testament on Possessions* (Grand Rapids: Eerdmans, 1995), 62.

15. So Johnson, *Literary Function*, 155.

both these things) can free a person to relinquish goods in the service of others (12:33).[16]

Reading the parable in light of the discourse on God and anxiety is justified based on their mutual proximity, the six lexical links they share (see ch. 5), and the specific connecting device (διὰ τοῦτο, "on account of this," 12:22) linking the two passages. The advice in 12:22–34 functions not only as a corollary of the parable but also, with 12:13–15 and 12:21, as one of its interpretive lenses.

The rich man in the parable exemplifies the antithesis of the lifestyle advocated in the subsequent discourse (trusting in God, selling one's goods, and giving alms). He displays a concern with his future eating (ἐσθίω) and drinking (πίνω; 12:19), and Jesus tells the disciples not to worry about what they are to eat (ἐσθίω; 12:22, 29) or drink (πίνω; 12:29). In contrast to the man's plan to build larger barns (ἀποθήκη; 12:18), Jesus cites approvingly the absence of any barns (ἀποθήκη) among the ravens (12:24).[17] Implied in the observation that God feeds the latter is an inability on the rich man's part to trust in God's provision (12:24b). Finally, as Jesus later claims, the rich man's plans prove impotent in prolonging his life (12:19, 25).

These multiple connections with the parable's literary context (12:22–34) invite reading 12:16–21 in light of sapiential conversations about anxiety. Anxiety is a motif in sapiential discussions of death and possessions, and it is possible that Luke appropriates and reconfigures this sapiential motif. Ben Sira links anxiety (μέριμνα) to the accumulation of wealth (χρῆμα; Sir 31:1–3). Lucian identifies worrying (φροντίζω) over acquiring an inheritance as a cause of premature death (*Dial. mort.* 16.4). Syriac Menander also sees undue anxiety as a cause of death (385–393). Seneca frequently links anxiety with the pursuit of luxury (*Ep.* 14.18; 42.7; 115.16; 119.15). He claims that anxiety stymies enjoyment (*Ep.* 14.18), and he posits a proportional relationship between one's "daily" worry and the measure of possessions a person acquires (*Ep.* 115.16). In Papyrus Insinger, God gives the "impious" person wealth so that he should worry daily (15.19). Other Egyptian texts eschew worry, recommending enjoyment instead.[18]

---

16. For an analysis of the tradition history and redaction of the saying in Luke 12:33, see Stephen R. Johnson, *Seeking the Imperishable Treasure: Wealth, Wisdom, and a Jesus Saying* (Eugene, Ore.: Cascade, 2008).

17. So Tannehill, *Luke*, 207

18. Statue of Nebneteru (*AEL* 3:18, 21–24); Inscription of Wennofer (*AEL* 3:56–57); cf. Ptahhotep (11; *AEL* 1:66).

When read in light of Luke 12:22–34, the rich man's response to the land's fruitful production can be understood as a manifestation of anxiety.[19] So, too, can the brother's interest in obtaining a share of the inheritance be regarded as a consequence of anxiety (12:13–15). Anxiety is embodied in specific practices related to possessions and in these instances is manifest in the pursuit of an inheritance and the plans to build larger barns and store goods for the future.[20] The rich man's plans to store his goods, moreover, evince a failure to trust in Jesus' subsequent characterization of God as one who will provide for his needs. This failure to trust in divine care is one reason that the rich man's plans constitute poverty vis-à-vis God (12:21b).[21]

I have argued previously that proposals for the use of possessions represent attempts to exert control given certain uncontrollable facets of death (death's inevitability, uncertain timing, potential imminence, etc.). Sapiential recommendations for the use of possessions function as a way to exert some modicum of control in the face of the loss of control that death represents.

Luke 12:13–34 makes two important contributions to this (largely sapiential) conversation. First, it identifies the fragility and uncertainties of life (of which death is one significant aspect) as a potential threat to one's sense of control. Life's fragility produces and fuels anxiety, which in turn stymies one's ability to live meaningfully. Anxiety hinders meaningful living, since it leads to the pursuit and amassing of possessions, an activity that (as noted above) not only fosters relational alienation but also fails to engender life (ζωή; 12:15).

Second, Luke 12:13–34 suggests that almost any effort to secure control through the use of possessions is a futile enterprise.[22] In Luke 12, enjoyment is seen not as an alternative to anxiety (*contra* Seneca) but as another possible symptom of it. Anxiety functions within this framework

19. So Caird, *The Gospel of St. Luke*, 163.

20. Plans that, admittedly, never come to fruition.

21. Eichholz sees in the discourse on anxiety the reason for the man's folly ("Vom reichen Kornbauern," 190–91). In this discourse, "all self-worries of a person are confronted with God's unique worries for people."

22. Johnson writes: "Possessions are what men use to preserve their life, to gain security against threat. But Jesus rejects this. The 'self' is not secured by possessions, and there is no correspondence between an increase in possessions and the state of a man's life" (*Literary Function*, 153).

as the sole fruit of the otherwise fruitless quest to exert control over one's life, either through the attempt to postpone death or through specific uses of possessions.

Luke's proposal of alms as a solution to anxiety is noteworthy precisely because this use of possessions most closely represents a relinquishing of the attempt to control life through one's possessions. In sharp contrast to the many methods whereby one might collect and accrue goods as a means of securing control, Luke upholds a use of goods (alms) that requires (a literal) letting go of control. Luke presents this precise use of goods as the vehicle through which one can store up treasure in heaven, thereby securing one's future relationship with God. As in Ben Sira, storing up riches does not "guarantee security" (Sir 11:10–11, 18–19, 20–21a, 23–24).[23] One rather achieves future security by relinquishing control of one's goods in the present. Releasing control is not, as in Seneca, an attitudinal detachment from possessions but rather a concrete act of selling and giving away of one's goods to the poor.

The parable suggests that greed is foolish because it harms both its owner, through the anxiety it produces, and others, through neglect. This focus upon the meaninglessness of avarice is a consequence of reading the parable in concert with Second Temple (sapiential) texts.

Why the Man Is (and Is Not) Called a Fool

I have proposed that the man's folly is best understood in terms of his limited imagination (in failing to practice any sapiential recommendations for the use of possessions in light of death's inevitability), the selfish and socially isolating nature of his greed, his saving for the future (and underlying assumption regarding the control he wields over his future), and the neglect of his own mortality. The benefit of reading Luke's parable in concert with Second Temple sapiential texts is evident when one compares the insights generated from this practice with prevailing yet ultimately unsatisfying understandings of the parable.

Many interpreters treat the description of the man as a "fool" (ἄφρων, 12:20) as the parable's *crux interpretum*.[24] As Eichholz maintains, the accu-

---

23. So Harrington, *Jesus Ben Sira*, 39.

24. So King, "The Man Who Was a Fool," 69–76; Eichholz, *Gleichnisse der Evangelien*, 185; Allen Verhey, *Remembering Jesus: Christian Community, Scripture, and the Moral Life* (Grand Rapids: Eerdmans, 2002), 108; cf. Dupont, *Les béatitudes*, 113.

sation of the man as a fool presents "the actual problem of the interpretation of our parable."[25] Seeking to clarify what the parable leaves unspecified, interpreters aim to discover the reason why the man is called a fool. In what does the man's folly consist?

Following Jeremias, most interpreters read the epithet "fool" in light of Ps 14:1a ("A fool [ἄφρων] said in his heart, 'There is no God'") and conclude that the rich man either is some type of atheist, has forgotten God, or has no relationship with God.[26] Reading the parable in light of Ps 14:1 coincides with a common tendency to depict the man's fault in (primarily) theological terms.[27] There is nothing amiss with speaking of the man's folly in such terms. Luke 12:21 invites such a reading, as does God's appearance in the parable and the prominent attention to God in 12:22–34. References to these latter verses would indeed buttress the arguments of those who use Ps 14:1 as the hermeneutical key to the parable.

But it is questionable if the single use of ἄφρων ("fool") in 12:20 justifies reading and understanding the parable through the primary lens of Ps 14:1.[28] There are indeed many problems with the assumption (usually

25. Eichholz, *Gleichnisse der Evangelien*, 185. He seeks to discover why the "clever" man "who acted so carefully" is called a fool. Eichholz insists on not prematurely evaluating the rich man in a negative manner; he views the man's initial response to the large production of his land as responsible (183–84). Eichholz suggests that the German passion for work has been improperly projected into the interpretation of this parable, resulting in premature (and unfair) criticisms of the rich man.

26. So Jeremias, *The Parables of Jesus*, 165; Danker, *Jesus and the New Age*, 247–48; Tannehill, *Luke*, 206; Wiefel, *Das Evangelium nach Lukas*, 237; Wright, "Parables on Poverty and Riches," 222; Scott, *Re-imagine the World*, 95; Snodgrass, *Stories with Intent*, 399.

27. Calvin accuses the man of not relying on God alone (*Commentary on a Harmony*, 150–51). King avers the man is a fool because he failed to recognize his dependence on God ("The Man Who Was a Fool"). Marshall, *Luke*: "The fool is the man who feels no need of God." Danker claims the rich man forgets God (*Jesus and the New Age*, 247–48). For Snodgrass, "the man left God out of the picture" (*Stories with Intent*, 399). One wonders if there is any influence here from von Rad, who defines folly as "practical atheism" (*Wisdom in Israel*, 65). The wide range of scholars who cite Ps 14:1 as a relevant parallel indicate that this strategy is widespread and not determined by one's geographic location, particular methodology, or type of theological commitment.

28. Interpreters who identify Ps 14:1 as an apt parallel also fail to explicate potential meanings of Ps 14:1, nor do they treat Ps 14:1 in its original literary context. It is

asserted without argument) that the appellation "fool" is best understood in light of Ps 14:1.

First, the evidence for employing Ps 14:1 as an interpretive lens to the parable (both texts use the term "fool," and no mention is made in the parable of the rich man's interaction with God) is paltry and, at best, circumstantial. The absence of an explicit reference to a relationship between God and the rich man is not sufficient evidence that he is an atheist or has disregard for God. The lack of a reference to God in 12:16–19 is typical of Lukan (and other Synoptic) parables. Characters in these parables are not regularly depicted as relating to God, and Luke 18:10–14 represents the sole exception.

Second, there is no indication that the only other instance of ἄφρων in Luke-Acts (Luke 11:40) should be read in light of Ps 14:1, nor has anyone suggested doing so. There are, however, compelling reasons for reading the parable in light of this other use of ἄφρων in Luke 11:40.[29] In the latter verse, ἄφρων immediately follows a reference to rapacity (ἁρπαγή; 11:39) and immediately precedes a reference to alms (ἐλεημοσύνη; 11:41). The presence of these two motifs in Luke 12:13–34 invites reading each episode in light of the other. When the parable is read in light of 11:39–41, the rich man's folly consists of greed and a failure to give away his goods in the form of alms.

Third, and most important, no argument is advanced for selecting Ps 14:1 over other potential intertexts that also use the term "fool." The arbitrary nature of the decision to understand Luke 12:19 through Ps 14:1 is curious, given the polyvalence of the term "fool." Several Hebrew Bible texts, for instance, associate folly with improper or excessive speech.[30] In light of such texts the man in the parable might be a fool because he speaks too frequently and before his time. God's explicit repudiation of the man's plans, that he will live for many years, might strengthen a case for such an argument. That the parable invites such a reading is just as unlikely as the argument for reading it in light of Ps 14:1.

---

puzzling that, despite its precise lexical parallel, Ps 53:2 (MT; LXX: 52:2) ("A fool said in his heart, 'There is no God'") has not been cited as a relevant text for Luke 12:20.

29. So Bovon, *L'Évangile selon Saint Luc*, 254.

30. Sir 20:7; Qoh 5:2; 10:14; Prov 10:8; cf. Sir 20:13; Qoh 10:12. See also Prov 6:12; 9:13; 10:18–19; 14:3; 15:2; 16:27; 17:7; 18:6–7; 19:1 (MT).

In light of Qoh 5:3, the man's folly might consist in delaying to fulfill a vow to God.[31] The parable gives no indication that the man either made or delayed a vow, and there is good reason that no one has argued for reading the parable in concert with Qoh 5:3. Yet just as little cause exists for reading the parable in light of Ps 14:1. Similarly, although folly is linked in the Hebrew Bible to adultery (Prov 7:7–27; 18:22 LXX), anger,[32] idolatry (Wis 14:8–13; 15:4–6, 14–15), and reviling God (Ps 74:18, 22), there is no legitimate basis for assuming that the rich man is guilty of any of these activities. The myriad vices associated with the epithet "fool" demonstrate the arbitrary nature of selecting only one of these (Ps 14:1) as the definitive text for explicating Luke 12:19.[33]

Even more puzzling than the singular fixation on Ps 14:1 is the neglect of texts that associate "fool" with the misuse or abuse of possessions, a motif germane to Luke's parable and its literary context. Jeremiah, for instance, describes a person who makes wealth unjustly (οὐ μετὰ κρίσεως) but whose riches later abandon him, leaving him to be a fool (ἄφρων) in his last days (Jer 17:11).[34] One might consider this parallel more apropos to Luke's parable than Ps 14:1, since, as in Jeremiah, Luke's rich man also finds himself on the verge of losing his possessions in his last days. The above examples from the Jewish Bible expand the potential semantic repertoire of the term "fool" beyond that of someone who fails to acknowledge God.

More helpful explanations for what constitutes the rich man's folly are found when the parable is situated among sapiential texts that focus on death and/or possessions,[35] for numerous wisdom texts associate folly with motifs that are germane to Luke's parable, namely, the (mis)use of possessions and/or faulty perceptions of death. For Proverbs, living in luxury (τρυφή) is not appropriate for a fool (ἄφρων; Prov 19:10), and foolish men (ἄφρων) swallow up a treasure (θησαυρός; Prov 21:20). Qoheleth contrasts the fool (ἄφρων) with the rich (πλούσιος; Qoh 10:6). One might

31. "Just as when you pray a vow to God, do not delay repaying it, for [God] has no pleasure in fools" (LXX).

32. Both θυμός (Qoh 7:9; Prov 29:11; Sir 31:30) and ὀργή (Prov 12:16; 27:3). Cf. Prov 14:17, 29.

33. Donahue offers a more sober approach, noting that the use of ἄφρων "recalls the wide OT polemic against 'folly'" (*The Gospel in Parable*, 178).

34. The analogy with the partridge (17:11a) suggests that the unjust amassing of wealth consists of taking it from others.

35. Bovon similarly claims that it is "necessary to plunge into Hebrew wisdom" to understand the meaning of "fool" in 12:20 (*L'Évangile selon Saint Luc*, 255).

consider the man in the parable a fool because, rather than mourning, he plans on enjoyment (εὐφροσύνη), an activity that Qoheleth associates with the "heart of fools [ἀφρόνων]" (Qoh 7:4). Ben Sira claims that every fool (ἄφρων) is taken captive by gold and that one's obsession with the metal leads to ruin and destruction (Sir 31:5–7).

Several extrabiblical sapiential texts also associate the term "fool" with an improper attitude toward, and use of, possessions. The Egyptian Instruction of Ankhsheshonq contains the following two statements in close proximity:

> Even if filled with soap, a storehouse yields a profit. (20.21).
> There is no fool who finds profit. (21.8; *AEL* 3:175)

Read in light of this pairing, the figure in Luke's parable can be understood as a fool because of his inability to yield a profit even when given ample opportunity by the production of his land and the presence of numerous storehouses (12:18).[36] When his death is announced (12:20), he has not yet found a profit from his land or storehouses. He has merely imagined it.

The eighth instruction of Papyrus Insinger contrasts the fool with the wise person within the context of a series of sayings on gluttony:

> The fool who does not control himself will be in want through gluttony.[37]
> The fool who has power, what happens to him is bad.
> It is the god who gives wealth; it is a wise man who guards <it>.
> The virtue of a wise man is to gather without greed.
> The great glory of a wise man is to control himself in his manner of life.
> The fool is in bad odor in the street because of gluttony. (5.13–18; *AEL* 3:189)

These sayings associate the fool with gluttony and insinuate, furthermore, that a fool is someone who gathers with greed (5.16). Each of these aspects of folly may be applied to the rich man in Luke's parable. In light of this critique of gluttony, the rich man's folly is evident in his plan to eat, drink, and enjoy.[38] The plans to tear down his barns and store his land's produce can be read as the acts of one who "gathers with greed" (5.16).[39]

---

36. The man is said to have "large barns" (Luke 12:18) and plans on building larger ones (12:18).

37. These sayings follow a warning that gluttony can lead to poverty (5.12).

38. For another link between the term "fool" and gluttony, see P. Ins. 7.9 (*AEL* 3:191).

39. On the other hand, the man's plans to protect the surplus of his field seems to

In light of the following sayings in Papyrus Insinger, one might identify gluttony as a cause of the rich man's imminent death:

> There is he who is weary from yesterday yet has a craving for wine.
> [There is] he who dislikes intercourse yet <spends> his surplus on women.
> [There is] he who dies in misery on account of gluttony.
> [The] evil that befalls the fool, his belly and his phallus bring it. (5.22–6.1; *AEL* 3:189)

Greco-Roman authors apply the term "fool" to those who misuse goods and to those who fail to live appropriately in light of death. On more than one occasion Seneca associates folly with planning for the future. After citing Epicurus approvingly ("The fool, with all his other faults, has this also, —he is always getting ready to live" [Frag. 494]), Seneca remarks:

> Reflect ... what this saying means, and you will see how revolting is the fickleness of men who lay down every day new foundations of life, and begin to build up fresh hopes *even at the brink of the grave*. Look within your own mind for individual instances; you will think of old men who are preparing themselves at that very hour for a political career, or for travel, or for business. (*Ep.* 13.16–17, emphasis added)

The man Seneca describes takes time while on the brink of death to make plans for the future. Luke's rich man follows a similar course; by preparing to live, he fails to live.

In a separate letter Seneca cites another saying of Epicurus: "The fool's life is empty of gratitude and full of fears; its course *lies wholly toward the future*" (*Ep.* 15.9, citing Frag. 491; emphasis added). In his comment on this quote, Seneca criticizes the making of future plans and the insatiability that prevents contentment.[40]

> And what sort of life do you think is meant by the fool's life? ... he means our own, for we are plunged by our blind desires into ventures which will

comport with the description of a "wise man" as one who guards the wealth that God gives (5.15). The wisdom of his decision to store up goods for the future is evident in light of the later description in the Eighth Instruction of a fool as one who "forgets the morrow," and who "will lack food in it" (7.6). It remains debatable whether the man gathers with or without greed (5:16).

40. The fool veers "from plan to plan" and is "inconsistent; nothing suits him for long" (Seneca, *Ep.* 52.1–2).

> harm us, but certainly will never satisfy us; for if we could be satisfied with anything, we should have been satisfied long ago; nor do we reflect how pleasant it is to demand nothing, how noble it is to be contented and not to be dependent upon Fortune. (*Ep.* 15.9–10)

Seneca links folly both with greed and the constant hope that one's life will last as long as possible. In addition to not being satisfied with their income, such people "grasp at the utmost space of time to which the life of man can be extended" (*Ep.* 120.17).[41] Seneca insists, to the contrary, that "we stand daily nearer the brink, and every hour of time thrusts us on towards the precipice over which we must fall" (*Ep.* 120.17–18). The fool fails to live meaningfully because of not recognizing death's potential imminence. It is this nearness of death that Luke's rich man neglects and about which God informs him.

Lucian associates folly (μάταιος) with two vices: hoarding money for unrelated heirs and thinking that one will live forever (*Dial. mort.* 22.7). The man in Luke's parable can with good reason be viewed as guilty on both counts; he hoards and does not dwell on the possible imminence of his death. Lucian's pairing of these two faults suggests a possible causal relationship between the two, namely, that hoarding is a consequence of a failure to face the reality (and potential imminence) of one's death.

As the above selections demonstrate, Ps 14:1 reflects one of many possible semantic associations for the term "fool." Because this epithet encompasses such a plethora of diverse behaviors and attitudes, it is irresponsible to insist that Luke 12:19 be understood in light of only one of these. This lexically myopic understanding of "fool" fails to explain adequately the rich man's folly.

In contrast to Ps 14:1, texts linking folly with improper attitudes toward death and possessions engender more insight why Luke's rich man is labeled a fool. Reading the parable in light of such texts provides a more richly textured and nuanced treatment of the characterization of the rich man. His folly reflects not a type of atheism but rather a twin failure to utilize possessions properly and to acknowledge and accept his own mortality.

---

41. Seneca notes that fools believe that the transition to death is a "dangerous reef" (*Ep.* 70.2).

8
Comparing the Parable of the Rich Fool in Luke and Thomas

The distinctive elements and contributions of Luke's parable are put into sharp relief when compared with the parallel version in the Coptic Gospel of Thomas.[1] Comparing Luke's version of the parable with that in Thomas provides an opportunity to reexamine some of the claims made in the previous three chapters regarding the benefit of reading the parable in concert with Second Temple texts whose focus is the interplay of death and possessions. Since my comparison makes extensive use of Thomas's parable, I will cite it in full.[2]

---

1. The comparison I undertake is primarily literary in nature and is not concerned with questions concerning which version predated the other or whether the Thomas saying is authentic to the historical Jesus. For these and general introductory issues related to Thomas, see Robert McL. Wilson, *Studies in the Gospel of Thomas* (London: Mowbray, 1960); H. E. W. Turner and Hugh Montefiore, *Thomas and the Evangelists* (SBT; Naperville, Ill.: Allenson, 1962); Gerant Vaughan Jones, *The Art and Truth of the Parables: A Study in Their Literary Form and Modern Interpretation* (London: SPCK, 1964), 230–40; Stephen J. Patterson, "The Gospel of Thomas within The Development of Early Christianity" (Ph.D. diss., Claremont Graduate University, 1988); Stephen J. Patterson and James M. Robinson, eds., *The Fifth Gospel: The Gospel of Thomas Comes of Age* (Harrisburg, Pa.: Trinity Press International, 1998); Jon Ma. Asgeirsson, April D. Deconick, and Risto Uro, eds., *Thomasine Traditions in Antiquity: The Social and Cultural World of the Gospel of Thomas* (NHMS 59; Leiden: Brill, 2006).

2. The Coptic text is from James Robinson, *The Coptic Gnostic Library: A Complete Edition of the Nag Hammadi Codices* (5 vols.; Leiden: Brill, 2000), 2:76–77. See also the Coptic text (and a Greek retroversion) in Uwe-Karsten Plisch, *The Gospel of Thomas: Original Text with Commentary* (trans. Gesine Schenke Robinson; Stuttgart: Deutsche Bibelgesellschaft, 2008), 154–55. For questions regarding the dating of Thomas, see Robinson, *The Coptic Gnostic Library*, 2:38–39. No Greek fragments are extant in Thomas for this saying.

ⲡⲉϫⲉ ⲓ̅ⲥ̅ | ϫⲉ ⲛⲉⲩⲛ̅ ⲟⲩⲣⲱⲙⲉ ⲙ̅ⲡⲗⲟⲩⲥⲓⲟⲥ ⲉⲩⲛ̅ⲧⲁϥ ⲙ̅|ⲙⲁⲩ ⲛ̅ϩⲁϩ ⲛ̅ⲭⲣⲏⲙⲁ ⲡⲉϫⲁϥ ϫⲉ ϯⲛⲁⲣ̅ⲭⲣⲱ ⲛ̅||ⲛⲁⲭⲣⲏⲙⲁ ϫⲉⲕⲁⲁⲥ ⲉⲉⲓⲛⲁϫⲟ ⲛ̅ⲧⲁⲱ[[ϩ]]ⲥϩ | ⲛ̅ⲧⲁⲧⲱϭⲉ ⲛ̅ⲧⲁⲙⲟⲩϩ ⲛ̅ⲛⲁⲉϩⲱⲣ ⲛ̅ⲕⲁⲣ`|ⲡⲟⲥ ϣⲓⲛⲁ ϫⲉ ⲛⲓⲣ̅ ϭⲣⲱϩ ⲗ̅ⲗⲁⲁⲩ ⲛⲁⲉⲓⲛⲉ|ⲛⲉϥⲙⲉⲉⲩⲉ ⲉⲣⲟⲟⲩ ϩⲙ̅ ⲡⲉϥϩⲏⲧ` ⲁⲩⲱ ϩⲛ̅ | ⲧⲟⲩϣⲏ ⲉⲧⲙ̅ⲙⲁⲩ ⲁϥⲙⲟⲩ ⲡⲉⲧⲉⲩⲙ̅ ⲙⲁϫⲉ || ⲙ̅ⲙⲟϥ` ⲙⲁⲣⲉϥ`ⲥⲱⲧⲙ̅

Jesus said, "There was a rich man who had many possessions. He said, 'I shall put my possessions[3] to use so that I may sow, reap, plant, and fill my storehouse with produce, with the result that I shall lack nothing.' Such were his intentions, but that same night he died. Let him who has ears hear." (Gos. Thom. 63)

Although the general outline of the story in the two versions is similar, there are few precise similarities that the two versions share in common.[4] The main character in each is a "rich" (πλούσιος / ⲡⲗⲟⲩⲥⲓⲟⲥ) man who articulates plans for the future that involve storing the land's produce in some type of storehouse. These plans are stymied, however, due to the man's death (announced in Luke, realized in Thomas) later on that night. In neither version does the man demonstrate any awareness of his imminent death. In both cases he is preoccupied, immediately before dying, with plans related to his possessions. This is where most of the resemblances end.

The two parables exhibit far more differences than similarities, and these divergences illuminate the distinctive voice and concerns of each version. Many of these disparities concern the contested sapiential con-

---

3. Aside from ⲛ̅ⲭⲣⲏⲙⲁ, the translation of the Coptic is that of Thomas Lambdin (Robinson, *The Coptic Gnostic Library*, 2:77). Plisch translates the two occurrences of ⲛ̅ⲭⲣⲏⲙⲁ as "possessions" (*The Gospel of Thomas*, 63); Lambdin translates the term as "money" both times. For the Greek χρῆμα, cf. LSJ, 2004–5. As Plisch notes, the plural of χρῆμα can mean "money."

4. Jones calls Thomas's version an "abbreviated" form of Luke's but does not draw attention to any of the differences between the parables (*Art and Truth*, 232). For Plisch, the "similarities in subject matter and structure show the core of the narrative still being the same" (*The Gospel of Thomas*, 155). Wolfgang Schrage sees far less similarities between the two versions and differentiates the identities of the two main characters (*Das Verhältnis des Thomas-Evangeliums zur synoptischen Tradition und zu den koptischen Evangelienübersetzungen* [BZNW 29; Berlin: Töpelmann, 1964], 131). His view reflects that of Johannes Leipoldt, who calls the man in Thomas a merchant and the man in Luke a farmer (*Das Evangelium nach Thomas* [TU 101; Berlin: Adademie, 1967], 68).

versation on the interplay of death and possessions. I will argue that some of the fundamental differences between the two versions highlight the important rhetorical function of character identification in Luke's parable.

Sapiential options for the use of possessions such as enjoyment, inheritance, and alms are lacking in Thomas. Thomas evinces no overt interest in the motif of enjoyment. The sole ideal and ultimate goal of Thomas's rich man is not rest, eating, drinking, nor enjoyment but self-sufficiency.[5] The envisioned result of his agricultural activities and filling his storehouse is that he will "lack nothing."

The issue of inheritance, an important element in the literary context of Luke's parable (12:13–15), is absent in the immediate context of Gos. Thom. 63. Thomas's version of the dispute regarding inheritance (Gos. Thom. 72; cf. Luke 12:13–15) neither immediately precedes nor occurs in close proximity to the parable of the rich man.[6] Even so, the question regarding the inheritance in Thomas lacks Luke 12:15, removing the explicit critique of avarice (πλεονεξία), which functions, in Luke, as the parable's introduction and one of its interpretive lenses. It is possible that the two pericopae were joined together in Thomas's source and that he separated them.[7] In any event, the absence of God's question concerning the future status of the man's possessions also removes inheritance from the parable's purview.

The critique of greed that frames and introduces Luke's version (12:15) is absent in Thomas. Neither do alms, Luke's alternative solution and antidote to greed (Luke 12:33; cf. 11:39, 41), appear in (or in close proximity to) Thomas's version. In short, Thomas addresses none of the sapiential recommendations regarding the use of possessions in light of death's inevitability that appear in Luke 12:13–34.

---

5. So Hugh Montefiore, "A Comparison of the Parables of the Gospel according to Thomas and of the Synoptic Gospels," in Montefiore and Turner, *Thomas and the Evangelists*, 57; Snodgrass, *Stories with Intent*, 393.

6. For a comparison of Gos. Thom. 72 and Luke 12:13–14, see Baarda, "Text and Transmission," 131–66. Thomas's version of the inheritance dispute (Gos. Thom. 72) reads as follows: "A [man said] to him, 'Tell my brothers to divide my father's possessions with me.' He said to him, 'O man, who has made me a divider?' He turned to his disciples and said to them, 'I am not a divider, am I?'" (Lambdin, *The Coptic Gnostic Library*, 2:81).

7. Both Luke and the Diatessaron place the episode of the inheritance dispute immediately prior to the Rich Fool parable.

A significant difference between Luke and Thomas is that the former's version provides (by virtue of its immediate literary context) constructive proposals (alms, giving to God) for how a person might use goods. Luke's rich man failed to do anything with his goods, but he did intend to enjoy them. Although the goal of self-sufficiency in Thomas's version does reflect certain sapiential emphases,[8] it does not reflect sapiential recommendations that occur in discussions about death. Ben Sira frames his warning against self-sufficiency within a discussion of the uncertain timing and potential imminence of death (Sir 11:24).

The crisis of the land's abundant production that introduces and frames Luke's parable is also absent in Thomas.[9] The dilemma in Luke, as identified by the rich man, is the lack of adequate storage for the abundant fruits (12:16), leading him to ask what he should do (12:17). The man recognizes that he "does not have where he will gather together his crops," and his proposed resolution (tearing down his barns and building larger ones) addresses this lack of storage capacity (12:17–18).

Nor is there in Thomas's version a catalyst for the man's plans regarding his possessions, aside from the fact that he has much of it. In Thomas, the man's intentions appear not in response to a specific event, as in Luke, but rather *ex nihilo*. It is as though we meet Thomas's man *in media res*, without being properly introduced to the setting of the story. Thomas's sayings do generally lack a narrative frame, but his capability of providing them is evident in the two parables immediately following that of the Rich Fool. His parable of the Banquet (Gos. Thom. 64) contains the same type of narrative frame one finds in the Synoptic parallels (Matt 22:1–10; Luke 14:16–24). The parable of the Vineyard Owner (Gos. Thom. 65) likewise includes a narrative frame that parallels those in the Synoptics (Mark 12:1–9; Matt 21:33–41; Luke 20:9–16).[10] Many other sayings in Thomas

8. Proverbs, for example, warns that those who are lazy are in danger of becoming poor (Prov 6:6–11; 10:4; 28:19).

9. The crisis facing the man concerns how he should respond to the land's abundant production.

10. These three parables in Thomas (63, 64, 65) may have been placed together because of the common word ⲣⲱⲙⲉ (ἄνθρωπος). Sayings 64 and 65 both have the word ϩⲙϩⲁⲗ (δοῦλος). Montefiore claims that sayings 64 and 65 are linked together because of their shared "warning about the dangers of materialism" ("Comparison of the Parables," 70).

also include some type of narrative introduction (Gos. Thom. 6, 12, 13, 18, 20, 21, 22, 24, 37, 43, 51–53, 60, 61, 79, 91, 99, 100, 104, 113, 114).

The lack of a specific reason to explain why Thomas's rich man puts his wealth to use might make it more difficult for readers/hearers to empathize or sympathize (and therefore identify) with him. Luke's rich man, by contrast, finds himself in a specific predicament (the land's abundant production coupled with a corresponding lack of adequate storage space) that might enable readers/hearers to imagine themselves in the same (or similar) quandary. Imagining the difficulty presented by such a crisis might increase the ability of readers/hearers to identify with the rich man in Luke's version.

There is another difference between Luke and Thomas that might more easily facilitate character identification on the part of readers/hearers with Luke's rich man. Whereas the rich man in Luke's version questions what course of action he should take (τί ποιήσω, "what might/should I do?"; 12:17), the man in Thomas proceeds without any similar query. Because the rich man in Thomas never questions what he might or will do, there is less opportunity for readers/hearers to put themselves in his place. Any crisis or predicament that might involve (and invite from readers/hearers) an imagined range of potentially disparate responses is absent. Thomas's conclusion to the parable ("Let him who has ears hear") is an explicit invitation for readers to reflect upon the parable and its meaning, but not necessarily to identify with the character of the rich man.

The rich man's question in Luke 12:17 (τί ποιήσω) enhances the possibility for both narrative tension and suspense as well as character identification. The repetition of τί ποιήσω in key moments of Luke's narrative has prepared the reader/hearer to expect some type of dénouement to the rich man's crisis.[11] The reader/hearer of Luke is thereby invited to wonder what course of action the rich man will undertake in response to the crisis of a justly acquired surplus. This question (τί ποιήσω) also has the potential rhetorical effect of inviting readers/hearers to ask themselves the same question. Luke's readers/hearers can make this question their own by asking how, especially given death's inevitability and potential imminence, they might make use of a justly acquired surplus.

The dissimilar descriptions of the rich man's death in the two versions points to another device in Luke that might encourage readers/hearers

11. Luke 3:10, 12, 14; 10:25; 16:3; 18:18, 41; 20:13, 15; Acts 2:37; 4:16; 22:10.

to identify with the rich man. Thomas relates the man's death in the past tense: "he died [ⲁϥⲙⲟⲩ]." It is an event that marks the conclusion both to the parable and to the man's life. Luke's version, in contrast, announces the man's death as a future (albeit imminent) event. Though announced, it has not yet taken place.

This difference is potentially significant, for it raises the question of how much time Luke's character might have between the announcement of his imminent death and its realization. Might the character in Luke's version have time to respond to the divine announcement by disposing of his goods in a certain manner? The announcement of a future death also enables (and potentially encourages) readers/hearers of Luke's version to consider their own use of possessions, in view of the possibility of death's imminence.[12] The declaration of the man's death in Thomas eliminates the possibility that he altered his behavior regarding the use of his goods.

Thomas's conclusion differs from Luke's in that its sole concern is the man's death. No interest is expressed regarding the ongoing life of the rich man's possessions. Thomas's interest in the possessions ends with the rich man's death. The question of the use of possessions appears, therefore, to play a more central role in Luke's version than in Thomas's. On the other hand, Thomas displays a keen interest in the handling of possessions.[13] Both versions describe the man as "rich" (πλούσιος / ⲙ̄ⲡⲗⲟⲩⲥⲓⲟⲥ), but only Thomas adds that he also had "much possessions [ⲛ̄ϩⲁϩ ⲛ̄ⲭⲣⲏⲙⲁ]." In Thomas, furthermore, the man plans to put his possessions (ⲭⲣⲏⲙⲁ) to use.

The two versions differ in regard to the role of the land. In Luke, the land produces abundantly, whereas in Thomas the man works the land (sowing, planting, reaping) *so that* it will produce abundantly. Thomas depicts a man who partners with (or manipulates?) the land to secure a surplus.[14] The abundant production of the land in Luke seems to be more of a (surprising) gift to the rich man. Luke's version stresses the *gifted* nature of the land in a way that Thomas does not. Thomas's version, on the

12. Stephen J. Patterson claims that the presence of God's announcement in Luke "makes explicit that which the Thomas version leaves to be discerned by the perceptive reader" ("Gospel of Thomas," 105).

13. Hugh Montefiore describes the concern in Thomas's version to be about "the dangers of commercial success" ("Comparison of the Parables," 54 n. 1).

14. In Luke, the man's plans for storage result from a surplus of goods. In Thomas, however, the man plans to use his wealth in order to *create* a surplus.

other hand, stresses the manner in which the man becomes a partner and co-worker with the land in its production of goods.

Luke's focus on the just acquisition of a surplus is more evident when compared with Thomas. Luke clarifies the source of (some of) the rich man's possessions by informing us that his land produced abundantly (12:16a). This clarification is important, given the regularity with which texts from Luke's milieu deride the unjust acquisition of wealth and issue proscriptions against it (e.g., Pseudo-Phocylides, *Sentences* 5). As noted previously, the Epistle of 1 Enoch *assumes* that all rich people have acquired their wealth unjustly. Thomas's failure to identify the source and means of the rich man's wealth, in light of this pervasive critique, leaves open the question whether or not his wealth was justly or unjustly acquired. Such a question might be of interest to a reader of the parable who was familiar with texts that deplore those who procure their wealth unjustly.

Finally, the presence of God as a character in Luke's parable is a striking difference with Thomas. The divine speech in Luke's version shows God to be keenly interested in the man's plans for his goods (12:20). God's important function is evident not only in his appearance as a literary character but also in the parable's conclusion (Luke 12:21). Whereas Thomas leaves readers/hearers to consider for themselves what the parable might mean ("Let him who has ears hear"), Luke identifies the man's storage of goods as an act of greed that constitutes poverty toward God (Luke 12:15, 21).[15] The absence of Luke 12:21 in Thomas (and Codex Bezae of Luke's version) lacks the Lukan insistence that the man's (selfish) storage of goods is both an ethical and theological act.[16]

15. Plisch notes that the conclusion in Thomas ("Let him who has ears hear") also appears as a variant in some manuscripts of Luke after 12:21 (*The Gospel of Thomas*, 156).

16. Given the external evidence for its inclusion, Metzger considers the absence of 12:21 in Codex Bezae and some old Latin versions to be "accidental" (*A Textual Commentary*, 135).

Conclusion: Illustrating Wisdom

Luke's parable of the rich fool is not a *Beispielerzählung*[1] merely providing a negative example to be avoided, nor is it simply a "critique of the rich."[2] The parable and its immediate literary context participate, reconfigure, and illustrate a highly contested Second Temple sapiential conversation regarding the meaningful use of goods given life's fragility and death's inevitability, uncertain timing, and potential imminence. Luke 12:13–34 reconfigures sapiential motifs by revealing a keen interest in the use of goods that are justly acquired and how to use these goods meaningfully, in light of the uncontrollable aspects of death such as its unpredictable timing. In light of the potential imminence of death, Luke 12:13–34 rejects as meaningless the pursuit of an inheritance, solitary enjoyment, and the storage of goods for one's own future use.

The parable and its immediate literary context not only eschew these uses of possessions but also champion a specific way of using goods. In light of death's inevitability and uncertain timing, Luke proposes alms as the optimal way to use possessions meaningfully. Alms are meaningful precisely in the context of death as an inevitable event whose timing is uncertain and potentially imminent. Alms are the primary antidote and alternative to greed and anxiety, vices that are manifest in social isolation and a selfish storage of goods for future use. Because giving alms provides one with an "unfailing treasure in heaven," it is meaningful not only for the poor to whom it is given but also for the one who gives it.[3] Giving alms is the primary way of being rich toward God and is, in light of death's

1. *Contra* Jülicher, *Die Gleichnisreden Jesu*, 2:viii; Bultmann, *History of the Synoptic Tradition*, 177–78; Seng, "Der Reiche Tor," 140–41; Fitzmyer, *The Gospel according to Luke*, 2:971; Wiefel, *Das Evangelium nach Lukas*, 236; Crossan, *In Parables*, 83; Bovon, *L'Évangile selon Saint Luc*, 245.

2. Tuckett, *Luke*, 96.

3. So Wheeler, *Wealth as Peril*, 63–64.

inevitability, uncertain timing, and potential imminence, the most meaningful option for the use of one's goods.

Proposing alms as the most fitting use of one's goods, given these uncontrollable facets of death, exemplifies Luke's participation in the (predominantly sapiential) conversation on death and possessions. No less important are the multiple ways in which Luke reconfigures aspects of this conversation by adapting sapiential motifs for his own existential, ethical, and theological interests. In doing so, Luke demonstrates both his indebtedness to sapiential discourse and the range of his own literary and theological creativity.

Further Implications

Luke's Parables as Sapiential Narratives

Chapters 5–7 demonstrate that the category *Beispeilerzählung* fails to capture or reflect adequately the rich texture of Luke 12:16–21. Classifying the parable as an "example narrative" mischaracterizes it because it only sees in the parable a warning against a certain behavior, in this case greed. But the parable evinces an interest in *why* such behavior is problematic and suggests that it is within a specific context (life's fragility and death's inevitability, uncertain timing, and potential imminence). As with many wisdom texts, the parable reflects on the kind of action that is appropriate for a specific "time" or situation.[4] Luke 12:16–21 reflects a wrestling with fundamentally existential questions related to the meaningful use of possessions in light of the aforementioned aspects of death. Luke's concern for questions related to meaningful living may prove to be a fruitful way of thinking about and analyzing his other parables.

Lukan parables display a special interest in the interplay of death and possessions. This twin motif appears most explicitly in Lazarus and the Rich Man (16:19–31) and the Unjust Steward (16:1–8), yet parables such as the Samaritan (10:30–36) and the Father and Two Sons (15:11–32) also reflect a concern, albeit more implicitly, with the use of goods within the context of a particular aspect of death. An analysis of these parables would provide a more nuanced and complete picture of Luke's attitude toward enjoyment, alms, luxury, saving for the future, generosity, hospitality, and

4. See, e.g., von Rad, *Wisdom in Israel*, 139.

inheritance. Within these parables Luke explores each of these options as potential vehicles of meaning, given the uncontrollable facets of death.

Common to many wisdom texts is a concern for negotiating where meaning is (and is not) located. James VanderKam, for example, defines wisdom literature as texts that "grapple in a more universal way with the meaning of life, with life's perplexities, and with how to live it properly."[5] Others have also observed the interest that wisdom texts have with living meaningfully.[6]

Luke's parables are similarly concerned with meaning and questions related to meaningful living. By "meaning" I refer to the symbolic domain from which people derive, and to which people ascribe, significance.[7] Although this "search for meaning" is first and foremost an existential endeavor,[8] it is inextricably bound up in Luke with ethical and theological concerns.

Luke's parables address the intersection of two specific motifs, death and possessions, each of which plays a significant role in the meaning that people construct for their lives. The interplay of these two motifs is not only a theme in Luke but also an important element of the narrative's rhetoric. By illustrating options for the use of possessions within the context of death's potential imminence and a postmortem judgment, Luke's parables engender reflection on the relative meaningfulness (or lack thereof) of dis-

5. James C. VanderKam, *An Introduction to Early Judaism* (Grand Rapids: Eerdmans, 2001), 115. Arguments regarding the definitions, boundaries, and chief characteristics of wisdom literature are manifold and complex. Crenshaw defines wisdom literature as a marriage between the form ("proverbial sentence or instruction, debate, intellectual reflection") and content ("self-evident intuitions about mastering life for human betterment, gropings after life's secrets with regard to innocent suffering, grappling with finitude, and quest for truth concealed in the created order and manifested in Dame Wisdom") of wisdom (*Old Testament Wisdom*, 19; see 11–25 for a fuller discussion). For various types of wisdom, see von Rad, *Old Testament Theology*, 1:418–59. Brueggemann describes wisdom as "the deposit of the best observations coming from a long history of reflection on experience" ("Epistemological Crisis," 86).

6. See, e.g., Seow, *Ecclesiastes*, 67; Gammie, "From Prudentialism to Apocalypticism," 482. It is noteworthy in this regard that Crenshaw entitles his chapter on Ecclesiastes "Chasing after Meaning" (*Old Testament Wisdom*, 116).

7. Clifford Geertz claims that the "imposition of meaning on life is the major end and primary condition of human existence" ("Deep Play: Notes on the Balinese Cockfight," in *The Interpretation of Cultures* [New York: Basic Books, 1973], 434).

8. Viktor Frankl argues that a person's primary concern is "to see a meaning in his life" (*Man's Search for Meaning* [New York: Washington Square Press, 1985], 136).

parate uses of possessions. This interest in meaningful living is not unlike Martha Nussbaum's understanding of the goal of Hellenistic philosophy as "human flourishing, or *eudaimonia*."[9]

Luke's parables share this interest, displayed in sapiential texts and Hellenistic philosophy, in meaningful living and illustrate it through the vehicle of narrative. His parables construct imaginative worlds in which the use of possessions is evaluated in light of life's fragility, death's inevitability, and a postmortem judgment. As narratives, Luke's parables illustrate sapiential concerns for meaning and provide the opportunity for literary characters and readers/hearers of Luke-Acts to evaluate their own use of possessions in light of the world constructed in the parable. For Luke, certain uses of possessions stymie one's capacity to live meaningfully. By contrast, other ways of using possessions enhance one's ability to live meaningfully.

In Luke's parable of the Rich Fool, this existential search for meaning is inseparable from ethical and theological concerns. The selfish storage of goods is deemed meaningless because it fails to include others, and this failure is considered poverty toward God. The use of alms is meaningful, by contrast, precisely because it enhances the lives of the giver and the recipient(s), and this act constitutes riches toward God.

Luke's parables thus function simultaneously as narratives of disorientation and reorientation.[10] Both of these functions are important. On the one hand, Luke's parables deconstruct certain behaviors (e.g., solitary enjoyment, selfish storage of goods for the future, neglect of suffering), revealing them to be inadequate sources of meaning. Yet parables do much more than merely subvert. They also construct worlds of possibility that by their very nature invite others to consider alternative ways of living. In particular, Luke's parables envision alternative ways of using possessions (e.g., hospitality, alms, generosity, and communal enjoyment). Luke's parables illustrate a rhetorical argument that these are meaningful uses of possessions, especially given one's inevitable death and postmortem judgment. It

9. Nussbaum underscores the emphasis of *eudaimonia* on "completeness of life" and prefers to translate the term as "human flourishing" (*Therapy of Desire*, 15).

10. On these terms, see Paul Ricoeur, "Biblical Hermeneutics," *Semeia* 4 (1975): 114–24; idem, *Conflict of Interpretations* (Evanston, Ill.: Northwestern University, 1974), 369–70. For an application of these terms to the Psalms, see Walter Brueggemann, "Psalms and the Life of Faith: A Suggested Typology of Function," *JSOT* 17 (1980): 5–21.

is precisely the context of death's uncertain timing, potential imminence, and postmortem judgment that makes these uses more meaningful than solitary enjoyment and saving for one's own future use.

Sapiential elements have been observed in the Synoptic Gospels,[11] and Jesus has been called a "teacher of aphoristic wisdom."[12] Indeed, Origen preferred "Wisdom" as the most appropriate title for Jesus.[13] Most scholarly attention on wisdom and the Gospels has neglected Luke, focusing rather on John, Q, or Matthew.[14]

Luke's Gospel, however, is replete with sapiential language, and he employs the term σοφία with more regularity than Mark or Matthew.[15]

---

11. Bultmann, *History of the Synoptic Tradition*, 69–108; William A. Beardslee, "The Wisdom Tradition and the Synoptic Gospels," *JAAR* 35 (1967): 231–40; idem, *Literary Criticism of the New Testament* (Philadelphia: Fortress, 1970), 30–41.

12. James G. Williams, *Those Who Ponder Proverbs: Aphoristic Thinking and Biblical Literature* (Bible and Literature Series 2; Sheffield: Almond, 1981), 16. See also Burton L. Mack, *A Myth of Innocence: Mark and Christian Origins* (Philadelphia: Fortress, 1988).

13. Origen, *Commentary on John* 1.109–124. Origen cites other titles for Jesus (e.g., Word, Life, Truth), but he favors Wisdom.

14. For John, see George W. MacRae ("Gnosticism and the Church of John's Gospel," in *Nag Hammadi, Gnosticism, and Early Christianity* [ed. C. W. Hedrick and R. Hodgson; Peabody, Mass.: Hendrickson, 1986], 84–96), who sees a "wisdom theology" in John's Gospel. For Q, see James M. Robinson, "Jesus as Sophos and Sophia: Wisdom Tradition and the Gospels," in *Aspects of Wisdom in Judaism and Early Christianity* (ed. Robert L. Wilken; Notre Dame, Ind.: University of Notre Dame Press, 1975), 1–16; James M. Robinson and Helmut Koester, *Trajectories through Early Christianity* (Philadelphia: Fortress, 1971), 71–113. For the identification of wisdom as the earliest stratum of the Q tradition, see Helmut Koester, "*Gnomai Diaphorai*: The Origin and Nature of Diversification in the History of Early Christianity," in Robinson and Koester, *Trajectories through Early Christianity*, 138; John S. Kloppenborg, *The Formation of Q: Trajectories in Ancient Wisdom Collections* (Philadelphia: Fortress, 1987), 317; cf. Mack, *A Myth of Innocence*, 59. For Matthew, see M. Jack Suggs, *Wisdom, Christology, and Law in Matthew's Gospel* (Cambridge: Harvard University Press, 1970). Blenkinsopp claims that Matthew, more than any other canonical Gospel, presents Jesus "as wise teacher" (*Wisdom and Law*, 181). For the Sermon on the Mount as a wisdom text, see Bernard Brendan Scott, "Jesus as Sage: An Innovative Voice in Common Wisdom," in Gammie and Perdue, *The Sage in Israel*, 399; Robert A. Guelich, *The Sermon on the Mount* (Waco, Tex.: Word, 1982), 323; Walter T. Wilson, "A Third Form of Righteousness: The Theme and Contribution of Matthew 6.19–7.12 in the Sermon on the Mount," *NTS* 53 (2007): 303–24.

15. The term σοφία occurs ten times in Luke-Acts (six in Luke, four in Acts). It appears only once in Mark (6:2) and only three times in Matthew (11:19; 12:42; 13:54).

Luke is alone among the Synoptics in personifying Wisdom and attributing speech to her (Luke 11:49). Luke also makes use of other sapiential terms, such as φρόνησις (1:17), σύνεσις (2:47), σόφος (10:21), and φρόνιμος (12:42; 16:8).[16] Luke consistently portrays wisdom positively,[17] and in the Gospel it is most frequently applied to Jesus.[18]

I suggest that Luke's parables can be profitably read as sapiential narratives. My reading has focused on one specific sapiential motif within these narratives, the interplay of death and possessions. Although not exclusive to other modes of thought (e.g., prophetic or apocalyptic), wisdom may prove to be one heuristic lens for illuminating other episodes and motifs in Luke-Acts.[19]

Parables and Character Formation

Specific types of wisdom literature have been characterized as "instructional,"[20] and character formation has been recognized as an

It does not occur in John. In Acts, wisdom is attributed to the seven men chosen to supervise the distribution of food to the widows (6:3), Stephen (6:10), Joseph (7:10), and Moses (7:22).

16. φρόνησις only appears one other time in the New Testament (Eph 1:8). On nine occasions in the Septuagint, the term translates חכמה. σύνεσις appears six other times in the New Testament. On four occasions in the Septuagint the term translates חכמה. φρόνιμος translates חכמה once in the Septuagint.

17. Luke does not exhibit any of the cautionary or critical tone toward wisdom that one finds, for example, in Paul (1 Cor 1:17–19; 2:1, 4, 13; 2 Cor 1:12). Nor does Luke distinguish, as does Paul, between "worldly" and godly wisdom (1 Cor 1:20–21; 2:5–7; 3:19).

18. It is twice used in descriptions of his development as a child (2:40, 52); Jesus' wisdom is greater than that of Solomon (11:31); and Jesus passes his wisdom on to the disciples (21:15).

19. Lohfink, for instance, has identified several similarities between the thought of Qoheleth and Luke's depiction of Jesus (*Qoheleth*, 16–17). Both, for example, conceive of God as a being who gives to people regardless of their moral status (Luke 6:35c). Although Qoheleth and Luke both share this view of God, it functions in the latter as a warrant for *imitatio dei*, namely, being kind to the wicked (Luke 6:35a–b).

20. Some (e.g., Kenton L. Sparks, "The Song of Songs: Wisdom for Young Jewish Women," *CBQ* 70 [2008]: 284) consider "instruction" to be the "chief purpose of wisdom texts." Many (e.g., Burkes, *God, Self, and Death*, 160–61) consider "instruction" to be a particular type of wisdom literature, finding expression, for example, in Ben Sira. Gammie ("From Prudentialism to Apocalypticism," 480) considers "instruc-

important component of wisdom instruction.[21] Many of the sapiential texts surveyed in this book reveal an interest in shaping character, particularly in regard to using possessions meaningfully in light of death's inevitability, uncertain timing, and potential imminence. An underlying premise of many such texts is that people are capable of adopting certain uses of possessions and eschewing other uses. Luke's parables seem to share this basic anthropological assumption. He depicts characters who make specific choices in regard to possessions, and he constructs narratives so as to encourage readers/hearers to evaluate these choice(s).

Luke's illustration and evaluation of characters' choices is a vehicle through which he facilitates character formation in his own readers and hearers. Luke's parables invite readers/hearers into contested sapiential conversations in which choices about possessions figure prominently. Luke illustrates his interest in the intersection of death and possessions through the specific vehicle of characterization.[22] Numerous characters in Luke-Acts are chiefly described in terms of their experience with death and their use (or misuse) of possessions.[23] Portraying the sapiential conversation on death and possessions in the specific form of narrative enables Luke's readers and hearers to see themselves reflected in the actions and choices of the literary characters.

Some of the differences between the Rich Fool parable in Luke and Thomas highlight ways in which Luke's version more easily facilitates

---

tion" to be one of the two types of paraenetic wisdom literature (e.g., Prov 1–9). Cf. Murphy, *Tree of Life*, 10.

21. Clements identifies character formation as a "primary goal of wisdom" (*Wisdom in Theology*, 34–35).

22. By "characterization," I refer to a narrative's depiction of specific characters. On the distinction between the terms "character" and "person," see Gail R. O'Day, "The Citation of Scripture as a Key to Characterization in Acts," in *Scripture and Traditions: Essays on Early Judaism and Christianity in Honor of Carl R. Holladay* (ed. Patrick Gray and Gail R. O'Day; NovTSup; Leiden: Brill, 2008), 207–21: "To speak of characters in any literary work, ancient or modern, is never to speak of persons, even if the character in question, as is the case in Acts, is based on a historical personage. Literary works have characters, not persons; the world has persons, but not characters. To read characters as if they were persons robs the literary character of its function and distinctive voice in its literary home" (211). On characterization in Luke-Acts, see John A. Darr, *On Character Building: The Reader and the Rhetoric of Characterization in Luke-Acts* (Louisville: Westminster John Knox, 1992).

23. These include, for example, Judas (Luke 22:4–5; Acts 1:16–20), Ananias and Sapphira (Acts 5:1–11), and John the Baptist (Luke 3:7–9, 12–14; 7:25).

opportunities to identify with the character of the rich man. A specific literary device Luke employs to construct both character identification and formation is the phrase τί ποιήσω ("What might/shall/must I do?").[24] In seven cases, the phrase τί ποιήσω is used to describe a potential use of possessions,[25] and in each instance the response to τί ποιήσω includes an illustration or teaching related to a specific use of possessions.[26]

The implicit assumption underlying each of the above sets of questions and responses is that a possibility exists for the questioner (the literary character) to live into the answer proposed in the narrative. It is feasible, in other words, for John's audience to share their food and clothing with the poor (3:10–14). So, too, can the lawyer share his goods and offer hospitality to those in need (10:37). The rich ruler is capable of selling all his goods and giving to the poor (18:22).[27]

Luke's readers/hearers are simultaneously invited to adopt these specific uses of possessions illustrated in the narrative. This process begins

24. The question τί ποιήσω (and its various forms) occurs in key episodes throughout Luke's narrative. The crowds respond to Peter's preaching by asking τί ποιήσωμεν (Acts 2:37). The owner of the vineyard decides to send his son, after asking τί ποιήσω (20:13). Saul responds to the risen Jesus by asking τί ποιήσω (Acts 22:10). For other uses of τί ποιήσω in Luke-Acts, see Luke 18:41; 20:13.

25. Luke 3:10, 12, 14; 10:25; 12:17; 16:3; 18:18. The crowds respond to John's preaching on repentance by asking what they should do (τί οὖν ποιήσωμεν; 3:10). The tax collectors and soldiers respond similarly, each asking the same question (τί ποιήσωμεν; 3:12, 14). The lawyer asks Jesus, τί ποιήσας ζωὴν αἰώνιον κληρονομήσω, which serves as the catalyst for the parable of the Samaritan (10:25). The same exact question (τί ποιήσας ζωὴν αἰώνιον κληρονομήσω) reappears on the lips of the rich ruler (Luke 18:18). The steward asks τί ποιήσω when faced with losing his job (16:3). Tannehill (*Luke*, 207) sees in the identical question (τί ποιήσω) of the rich fool and the steward in 16:1–8 (cf. 12:17; 16:3) a contrast between the two characters; the former is a ἄφρων (12:20), and the latter is φρονίμως (16:8). Tannehill's claim that the steward is wise because he gives away "property in his control," reads, however, against the parable's own plain sense.

26. John instructs the crowds, tax collectors, and soldiers concerning the giving and taking of specific possessions (food, clothing, money; 3:10, 12, 14). The rich man decides to build larger barns and anticipates the future enjoyment of his goods (12:17–19). The steward implements his plan to reduce debts that others owe his master (16:3). Jesus' reply to the lawyer details the Samaritan's generous sharing of goods and money on behalf of the wounded man (10:25). The rich ruler is told to sell all he has and give to the poor (18:22).

27. For how Luke 12:13–34 fits into Luke's broader ethics regarding wealth and possessions, see Hays, *Luke's Wealth Ethics*, 125–29.

with Luke's readers/hearers making the question "What would I do?" their own and reflecting upon how they might use possessions meaningfully. Luke's parables thus serve a dual function: they construct both alternative worlds of meaningful living and characters and communities capable of inhabiting and embodying these alternative worlds.

The world imagined in Luke's parables is one in which possessions are used meaningfully when they serve relational ends.[28] The descriptions of the communities in Acts 2:42–47 and 4:32–35 function literarily as a realization (idealized or not) of this imagined world.[29] Luke imagines this world for his literary characters and readers/hearers, and he invites them to live into it by going about the difficult work of constructing this world for themselves and their communities.[30] Luke's parables propose that the actualization of this imagined world is an act whose meaning is not only maintained in the face of the uncertain and uncontrollable aspects of death, but even enhanced in this specific context.

---

28. This preference for the relational use of possessions explains, in part, why the steward is praised for reducing the amount that debtors owe to his master (16:1–8a).

29. Acts 2 and 4 describe the beginnings of a structure that allows for the implementation of some of the teaching and illustration about possessions in Luke.

30. These two episodes signal Luke's interest in the construction of communities, and not only individuals.

Bibliography

Aalen, Sverre. "St. Luke's Gospel and the Last Chapters of 1 Enoch." *NTS* 13 (1966–1967): 1–13.

Aland, Barbara, Kurt Aland, Eberhard Nestle, and Erwin Nestle, eds. *Nestle-Aland NovT Graece*. 27th ed. Stuttgart: Deutsche Bibelgesellschaft, 1993.

Allison, Dale C. *Testament of Abraham*. CEJL. Berlin: de Gruyter, 2003.

Anat, M. A. "The Lament on the Death of Humanity in the Scroll of Qohelet." *Beth Mikra* 15 (1970): 375–80.

Argal, Randal A. *1 Enoch and Sirach: A Comparative Literary and Conceptual Analysis of the Themes of Revelation, Creation and Judgment*. SBLEJL 8. Atlanta: Scholars Press, 1994.

Arterbury, Andrew. *Entertaining Angels: Early Christian Hospitality in Its Mediterranean Setting*. NTM 8. Sheffield: Sheffield Phoenix, 2005.

Asensio, Victor Morla. "Poverty and Wealth: Ben Sira's View of Possessions." Pages 150–78 in *Der Einzelne und seine Gemeinschaft bei Ben Sira*. Edited by Renate Egger-Wenzel and Ingrid Krammer. BZAW 270. Berlin: de Gruyter, 1998.

Asgeirsson, Jon Ma., April D. Deconick, and Risto Uro, eds. *Thomasine Traditions in Antiquity: The Social and Cultural World of the Gospel of Thomas*. NHMS 59. Leiden: Brill, 2006.

Assman, Jan. *Death and Salvation in Ancient Egypt*. Translated by David Lorton. Ithaca, N.Y.: Cornell University Press, 2005.

———. "A Dialogue Between Self and Soul: Papyrus Berlin 3024." Pages 384–403 in *Self, Soul and Body in Religious Experience*. Edited by A. I. Baumgarten et al. SHR 78. Leiden: Brill, 1998.

Athanasius of Alexandria. *Apologia de fuga sua*. Edited by Jan-M. Szymusiak. SC 56. Paris: Cerf, 1958.

Augustine. *De Trinitate*. Translated by Gareth B. Matthews. Cambridge: Cambridge University Press, 2002.

———. *Enarrationes in Psalmos 1–32*. Edited by Clemens Weidmann. CSEL 43.1a. Vienna: Verlag der Österreichischen Akademie der Wissenschaften, 2003.

———. *Enarrationes in Psalmos 1–50*. Edited by P.-P. Verbraken et al. CCSL 38. Turnhout: Brepols, 1956.

———. *Sermones de Vetere Testamento*. CCSL 41. Turnhout: Brepols, 1961.

———. *Sermones in Matthaeum*. Edited by P.-P. Verbraken et al. CCSL 41Aa. Turnhout: Brepols, 2008.

Baarda, Tjitze. "Luke 12, 13–14: Text and Transmission from Marcion to Augustine." Pages 107–62 in vol. 1 of *Christianity, Judaism, and other Greco-Roman Cults: Studies for Morton Smith at Sixty*. Edited by Jacob Neusner. SJLA 12. 4 vols. Leiden: Brill, 1975. Repr. as pages 117–72 in *Early Transmission of Words of Jesus: Thomas, Tatian, and the Text of the New Testament*. Edited by Tjitze Baarda. Amsterdam: Boekhandel/Utgeverij, 1983.

———, trans. "The Sentences of the Syriac Menander: A New Translation and Introduction." Pages 583–606 in vol. 2 of *The Old Testament Pseudepigrapha*. Edited by James H. Charlesworth. 2 vols. New York: Doubleday, 1983–1985.

Baasland, Ernst. "Zum Beispiel der Beispielerzählungen: Zur Formenlehre der Gleichnisse und zur Methodik der Gleichnisauslegung." *NovT* 28 (1986): 193–219.

Bailey, Kenneth E. *Poet and Peasant: A Literary-Cultural Approach to the Parables in Luke*. Grand Rapids: Eerdmans, 1976.

———. *Through Peasant Eyes: More Lucan Parables, Their Culture and Style*. Grand Rapids: Eerdmans, 1980.

Barclay, J. M. G. *Jews in the Mediterranean Diaspora, from Alexander to Trajan (323 BCE—117 CE)*. Edinburgh: T&T Clark, 1996.

Bartsch, Shadi, and David Wray, eds. *Seneca and the Self*. Cambridge: Cambridge University Press, 2009.

Bauer, Walter, Frederick Danker, W. F. Arndt, and F. W. Gingrich. *A Greek-English Lexicon of the New Testament and other Early Christian Literature*. 3rd ed. Revised and edited by Frederick Danker. Chicago: University of Chicago Press, 2000.

Beardslee, William A. *Literary Criticism of the New Testament*. Philadelphia: Fortress, 1970.

———. "The Wisdom Tradition and the Synoptic Gospels." *JAAR* 35 (1967): 231–40.

Beavis, Mary Ann. "The Foolish Landowner (Luke 12:16b–20)." Pages 55–68 in *Jesus and His Parables: Interpreting the Parables of Jesus Today*. Edited by V. George Shillington. Edinburgh: T&T Clark, 1997.

Beentjes, Pancratius C., ed. *The Book of Ben Sira in Hebrew: A Text Edition of All Extant Manuscripts and a Synopsis of All Parallel Hebrew Ben Sira Texts*. VTSup 68. Leiden: Brill, 1997.

———. "God's Mercy: 'Racham' (pi.), 'Rachum', and 'Rachamim' in the Book of Ben Sira." Pages 231–48 in *'Happy the One who Meditates on Wisdom' (Sir 14.20): Collected Essays on the Book of Ben Sira*. Edited by Pancratius C. Beentjes. Biblical Exegesis and Theology 43. Leuven: Peeters, 2006.

Betz, Hans Dieter. *Lukian von Samosata und das Neue Testament: Religiongeschichtliche und paränetische Parallelen*. Ein Beitrag zum Corpus Hellenisticum Novi Testamenti 76. Berlin: Akademie, 1961.

Bickermann, Elias. *Four Strange Books of the Bible*. New York: Schocken, 1967.

Blenkinsopp, Joseph. *Wisdom and Law in the Old Testament: The Ordering of Life in Israel and Early Judaism*. Oxford: Oxford University Press, 1995.

Blount, Brian. *Cultural Interpretation: Reorienting New Testament Criticism*. Minneapolis: Fortress, 1995.

Bonner, Campbell, ed. *The Last Chapters of Enoch in Greek*. London: Christophers, 1937. Repr., Stuttgart: Wissenshacftliche Buchgesellschaft, 1968.

Bornkamm, Günther. *Jesus of Nazareth*. Translated by Irene and Fraser McLuskey with James M. Robinson. New York: Harper & Row, 1960.

Boucher, Madeleine I. *The Parables*. Wilmington, Del.: Glazier, 1981.

Bovon, François. *L'Évangile selon saint Luc 9,51–14,35*. Commentaire du Nouveau Testament Deuxième Série 3b. Geneva: Labor et Fides, 1996.

———. "The Reception and Use of the Gospel of Luke in the Second Century." Pages 379–400 in *Reading Luke: Interpretation, Reflection, Formation*. Edited by Craig G. Bartholomew, Joel B. Green, and Anthony C. Thiselton. Grand Rapids: Zondervan, 2005.

Box, G. H., ed. *The Testament of Abraham: Translated from the Greek Text with Introduction and Notes*. London: SPCK, 1927.

Braun, Rainer. *Kohelet und die frühhellenistische Populärphilosophie*. BZAW 130. Berlin: de Gruyter, 1973.

Bremer, Jan Maarten. "Death and Immortality in Some Greek Poems." Pages 109–24 in *Hidden Futures: Death and Immortality in Ancient Egypt, Anatolia, the Classical, Biblical and Arabic-Islamic World*. Edited by J. M. Bremmer, Th. P. J. van den Hout, and R. Peters. Amsterdam: Amsterdam University Press, 1994.

———. "The Soul, Death, and the Afterlife in Early and Classical Greece." Pages 91–106 in *Hidden Futures: Death and Immortality in Ancient Egypt, Anatolia, the Classical, Biblical and Arabic-Islamic World*. Edited by J. M. Bremmer, Th. P. J. van den Hout, and R. Peters. Amsterdam: Amsterdam University Press, 1994.

Brown, Francis, Samuel Rolles Driver, and Charles A. Briggs. *A Hebrew and English Lexicon of the Old Testament, with an Appendix, Containing the Biblical Aramaic*. Peabody, Mass.: Hendrickson, 1996.

Brown, William P. *Character in Crisis: A Fresh Approach to the Wisdom Literature of the Old Testament*. Grand Rapids: Eerdmans, 1996.

———. *Ecclesiastes*. IBC. Louisville: John Knox, 2000.

Bruce, Alexander Balmain. *The Parabolic Teaching of Christ: A Systematic and Critical Study of the Parables of our Lord*. 3rd ed. New York: Armstrong & Son, 1898.

Brueggemann, Walter A. "The Epistemological Crisis of Israel's Two Histories (Jer 9:22–23)." Pages 85–105 in *Israelite Wisdom: Theological and Literary Essays in Honor of Samuel Terrien*. Edited by John G. Gammie et al. Missoula, Mont.: Scholars Press, 1978.

———. "Psalms and the Life of Faith: A Suggested Typology of Function." *JSOT* 17 (1980): 3–32.

Bultmann, Rudolf. *The History of the Synoptic Tradition*. Translated by John Marsh. Oxford: Blackwell, 1963.

———. *Theology of the New Testament*. Translated by Kendrick Grobel. New York: Charles Scriber's Sons, 1951, 1955.

Burkes, Shannon. *Death in Qoheleth and Egyptian Biographies of the Late Period*. SBLDS 170. Atlanta: Society of Biblical Literature, 1999.

———. *God, Self, and Death: The Shape of Religious Transformation in the Second Temple Period*. JSJSup 79. Leiden: Brill, 2003.

Byargeon, Ricky William. "The Significance of the Enjoy Life Concept in Qoheleth's Challenge of the Wisdom Tradition." Ph.D. diss., Southwestern Baptist Theological Seminary, 1991.

Cadoux, Arthur T. *The Parables of Jesus: Their Art and Use*. London: James Clark, 1931.

Caird, George Bradford. *The Gospel of St. Luke*. New York: Seabury, 1963.

———. *New Testament Theology*. Edited by L. D. Hurst. Oxford: Clarendon, 1994.

Calduch-Benages, Nuria, Joan Ferrer, and Jan Liesen. *La Sabiduría del Escriba: Edición diplomática de la versión siriaca del libro de Ben Sira según el Códice Ambrosiano, con traducción española e inglesa*. Biblioteca Midrásica 26. Estella, Navarra: Editorial Verbo Divino, 2003.

Calvin, Jean. *Commentary on a Harmony of the Evangelists: Matthew, Mark, and Luke*. Translated by William Pringle. 3 vols. Grand Rapids: Eerdmans, 1949.

Caquot, André. "Israelite Perceptions of Wisdom and Strength in the Light of the Ras Shamra Texts." Pages 25–33 in *Israelite Wisdom: Theological and Literary Essays in Honor of Samuel Terrien*. Edited by John G. Gammie et al. Missoula, Mont.: Scholars Press, 1978.

Cassian, John. *The Institutes*. Translated by Boniface Ramsey. ACW 58. Mahwah, N.J.: Paulist, 2000.

———. *Institutions Cénobitiques*. Edited by Jean-Claude Guy. SC 109. Paris: Cerf, 2001.

Champlin, Edward. *Final Judgments: Duty and Emotion in Romans Wills, 200 B.C.–A.D. 250*. Berkeley: University of California Press, 1991.

Charlesworth, James H., ed. *The Old Testament Pseudepigrapha*. 2 vols. New York: Doubleday, 1983–1985.

Chen, Diane G. *God as Father in Luke-Acts*. Studies in Biblical Literature 92. New York: Lang, 2006.

Chopineau, Jacques. "Hèvèl en hébreu biblique: Contribution à l'étude des rapports entre sémantique et exégèse de l'Ancien Testament." Ph.D. diss., University of Strasbourg, 1971.

Christianson, Eric S. *A Time to Tell: Narrative Strategies in Ecclesiastes*. JSOTSup 280. Sheffield: Sheffield Academic Press, 1998.

Chrysostom, John. *Homilae in Matthaeum*. PG 57:13–472; 58:471–94.

———. *In Eutropium*. PG 52: 391–96.

Clement of Alexandria. *Le Pédagogue*. Edited by C. Mondésert et al. 3 vols. SC 108. Paris: Cerf, 1960–1970.

———. *Les Stromates*. Vols. 4, 6. Edited by M. Patrick Descourtieux and Annewies van den Hoek. SC 446, 463. Paris: Cerf, 1999, 2001.

———. *Stromata Buch 1–VI*. Edited by O. Stählin and Ludwig Früchtel. 3rd ed. Vol. 2 of *Clemens Alexandrinus*. Die Friechischen Christlichen Schriftsteller der ersten drei Jahrhunderte. Leipzig: Hinrichs, 1960.

———. "Who Is the Rich Man That Shall Be Saved?" Pages 591–603 in vol. 2 of *Ante-Nicene Fathers*. Translated by William Wilson. Edited by Alexander Roberts and James Donaldson. 10 vols. 1885–1887. Repr., Peabody, Mass.: Hendrickson, 1994.

Clements, Ronald E. *Wisdom in Theology*. Grand Rapids: Eerdmans, 1992.

Clines, David J. A., ed. *The Dictionary of Classical Hebrew*. Sheffield: Sheffield Academic Press, 1993–.

Collins, John J. *Between Athens and Jerusalem: Jewish Identity in the Hellenistic Diaspora*. 2nd ed. Grand Rapids: Eerdmans, 2000.

———. *Jewish Wisdom in the Hellenistic Age*. OTL. Louisville: Westminster John Knox, 1997.

———. "Wisdom, Apocalypticism, and Generic Compatibility." Pages 165–85 in *In Search of Wisdom: Essays in Memory of John G. Gammie*. Edited by Leo G. Perdue, Bernard Brandon Scott, and William Johnston Wiseman. Louisville: Westminster John Knox, 1993. Repr. as pages 385–404 in John J. Collins, *Seers, Sybils and Sages in Hellenistic-Roman Judaism*. JSJSup 54. Leiden: Brill, 1997.

Conzelmann, Hans. *Die Mitte Der Zeit*. Tübingen: Mohr Siebeck, 1953.

Corley, Jeremy. *Ben Sira's Teaching on Friendship*. BJS 316. Providence, R.I.: Brown Judaic Studies, 2002.

———. "God as Merciful Father in Ben Sira and the New Testament." Pages 33–38 in *Ben Sira's God: Proceedings of the International Ben Sira Conference Durham–Ushaw College 2001*. Edited by Renate Egger-Wenzel. BZAW 321. Berlin: de Gruyter, 2002.

Coughenour, Robert A. "Enoch and Wisdom: A Study of the Wisdom Elements in the Book of Enoch." Ph.D. diss., Case Western Reserve, 1972.

———. "The Woe Oracles in Ethiopic Enoch." *JSJ* 9 (1978): 192–97.

Craddock, Fred B. *Luke*. IBC. Louisville: John Knox, 1990.

Crenshaw, James L. "The Concept of God in Old Testament Wisdom." Pages 1–18 in *In Search of Wisdom: Essays in Memory of John G. Gammie*. Edited by Leo G. Perdue, Bernard Brandon Scott, and William Johnston Wiseman. Louisville: Westminster John Knox, 1993.

———. *Ecclesiastes*. OTL. Louisville: Westminster John Knox, 1987.

———. "Method in Determining Wisdom Influence Upon 'Historical' Literature." *JBL* 88 (1969): 129–42.

———. *Old Testament Wisdom: An Introduction*. 3rd ed. Louisville: Westminster John Knox, 2010.

———. "The Shadow of Death in Qoheleth." Pages 205–16 in *Israelite Wisdom: Theological and Literary Essays in Honor of Samuel Terrien*. Edited by John G. Gammie et al. Missoula, Mont.: Scholars Press, 1978.

Cross, F. M. "The Oldest Manuscripts from Qumran." *JBL* 74 (1955): 147–72.

Crossan, John Dominic. *The Dark Interval: Towards a Theology of Story*. Niles, Ill.: Argus Communications, 1975.

———. *In Parables: The Challenge of the Historical Jesus*. New York: Harper & Row, 1973.

———. "Parable and Example in the Teaching of Jesus." *NTS* 18 (1971–1972): 285–307.

Cyprian. *Ad Quirinum testimonia adversus Judaeos*. Edited by R. Weber. CCSL 3. Turnhout: Brepols, 1972.

———. *La Bienfaisance et Les Aumônes*. Edited by Michel Poirer. SC 440. Paris: Cerf, 1999.

———. *De dominica oratione*. Edited by C. Moreschini. CCSL 3A. Turnhout: Brepols, 1976.

———. *De Opere et Eleemosynis*. Edited by Manlio Simonetti. CCSL 3A. Turnhout: Brepols, 1976.

Cyril of Alexandria. *The Gospel of Saint Luke*. Translated by R. Payne Smith. Long Island, N.Y.: Studion, 1983.

D'Alario, Vittoria. "La réflexion sur le sens de la vie en Sg 1–6: Une réponse aux questions de Job et de Qohélet." Pages 313–29 in *Treasures of Wisdom: Studies in Ben Sira and the Book of Wisdom (Festschrift M. Gilbert)*. Edited by N. Calduch-Benages and J. Vermeylen. Leuven: Leuven University Press, 1999.

Danker, Frederick W. *Jesus and the New Age: A Commentary on St. Luke's Gospel*. Rev. ed. Philadelphia: Fortress, 1988.

Darr, John A. *On Character Building: The Reader and the Rhetoric of Characterization in Luke-Acts*. Louisville: Westminster John Knox, 1992.

Delcor, Mathias. "Jewish Literature in Hebrew and Aramaic in the Greek Era." Pages 352–84 in *The Hellenistic Age*. Vol. 2 of *The Cambridge History of Judaism*. Edited by W. D. Davies and Louis Finkelstein. 4 vols. Cambridge: Cambridge University Press, 1989.

———. *Le Testament d'Abraham*. SVTP 2. Leiden: Brill, 1973.

Dell, Katherine. *'Get Wisdom, Get Insight': An Introduction to Israel's Wisdom Literature*. Macon, Ga.: Smith & Helwys, 2000.

Derchain, Philippe. "Death in Egyptian Religion." Pages 111–15 in vol. 1 of *Mythologies*. Edited by Yves Bonnefoy. 2 vols. Chicago: University of Chicago Press, 1991.

Derrett, J. D. "The Rich Fool: A Parable of Jesus Concerning Inheritance." *HeyJ* 18 (1977): 131–51.

Dibelius, Martin. *From Tradition to Gospel*. Translated by Bertram Lee Woolf. New York: Charles Scribner's Sons, 1935.

Dieleman, Jacco. *Priests, Tongues, and Rites: The London-Leiden Magical Manuscripts and Translation in Egyptian Ritual (100–300 CE)*. Leiden: Brill, 2005.

Dodd, Charles Harold. *The Parables of the Kingdom*. Rev. ed. New York: Charles Scribner's Sons, 1961.

Donahue, John R. *The Gospel in Parable: Metaphor, Narrative and Theology in the Synoptic Gospels*. Philadelphia: Fortress, 1988.

Donaldson, Terence L. "Parallels: Use, Misuse, and Limitations." *EvQ* 55 (1983): 193–210.

Dupont, Jacques. *Les béatitudes 3: Les évangélistes*. 3 vols. Paris: Gabalda, 1973.

Eichholz, Georg. *Gleichnisse der Evangelien: Form Überlieferung Auslegung*. Neukirchen-Vluyn: Neukirchener, 1971.

Elliger, K., and W. Rudolph, eds. *Biblia Hebraica Stuttgartensia*. 5th ed. Stuttgart: Deutsche Bibelgesellschaft, 1997.

Ephrem the Syrian. *Letter to Publius*. Edited by Kathleen McVey. Translated by Edward G. Matthews Jr. and Joseph P. Amar. FC 91. Washington, D.C.: The Catholic University of America Press, 1994.

Erasmus. *Paraphrase on Luke 11–24*. Vol. 48 of *Collected Works of Erasmus*. Translated by Jane E. Phillips. Toronto: University of Toronto Press, 2003.

Esler, Philip Frances. *Community and Gospel in Luke-Acts: The Social and Political Motivations of Lucan Theology*. Cambridge: Cambridge University Press, 1987.

Evans, Christopher F. *Saint Luke*. TPI New Testament Commentaries. Philadelphia: Trinity Press International, 1990.

Fichtner. Johannes. "Jesaja unter den Weisen." *TLZ* 74 (1949): 75–80.

Fisch, Harold. *Poetry with a Purpose: Biblical Poetics and Interpretation*. Bloomington: Indiana University Press, 1998.

Fischer, Susanna E. *Seneca als Theologe: Studien zum Verhaltnis von Philosophie und Tragödiendichtung*. Beiträge zur Altertumskunde 259. Berlin: de Gruyter, 2008.

Fitzgerald, John T. "Last Wills and Testaments in Graeco-Roman Perspective." Pages 637–72 in *Early Christianity and Classical Culture: Comparative Studies in Honor of Abraham J. Malherbe*. Edited by John T. Fitzgerald, Thomas H. Olbricht, and L. Michael White. Leiden: Brill, 2003.

Fitzmyer, Joseph A. *The Gospel according to Luke: Introduction, Translation, and Notes*. AB 28–28A. 2 vols. Garden City: Doubleday, 1981–1985.

Foucault, Michel. *The Archaeology of Knowledge*. London: Routledge, 1972.

Fowden, Garth. *Egyptian Hermes: A Historical Approach to the Late Pagan Mind*. Cambridge: Cambridge University Press, 1986.

Fox, Michael V. "Aging and Death in Qohelet 12." *JSOT* 42 (1988): 55–77.

———. *Ecclesiastes: קהלת*. *The Traditional Hebrew Text with the New JPS Translation*. Philadelphia: Jewish Publication Society, 2004.

———. "The Meaning of HEBEL for Qohelet." *JBL* 105 (1986): 409–27.

———. *Qohelet and His Contradictions*. Sheffield: Almond, 1989.

———. *A Time to Tear Down and a Time to Build Up: A Rereading of Ecclesiastes*. Grand Rapids: Eerdmans, 1999.

Frankemölle, Hubert. "Zum Thema des Jakobusbriefes im Kontext der Rezeption von Sir 2, 1–18 und 15, 11–20." *BN* 48 (1989): 21–49.

Frankl, Viktor. *Man's Search for Meaning*. New York: Washington Square Press, 1985.

Funk, Robert W. *Parables and Presence: Forms of the New Testament Tradition*. Philadelphia: Fortress, 1982.

Galling, Kurt. *Die Krise der Aufklärung in Israel*. Mainzer Universitätsreden 19. Mainz: Gutenberg-Buchhandlung, 1952.

———. "Das Rätsel der Zeit im Urteil Kohelets (Koh 3, 1–15)." *ZTK* 58 (1961): 1–15.

Gammie, John G. "From Prudentialism to Apocalypticism: The Houses of the Sages amid the Varying Forms of Wisdom." Pages 479–97 in *The Sage in Israel and the Ancient Near East*. Edited by John G. Gammie and Leo G. Perdue. Winona Lake, Ind.: Eisenbrauns, 1990.

———. "The Sage in Sirach." Pages 355–72 in *The Sage in Israel and the Ancient Near East*. Edited by John G. Gammie and Leo G. Perdue. Winona Lake, Ind.: Eisenbrauns, 1990.

Gardiner, Alan H. *The Attitude of the Ancient Egyptians to Death and the Dead*. Cambridge: Cambridge University Press, 1935.

Garland, Robert. *The Greek Way of Death*. London: Duckworth, 1985.

Geertz, Clifford. "Deep Play: Notes on the Balinese Cockfight." Pages 412–53 in *The Interpretation of Cultures*. Edited by Clifford Geertz. New York: Basic Books, 1973.

Gerhardsson, Birger. "If We Do Not Cut the Parables Out of Their Frames." *NTS* 37 (1991): 321–35.

Gesenius, Wilhelm. *Thesaurus philologicus criticus linguae hebraeae et Thesaurus chaldaeae Veteris Testamenti*. 3 vols. Leipzig: Vogel, 1829–1842.

Gianto, Agustinos. "The Theme of Enjoyment in Qohelet." *Bib* 73 (1992): 528–32.

Gilbert, Maurice. *Les cinq livres des Sages: Les Proverbes de Salomon, Le livre de Job, Qohélet ou l'Écclésiaste, Le livre de ben Sira, La Sagesse de Salomon*. Paris: Cerf, 2003.

———. "La description de la vieillesse en Qohelet XII 1–7 est-elle allégorique?" Pages 96–109 in *Congress Volume: Vienna, 1980*. Edited by J. A. Emerton. VTSup 32. Leiden: Brill, 1981.

Ginsburg, Christian D. *Coheleth*. London: Longman, Green & Roberts, 1861. Repr., New York: Ktav, 1970.

Gordis, Robert. *Koheleth—the Man and his World. A Study of Ecclesiastes*. 3rd ed. New York: Schocken, 1955.

———. "Quotations in Biblical, Oriental and Rabbinic Literature." *HUCA* 22 (1949): 157–219.

———. "Quotations in Wisdom Literature." *JQR* 30 (1939–1940): 123–47. Repr. as pages 220–44 in *Studies in Ancient Israelite Wisdom*. Edited by James L. Crenshaw. New York: Ktav, 1976.

Gould, E. P. *St. Mark*. ICC. New York: Charles Scribner's Sons, 1896.

Green, Joel. *The Gospel of Luke*. NICNT. Grand Rapids: Eerdmans, 1997.

Gregory. *Gregory the Great: Forty Gospel Homilies*. Translated by David Hurst. Kalamazoo, Mich: Cistercian, 1990.

Gregory of Nazianzen. *On His Father's Silence*. PG 35:933–45.

Gregory of Nyssa. *Homélies sur l'Ecclésiaste*. Translated by P. Alexander. SC 46. Paris: Cerf, 1996.

Gregory Thaumaturgos. *Gregory Thaumaturgos' Paraphrase of Ecclesiastes*. Translated by John Jarick. SBLSCS 29. Atlanta: Scholars Press, 1990.

Gregory, Andrew. "Looking for Luke in the Second Century: A Dialogue with François Bovon." Pages 401–15 in *Reading Luke: Interpretation, Reflection, Formation*. Edited by Craig G. Bartholomew, Joel B. Green, and Anthony C. Thiselton. Grand Rapids: Zondervan, 2005.

———. *The Reception of Luke and Acts in the Period before Irenaeus*. WUNT 2/169. Tübingen: Mohr Siebeck, 2003.

Gressmann, Hugo. *Vom reichen Mann und armen Lazarus: Eine literargeschichtliche Studie*. Abhandlungen der königlich preussischen Akademie der Wissenschaften: Philosophisch-historische Klasse, 1918, 7. Berlin: Verlag der königlich Akademie der Wissenschaften, 1918.

Grobel, Kendrick. "'...Whose Name Was Neves.'" *NTS* 10 (1963–1964): 373–82.

Gryson, Roger, ed. *Biblia Sacra: Iuxta Vulgata Versionem*. 4th ed. Stuttgart: Deutsche Bibelgesellschaft, 1994.

Guelich, Robert A. *The Sermon on the Mount*. Waco, Tex.: Word, 1982.

Harrington, Daniel J. *Jesus Ben Sira of Jerusalem: A Biblical Guide to Living Wisely*. Collegeville, Minn.: Liturgical Press, 2005.

Hartin, Patrick J. "'Who Is Wise and Understanding Among You?' (James 3:13): An Analysis of Wisdom, Eschatology, and Apocaypticism in the Letter of James."

Pages 149–68 in *Conflicted Boundaries in Wisdom and Apocalypticism*. Edited by Benjamin G. Wright III and Lawrence M. Wills. SBLSymS 35. Atlanta: Society of Biblical Literature, 2005.

Hays, Christopher M. *Luke's Wealth Ethics: A Study in Their Coherence and Character*. WUNT 275. Tübingen: Mohr Siebeck, 2010.

Hays, Richard B. *The Conversion of the Imagination: Paul as Interpreter of Israel's Scripture*. Grand Rapids: Eerdmans, 2005.

———. *Echoes of Scripture in the Letters of Paul*. New Haven: Yale University Press, 1989.

———. *The Moral Vision of the New Testament*. San Francisco: Harper SanFrancisco, 1996.

Hays, Richard B., and Joel B. Green, "The Use of the Old Testament by New Testament Writers." Pages 222–38 in *Hearing the New Testament: Strategies for Interpretation*. Edited by Joel B. Green. Grand Rapids: Eerdmans, 1995.

Hedrick, Charles. *Parables as Poetic Fictions: The Creative Voice of Jesus*. Peabody, Mass.: Hendrickson, 1994.

Hendrickx, Herman. *The Parables of Jesus*. Rev. ed. Studies in the Synoptic Gospels. San Francisco: Harper & Row, 1986.

Hengel, Martin. *Judaism and Hellenism*. Translated by John Bowden. 2 vols. Philadelphia: Fortress, 1974.

Herzog, William R. Parables as Subversive Speech: Jesus as Pedagogue of the Oppressed. Louisville: Westminster John Knox, 1994.

Hock, Ronald F. "The Parable of the Foolish Rich Man (Luke 12:16–20) and Graeco-Roman Conventions of Thought and Behavior." Pages 181–96 in *Early Christianity and Classical Culture: Comparative Studies in Honor of Abraham J. Malherbe*. Edited by John T. Fitzgerald, Thomas H. Olbricht, and L. Michael White. Leiden: Brill, 2003.

Holladay, William L., ed. *A Concise Hebrew and Aramaic Lexicon of the Old Testament*. Leiden: Brill, 1988.

Hollander, John. *The Figure of Echo: A Mode of Allusion in Milton and After*. Berkeley: University of California Press, 1981.

Hoppe, Rudolf. *Der theologische Hintergrund des Jakobusbriefes*. Forschung zur Bibel 28. Wurzburg: Echter, 1977.

Horsley, Richard A. "The Politics of Cultural Production in Second Temple Judea: Historical Context and Political-Religious Relations of the Scribes Who Produced 1 Enoch, Sirach, and Daniel." Pages 123–45 in *Conflicted Boundaries in Wisdom and Apocalypticism*. Edited by Benjamin G. Wright III and Lawrence M. Wills. SBLSymS 35. Atlanta: Society of Biblical Literature, 2005.

Horst, Pieter W. van der. "Pseudo-Phocylides Revisited." *JSP* 3 (1988): 3–30. Repr. as pages 35–62 in idem, *Essays on the Jewish World of Early Christianity*. Göttingen: Vandenhoeck & Ruprecht, 1990.

Hultgren, Arland J. *The Parables of Jesus: A Commentary*. Grand Rapids: Eerdmans, 2000.

Hunter, Alastair. *Wisdom Literature*. London: SCM, 2006.

James, Montague Rhodes. *The Testament of Abraham: The Greek Text Now First Edited with an Introduction and Notes*. TS 2/2. Cambridge: Cambridge University Press, 1892.

Jastrow, Marcus, ed. *Dictionary of the Targumim, the Talmud Babli and Yerushalmi, and the Midrashic Literature*. Peabody, Mass.: Hendrickson, 2005.

Jeremias, Joachim. *The Parables of Jesus*. Translated by S. H. Hooke. 2nd ed. Upper Saddle River, N.J.: Prentice Hall, 1972.

Johnson, Luke Timothy. *The Gospel of Luke*. SP 3. Collegeville, Minn.: Liturgical Press, 1991.

———. *The Letter of James: A New Translation with Introduction and Commentary*. AB 37A. New York: Doubleday, 1995.

———. *The Literary Function of Possessions in Luke-Acts*. SBLDS 39. Missoula, Mont.: Scholars Press, 1977.

———. "The Lukan Kingship Parable." *NovT* 24 (1982): 139–59.

Johnson, Stephen R. *Seeking the Imperishable Treasure: Wealth, Wisdom, and a Jesus Saying*. Eugene, Ore.: Cascade, 2008.

Johnston, Sarah Iles. *Restless Dead: Encounters between the Living and the Dead in Ancient Greece*. Berkeley: University of California Press, 1999.

Jones, Gerant Vaughan. *The Art and Truth of the Parables: A Study in Their Literary Form and Modern Interpretation*. London: SPCK, 1964.

Jülicher, Adolf. *Die Gleichnisreden Jesu*. 2 vols. Tübingen: Mohr Siebeck, vol. 1, 1888; vols. 1–2, 1899. Repr., 1910.

Kasher, Aryeh. *The Jews in Hellenistic and Roman Egypt: The Struggle for Equal Rights*. TSAJ 7. Tübingen: Mohr Siebeck, 1985.

Kennedy, George A. *Aristotle on Rhetoric: A Theory of Civic Discourse*. New York: Oxford University Press, 1991.

King, Martin Luther, Jr. "The Man Who Was a Fool." Pages 69–76 in *Strength to Love*. Edited by Martin Luther King Jr. Philadelphia: Fortress, 1981.

Kissinger, Warren S. *The Parables of Jesus: A History of Interpretation and Bibliography*. ATLA Bibliography Series 4. Metuchen, N.J.: American Theological Library Association, 1979.

Kister, Menahem. "Some Observations on Vocabulary and Style in the DSS." Pages 137–65 in *Diggers at the Well: Proceedings of a Third International Symposium on the Hebrew of the Dead Sea Scrolls and Ben Sira*. Edited by T. Muraoka and J. F. Elwolde. Leiden: Brill, 2000.

Kittel, Gerhard, and Gerhard Friedrich, eds. *Theological Dictionary of the New Testament*. Translated by G. W. Bromiley. 10 vols. Grand Rapids: Eerdmans, 1964–1976.

Kloppenborg, John S. *The Formation of Q: Trajectories in Ancient Wisdom Collections*. Philadelphia: Fortress, 1987.

Klostermann, Erich, and Hugo Gressmann, *Das Lukasevangelium*. HNT 2.1. Tübingen: Mohr Siebeck, 1919.

Koch, Klaus. "Gibt es ein Vergeltungsdogma im Alten Testament?" Pages 130–80 in *Um das Prinzip der Vergeltung in Religion und Recht des Alten Testaments*. Edited by Klaus Koch. Wege der Forschung 125. Darmstadt: Wissenshcaftliche Buchgesellschaft, 1972.

Koehler, Ludwig, and Walter Baumgartner, eds. *The Hebrew and Aramaic Lexicon of the Old Testament*. 5 vols. Leiden: Brill, 1967–1995.

Koester, Helmut. "*Gnomai Diaphorai*: The Origin and Nature of Diversification in the History of Early Christianity." Pages 114–57 in James M. Robinson and Helmut Koester, *Trajectories through Early Christianity*. Philadelphia: Fortress, 1971.

Koetsveld, C. E. van. *De Gelijkenissen van den Zaligmaker*. 2 vols. Utrecht: Schoonhoven, 1869.

Kolarcik, Michael. *The Ambiguity of Death in the Book of Wisdom 1–6*. AnBib 127. Rome: Pontifical Biblical Institute, 1991.

Kolenkow, Anitra Bingham. "The Genre Testament and the Testament of Abraham." Pages 139–52 in *Studies on the Testament of Abraham*. Edited by George W. E. Nickelsburg. SBLSCS 6. Missoula, Mont.: Scholars Press, 1972.

Kristeva, Julia. *Semiotiké: Recherches pour une sémanalyse*. Collections Tel Quel. Paris: Le Seuil, 1969.

Krüger, Thomas. *Qoheleth: A Commentary*. Translated by O. C. Dean Jr. Hermeneia. Minneapolis: Fortress, 2004.

Kugel, James L. "Qohelet and Money." *CBQ* 51 (1989): 32–49.

Kümmel, Werner Georg. *The Theology of the New Testament: According to Its Major Witnesses: Jesus, Paul, John*. Translated by John E. Steely. Nashville: Abingdon, 1973.

Kurtz Donna C., and John Boardman. *Greek Burial Customs*. Aspects of Greek and Roman Life. Ithaca, N.Y.: Cornell University Press, 1971.

Lagarde, Paul de. *Libri Veteris Testamenti Apocryphi Syriace*. London: Williams & Norgate, 1861.

Landes, George M. "Jonah: A *Māšāl*?" Pages 137–58 in *Israelite Wisdom: Theological and Literary Essays in Honor of Samuel Terrien*. Edited by John G. Gammie et al. Missoula, Mont.: Scholars Press, 1978.

Lattimore, Richmond. *Themes in Greek and Latin Epitaphs*. Illinois Studies in Language and Literature 28. Urbana: University of Illinois Press, 1942.

Lavoie, Jean-Jacques. *La penseé du Qohélet: Étude exégétique et intertextuelle*. Quebec: Fides, 1992.

Lee, Eunny P. *The Vitality of Enjoyment in Qohelet's Theological Rhetoric*. BZAW 353. Berlin: de Gruyter, 2005.

Leipoldt, Johannes. *Das Evangelium nach Thomas*. TU 101. Berlin: Adademie, 1967.

Levi, Israel. *The Hebrew Text of the Book of Ecclesiasticus*. SSS 3. Leiden: Brill, 1904.

Lichtheim, Miriam. *Ancient Egyptian Literature: A Book of Readings*. 3 vols. Berkeley: University of California Press, 1973–1980.

———. *Late Egyptian Wisdom Literature in the International Context: A Study of Demotic Instructions*. OBO 52. Fribourg: Universitätsverlag; Göttingen: Vandenhoeck & Ruprecht, 1983.

Liddell, Henry George, and Robert Scott. *A Greek-English Lexicon*. 9th ed. Revised by Henry Stuart Jones. Oxford: Clarendon, 1996.

Lindblom, Johannes. "Wisdom in the Old Testament Prophets." Pages 192–204 in *Wisdom in Israel and the Ancient Near East*. Edited by M. Noth and D. W. Thomas. VTSup 3. Leiden: Brill, 1955.

Linnemann, Eta. *Parables of Jesus: Introduction and Exposition*. London: SPCK, 1975.

Lips, Hermann von. *Weisheitliche Traditionen im Neuen Testament*. WUNT 64. Neukirchen-Vluyn: Neukirchener, 1990.

Lohfink, Norbert. "Qoheleth 5:17–19—Revelation by Joy." *CBQ* 52 (1990): 625–35.

———. *Qoheleth: A Continental Commentary*. Translated by Sean McEvenue. Minneapolis: Fortress, 2003.

Longman, Tremper, III. *The Book of Ecclesiastes*. Grand Rapids: Eerdmans, 1998.

Loretz, Oswald. *Qohelet und der alte Orient*. Freiburg: Herder, 1964.

Lucian. Translated by A. M. Harmon et al. 8 vols. LCL. Cambridge: Harvard University Press, 1915–1967.

Ludlow, Jared Warner. *Abraham Meets Death: Narrative Humor in the Testament of Abraham*. JSPSup 41. Sheffield: Sheffield Academic Press, 2002.

Luther, Martin. *1 Timothy*. Edited by Hilton C. Oswald. Translated by Richard J. Dinda. Vol. 28 of *Luther's Works*. Saint Louis: Concordia, 1973.

———. *Commentary on Habbakkuk*. Edited by Hilton C. Oswald. Translated by Martin H. Bertram. Vol. 19 of *Luther's Works*. Saint Louis: Concordia, 1955.

———. *Commentary on Isaiah 1: Lectures on Isaiah Chapters 1–39*. Edited by Jaroslav Pelikan. Translated by Herbert J. A. Bouman. Vol. 16 of *Luther's Works*. Saint Louis: Concordia, 1969.

———. *Fourteen Consolations*. Edited by Martin O. Dietrich. Translated by Martin H. Bertram. Vol. 42 of *Luther's Works*. Philadelphia: Fortress, 1969.

———. *Notes on Ecclesiastes*. Edited and translated by Jaroslav Pelikan. Vol. 15 of *Luther's Works*. Saint Louis: Concordia, 1972.

———. *The Sermon on the Mount*. Edited and translated by Jaroslav Pelikan. Vol. 21 of *Luther's Works*. Saint Louis: Concordia, 1956.

———. *Sermons of Martin Luther: The House Postils*. Translated and edited by Eugene F. A. Klug et al. 3 vols. Grand Rapids: Baker, 1996.

———. *Trade and Usury*. Edited by Walther I. Brandt. Translated by Charles M. Jacobs. Vol. 45 of *Luther's Works*. Philadelphia: Muhlenberg, 1962.

Mack, Burton L. *A Myth of Innocence: Mark and Christian Origins*. Philadelphia: Fortress, 1988.

MacLeod, M. D. Preface and introductions to vol. 8 of *Lucian*. LCL. Translated by M. D. MacLeod. Cambridge: Harvard University Press, 1967.

MacRae, George W. "Gnosticism and the Church of John's Gospel." Pages 84–96 in *Nag Hammadi, Gnosticism, and Early Christianity*. Edited by C. W. Hedrick and R. Hodgson. Peabody, Mass.: Hendrickson, 1986.

Malherbe, Abraham. "The Christianization of a *Topos* (Luke 12:13–34)." *NovT* 38 (1996): 123–35.

———, ed. *The Cynic Epistles: A Study Edition*. SBLSBS 12. Missoula, Mont.: Scholars Press, 1977.

———. "Hellenistic Moralists and the New Testament." *ANRW* 2.26.1:267–333.

Marböck, Johann. *Weisheit im Wandel: Untersuchungen zur Weisheitstheologie bei Ben Sira*. BBB 37. Bonn: Hanstein, 1971.

Marshall, I. Howard. *Luke: Historian and Theologian*. Exeter: Paternoster, 1970.

May, John R. "Visual Story and the Religious Interpretation of Film." Pages 23–43 in *Religion in Film*. Edited by John R. May and Michael Bird. Knoxville: University of Tennessee Press, 1982.

McCall, Marsh H. *Ancient Rhetorical Theories of Simile and Comparison*. Cambridge: Harvard University Press, 1969.

McKane, William. *Prophets and Wise Men*. SBT 44. London: SCM, 1965.

Metzger, Bruce M. *A Textual Commentary on the Greek New Testament: A Companion Volume to the United Bible Societies' Greek New Testament*. 4th ed. Stuttgart: Deutsche Bibelgesellschaft/United Bible Societies, 1994.

Metzger, James A. *Consumption and Wealth in Luke's Travel Narrative*. Biblical Interpretation Series 88. Leiden: Brill, 2007.

Meyer, Elizabeth A. "Explaining the Epigraphic Habit in the Roman Empire: The Evidence of Epitaphs." *JRS* 80 (1990): 74–96.

Middendorp, Theophil. *Die Stellung Jesu Ben Siras zwischen Judentum und Hellenismus*. Leiden: Brill, 1973.

Milde, Henk. "'Going Out into the Day': Ancient Egyptian Beliefs and Practices concerning Death." Pages 15–34 in *Hidden Futures: Death and Immortality in Ancient Egypt, Anatolia, the Classical, Biblical and Arabic-Islamic World*. Edited by J. M. Bremmer, Th. P. J. van den Hout, and R. Peters. Amsterdam: Amsterdam University Press, 1994.

Montefiore, Hugh. "A Comparison of the Parables of the Gospel according to Thomas and of the Synoptic Gospels." Pages 40–78 in *Thomas and the Evangelists*. Edited by Hugh Montefiore and H. E. W. Turner. SBT. London: SCM, 1962.

Mosely, A. W. "Jesus' Audiences in the Gospels of St. Mark and St. Luke." *NTS* 10 (1963): 139–49.

Motto, Anna Lydia. *Seneca Sourcebook: Guide to the Thought of Lucius Annaeus Seneca. in the Extant Prose Works—Epistulae Morales, the Dialogi, De Beneficiis, De Clementia, and Quaestiones Naturale*. Amsterdam: Hakkert, 1970.

Moxnes, Halvor. *The Economy of the Kingdom: Social Conflict and Economic Relations in Luke's Gospel*. OBT 23. Philadelphia: Fortress, 1988.

Muilenberg, James. "A Qoheleth Scroll from Qumran." *BASOR* 135 (1954): 20–28.

Murphy, Roland E. "The Sage in Ecclesiastes and Qoheleth the Sage." Pages 263–71 in *The Sage in Israel and the Ancient Near East*. Edited by John G. Gammie and Leo G. Perdue. Winona Lake, Ind.: Eisenbrauns, 1990.

———. *The Tree of Life: An Exploration of Biblical Wisdom Literature*. 3rd ed. Grand Rapids: Eerdmans, 2002.

———. "Wisdom—Theses and Hypotheses." Pages 35–42 in *Israelite Wisdom: Theological and Literary Essays in Honor of Samuel Terrien*. Edited by John G. Gammie et al. Missoula, Mont.: Scholars Press, 1978.

Murphy, Roland E., and Elizabeth Huwiler. *Proverbs, Ecclesiastes, Song of Songs*. NIBC. Peabody, Mass.: Hendrickson, 1999.

Nelson, Milward Douglas. *The Syriac Version of the Wisdom of Ben Sira Compared to the Greek and Hebrew Materials*. SBLDS 107. Atlanta: Scholars, 1988.

Newhauser, Richard. *The Early History of Greed: The Sin of Avarice in Early Medieval Thought and Literature*. Cambridge: Cambridge University Press, 2000.

Newsom, Carol. A. "The Development of 1 Enoch 6–19: Cosmology and Judgment." *CBQ* 42 (1980): 310–29.

Nickelsburg, George W. E. *1 Enoch 1: A Commentary on the Book of 1 Enoch, Chapters 1–36; 81–108*. Hermeneia. Minneapolis: Fortress, 2001.

———. "Eschatology in the Testament of Abraham: A Study of the Judgment Scene in the Two Recensions." Pages 23–64 in *Studies on the Testament of Abraham*. Edited by George W. E. Nickelsburg. SBLSCS 6. Missoula, Mont.: Scholars Press, 1972.

———. "Revisiting the Rich and the Poor in 1 Enoch 92–105 and the Gospel according to Luke." Pages 579–605 in *Society of Biblical Literature 1998 Seminar Papers*. Atlanta: Scholars Press, 1998.

———. "Riches, the Rich and God's Judgment in 1 Enoch 92–105 and the Gospel according to Luke." *NTS* 25 (1978–1979): 324–44.

———. "Social Aspects of Palestinian Jewish Apocalypticism," Pages 641–54 in *Apocalypticism in the Mediterranean World and the Near East*. Edited by D. Hellholm. 2nd ed. Tübingen: Mohr Siebeck, 1989.

———. "Structure and Message in the Testament of Abraham." Pages 85–93 in *Studies on the Testament of Abraham*. Edited by George W. E. Nickelsburg. SBLSCS 6. Missoula, Mont.: Scholars Press, 1972.

———. "Summary and Prospects for Future Work." Pages 289–98 in *Studies on the Testament of Abraham*. Edited by George W. E. Nickelsburg. SBLSCS 6. Missoula, Mont.: Scholars Press, 1972.

Nickelsburg, George W. E., and James C. VanderKam, trans. *1 Enoch: A New Translation*. Minneapolis: Fortress, 2004.

Noël, Filip. *The Travel Narrative in the Gospel of Luke: Interpretation of Lk 9,51–19,28*. Collectanea Biblica et Religiosa Antiqua 5. Brussels: Koninklijke Vlaamse Academie van België voor Wetenschappen en Kunsten, 2004.

Nolland, John. "The Role of Money and Possessions in the Parable of the Prodigal Son (Luke 15:11–32): A Test Case." Pages 178–209 in *Reading Luke: Interpretation, Reflection, Formation*. Edited by Craig G. Bartholomew, Joel B. Green, and Anthony C. Thiselton. Scripture and Hermeneutics Series 6. Grand Rapids: Zondervan, 2005.

Nussbaum, Martha C. *The Therapy of Desire: Theory and Practice in Hellenistic Ethics*. Princeton: Princeton University Press, 1994.

O'Day, Gail R. "The Citation of Scripture as a Key to Characterization in Acts." Pages 207–21 in *Scripture and Traditions: Essays on Early Judaism and Christianity in Honor of Carl R. Holladay*. Edited by Patrick Gray and Gail R. O'Day. NovTSup. Leiden: Brill, 2008.

Ogden, Graham. "Qoheleth's Use of the 'Nothing is Better'-Form." *JBL* 98 (1979): 339–50.

Palahniuk, Chuck. *Fight Club*. New York: W. W. Norton, 1996.

Pao, David W. *Acts and the Isaianic New Exodus*. WUNT 2/130. Tübingen: Mohr Siebeck, 2000.

Patterson, Stephen J. "The Gospel of Thomas within the Development of Early Christianity." Ph.D. diss., Claremont Graduate University, 1988.

Patterson, Stephen J., and James M. Robinson, eds. *The Fifth Gospel: The Gospel of Thomas Comes of Age*. Harrisburg, Pa.: Trinity Press International, 1998.

Perdue, Leo G. "Cosmology and the Social Order in the Wisdom Tradition." Pages 457–78 in *The Sage in Israel and the Ancient Near East*. Edited by John G. Gammie and Leo G. Perdue. Winona Lake, Ind.: Eisenbrauns, 1990.

Perkins, Pheme. *Hearing the Parables of Jesus*. New York: Paulist, 1981.

Peursen, W. Th. van. *Language and Interpretation in the Syriac Text of Ben Sira: A Comparative Linguistic and Literary Study*. Monographs of the Peshitta Institute: Studies in the Syriac Versions of the Bible and Their Cultural Contexts 16. Leiden: Brill, 2007.

Plisch, Uwe-Karsten. *The Gospel of Thomas: Original Text with Commentary*. Translated by Gesine Schenke Robinson. Stuttgart: Deutsche Bibelgesellschaft, 2008.

Plutarch. Moralia. Translated by Phillip H. De Lacy et al. 15 vols. LCL. Cambridge: Harvard University Press, 1927–1969.

Poortman, Bartel. "Death and Immortality in Greek Philosophy: From the Presocratics to the Hellenistic Era." Pages 197–220 in *Hidden Futures: Death and Immortality in Ancient Egypt, Anatolia, the Classical, Biblical and Arabic-Islamic World*. Edited by J. M. Bremmer, Th. P. J. van den Hout, and R. Peters. Amsterdam: Amsterdam University Press, 1994.

Quaegebeur, Jan. "Cultes égyptiens et grecs en Egypte hellénistique: L'exploitation des sources." Pages 303–24 in *Egypt and the Hellenistic World: Proceedings of the International Colloquium, Leuven 24–26 May 1982*. Edited by E. van't Dack, P. van Dessel, and W. van Gucht. Leuven: Orientaliste, 1983.

Rad, Gerhard von. *Old Testament Theology*. Translated by D. M. G. Stalker. 2 vols. Louisville: Westminster John Knox, 1962.

———. *Wisdom in Israel*. London: SCM, 1972.

Rahlfs, Alfred, ed. *Septuaginta*. Stuttgart: Deutsche Bibelgesellschaft, 1979.

Reines, C. W. "Koheleth on Wisdom and Wealth." *JJS* 5 (1954): 80–84.

Reiterer, Friedrich V. "Deutung und Wertung des Todes durch Ben Sira." Pages 203–36 in *Die alttestamentliche Botschaft als Wegweisung: Festschrist für Heinz Reinelt*. Edited by Josef Zmijewski. Stuttgart: Katholishces Bibelwerk, 1990.

———. "Review of Recent Research on the Book of Ben Sira (1980–1996)." Pages 23–60 in *The Book of Ben Sira in Modern Research: Proceedings of the First International Ben Sira Conference 28–31 July 1996 Soesterberg, Netherlands*. Edited by Pancratius C. Beentjes. Berlin: de Gruyter, 1997.

———. *Zählsynopse zum Buch Ben Sira*. Fontes et Subsidia ad Bibliam pertinentes 1. Berlin: de Gruyter, 2003.

Rengstorf, Karl Heinrich. *Das Evangelium nach Lukas*. 3 vols. Göttingen: Vandenhoeck & Ruprecht, 1952.

Ricoeur, Paul. "Biblical Hermeneutics." *Semeia* 4 (1975): 29–148.

———. *Conflict of Interpretations*. Evanston: Northwestern University, 1974.

Riggs, Christina. *The Beautiful Burial in Roman Egypt: Art, Identity, and Funerary Religion*. Oxford: Oxford University Press, 2005.

Rindge, Matthew S. "Jewish Identity under Foreign Rule: Daniel 2 as a Reconfiguration of Genesis 41." *JBL* 129 (2010): 85–104.

———. "Mortality and Enjoyment: The Interplay of Death and Possessions in Qoheleth." *CBQ* 73 (2011): 265–80.

Robbins, Vernon K. *Exploring the Texture of Texts: A Guide to Socio-rhetorical Interpretation*. Harrisburg, Pa.: Trinity Press International, 1996.

———. *The Tapestry of Early Christian Discourse: Rhetoric, Society and Ideology*. New York: Routledge, 1996.

Robinson, James M., ed. *The Coptic Gnostic Library: A Complete Edition of the Nag Hammadi Codices*. 5 vols. Leiden: Brill, 2000.

———. "Jesus as Sophos and Sophia: Wisdom Tradition and the Gospels." Pages 1–16 in *Aspects of Wisdom in Judaism and Early Christianity*. Edited by Robert L. Wilken. Notre Dame, Ind.: University of Notre Dame Press, 1975.

Robinson, James M., and Helmut Koester. *Trajectories through Early Christianity*. Philadelphia: Fortress, 1971.

Roddy, Nicolae. *The Romanian Version of the Testament of Abraham: Text, Translation, and Cultural Context*. SBLEJL 19. Atlanta: Society of Biblical Literature, 2001.

Rousseau, François. "Structure de Qohélet I 4–11 et plan du livre." *VT* 31 (1981): 200–217.

Rudd, Niall. *Themes in Roman Satire*. London: Duckworth, 1986.

Rudman, Dominic. *Determinism in the Book of Ecclesiastes*. Sheffield: Sheffield Academic Press, 2001.

Sacks, Sheldon. *Fiction and the Shape of Belief*. Berkeley: University of California Press, 1966.

Salyer, Gary D. *Vain Rhetoric: Private Insight and Public Debate in Ecclesiastes*. JSOTSup 327. Sheffield: Sheffield Academic Press, 2001.

Sanders, E. P. "Testament of Abraham." Pages 871–902 in vol. 1 of *The Old Testament Pseudepigrapha*. Edited by James H. Charlesworth. 2 vols. New York: Doubleday, 1983–1985.

Sanders, Gabriel. *Lapides memores: Païens et chrétiens face à la mort: Le térmoignage de l'épigraphie funéraire latine*. Edited by Angela Donati, Dorothy Pikhuis, and Marc van Uytfanghe. Epigrafia e antichità 11. Faenza: Fratelli Lega, 1991.

Sanders, Jack T. *Ben Sira and Demotic Wisdom*. SBLMS 28. Chico, Calif.: Scholars Press, 1983.

Sandmel, Samuel. "Parallelomania." *JBL* 81 (1962): 1– 13.

Sandoval, Timothy J. *The Discourse of Wealth and Poverty in the Book of Proverbs*. Biblical Interpretation Series 77. Leiden: Brill, 2006.

Scaer, Peter J. *The Lukan Passion and the Praiseworthy Death*. NTM 10. Sheffield: Sheffield Phoenix, 2005.

Schlatter, Adolf. *The History of the Christ: The Foundation for New Testament Theology*. Translated by Andreas J. Köstenberger. Grand Rapids: Baker, 1997.

Schmidt, Francis. "Le Testament d'Abraham: Introduction, edition de la recension courtre, traduction et notes." 2 vols. Ph.D. diss., University of Strasbourg, 1971.

———. *Le Testament grec d'Abraham: Introduction, édition critique des deux recensions grecques, traduction*. Tübingen: Mohr Siebeck, 1986.

Schottroff, Luise. *Die Gleichnisse Jesu.* Gütersloh: Gütersloher Verlaghaus, 2005.

Schrader, Lutz. "Beruf, Arbeit und Mue als Sinnerfüllung bei Jesus Sirach." Pages 117–49 in *Der Einzelne und seine Gemeinschaft bei Ben Sira.* Edited by Renate Egger-Wenzel and Ingrid Krammer. BZAW 270. Berlin: de Gruyter, 1998.

Schrage, Wolfgang. *Das Verhältnis des Thomas-Evangeliums zur synoptischen Tradition und zu den koptischen Evangelienübersetzungen.* BZNW 29. Berlin: Töpelmann, 1964.

Schwienhorst-Schönberger, Ludger. *Nicht im Menschen Gründet das Glück (Koh 2:24): Kohelet im Spannungsfeld jüdischer Weisheit und hellenistischer Philosophie.* Freiburg: Herder, 1994.

Scott, Bernard Brandon. *Hear Then the Parable: A Commentary on the Parables of Jesus.* Minneapolis: Fortress, 1989.

———. "Jesus as Sage: An Innovative Voice in Common Wisdom." Pages 399–415 in *The Sage in Israel and the Ancient Near East.* Edited by John G. Gammie and Leo G. Perdue. Winona Lake, Ind.: Eisenbrauns, 1990.

———. *Re-imagine the World: An Introduction to the Parables of Jesus.* Santa Rosa, Calif.: Polebridge, 2001.

Seccombe, David Peter. *Possessions and the Poor in Luke-Acts.* Linz: Fuchs, 1983.

Sellew, Philip. "Interior Monologue as a Narrative Device in the Parables of Luke." *CBQ* 54 (1992): 239–53.

Seneca. Ad Lucilium Epistulae Morales. Translated by Richard M. Gummere. 3 vols. LCL. Cambridge: Harvard University Press, 1917–1925.

Seng, Egbert W. "Der Reiche Tor: Eine Untersuchung von Lk. Xii 16–21 unter besonderer Berücksichtigung form- und motivgeschichtlicher Aspekte." *NovT* 20 (1978): 136–55.

Seow, C. L. *Ecclesiastes: A New Translation with Introduction and Commentary.* AB 18C. New York: Doubleday, 1997.

———. "Linguistic Evidence and the Dating of Qoheleth." *JBL* 115 (1996): 643–66.

Simon, Louis. *Une Ethique de la Sagesse: Commentaire de l'epitre de Jacques.* Geneve: Labor et Fides, 1961.

Skehan, Patrick W., and Alexander Di Lella, *The Wisdom of Ben Sira: A New Translation with Notes, Introduction, and Commentary.* AB 39. Garden City, N.Y.: Doubleday, 1987.

Snodgrass, Klyne. *Stories with Intent: A Comprehensive Guide to the Parables of Jesus.* Grand Rapids: Eerdmans, 2008.

Sokoloff, Michael, ed. *A Dictionary of Jewish Palestinian Aramaic of the Byzantine Period.* 2nd ed. Ramat-Gan, Israel: Bar Ilan University, 2002.

Sommer, Benjamin D. *A Prophet Reads Scripture: Allusion in Isaiah 40–66.* Stanford, Calif.: Stanford University Press, 1998.

Sparks, Kenton L. "The Song of Songs: Wisdom for Young Jewish Women." *CBQ* 70 (2008): 277–99.

Spencer, Alan Jeffrey. *Death in Ancient Egypt.* 2nd ed. Harmondsworth: Penguin, 1984.

Stacy, R. Wayne. "Luke 12:13–21: The Parable of the Rich Fool." *RevExp* 94 (1997): 285–92.

Stagg, Frank. *Studies in Luke's Gospel.* Nashville: Convention, 1965.

Sterling, Gregory E. "*Mors Philosophi:* The Death of Jesus in Luke." *HTR* 94 (2001): 383–402.

Stone, Michael. E., trans. *The Testament of Abraham: The Greek Recensions.* SBLTT 2. Missoula, Mont.: Scholars Press, 1972.

Strauss, David Friedrich. *The Life of Jesus Critically Examined.* Translated by George Eliot from the 4th German edition. Philadelphia: Fortress, 1972.

Stuckenbruck, Loren. *1 Enoch 91–108.* CEJL. Berlin: de Gruyter, 2007.

Suggs, M. Jack. *Wisdom, Christology, and Law in Matthew's Gospel.* Cambridge: Harvard University Press, 1970.

Talbert, Charles H. *Reading Luke: A Literary and Theological Commentary on the Third Gospel.* New York: Crossroad, 1982.

Tannehill, Robert C. *Luke.* ANTC. Nashville: Abingdon, 1996.

———. *The Narrative Unity of Luke-Acts: A Literary Interpretation.* 2 vols. Philadelphia: Fortress, 1986.

Taylor, Charles. *The Dirge of Coheleth in Ecclesiastes XII, Discussed and Literally Interpreted.* London: Williams & Norgate, 1874.

Tcherikover, Victor. "Jerusalem on the Eve of the Hellenistic Reform." Pages 117–51 in *Hellenistic Civilization and the Jews.* Edited by Victor Tcherikover. Philadelphia: Jewish Publication Society of America, 1961.

Terrien, Samuel. "Amos and Chokmah." Pages 108–15 in *Israel's Prophetic Heritage.* Edited by B. W. Anderson and W. Harrelson. New York: Harper & Bros., 1962.

Tertullian. *Opera.* CCSL 1. Turnhout: Brepols, 1954.

Tucker, Jeffrey T. *Example Stories: Perspectives on Four Parables in the Gospel of Luke.* JSNTSup 162. Sheffield: Sheffield Academic Press, 1998.

Tuckett, Christopher M. *Luke.* NTG. Sheffield: Sheffield Academic Press, 1996.

Turner, H. E. W., and Hugh Montefiore. *Thomas and the Evangelists.* SBT. Naperville, Ill.: Allenson, 1962.

Turner, Nigel. "The Testament of Abraham: A Study of the Original Language, Place of Origin, Authorship, and Relevance." Ph.D. diss., University of London, 1953.

Ulrich, Eugene. "Ezra and Qoheleth Manuscripts from Qumran (4QEzra, 4QQoh$^{A, B}$)." Pages 139–57 in *Priests, Prophets and Scribes: Essays on the Formation and Heritage of Second Temple Judaism in Honour of Joseph Blenkinsopp.* Edited by Eugene Ulrich et al. JSOTSup 149. Sheffield: JSOT Press, 1992.

VanderKam, James C. *An Introduction to Early Judaism.* Grand Rapids: Eerdmans, 2001.

Venit, Marjorie S. *Monumental Tombs of Ancient Alexandria: The Theater of the Dead.* New York: Cambridge University Press, 2002.

Verhey, Allen. *Remembering Jesus: Christian Community, Scripture, and the Moral Life.* Grand Rapids: Eerdmans, 2002.

Via, Dan Otto. *The Parables: Their Literary and Existential Dimension.* Philadelphia: Fortress, 1967.

Volz, Paul. *Hiob und Weisheit.* 2nd ed. Die Schriften des Alten Testaments 3/2. Göttingen: Vandenhoeck & Ruprecht, 1921.

Wailes, Stephen L. *Medieval Allegories of Jesus' Parables.* UCLA Center for Medieval and Renaissance Studies 23. Berkeley: University of California Press, 1987.

Ward, James M. "The Servant's Knowledge in Isaiah 40–55." Pages 121–36 in *Israelite Wisdom: Theological and Literary Essays in Honor of Samuel Terrien*. Edited by John G. Gammie et al. Missoula, Mont.: Scholars Press, 1978.

Weeber, Karl-Wilhelm. *Luxus im alten Rom: Die öffentliche Pracht*. Darmstadt: Primus, 2006.

Wenham, David. "The Purpose of Luke-Acts: Israel's Story in the Context of the Roman Empire." Pages 79–103 in *Reading Luke: Interpretation, Reflection, Formation*. Edited by Craig G. Bartholomew, Joel B. Green, and Anthony C. Thiselton. Scripture and Hermeneutics Series 6. Grand Rapids: Zondervan, 2005.

Werline, Rodney A. "*The Psalms of Solomon* and the Ideology of Rule." Pages 69–87 in *Conflicted Boundaries in Wisdom and Apocalypticism*. Edited by Benjamin G. Wright III and Lawrence M. Wills. SBLSymS 35. Atlanta: Society of Biblical Literature, 2005.

Westermann, Claus. *Grundformen prophetischer Rede*. Munich: Kaiser, 1964.

Whedbee, J. William. *Isaiah and Wisdom*. Nashville: Abingdon, 1971.

Wheeler, Sondra Ely. *Wealth as Peril and Obligation: The New Testament on Possessions*. Grand Rapids: Eerdmans, 1995.

Whitley, Charles. *Koheleth, His Language and Thought*. BZAW 148. Berlin: de Gruyter, 1979.

Whybray, R. N. *Ecclesiastes*. NCBC. Grand Rapids: Eerdmans, 1989.

———. "The Identification and Use of Quotations in Ecclesiastes." Pages 435–51 in *Congress Volume: Vienna, 1980*. Edited by J. A. Emerton. VTSup 32. Leiden: Brill, 1981.

———. "Prophecy and Wisdom." Pages 181–99 in *Israel's Prophetic Tradition*. Edited by R. Coggins et al. Cambridge: Cambridge University Press, 1982.

———. "Qoheleth, Preacher of Joy." *JSOT* 23 (1982): 87–98.

Wiefel, Wolfgang. *Das Evangelium nach Lukas*. Berlin: Evangelische Verlagasanstalt, 1988.

Williams, James G. *Those Who Ponder Proverbs: Aphoristic Thinking and Biblical Literature*. Bible and Literature Series 2. Sheffield: Almond, 1981.

———. "What Does It Profit a Man? The Wisdom of Koheleth." Pages 375–89 in *Studies in Ancient Israelite Wisdom*. Edited by James L. Crenshaw. New York: Ktav, 1976.

Williamson, Robert, Jr., "Death and Symbolic Immortality in Second Temple Wisdom Instructions." Ph.D. diss., Emory University, 2011.

Wilson, Robert McL. *Studies in the Gospel of Thomas*. London: Mowbray, 1960.

Wilson, Walter T. *Love without Pretense: Romans 12:9–21 and Hellenistic-Jewish Wisdom Literature*. WUNT 2/46. Tübingen: Mohr Siebeck, 1991.

———. *The Mysteries of Righteousness: The Literary Composition and Genre of the Sentences of Pseudo-Phocylides*. TSAJ 40. Tübingen: Mohr Siebeck, 1994.

———. *The Sentences of Pseudo-Phocylides*. CEJL. Berlin: de Gruyter, 2005.

———. "A Third Form of Righteousness: The Theme and Contribution of Matthew 6.19–7.12 in the Sermon on the Mount." *NTS* 53 (2007): 303–24.

Winter, Michael M. "Theological Alterations in the Syriac Translation of Ben Sira." *CBQ* 70 (2008): 300–312.

Wolff, H. W. *Amos the Prophet*. Philadelphia: Fortress, 1973.
Wolter, Michael. *Das Lukasevangelium*. HNT 5. Tübingen: Mohr Siebeck, 2008.
Wright, Benjamin G., III. "The Discourse of Riches and Poverty in the Book of Ben Sira." Pages 559–78 in vol. 2 of *Society of Biblical Literature 1998 Seminar Papers*. Atlanta: Scholars Press, 1998.
———. "New Perspectives on Biblical Vocabulary and Translation Technique: Sirach in Relation to Its Presumed Hebrew 'Vorlage.'" Ph.D. diss., University of Pennsylvania, 1988.
———. *No Small Difference: Sirach's Relationship to its Hebrew Parent Text*. SBLSCS 26. Atlanta: Scholars Press, 1989.
———. "Putting the Puzzle Together: Suggestions concerning the Social Location of the Wisdom of Ben Sira." Pages 89–112 in *Conflicted Boundaries in Wisdom and Apocalypticism*. Edited by Benjamin G. Wright III and Lawrence M. Wills. SBLSymS 35. Atlanta: Society of Biblical Literature, 2005.
Wright, Stephen I. "Parables on Poverty and Riches (Luke 12:13–21; 16:1–13; 16:19–31)." Pages 217–39 in *The Challenge of Jesus' Parables*. Edited by Richard N. Longenecker. Grand Rapids: Eerdmans, 2000.
Zandee, Jan. *Death as an Enemy: According to Ancient Egyptian Conceptions*. SHR 5. Leiden: Brill, 1960.
Ziegler, Joseph, ed. *Sapientia Iesu Filii Sirach*. Septuaginta, Vetus Testamentum Graecum 12.2. Göttingen: Vandenhoeck & Ruprecht, 1965.

Index of Ancient Sources

Hebrew Bible

(LXX chapter numbers are in parentheses when they differ from MT numbers.)

Deuterocanonical Works

Dead Sea Scrolls

Pseudepigrapha

Ancient Jewish Writers

New Testament

Greek and Roman Sources

Miscellaneous

Index of Modern Authors

www.ingramcontent.com/pod-product-compliance
Lightning Source LLC
Chambersburg PA
CBHW031937110726
47902CB00001B/209

9781589836143